# Women & Public Policy in Canada

## Neo-liberalism and After?

# Women
# & Public Policy
# in Canada
## Neo-liberalism and After?

Alexandra Dobrowolsky

**OXFORD**
UNIVERSITY PRESS

# OXFORD
UNIVERSITY PRESS

70 Wynford Drive, Don Mills, Ontario M3C 1J9
www.oupcanada.com

Oxford University Press is a department of the University of Oxford.
It furthers the University's objective of excellence in research, scholarship,
and education by publishing worldwide in

Oxford    New York

Auckland   Cape Town   Dar es Salaam   Hong Kong   Karachi
Kuala Lumpur   Madrid   Melbourne   Mexico City   Nairobi
New Delhi   Shanghai   Taipei   Toronto

With offices in

Argentina   Austria   Brazil   Chile   Czech Republic   France   Greece
Guatemala   Hungary   Italy   Japan   Poland   Portugal   Singapore
South Korea   Switzerland   Thailand   Turkey   Ukraine   Vietnam

Oxford is a trade mark of Oxford University Press
in the UK and in certain other countries

Published in Canada
by Oxford University Press

**Library and Archives Canada Cataloguing in Publication Data**

Women and public policy in Canada : neoliberalism and after? / edited by
Alexandra Z. Dobrowolsky.

Includes bibliographical references and index.
ISBN 978-0-19-543061-5

1. Women—Government policy—Canada.   2. Neoliberalism—Canada.
I. Dobrowolsky, Alexandra Z. (Alexandra Zorianna), 1964–

HQ1236.5.C2 W6264 2009          305.420971          C2009-900639-1

Cover Image: Storman/iStockphoto

1  2  3  4  –  12  11  10  09

This book is printed on permanent (acid-free) paper ⊖.
Printed in Canada

# Contents

# Acknowledgements

The seeds of this collection were planted as a result of a rich and fertile collaboration between a number of colleagues and friends, mostly based at the Université de Montréal, for which I am incredibly grateful. A generous Social Science and Humanities Research Council of Canada strategic research grant on the topic of 'social cohesion' facilitated a range of opportunities (through meetings, conference calls, workshops, and national and international panels) to discuss, debate, dispute, and delineate the core ideas, institutions, interests, and identities at stake with respect to both neo-liberalism and social investment. I am personally and intellectually indebted to the members of this 'social cohesion' research team—Paul Bernard, Pascale Dufour, Jane Jenson, Denis Saint-Martin, and Deena White—as well as to the many research assistants (at the Université de Montréal and Saint Mary's University) who worked on this project, all of whom have since graduated and gone on to other challenging forms of work and study. Sincere thanks also to those who provided their cogent reflections and cross-national comparisons via various project-sponsored colloquia and project-sparked personal interactions; with extra special thanks for their insights and support to Wendy Larner, Ruth Lister, Martin Powell, George Ross, Fiona Williams, and Gareth Williams.

The majority of the papers in this volume were first presented as part of a workshop I organized as the Women, Gender and Politics Section Head for the annual conference of the Canadian Political Science Association Annual (CPSA) held at York University in the spring of 2006. Presenters came from across Canada and abroad to take part in this somewhat controversial, albeit highly stimulating, session that grappled with the contentious and contested nature of both contemporary neo-liberalism and social investment vis-à-vis women. I have been inspired by, and am especially grateful to, the participants who later agreed to re-work and, in many cases, re-write their workshop papers to produce chapters for this collection. I am also extremely thankful for the contributors who were enlisted after the fact in the months that followed the conference, and who agreed to engage in this challenging endeavour. Thanks to all the contributors for their hard work, patience, and perseverance.

I would also like to acknowledge Saint Mary's Political Science Honours student, Phoebe Smith (whom I hired as an editorial assistant by way of a student summer-employment grant) for her diligence and professionalism in doing an early copy edit and reference check of the draft manuscript.

Of course, sincere thanks also go out to the Oxford University Press Canada team in general and, in particular, to Peter Chambers, Freya Godard, Katherine

Skene, and Janice Evans, as well as the anonymous reviewers of the collection, for their assistance and helpful comments.

Finally, I would like to express my profound and heartfelt thanks to my family (encompassing a wide array of immediate and extended, as well as 'adopted', members, even those of the canine variety) who have provided unfailing love, support, and encouragement, and who continue to spoil me in immeasurable ways. Here, I must also single out my (long-suffering) partner, Richard Devlin and say, simply, thanks for everything.

This book is dedicated to my mother, Halyna Dobrowolsky; my sisters, Roma Dobrowolsky and Sonia McCaul; my nieces, Kalina and Emma McCaul and Alexa Gilbert; and to the memory of my late nephew Michael Devlin.

# Introduction:

## Neo-liberalism and After?

Alexandra Dobrowolsky

In many ways, the years approaching 2010 are reminiscent of the tumultuous 1970s. With the extreme fluctuations in oil prices, the rising cost of basic foods, like bread and rice, and the world threatened by the repercussions of a recession in the US, one is starkly reminded of the oil shocks, shortages, and stagflation (a combination of inflation and high unemployment) that stultified many countries in the 1970s and shattered the post-war Keynesian consensus. In its place, by the late 1970s, through the 1980s, and into the 1990s, a new economic and political paradigm—*neo-liberalism*—took hold and was consolidated. Does today's socio-economic and political turmoil, then, suggest cracks in, or even a crisis of, neo-liberalism? Have we seen any evidence of 'post–neo-liberal' priorities, or projects that offer policy directions 'after neo-liberalism'? Or, as some have argued, is 'neo-liberalization' simply 'rolling out' and penetrating ever wider social spaces and mindsets (Peck and Tickell 2002)? The authors in this collection critically examine recent neo-liberal as well as potentially 'post–neo-liberal' trajectories (that is, competing, contingent, and contested ideas, institutions, instruments, and identities) in a range of policy areas and consider their implications for a diversity of Canadian women.

At its core, neo-liberalism refers to a highly influential market rationality that has grown in depth and scope to encompass a daunting array of economic, political, social, and cultural phenomena. Across both the global North and South, neo-liberalism gained sway as a complex 'composite ideological structure'. That structure

> is not simply an expression of free-market libertarianism, nor is it just an outgrowth of neoconservative moral authoritarianism, but it reflects both. Neoliberalism was not only a reactionary response to fiscal and debt crises, nor is it merely a handmaiden of financialization and corporate globalization, but it is both. Neoliberalism-in-general is a loose and contradiction-laden ideological framework. (Peck 2004, 403)

Neo-liberal ideas advanced in the 1970s and developed into formidable state projects in the 1980s and 1990s. In countries around the world, the promulgation of neo-liberal policies resulted in the

> bleeding of social services, reduction of state governments . . . the ongoing liquidation of job security, the increasing elimination of a decent social wage, the creation of a society of low-skilled workers, and the emergence of a culture of permanent insecurity and fear . . . [that often hid] behind appeals to common sense and alleged immutable laws of nature. (Giroux 2008, 7)

More recently, however, some analysts have begun to question the exhaustive reach and extensive hold of neo-liberalism. Indeed, some have asserted that, as a concept, neo-liberalism is now 'entirely overworked' and even a 'cliché' (Smith 2008, 156–7). John Clarke pinpointed the nature of the problem when he wrote that the term neo-liberalism

> has been stretched too far to be productive as a critical analytical tool. Neo-liberalism suffers from promiscuity (hanging out with various theoretical perspectives), omnipresence (treated as a universal or global phenomenon), and omnipotence (identified as the cause of a wide variety of social, political and economic changes. (2008a, 135)

Although it may be overstating the case to call neo-liberalism a cliché, most would now agree that neo-liberalism is not an unchanging, immutable force and that it plays out in different ways in different places for different people. We have seen not only 'variations of neo-liberal discourses, technologies, and interventions' around the world, but also, increasingly, 'the changing repertoire of neo-liberalism over time' (Clarke 2008a, 140). For instance, Sylvia Bashevkin's research shows how the Canadian Conservative governments that first advocated neo-liberal state projects in the 1980s and early 1990s produced something more akin to neo-liberalism 'lite' in comparison to the early, heavy-handed approaches adopted by Conservative leaders in the United States and Britain. In those two countries, the coercive and punitive aspects of neo-liberalism were very real and were often combined with neo-conservative moralistic dictates that put women 'on the defensive' (Bashevkin 1998) and targeted specific, disadvantaged groups, among them lone mothers (2002). In contrast, Canadian neo-liberalism at the federal level, initially at least, contained less of this social-conservative and targeted punch. Moreover, Canadian neo-liberal blows came faster and harder after the Mulroney and Campbell Conservatives left office, that is, under the Liberals, particularly the Chrétien government in the mid-1990s.

Beyond some concession to the different manifestations of neo-liberalism, however, there is less consensus when it comes to the status of neo-liberalism in Canada today. Several contributors to this volume firmly believe not only that neo-liberalism has solidified, but that its scope has spread. From this perspective, just as structural factors like the relations of capitalism are ultimately

determinative, so too have neo-liberal, individualizing, market-driven mandates become hegemonic. Some go even further, arguing that neo-liberalism
not only becomes more embedded over time, but is normalized and extends
beyond political and economic policy initiatives, infiltrating social imperatives
as well (see, for example, Harder in this volume). In other words, at present,

> new ways of thinking, new political formations, and new institutional forms … can be
> characterized as neo-liberal because they involve both the *direct* expansion of the scope
> and reach of corporate capital and the *indirect* 'economization' of areas of social and
> political life. (Clarke 2008a, 136)

Conversely, other contributors shed light on several contemporary developments in Canada and abroad which, in their view, illustrate that more has been
going on than just neo-liberalism, end of story. From this vantage point, not only
inconsistencies and interruptions in neo-liberalism, but even digressions from
neo-liberalism are possible and will likely become more apparent over time.

Just as there are varieties of capitalism (Hall and Soskice 2001), there have
also been radically different varieties of liberalism (O'Connor et al. 1999;
Mahon in this volume). An acceptance of the spatial and increasingly temporal
variability of neo-liberalism helps us to theorize it as a 'multi-vocal and contradictory phenomenon' (Larner 2000, 21). Moreover, as Ong observes:

> A context specific inquiry allows us to capture how opposing interpretations and claims
> can and do interrupt, slow down, deflect, and negotiate neoliberal logics and initiatives.
> The temporality of transmission, translation, and negotiation in this fluctuating space
> is fraught with political complication, contingency, and ambiguity. (2006, 17)

With a suitable theoretical lens and the close study of policies, anomalies in
neo-liberalism can be seen at 'macro', 'meso', and 'micro' levels in studies that
home in on specific policies, institutions, ideas, interests, and identities and
their interrelations (Vickers 2008). Canada's federal system is illustrative.
Despite fairly standardized federal fiscal arrangements (some of which betray
a neo-liberal logic, like the Canada Health and Social Transfer, discussed below),
Canada still 'has a patchwork of varying provincial programs, characterized by
diverse institutional arrangements and bases of entitlement, as well as varying
levels and forms of expenditures' (Prentice 2004, 194). This reflects the sway of
different sets of political actors in different socio-economic, political, and cultural contexts at the sub-national level. Careful contextual analyses at such
'meso' levels (Vickers 2008), then, are more likely to show that 'attempts to
install neo-liberal strategies, techniques, and politics have been far from uniform or uniformly successful' (Clarke 2008b, 259).

It is also not surprising that, with close attention paid by analysts to context
and the specifics of space and time, there are also those who have identified
new perspectives beyond straight neo-liberalism, such as 'inclusive liberalism'

(for a definition and discussion, see Mahon in this volume), or 'social investment' (see Jenson in this volume). Although the latter will be detailed below, suffice it to say for now that after Canada's neo-liberal high-water mark in the mid-1990s, changing ideas, representations, and policy instruments at most raised the possibility of a paradigm shift away from neo-liberalism, or at the very least, introduced discourses that reflected something more than 'pure', unadulterated neo-liberalism. Therefore, as social investment discourses in Canada (and elsewhere) became more pervasive at the end of the 1990s and well into the 2000s, the prospect of changes in, and even departures from, neo-liberalism emerged.

Of course, the nature and extent of change is deeply disputed, as the various chapters in this volume make clear. For example, as many contributors point out, the social investment perspective shares some patently neo-liberal preoccupations. In fact, some analysts have referred to social investment priorities as being akin to a 'neoliberal wolf in lamb's clothing' (McKeen 2007). Yet, as other contributors to this volume attest, the similarities to neo-liberalism do not necessarily rule out the possibility of some inconsistencies or noteworthy differences. And, if we analyze social investment and other potential changes to neo-liberalism, the idea that neo-liberalism is not monolithic becomes more plausible.

This exploration of both continuity *and* change is timely and relevant, especially when leading state and social policy studies are often prone to highlight the former. Consider studies that emphasize the resilience of welfare states, deeply entrenched policy legacies, or leading 'path dependent' policies (Pierson 1994; Bonoli 2003). Although this literature is insightful and still highly influential, it is susceptible to the critique that its exclusive focus on continuity 'misses discontinuities that are also occurring' (McBride and McNutt 2007, 179). It also tends to give short shrift to the influence of a wider range of political actors, beyond the 'usual suspects' (Dobrowolsky and Saint-Martin 2005). And so, while acknowledging the tenacity of neo-liberal logic and projects, this collection turns our attention to the dynamics and dimensions of change (see also Powell 1999; Hemerijck 2002; Jenson and Saint-Martin 2003, 2006; Streeck and Thelen 2005; Jenson 2008) and to the roles played by a broader array of political actors.

To be sure, the contributors to this volume do agree upon some fundamental issues. Firstly, the contributors emphatically agree that Canadian women, in general, have not fared well under neo-liberalism and that certain groups of women have had a much harder time than others. Whereas some women's situations have undoubtedly improved, we see growing differences between women. Secondly, few, if any, of the contributors to this volume would suggest that social investment policies have advanced women's socio-economic and political status (see also Dobrowolsky and Jenson 2004; Dobrowolsky 2006). In fact, the exact opposite may be the case (see Jenson in this volume), and again, some women are even more prone to marginalization (see also Dobrowolsky with Lister 2006; as well as McNutt and Hawryluk, and Altamirano-Jiménez in this volume). Women, overall, have increasingly been made invisible; that is, they disappear from the policy agenda, but certain groups of women are 'instrumentalized', because some women's identities are used strategically by the state and in the media (see Dobrowolsky 2008b and Abu-Laban in this volume). Thirdly, no one in this volume claims that there has been a linear progression from neo-liberalism to social investment policies (see Collier in this volume) nor a straightforward move from neo-liberalism to something else, for that matter. Yet, all the authors in this collection do acknowledge new developments. In particular, all remark upon the return of 'the social': from the profusion of references to 'social risks' to the preponderance of 'social inclusion and exclusion' and 'social cohesion' discourses.

On this last point, however, analyses also vary considerably. Some remind us that the re-emergence of a vocabulary around the social runs counter to the main tenets of neo-liberalism and therefore supports the position that a distinctive social investment perspective has materialized. Conversely, others argue that such discourses still, ultimately, perpetuate the forces of neo-liberal marketization. They illustrate this with reference to the constrained ways that goals like social cohesion are pursued in some of Canada's once-revered and widely emulated policies, for example, health (see Armstrong in this volume) as well as immigration and multiculturalism (see Abu-Laban in this volume). Still others draw attention to the paradoxes involved when governmental concern over faltering social cohesion has not been made manifest in key policy areas, even those that are attracting great attention and concern of late, such as climate change (see McNutt and Hawryluk in this volume).

The debate runs deep over whether we are seeing substantially different dynamics at play in, and beyond, neo-liberalism. Yet to reach an agreement on this highly contentious concern is not the intent of this volume. Rather, the aim is to open up the conversation by advancing more nuanced, context-specific studies that evaluate the contemporary state of women and public policy in Canada from many vantage points from varied perspectives, and through several lenses and layers of analysis. It is only by exploring continuities, changes, and contradictions that we can re-assert the vital role of political struggle, broadly conceived. By treating neo-liberalism as more contingent and contested, by keeping neo-liberalism more 'open', we are prodded to consider alternatives and to think 'about what is not neo-liberal and thus the possibility of living without neoliberalism' (Clarke 2008a, 145).

But before we discuss such matters further, more background about what neo-liberalism is and how it has unfolded in Canada would be beneficial.

## Fleshing Out Neo-liberalism

It is widely acknowledged that neo-liberalism first took hold in the United States and Britain, where it was spearheaded by two conservative leaders, Ronald Reagan and Margaret Thatcher, respectively. Given intensified globalization, neo-liberal ideas and practices quickly spread to parties of other political stripes (see, for example, Hay 1999), and influential political actors adopted them in other places of governance (George 2000; Peck 2004). The result was substantial political, economic, and social transformations around the world:

> There has everywhere been an emphatic turn towards neoliberalism in political-economic practices and thinking since the 1970's. . . . Almost all states, from those newly minted after the collapse of the Soviet Union to old-style social democracies and welfare states such as New Zealand and Sweden, have embraced, sometimes voluntarily and in other instances in response to coercive pressures, some version of neoliberal theory and adjusted at least some policies and practices accordingly. (Harvey 2005, 2–3)

Neo-liberalism has many complex elements, and although the emphases shift over space and time, its most distinctive traits can be distilled as follows. First and foremost, the term neo-liberalism 'denotes new forms of political-economic governance premised on the extension of market relationships' (Larner 2000, 5). For neo-liberals, the market must remain unfettered and thus 'free mobility of capital between sectors, regions, and countries is regarded as crucial' (Harvey 2005, 66). Furthermore, with the economy as the driver, both 'the political' and 'the social' take a back seat. The space for politics shrinks, not only in terms of the size and scope of the state, but also with respect to the legitimacy of collective action. In place of collective struggle, neo-liberalism heralds the individual. These premises explain why Margaret Thatcher declared, 'There is no such thing as society'!

Neo-liberalism calls for state cutbacks: downsizing, deficit and debt reduction, devolution, and deregulation are dominant ideals and practices. The market is maximized, and the state minimizes its role with respect to social well-being. As public space contracts, more scope is given to the private, including the assigning of individual solutions to societal problems. Individual 'choice' and self-sufficiency are championed. Individuals' duties and obligations are trumpeted over deeper and broader citizenship rights, like social rights, to which the welfare state was committed under Keynesianism (Marshall 1965). Under neo-liberalism, those who rely on the state are considered wastrels and scroungers, and those mobilizing for an active state and alternative agendas are written off as pesky 'special interests'. Neo-liberalism's reduced state responsibilities and its program 'streamlining', along with deregulation and privatization, have also effectively resulted in off-loading onto the family. And, given the gendered construction of social reproduction, women are usually compelled to take up much of the slack.

As Larner carefully explains, neo-liberalism can be variously construed. It can be viewed as a *policy framework*, 'marked by a shift from Keynesian welfarism towards a political agenda favouring the relatively unfettered operation of markets' (2000, 6). In addition, it can be considered to be an *ideology* where the approach to neo-liberalism is more 'sociological' and 'in which a wider range of institutions, organizations and processes are considered' (2000, 9). Neo-liberalism can also be interpreted as *governmentality* (a neologism of governance and rationality coined by Michel Foucault—see Murray 2007, 162) where, beyond ideology, discourses are involved, and discourse is understood

> not simply as a form of rhetoric disseminated by hegemonic economic and political groups, nor as the framework within which people represent their lived experience, but rather as a system of meaning that constitutes institutions, practices and identities in contradictory and disjunctive ways. (2000, 12)

So, for example, Wendy Brown contends that neo-liberalism is not merely 'a bundle of economic policies with inadvertent political and social consequences' but that it represents a 'social analysis that, when deployed as a form of governmentality, reaches from the soul of the citizen-subject to education policy to practices of empire.' As a 'regulating strategy of governance, neo-liberal rationality exercises its hegemony as an administrative project that defines all aspects of life ... extending market values to all institutions and social action' (2005, 38, 39–40).

In this book, all three definitions can be found, and references to all three dimensions of neo-liberalism will be made in this introduction. An awareness of these many meanings is vitally important because, as Larner suggests:

> Most immediately, we are alerted to the possibility that there are different configurations of neo-liberalism, and that close inspection of particular neo-liberal projects is more likely to reveal a complex and hybrid political imaginary, rather than the straight-forward implementation of a unified and coherent philosophy. Moreover, in making visible the claims of those all too often portrayed as the 'victims' of welfare state restructuring ... [one can] emphasize that new welfare state arrangements emerge out of political struggle, rather than being imposed in a top down manner. (2000, 12)

And so, let us briefly review how neo-liberal policy frameworks, ideologies, and governmentality became manifest in Canada.

Here, as elsewhere, marketization, trade liberalization, privatization, deregulation, downsizing, and devolution became the economic and political norms of the 1980s, and well into the 1990s in both ideology and policy. As has been profusely documented, women bore the brunt of the neo-liberal restructuring that took place. For example, they grappled with extensive job losses in areas hit hardest by free trade (Gabriel and Macdonald 1996; Macdonald 2003), the result of the Mulroney government's crowning neo-liberal achievement: the 1989 Canada–US Free Trade Agreement (FTA). The free-trade agenda was then expanded, resulting in the North American Free Trade Agreement (NAFTA), which was subsequently endorsed by the Chrétien government, despite earlier Liberal denunciations of the FTA. The Canadian state remained oblivious to the negative impact that free trade had on women, particularly women who were already marginalized (Gabriel and Macdonald 1996). It also ignored the fact that women, in general, relied disproportionately on programs that were rescinded or privatized as a result of neo-liberal state projects. Women also had to contend with heavier workloads, the consequence of juggling multiple responsibilities in increasingly more precarious paid employment, as well in their unpaid work in the home and in their communities (Brodie 1996; Bakker 1996; Evans and Wekerle 1997; Bashevkin 1998, 2002; Cossman and Fudge 2002; McKeen and Porter 2003). Beyond gender, intersecting identities such as race, ethnicity, Indigeneity, disability, and class, as well as other notable differences such as citizenship status, contributed to growing inequalities, not only between women and men, but between women as well.

Ironically, although Brian Mulroney's Conservatives used neo-liberal words, beyond free trade, most neo-liberal policy deeds were done by subsequent Liberal governments. As Whitaker notes, 'the Mulroney neo-liberal project, while strong on rhetorical formulation, was weak on consistency and follow-through' (2006, 7). Jean Chrétien's Liberal government, however, consistently followed through, methodically meeting neo-liberal policy objectives. The Liberals succeeded in ways that the Conservatives could not by

> deliberately eschewing the ideological rhetoric of their predecessors. Making no claims to a broader neo-liberal vision, downplaying the ideological antimonies of 'markets' versus 'politics', and avoiding rhetorical attacks on 'big government' and exhortations to 'free enterprise', the Liberals instead focused on practical results. (Whitaker 2006, 8)

Thus, despite the 'welfare liberal' promises contained in the Liberals' *Red Book*, on the basis of which they rode to power in 1993, the Chrétien government proceeded to take a sharp rightward turn. Chrétien's Liberals adopted a neo-liberal policy framework in many areas, from the economic domain (for example, adopting NAFTA) and political realm of the state (for example, drastically downsizing the civil service) to the social sphere (for example, 'streamlining' social services and slashing support to groups and movements in civil society) (for details see Clarkson 2005; and Smith 2005).

Undoubtedly there were members of the Liberal government who were not fully supportive of this embracing of neo-liberalism. For example, there were those who wanted to follow the alternative policy directions taken in the Social Security Review (SSR), conducted in the government's first year in office, many of which reflected more 'welfare-liberal', and in hindsight, 'social investment', priorities. Nevertheless, Liberal Finance Minister Paul Martin's neo-liberal agenda—doing away with the deficit, curtailing spending on social programs, and promoting policy flexibility—ultimately took precedence. And so, it was under the Liberals, in the mid-1990s, that downsizing reached devastating levels:

> The federal government's policy change [was] widely seen as a disjuncture—an 'epiphany in fiscal federalism and national social policy'... or as the end of an era.... Yet it followed on years of policy tinkering or 'drift', which had prepared the ground and, arguably, made the departure less dramatic than it would otherwise have been. (McBride and McNutt 2007, 178)

From unemployment insurance rates to funding for advocacy groups, the cuts came fast and furious. As the chapters in this collection remind us, many core government programs and agencies were negatively affected, from the generous Canada Assistance Plan (CAP), which was replaced by the highly circumscribed Canada Health and Social Transfer (CHST), to the the Canadian Advisory Council on the Status of Women (CACSW), which was abolished. The deleterious repercussions of these neo-liberal policy decisions on women have been documented in various studies, books, and articles; the purpose of this book is to describe and evaluate what took place *after* this period of intense restructuring.

## From Neo-liberalism to the Social Investment Perspective

By the late 1990s, in response to worsening social conditions and political unrest, the definition of problems, policy priorities, and policy instruments began to be modified at both the national and sub-national levels. Provincial leaders were not happy with the reduced funds they received from the federal government as a result of the institutionalization of the CHST; Canadians, in general, had had enough of belt-tightening and lack of services; and most women's groups continued to oppose political agendas that were based purely on economic calculations. Moreover, and significantly, by this point, Canada had entered into an era of post-deficit politics. Having slain the deficit dragon, and with growing surpluses on which to draw, the Liberal government could now spend. It is here that the discourse of 'the social' is re-introduced.

To begin with, because the word 'spending' was associated with the 'tax and spend' Keynesian era, governments now spoke of 'social investments' in areas like health and education, where there were promises of not just societal but also fiscal returns (Dobrowolsky 2002; Lister 2003; Jenson and Saint-Martin 2003; Dobrowolsky and Jenson 2004, 2005; Dobrowolsky and Saint-Martin 2005; Dobrowolsky and Lister 2008). From this perspective, because Keynesianism was marred by profligate consumption, social investment would be marked by production, now and into the future. Put simply, the overarching objective of the social investment approach was to promote employability, that is, to get people into paid work. Because the goal was to create knowledgeable, skilled workers to make Canada more competitive in a challenging global marketplace, the boosting of human capital became a prime policy objective.

Social capital also became a stated consideration, with more emphasis being placed not just on families, but also on communities and the voluntary sector. Here and elsewhere, the 'social' became more conspicuous in state concerns. For instance, '[g]overnment sponsored policy templates such as social cohesion, social exclusion, civic engagement and the voluntary sector have been advanced as legitimate responses to the numerous social ills that plague societies' (Orsini and Smith 2007, 2). The rationale here was that investing in the 'social' now could prevent costly societal transgressions in future.

At the same time, in lieu of flat-out neo-liberal state 'off-loading' and privatization, 'partnerships' became the new buzzword. Notably, this did not entail just partnerships between the state and business, which is a typical neo-liberal tactic, but also between the federal government and the provinces, some Aboriginal organizations (see Altamirano-Jiménez in this volume), and certain elements of the voluntary sector (Brock 2006). And so, discourses of 'streamlining' and 'downsizing', or the omnipresent castigation of countless 'special interests' that were prevalent at the height of the neo-liberal state project were now re-jigged in favour of a range of 'strategic partnerships'. Consider the federal–provincial partnerships constructed in the 1999 Social Union Framework Agreement (SUFA) (Phillips 2001) or third-sector partnerships as evidenced by the Caledon Institute's central role in the policy design of new national programs like the National Child Benefit (NCB) (Dobrowolsky and Saint-Martin 2005; Saint-Martin and Dobrowolsky 2005).

Neo-liberalism called for a passive state (for example, hollowing out the state by scaling back on social spending, downsizing, deregulating, and devolving); the *social investment perspective*, on the other hand, required the state to be more active. However, unlike the welfare state that 'rowed', here the state 'steered' towards investments that would reap future rewards. Whereas the welfare state provided services directly, from the social investment perspective the state should act as an 'enabler'. Whereas the welfare state constructed a protective social safety net for the here and now, social investment has been likened to a trampoline, where citizens would be equipped to spring forward into the future (Saint-Martin 2007). Investments in education, innovation, healthcare, and children (particularly, children *at risk*) would 'pay off' later by producing skilled, productive workers and preventing a host of expensive social ills. And so, in the preface to the Liberal's 2000 election pamphlet, Prime Minister Chrétien asserted:

> we have invested for the future—in health care, education, innovation, children, the environment, and the social programs that are the foundation of a strong society. In fact, close to 75 per cent of our spending since 1997 has been in these areas. . . . Our

purpose will be . . . to [continue to] do better for ourselves and our children. (cited in Dobrowolsky 2006, 187)

Elsewhere, he explained:

> In the new, global economy of the 21st century prosperity depends on innovation, which, in turn, depends on the investments that we make in the creativity of our people. We must invest not only in technology and innovation but also, in the Canadian way, to create an environment of inclusion in which all Canadians can take advantage of their talents, their skills and their ideas. (in Dobrowolsky 2006, 187)

Despite the fact that the Liberal prime minister called this the 'Canadian way' and described his government's combination of debt repayment and renewed expenditures in selective social programs as this country's unique 'balanced' approach, the 'social investment' turn had wider provenance.

The term social investment derives from the work of the British social theorist Anthony Giddens (1998). It also coincided with the post-Conservative, or 'third-way', thinking that was first articulated by President Bill Clinton but was soon emulated elsewhere. Moreover, the social investment approach was in line with child- and family-centred welfare reform agendas promoted in core European policy documents (Jenson and Saint-Martin 2006; Saint-Martin 2007). Indeed, after the third way was heralded in Britain (Hale et al. 2004), it was actually the social investment perspective that became the new, defining paradigm for consecutive New Labour governments (Dobrowolsky and Jenson 2005; Wincott 2006; Dobrowolsky and Lister 2008). In Britain, for example, unparalleled resources were expended in areas such as childcare and the eradication of child poverty. Social investment rationales could also be found in other liberal democratic states, such as New Zealand (Larner and Craig 2005).

In brief, the basic principles of the social investment model are as follows. Social policy reforms are initiated with a view to excelling in a competitive, global marketplace. Human-capital formation, which increases the capacity of everyone to engage in paid work, becomes a primary goal. Investing in human capital involves state sponsorship of a range of training and education initiatives. The idea is to expand 'opportunities' in order to promote employability. All ages are included in, for instance, the endorsement of 'life-long learning'; however, unprecedented attention is paid to the young, especially to children. Consider here the encouragement of 'early childhood education'. There are also prominent pledges to tackle child poverty and even end it! The policies that arise from these promises also show that beyond human capital, social capital (for example, family and community networks) is significant. Investments in human and social capital are seen as ways to deal with social exclusion and foster social inclusion and cohesion. The long-term goal of the social investment approach, then, is to create prosperity and produce a more inclusive society filled with good 'citizen workers' (Lister 2003).

Obviously, the social investment perspective shares some core neo-liberal assumptions. For example, investments are often chosen through the use of managerial indicators and are monitored and tracked methodically through benchmarking. Both neo-liberalism and social investment paradigms favour balanced budgets and are highly market-oriented. Consider the economic terminology of social investment policy ('investments', 'human capital', and 'social capital'). Moreover, both neo-liberalism and social investment models promote productive labour and take women's social reproductive labour for granted.

Nevertheless, with a social investment agenda, the state is actively involved in capacity building. It thus embarks upon social policy redesign, although, again, always with an eye on enhancing economic competitiveness. Social policy, consequently, becomes 'productive'. Indeed, with social investment, social policy becomes increasingly intertwined with economic policy, and the preferred policy instruments change. The use of tax credits and tax benefits, which Bashevkin dubbed the 'taxification' of social policy (2002), is illustrative. Notably, although policy instruments like tax credits reduce state revenue, the taxification of social policy is *not* depicted as state spending; rather, it is dubbed a social *investment* and is portrayed as the converse of 'wasteful consumption' (Jenson 2008). Thus, gone are the universal welfare-state programs of yore. And yet, the new policy instruments can conceivably be geared towards redistribution, albeit targeted redistribution, although usually by stealth (Dobrowolsky and Lister 2008).

What is distinctive here is that there is a focus on social policy and the 'social' more broadly and there are, actually, state 'investments' to consider. Furthermore, social investment policy goals are somewhat different than those that are pursued in a neo-liberal project. Competitiveness is crucial, but so too are social inclusion and cohesion. As will be become apparent, these aims are not without serious limitations; however, some would argue that they do suggest a shift from straight-up neo-liberalism.

In Canada, social investment priorities became evident by the end of the 1990s and into the new millennium, at the end of Prime Minister Jean Chrétien's time in office. They also continued under Paul Martin, but this time as part of Martin's prime ministerial legacy, ironically, ten years after he had instigated the deep neo-liberal cuts in the first place! Given, for example, the high profile of social investment in Speeches from the Throne, press releases, and campaign literature, and given renewed investments or different policy designs in strategic areas in this period—for example, the National Child Benefit (NCB), the Canada Child Tax Benefit (CCTB), and the National Child Benefit Supplement (NCBS)—many would acknowledge that some shifts had occurred. However, once again, there is far less agreement about the extent and effects of these changes. In other words, there are debates over whether modifications occurred only at the level of rhetoric, or whether the social investment approach had some real impact on policy development and on the socio-economic conditions of Canadian citizens, particularly women.

## Where Are the Women?

As this volume attests, there are huge disputes over the nature of these developments and what they mean for neo-liberalism and for politics in Canada. There is more agreement when it comes to the ultimate outcome for women. With talk of social investment and the priorization of human capital, as well as with efforts to combat social exclusion, some children were obviously in the picture, but women were noticeably out of it. Children symbolized the ideal investments for the future (Jenson 2001; Dobrowolsky and Jenson 2004; Jenson and Saint-Martin 2003, 2006; Saint-Martin 2007). And so, for example, child poverty was cause for concern, but there was no mention that most poor children were being raised by poor mothers who were caught in the downward spiral of the feminization of poverty. Beyond some references to Aboriginal children, the children invoked were not differentiated by gender, race, or ethnicity, among other markers of difference (Dobrowolsky 2002; see Altimirano-Jiménez in this volume). What became increasingly clear was that women's concerns and needs had fallen off the agenda (see Jenson in this volume). For instance, with the promotion of discourses of social inclusion, exclusion, and cohesion, one of the rallying cries and mobilizing features of the women's movement in Canada, that of *equality*, was removed from the political lexicon. It was simply assumed—erroneously—that women's equality was a given (Dobrowolsky 2008a; see Dobrowolsky in this volume).

Granted, Canadian women today 'have one of the highest labour force participation rates in the world, a rate that is converging with that of men' in that the participation rate for citizens aged 25–54 was 91 per cent for men and 81 per cent for women (Statistics Canada, 2006a). Although this may have contributed to women's socio-economic progress over the last few decades, one would be hard pressed to find concrete evidence that women are men's economic equals. Indeed, for some groups of women, economic inequality is growing despite the fact that Canada's federal government has produced successive fiscal surpluses in recent years.

Although Canada has pay and employment equity legislation, here too there have been setbacks and shortfalls. The cost of enforcing pay-equity legislation led some provinces to repeal such legislation and amend provincial human-rights codes, or refuse to pay the expenses involved (see Dobrowolsky in this volume). Although some of the recommendations made in 1983 by the Abella Commission (the Royal Commission on Equality in Employment) were accepted by the Conservative government of Brian Mulroney, resulting in 1986 in the *Employment Equity Act*, there were serious limitations (Timpson 2001) and subsequent Liberal government reforms gave the Act 'more teeth' but 'less bite' (Lum and Williams 2000, 198).

Despite such legislation and the fact that more Canadian women are engaged in paid employment than ever before, women's work is still ghettoized and women are underpaid, in general and in comparison to men. By July 2006, the average hourly wage for Canadian women employees was $17.73 and $21.11 for men (Statistics Canada 2006), and women were still doing significantly more unpaid social-reproduction work and thus having less free time than men. Moreover, the disparities between women have become even starker. The 71 cents that women make for every dollar earned by a man drops to 46 cents for Aboriginal women (Altamirano-Jiménez in this volume).

The economic situation is a difficult one for many Canadian women, but it can be dire for others, particularly single women, lone mothers, senior women, racialized women, Aboriginal women, women with disabilities, and recent immigrant women:

> Canadian women are more likely to be poor than are Canadian men. . . . Forty-eight percent of unattached senior women and 53 percent of all families headed by lone-parent mothers had incomes falling below the low income cut-offs. . . . Single-parent families, elderly women, and visible minority women are much more likely to experience unemployment, underemployment and poverty. . . . Aboriginal women in Canada tend to suffer even more from unemployment and lower incomes, as well as lower life expectancy, greater heath problems, and domestic violence. (Jacquetta Newman and Linda White 2006, 221–2)

Women's equality is not a given in the political realm either. When it comes to basic, numerical representation of women in formal politics, women's numbers in the House of Commons have stalled at about 20 per cent (after reaching a peak of 21.1 per cent in 2004, they dipped to 20.8 per cent after the 2006 election). Only three Aboriginal women have been elected to the lower chamber since 1867, and, at the start of the new millennium, there were just four visible-minority women in the House (Trimble and Arscott 2003, 29). Women have attained a 'critical mass' in Quebec's legislature, but their representation in provincial and territorial legislatures overall matches that of the federal level; and the situation is only marginally better municipally. Moreover, the vexing question of whether numerical representation translates into substantive representation of women remains unresolved (see Dobrowolsky in this volume).

Efforts to build up a concentrated 'femocracy' within the Canadian state in the 1970s have been abandoned in favour of gender 'mainstreaming' (Hankivsky 2007). Whereas the Liberal government closed the doors of the CACSW, when the Conservatives came into power in 2006 they shut down 12 of 16 Status of Women Canada (SWC) regional offices and reduced the SWC's modest budget by another $5 million. The Harper government also stifled the SWC's research capacity, made sure it was divorced from any advocacy initiatives, and even removed 'equality' from its mandate. It then proceeded to close off other routes to equality, like the Court Challenges Program.

This political and economic situation not only affects women negatively within the state but also hinders their political mobilization outside the state. Core funding to women's groups, provided by the SWC Women's Program, long ago became a thing of the past. But now, partly as a result of funding cuts, national equality-seeking organizations that had high profiles in the 1980s and early 1990s, like the National Association of Women and the Law (NAWL), the National Action Committee on the Status of Women (NAC), the Native Women's Association of Canada (NWAC), the DisAbled Women's Network (DAWN), the National Organization of Immigrant and Visible Minority Women (NOIVM), and the Women's Legal Education and Action Fund (LEAF), are either gone or are dramatically diminished. If they are still in existence, their efforts are seldom lauded. Indeed, the opposite is usually the case. Attacks in academia (Morton and Knopff 2000; Brodie 2002) have been taken up by the media and are currently parroted by government officials (Dobrowolsky 2008a; Dobrowolsky in this volume), who seem only to have time for anti-feminist lobby groups like REAL Women (see Jenson in this volume).

Although women's concerns and needs started to disappear well before 2006, the increasing delegitimizing and under-funding of the women's movement, combined with a Conservative government with a retrogressive mandate, have made women even more invisible (although some women are still strategically deployed; see Altarmirano-Jiménez and Abu-Laban in this volume). As a consequence, now, perhaps more than ever before, there is a greater urgency to this exercise: that is, evaluating the shapes and forms that public policies have taken over the last 10 to 15 years; their inconsistencies, and interruptions; and how these policies impact Canadian women in all their diversity.

## Analyzing and Assessing Current Trends

For many academics and activists, what has happened most recently merely reflects shifts within a deeper and wider, albeit patchy, process of neo-liberalization. From this standpoint, any new policies, institutions, ideologies, discourses, and governmentalities represent efforts to consolidate and stabilize neo-liberalism. This may either involve the 'flanking' of neo-liberalism, that is, with the incorporation of some non-market, 'third-way' social logic (Jessop 2002), or the 'rolling out' of neo-liberal marketization into broader areas that include social life (Peck and Tickell 2002; Tickell and Peck 2003).

For other analysts, however, politics and policy have taken, or can still take, notable new turns (Esping-Andersen 2002). This is evident not only in the rise of the social investment perspective, but also in less uniform policy priorities, institutions, and forms of program delivery. From the vantage point of change, while there are no doubt important continuities with neo-liberalism, there are also some significant discontinuities. Jane Jenson directs our attention to both a change in ideas and the rolling out of new instruments, from tax-based income supplementation to early childhood education programs (2008).

In particular, in this volume we see divergences that arise at the 'meso' and 'micro' levels. The childcare policies across Canada, as noted in several chapters, are a prime example of what Susan Prentice describes as 'intra-regime variants'; moreover, '[s]uch variation points to the significance of close study of similarities and differences in policy design and political arrangements, including the role of social actors' (2004, 194). Similarly, in this volume, we see changes to the roles and significance of political actors, partisan and otherwise, that is, from agenda-shifting politicians and judges to influential feminist activists and women's organizations. This collection also shows that just as changing political actors (broadly conceived) matter, so too do different policy realms. Neo-liberal ideas and policy frameworks were taken up quite quickly in some policy fields, whereas in others their effects have taken longer to be felt (for example, their delayed impact on the Charter and the courts; see Dobrowolsky in this volume). Similarly, whereas social investment is quite apparent in some areas, it is largely absent in others (see Abu-Laban and McNutt and Hawryluk in this volume).

It becomes evident that even if one accepts that there was a move from neo-liberalism to social investment models, this is by no means a linear process. The shift in policy directions that occurred between the Martin Liberal and Harper Conservative governments (for example, from universal childcare to a paltry childcare credit), or changes from New Democratic to Conservative or Liberal governments at the provincial level (Collier in this volume), underscore this point. In short, despite the fundamental debates within it, what this collection clearly illustrates is that political struggle matters.

## Queries, Structure, and Aspirations

Are we seeing the entrenchment of a hegemonic neo-liberalism, or is neo-liberalism at an impasse? Is *post–neo-liberalism* possible? If so, what comes *after* neo-liberalism, and what are the implications for public policy in Canada? What and who are 'at risk'? Is the situation for Canadian women getting better or worse, or is it at a standstill? Where are we when it comes to the nature and effects of gender equality today, and what about the future? Which policies and which women are we considering when we pose such questions? To be sure, the answers will vary considerably given changes across space and time, nationally and across provinces, given different policy areas, as well as different levels of analysis, and, of course, given differences among women. And so, the purpose of this volume is to delve more deeply into these highly contested areas and offer greater insight by including chapters that are sensitive to both continuities and changes, that consider both structure and agency, and that are attentive to issues of women's equality, difference, and diversity.

The hope is that through careful contextual analysis we can begin to discern (1) whether there may be 'residual attachments that cannot be adequately incorporated or displaced' by neo-liberalism; (2) whether there can be 'appropriations that come loose from their neo-liberal fixings'; and (3) whether there might even be 'other rationalities, political imaginaries, and projects' (Clarke 2008a, 142) after neo-liberalism.

## Structure of the Volume

This introduction highlights the complexities of neo-liberalism and lays out the parameters of the debates around neo-liberalism *and after*, paying close attention to the premises and propositions of the social investment perspective. The chapters that follow consider recent developments in a wide range of policy areas, some that are more woman-focused (for example, gender equality, and violence against women) than others, but all clearly delve into policy dynamics that reflect the contested relations of gender as well as class, race, ethnicity, Indigeneity, sexuality, and even age, and their complicated intersections. While most of the chapters focus on policies at the national level, many also take into consideration sub-national, regional, and provincial perspectives and their variations and interrelations.

In Chapter 1, Jane Jenson provides a comprehensive overview of pivotal, political developments in Canada and in Quebec of late. Through a double comparison (not only of Canada and Quebec, but of two policy fields: gender equality and childcare), and from an institutionalist perspective, she makes the case for why neo-liberalism *cannot* account for everything. Instead, she analyzes the stark repercussions of social investment discourses and practices, how they have accelerated a process that began with Liberal governments' neo-liberal governing project, and how this has resulted in the present situation, where women's needs and concerns have been 'written out of' the story.

Jenson's survey is followed by chapters that examine both neo-liberalism and the social investment perspective vis-à-vis particular policies, at particular levels, and often for particular groups of women. For example, in Chapter 2, Rianne Mahon homes in on childcare policy. Mahon studies several significant strands of liberalism and how they relate to strategies for non-parental childcare that have been pursued in Canada. For example, she describes how and why Canada's narrowly targeted childcare policy expanded substantially in 2003 to a pan-Canadian childhood learning and care system that reflected 'inclusive liberalism'; and then, how and why Canada's latest childcare option, adopted by the Harper government upon coming to power in 2006, contracted not only because of its neo-liberal, but also because of its neo-conservative, underpinnings.

In Chapter 3, Martha MacDonald provides a detailed examination of the intricacies of the unemployment/employment insurance program (UI/EI). She directly addresses the question of whether the different components of, and the many revisions to, the 1996 *Employment Insurance Act* reflect changes in state discourses and/or practices, and assesses the gendered outcomes of these components and changes. She points to some dramatic modifications in the Special EI Benefits that are consistent with the social investment model (for example, in relation to Parental Benefits and the new Compassionate Care Benefit). When it comes to regular EI, aside from shifts in discourse (for example, the language has 'softened'), and some slight modifications in its substance (for example, some of the most punitive elements have been removed), there are notable neo-liberal continuities (for example, Regular EI Benefits are still much lower than those under UI; there are lingering issues around targeting and means-testing). MacDonald also considers how this national program plays out differently in different regions (for example, its impact on the Atlantic provinces and also with respect to Quebec). Throughout, women's gains and losses are evaluated, with, for instance, MacDonald underscoring the gendered assumptions that underlie the social investment perspective as it reinforces women's responsibility for care.

Pat Armstrong, in Chapter 4, reflects upon recent concerns with respect to healthcare policy and relates them to radically divergent models of fostering social cohesion. She takes issue with how social cohesion is currently being deployed to remedy the social ills created by neo-liberalism. In her view, the shapes that social cohesion currently takes, that is, with their neo-liberal underpinnings, only exacerbate existing disparities. Armstrong illustrates how the healthcare strategies that have been, and are being, adopted ultimately undercut collective support for, and democratic control over, care and how this harms women's access to, and work in, care. Instead, Armstrong argues for an alternative approach to social cohesion—one that supports communities by way of a strong state that advances equitable and secure social programs, social, and political rights.

In Chapter 5, Kathleen McNutt and Sara Hawryluk also call into question social cohesion, and do so in relation to its scope in light of an area of rapidly growing concern for post-millennial governments: that of climate change. They criticize Canadian governments' narrow climate-change focus that (1) has been limited to environmental and economic risks; (2) fails to consider the social risks involved; and (3) ignores the gendered impacts of global warming. McNutt and Hawryluk illustrate why a consideration of women is crucial to the climate-change debate and how the threat of climate change to social cohesion has gendered outcomes. They also consider differential impact, such as the disproportionately negative consequences of global warming for women in Canada's North, as well as Aboriginal women's unique concerns vis-à-vis climate change. Like Armstrong, McNutt and Hawryluk also make a number of concrete recommendations. They detail several mechanisms and necessary actions for 'writing women into' an agenda that has, heretofore, ignored them entirely. Thus, McNutt and Hawryluk make a case for women's equality *as* a social investment that produces social inclusion and cohesion.

In Chapter 6, Isabel Altamirano-Jiménez specifically addresses racialized gender, citizenship, and the welfare state by challenging the assumed neutrality, and 'whiteness', of the latter. She traces continuities and changes to both neo-liberalism and the social investment model and their effects on different women by focusing on race inequalities, on Indigenous people in general, and on Indigenous women in particular. Her chapter illuminates how policies influenced by both neo-liberalism and social investment perpetuate racialized constructions of Indigenous peoples and produce a reconfigured Indigenous citizenship. Indigenous peoples' socio-economic, racial, and political conditions are now viewed as problems to be 'solved'. This is especially apparent when it comes to Indigenous women, who are constructed as 'victim-subjects', unknowing subjects and actors. In that way, state interventions and interference in Aboriginal self-government are justified as 'rescuing women from their own culture'. At the same time, Altamirano-Jiménez also acknowledges the role being played by new citizenship discourses and practices that, paradoxically and problematically, treat women as both victim-subjects and empowered citizens. These contradictory portrayals not only undermine Indigenous peoples' self-government claims, but also excuse the Canadian state's resistance to realizing Indigenous entitlements.

Yasmeen Abu-Laban continues the critical interrogation of the role played by the state (as well as the nation) in responding to issues of equality and diversity. In Chapter 7, moving beyond a consideration of the neo-liberal threat to the welfare state, she problematizes two faulty assumptions frequently being made in scholarship on contemporary liberal democracies: that is, that both immigration and multiculturalism are also posing threats to the welfare state. Here too, we see women depicted instrumentally, but in this case, it is female immigrants who are cast as victims of 'patriarchal cultures' whose status in the private sphere threatens the gains made by Western women as rights-bearing citizens. As in many of the other contributions to this volume, 'risk' and integrationist discourses and rationales are prominent. However, Abu-Laban highlights the troubling associations that are being made between 'risk' and concepts like social cohesion vis-à-vis immigrants, refugees, and racialized groups, especially in a security-obsessed post–September 11 environment. In other words, now immigrants and ethnic, racial, and cultural diversity are being labelled as 'risky' and blamed for insecurity. Hence, Abu-Laban makes the links explicit between not only neo-liberalism and changes to immigration and multicultural policy, but also between the latter and the logic of integration, social cohesion, and national attachment and national-security concerns.

From the national level, Cheryl N. Collier moves the discussion to the provincial level. In Chapter 8 she compares anti-violence policies pursued by Ontarian and British Columbian governments between 1994 and 2007. This case study of a woman-focused policy arena poses a number of pertinent questions: Are all policy fields affected by neo-liberalism and post–neo-liberalism in the same ways? Have governments of different political stripes differed in their responses? What has been the impact of other political actors, such as those involved in women's movements? In the end, Collier's analysis of anti-violence policy demonstrates the significance of partisan political variation, as well as the importance of changes in political contexts and actors to neo-liberalism and post–neo-liberalism. For example, even in neo-liberal times, left-wing regimes were more willing to accept feminist critiques and solutions to violence against women. Right-wing regimes were more reluctant, even when they were prepared to re-invest in anti-violence services. Through this study, Collier also makes it clear that the move from neo-liberalism to post–neo-liberalism is not an uncomplicated, chronological process.

The following two chapters examine the impact of neo-liberalism and post–neo-liberalism on policy and legislation, as well as on court cases. In Chapter 9, Lois Harder directs our attention to how the state is implicated in the families, sexual lives, and identities of citizens through the regulation of intimate life. Her chapter explores the state's regulation of marriage and 'marriage-like' relationships and the contradictions that have developed in light of rationales of political membership and economic efficiency. Harder considers conjugality at a pan-Canadian level, but also in relation to policy decisions taken in Alberta. She relates changes in policies concerning conjugality to the entrenchment and normalization of neo-liberalism and makes the links to social investment, especially given the growing familial obligations involved in both neo-liberal and social investment governing projects.

Chapter 10 explores why neo-liberalism was slower to take hold at the level of the Charter of Rights and Freedoms and the Supreme Court. Alexandra Dobrowolsky details how, in these realms, equality gains were ostensibly being made in the midst of neo-liberal consolidation. However, she unpacks assessments of women as either 'winners' or 'losers' with the Charter and the courts by showing how cases that were once considered banner 'victories' are not so clear-cut, and how feminist losses are similarly not as one-dimensional as they seem at first. Instead, she points to changing institutions and ideas, interests and identities, to explain the attenuation of substantive equality, particularly in the context of marketization and the coming to power of the Conservatives.

Last but not least, in Chapter 11 Isabella Bakker considers national and international developments by delving into what is actually happening to Canada's international commitments like the Beijing Platform for Action, the Convention for the Elimination of Discrimination against Women, and the Millennium Development Goals. She contrasts federal government rhetoric in relation to the financing of these goals with the failure to keep these promises, and with the decline in gender-based monitoring mechanisms that has made it more difficult to 'follow the money'. Bakker examines critically how 'macro' policies are defined in light of neo-liberal priorities, as well as the growing fiscalization of social policy that comes with the social investment perspective, and how both undervalue women's unpaid labour.

## Conclusion

The development of neo-liberalism has not been even. In his sweeping account of its history and evolution, even David Harvey writes that various 'forces and fluxes' have affected the degree of neo-liberalization (2005, 115) and he concedes that 'some attention must be paid to contextual conditions and institutional arrangements' (116). And thus, the explicit objective of this collection is to stimulate discussions and debates on the state of neo-liberalism and the status of women when it comes to public policy in Canada, by advancing more nuanced, context-specific analyses, at several levels—macro, meso, and micro. When we do so, it becomes clearer that neo-liberalism is neither unified nor uniform.

What then follows is the volume's more destabilizing aim. As Clarke stresses, it is important to 'imply a way of thinking about neo-liberalism that reduces its density and totalizing weight—and the analytical and political breathlessness that such weight induces' (2008a, 145). By problematizing the breadth and depth of neo-liberalism, plumbing its internal contradictions, and pursuing contending ideas and developments, we can begin to identify and assess both competing, and better still, alternative, discourses and practices. For only by proceeding in these ways can 'we make visible the contestations and struggles that we are currently engaged in' (Larner 2000, 21) and, ideally, prime progressive politics for other potentialities.

### Note

I would like to once again acknowledge and thank Paul Bernard, Pascal Dufour, Jane Jenson, Denis Saint-Martin, and Deena White for their painstaking efforts to map out the parameters of the social investment perspective. I am also grateful for Wendy Larner's careful work on neo-liberalism, and her helpful comments on an earlier version of this chapter, and for the anonymous reviewers' feedback.

### References

Bashevkin, Sylvia. 1998. *Women on the Defensive: Living through Conservative Times*. Toronto: University of Toronto Press.

———. 2002. *Welfare Hot Buttons: Women, Work, and Social Policy Reform*. Toronto: University of Toronto Press.

Bakker, Isabella, ed. 1996. *Rethinking Restructuring: Gender and Change in Canada*. Toronto: University of Toronto Press.

Bonoli, Guiliano. 2003. 'Social Policy through Labour Markets: Understanding National Differences in the Provision of Economic Security to Wage Earners, *Comparative Political Studies* 36 (9): 1007–30.

Brock, Kathy. 2006. 'The Devil's in the Detail: The Chrétien Legacy for the Third Sector'. In Lois Harder and Steve Patten, eds, *The Chrétien Legacy: Politics and Public Policy in Canada*, 255–75. Montreal: McGill-Queen's University Press.

Brodie, Ian. 2002. *Friends of the Court: The Privileging of Interest-Group Litigants in Canada*. Albany: State University of New York Press.

Brodie, Janine, ed. 1996. *Women and Canadian Public Policy*. Toronto: Harcourt Brace.

Brown, Wendy. 2005. *Edgework: Critical Essays on Knowledge and Politics*. Princeton: Princeton University Press.

Clarke, John. 2008a. 'Living with/in and without Neo-liberalism', *Focaal: European Journal of Anthropology* 51: 135–47.

———. 2008b. 'Reply: Power, Politics, and Places: What's Not Neo-liberal?' *Focaal: European Journal of Anthropology* 51: 158–60.

Clarkson, Stephen. 2005. *The Big Red Machine: How the Liberal Party Dominates Canadian Politics*. Vancouver: University of British Columbia Press.

Cossman, Brenda, and Judy Fudge, eds. 2002. *Privatization, Law, and the Challenge to Feminism*. Toronto: University of Toronto Press.

Dobrowolsky, Alexandra. 2002. 'Rhetoric versus Reality: The Figure of the Child and New Labour's Strategic Social Investment State', *Studies in Political Economy* 29: 43–73.

———. 2006. 'The Chrétien Legacy and Women: Changing Policy Priorities with Little Cause for Celebration'. In Lois Harder and Steve Patten, eds, *The Chrétien Legacy: Politics and Public Policy in Canada*, 181–219. Montreal: McGill Queen's University Press.

———. 2008a. 'The Women's Movement in Flux: Feminist and Framing, Passion and Politics'. In Miriam Smith, ed., *Group Politics and Social Movements in Canada*, 159–80. Peterborough: Broadview Press.

———. 2008b. 'Interrogating "Invisibilization" and "Instrumentalization": Women and Current Citizenship Trends in Canada', *Citizenship Studies* 12 (5): 465–79.

———, and Jane Jenson. 2004. 'Shifting Representations of Citizenship: Canadian Politics of "Women" and "Children" ', *Social Politics* 11 (2): 154–10.

———, and ———. 2005. 'Social Investment Perspectives and Practices: A Decade in British Politics'. In Martin Powell, Linda Bauld, and Karen Clarke, eds, *Social Policy Review 17: Analysis and Debate in Social Policy, 2005*, 203–30. Bristol: Policy Press.

———, with Ruth Lister. 2006. 'Social Exclusion and Changes to Citizenship: Women and Children, Minorities and Migrants'. In Evangelia Tastsoglou and Alexandra Dobrowolsky, eds, *Women, Migration and Citizenship: Making Local, National and Transnational Connections*, 149–81. Aldershot: Ashgate Press.

———, and ———. 2008. 'Social Investment: The Discourse and the Dimensions of Change'. In Martin Powell, ed., *Modernising the Welfare State: The Blair Legacy*, 125–42. Bristol: Policy Press.

———, and Denis Saint-Martin. 2005. 'Agency, Actors and Change in a Child Focused Future: Problematising Path Dependency', *Journal of Commonwealth and Comparative Politics* 43: 1, 1–33.

Esping-Andersen, Gøsta. 2002. *Why We Need a New Welfare State*. Oxford: Oxford University Press.

Evans, Patricia M., and Gerda R. Wekerle, eds. 1997. *Women and the Canadian Welfare State: Challenges and Change*. Toronto: University of Toronto Press.

Gabriel, Christina, and Laura Macdonald. 1996. 'NAFTA and Economic Restructuring: Some Gender and Race Implications'. In Isabella Bakker, ed., *Rethinking Restructuring: Gender and Change in Canada*, 165–86. Toronto: University of Toronto Press.

George, Susan. 2000. 'A Short History of Neoliberalism: Twenty Years of Elite Economics and Emerging Opportunities for Structural Change'. In W. Bello, N. Bullard, and K. Malhotra, eds, *Global Finance: New Thinking on Regulating Capital Markets*, 27–35. London: Zed.

Giddens, Anthony. *The Third Way: The Renewal of Social Democracy*. Cambridge: Polity Press.

Hale, Sarah, Will Leggett, and Luke Martell, eds. 2004. *The Third Way and Beyond: Criticisms, Futures, Alternatives*. Manchester: Manchester University Press.

Hall, Peter A., and David Soskice. 2001. *Varieties of Capitalism: The Institutional Foundations of Comparative Advantage*. Oxford: Oxford University Press.

Hankivsky, Olena. 2007. 'Gender Mainstreaming in the Canadian Context: "One Step Forward and Two Steps Back" '. In Michael Orsini and Miriam Smith, eds, *Critical Policy Studies*, 111–35. Vancouver: UBC Press.

Harvey, David. 2005. *A Brief History of Neoliberalism*. Oxford: Oxford University Press.

Hay, Colin. 1999. *The Political Economy of New Labour*. Manchester: Manchester University Press.

Hemerijck, Anton. 2002. 'The Self-Transformation of the European Social Model(s)'. In Gøsta Esping-Andersen, with Duncan Gallie, Anton Hemerijck, and John Myles, eds, *Why We Need a New Welfare State*. Oxford: Oxford University Press.

Jenson, Jane. 2001. 'Canada's Shifting Citizenship Regime: Investing in Children'. In Trevor C. Salmon and Michael Keating, eds, *The Dynamics of Decentralization*, 107–24. Montreal: McGill-Queen's University Press.

———. 2008. 'Explaining Social Policy'. Presentation for workshop roundtable, 'Explaining Social Policy'. Canadian Political Science Association Annual Conference. June 4–6, University of British Columbia.

———, and Denis Saint-Martin. 2003. 'New Routes to Social Cohesion? Citizenship and the Social Investment State', *Canadian Journal of Sociology* 28 (1): 77–99.

———, and ———. 2006. 'Building Blocks for a New Social Architecture: The Lego Paradigm of an Active Society', *Policy and Politics* 34 (3): 429–51.

Jessop, Bob. 2002. 'Liberalism, Neoliberalism and Urban Governance: A State-Theoretical Perspectives', *Antipode* 34 (2): 452–72.

Larner, Wendy. 2000. 'Neo-liberalism, Policy, Ideology, Governmentality', *Studies in Political Economy* 63: 3–25.

———, and David Craig. 2005. 'After Neoliberalism? Community Activism and Local Partnerships in Aotearoa New Zealand', *Antipode* 37 (3): 401–24.

Lister, Ruth. 2003. 'Investing in the Citizen-Workers of the Future: Transformations in Citizenship and the State under New Labour', *Social Policy and Administration* 37 (5): 427–43.

Lum, Janet, and A. Paul Williams. 'Out of Sync with a "Shrinking State": Making Sense of the Employment Equity Act (1995)?'. In Mike Burke, Colin Mooers, and John Shields, *Restructuring and Resistance: Canadian Public Policy in an Age of Global Capitalism*, 194–211. Halifax: Fernwood Press.

McBride, Stephen, and Kathleen McNutt. 2007. 'Devolution and Neoliberalism in the Canadian Welfare State: Ideology, National and International Conditioning Frameworks, and Policy Change in British Columbia', *Global Social Policy* 7 (2): 177–201.

Macdonald, Laura. 2003. 'Gender and Canadian Trade Policy: Women's Strategies for Access and Transformation'. In Claire Turenne Sjolander, Heather A. Smith, and Deborah Steinstra, eds, *Feminist Perspectives on Canadian Foreign Policy*, 40–54. Toronto: Oxford University Press.

McKeen, Wendy. 2007. 'The National Children's Agenda: A Neoliberal Wolf in Lamb's Clothing', *Studies in Political Economy* 80: 151–73.

———, and Ann Porter. 2003. 'Politics and Transformation: Welfare State Restructuring in Canada'. In Wallace Clement and Leah Vosko, eds, *Changing Canada: Political Economy as Transformation*. Montreal: McGill-Queens University Press.

Marshall, T.H. 1965. *Class, Citizenship and Social Development: Essays*. Garden City, NY: Anchor Books.

Morton, F.L., and Rainer Knopff. 2000. *The Charter Revolution and the Court Party*. Peterborough: Broadview Press.

Murray, Karen Bridget. 2007. 'Governmentality and Shifting Winds of Policy Studies'. In Michael Orsini and Miriam Smith, eds, *Critical Policy Studies* 161–84. Vancouver: UBC Press.

Newman, Jacquetta, and Linda A. White. 2006. *Women, Politics and Public Policy: The Political Struggles of Canadian Women.* Toronto: Oxford University Press.

O'Connor, Julia S., Ann Shola Orloff, and Sheila Shaver. 1999. *States, Markets, Families: Gender, Liberalism and Social Policy in Australia, Canada, Great Britain and the United States.* Cambridge: Cambridge University Press.

Ong, Aihwa. 2006. *Neoliberalism as Exception: Mutations in Citizenship and Sovereignty.* Durham, NC: Duke University Press.

Orsini, Michael, and Miriam Smith. 2007. 'Critical Policy Studies'. In Michael Orsini and Miriam Smith, eds, *Critical Policy Studies*, 1–16. Vancouver: UBC Press.

Peck, Jamie. 2004. 'Geography and Public Policy Constructions of Neoliberalism', *Progress in Human Geography* 28 (3): 392–405.

———, and Adam Tickell. 2002. 'Neoliberalizing Space', *Antipode* 34 (3): 380–404.

Phillips, Susan D. 2001. 'SUFA and Citizen Engagement: Fake or Genuine Masterpiece?' *Policy Matters* 2 (7): 1–36.

Pierson, Paul. *1994. Dismantling the Welfare State? Reagan, Thatcher and the Politics of Retrenchment.* Cambridge: Cambridge University Press.

Powell, Martin. 1999. *New Labour, New Welfare State?* Bristol: Policy Press.

Saint-Martin, Denis. 2007. 'From the Welfare State to the Social Investment State: A New Paradigm for Canadian Social Policy?'. In Michael Orsini and Miriam Smith, eds, *Critical Policy Studies*, 279–98. Vancouver: UBC Press.

———, and Alexandra Dobrowolsky. 2005. 'Social Learning, Third Way Politics, and Welfare State Redesign'. In André Lecours, ed., *New Institutionalism Theory and Analysis*, 245–75. Toronto: University of Toronto Press.

Smith, Miriam. 2005. *A Civil Society? Collective Actors in Political Life.* Peterborough, Ont.: Broadview Press.

Smith, Neil. 2008. 'Comment: Neo-liberalism: Dominant but Dead', *Focaal: European Journal of Anthropology* 51: 155–7.

Statistics Canada. 2006. 'General Social Survey: Paid and Unpaid Work'. http://www.statcan.ca/Daily/English/0607/19/d060719b.htm.

Streeck, Wolfgang, and Kathleen Thelen. 2005. *Beyond Continuity: Institutional Change in Advanced Political Economies.* Oxford: Oxford University Press.

Tickell, Adam, and Jamie Peck. 2003. 'Making Global Rules: Globalization of Neoliberalization?'. In Jamie Peck and Henry Wai-chung Yeung, eds, *Remaking the Global Economy: Economic-Geographic Perspectives.* London: Sage.

Timpson, Annis May. 2001. *Driven Apart: Women's Employment Equality and Child Care in Canadian Public Policy.* Vancouver: UBC Press.

Trimble, Linda, and Jane Arscott. 2003. *Still Counting: Women in Politics across Canada.* Peterborough, Ont.: Broadview Press.

Vickers, Jill. 2008. 'Do Feminist Organizations Need a Coordinating "Peak" Agency to Influence State Policies in Federations?' Presentation for panel 'Before, During and After the National Action Committee on the Status of Women'. Canadian Political Science Association Annual Conference. June 4–6, University of British Columbia.

Whitaker, Reg. 2006. 'The Chrétien Legacy'. In Lois Harder and Steve Patten, eds, *The Chrétien Legacy: Politics and Public Policy in Canada*, 3–36. Montreal: McGill Queen's University Press.

Wincott, Daniel. 2006. 'Paradoxes of New Labour Social Policy: Toward Universal Child Care in Europe's "Most Liberal" Welfare Regime', *Social Politics* 13 (2): 286–312.

# CHAPTER 1

# Writing Gender Out:

## The Continuing Effects of the Social Investment Perspective

Jane Jenson

## Introduction

In federal politics there is much less talk these days about gender equality, and many policies and institutions that feminists claimed and constructed are no more. Assaults against those institutions were dramatic in the first months of the Harper government that was elected in 2006. In their 2006 campaign book, the Conservatives, using the classic neo-liberal language of 'choice', advocated the rolling back of the 'one-size-fits-all plan to build a massive childcare bureaucracy' and promised to 'let parents chose [*sic*] what's best for their children, . . . whether that means formal childcare, informal care through neighbours or relatives, or a parent staying at home.'[1] Years of research and advocacy about the advantages of high-quality early-childhood services were ignored in this position. It was driven by analyses such as those of REAL Women of Canada which propounded the notion that children needed to be rescued from childcare.[2] Thus, the beginnings of a pan-Canadian childcare program finally laid down by the Liberal government of Paul Martin was dismantled immediately and replaced by an allowance whose full benefit would go to two-parent families with a single earner, that is, families with a stay-at-home and non-earning parent. In response, numerous groups rose up in protest and coalitions were stitched together. Opposition to the Conservatives' stance on childcare was the rallying point for numerous progressive forces opposed to the government (Holly 2009).

In addition to this backtracking on a key service needed by many women, the political representation of women was significantly reduced. The first cabinet named by Stephen Harper had fewer women than that of Paul Martin, and no woman was named to a major portfolio. In fall 2006, state and quasi-public institutions that housed or protected feminist analyses were the target. The Court Challenges Program was cancelled, and the Law Commission of Canada dismantled. Most dramatically, Status of Women Canada, already limping along as a minor agency within the government, saw its budget slashed while the very word 'equality' was excised from its mandate and the rules changed so that women's groups could not use federal funding for advocacy or lobbying. And yet there was much less mobilization than around the childcare issue. As long-time feminist and former president of the National Action Committee on the Status of Women, Judy Rebick put it: 'In one way, the Harper changes are the nail in the coffin, which may be why they are receiving so little attention' (Rebick 2006).

How can we understand these assaults on services and on the institutionalized representation of women? One explanation would be simply to point to the neo-liberalism of the Harper government and use that to tell the story of yet more sliding away from the policy and political forms established in the forty years after 1945. But such a story is too simple. It cannot tell us why the retreat from childcare generated mobilization by advocates, whereas the cuts to the representation of women provoked much less. Nor can it account for differences between neo-liberal governments in power at the same time. If we look at the neo-liberal government of Quebec under the Liberals led by Premier Jean Charest since 2003, we see a quite different story of childcare services and the representation of women.

There is no denying that the Charest government took office with classically neo-liberal positions and that many of the tenets of neo-liberalism, such as privileging tax cuts and expecting practically everyone to be in the paid labour force, continue to guide its politics (Boismenu et al. 2004). It also dragged its feet on pay equity, initially capped the expansion of childcare, and increased the private-sector component of the system (Jenson 2008b). There were proposals to eliminate the thirty-year-old Conseil du statut de la femme (CSF) by folding it into a Conseil de l'égalité (Equality Council). Such actions were justified by the government's goal of re-engineering the Quebec model of society to modernize it and make it competitive in a globalized world, partly by reducing public spending and opening more space for market forces.

Yet, efforts to undermine programs supporting women and gender equality have been tempered. After significant mobilization by civil society, the CSF's mandate and its focus on gender equality were maintained.[3] The cabinet that Jean Charest named after the 2007 elections was 50 per cent female, a first in Quebec and Canada. It also included the first Black female minister, and two of the most important positions (finance and deputy prime minister) were held by powerful women. These firsts were all hailed by the main women's organization, the Fédération des femmes du Québec.[4] In its 2008 budget, the government, despite the bleak economic outlook, announced new spending on childcare, promising to support funding for the creation of 20,000 new spaces over five years. Moreover, in doing so it explicitly *rejected* the proposal of the official opposition to 'compensate' parents not using subsidized services with a substantial monthly payment. In other words, while the Action démocratique du Québec (ADQ) advocated a made-in-Quebec measure very similar to the Harper government's so-called Universal Child Care Benefit and made the same criticisms of public support for non-parental childcare, the Liberals explicitly rejected those views in the name of gender equality. As the policy document prepared for the 2008 policy conference explicitly put it:

> [T]he Quebec Liberal Party is strongly opposed to any program such as the one proposed by Mario Dumont of the ADQ that would have the indirect effect of encouraging people to withdraw from the labour market and of reducing women's financial independence. Facing a major demographic challenge, Quebec needs everyone's shoulder at the wheel. As a society we cannot afford to spend more than a billion dollars to push people to choose to stay at home. Such a program is not a good solution. (QLP 2008, 15, my translation)

It is not enough, then, simply to see the neo-liberalism of the Harper government as the reason for its assault against policies and institutions representing women and feminism as well as the services on which women depend. Instead, this chapter will claim that much that the Harper government did was made possible by the move under the Liberal governments of Jean Chrétien and Paul Martin towards the social investment perspective on social policy. This reorientation, where it is fully developed, has brought not only new policy goals and actions but also a discourse focused on children and young people. There are consequences of this shift for the kind of attention that women and gender equality receive. A key social mechanism is at work. It is the writing out of women and gender.[5] Where women's circumstances and needs used to be present in policy discourse and action, they are no more.[6] State actions are justified in terms other than the advancement of equality between women and men, and mobilization by civil society is organized in the name of actors other than women and to overturn something other than unequal gender relations.

The same shift to the social investment perspective did not occur in Quebec, either under the Parti Québécois governments from 1994 to 1998 or the Liberals between 2003 and 2007 (Dufour et al. 2008). There, the story of policy change is different. Although the Quebec childcare system has a much larger place for the private sector now than in its original design, the government supports this public policy more now than it did before its election in 2003 (Jenson 2008b; 2002). Although the women's movement is critical of the government on many fronts, it is still represented both in and by the CSF. The status of women secretariat (Secrétariat à la condition féminine) still describes its mandate as supporting and developing the actions of all government agencies in order to advance gender equality.[7] The parity between women and men in the Quebec cabinet is in sharp contrast to the Harper cabinet named in January 2006, only 21 per cent of whose members were women. This number is low by international standards as well as in comparison to earlier federal cabinets.[8] In other words, although the Liberal government of Quebec is neo-liberal on many issues, its assaults against women and principles of gender equality are much less dramatic, and this despite a strong emphasis on family policy. The writing out of gender equality that we see clearly at the federal level is less obvious in Quebec. Why might this be so?

# Why 'Neo-liberalism' Cannot Explain Everything

How can we understand the greater mobilization against the childcare positions of the Harper government than against its virtual elimination of, among other things, the last redoubt of the 'women's state'?[9] And what would help us to understand why two neo-liberal governments behave quite differently? Several approaches are available. One would focus simply on the right-wing positions adopted by the Harper and Charest governments and the individual men who lead them. Numerous accounts exist, for example, of the Harper government's neo-liberalism and its strong ties to the anti-feminist REAL Women network.[10] The Charest Liberals are also frequently painted with the colours of neo-liberalism, whether by their opponents on the left, for example, the Forum social québécois (Canet 2007) or by academics (Rouillard et al. 2003). I do not dispute that they are neo-liberal, but nonetheless they have acted differently.

Other analysts would adopt a much more general level of analysis, attributing positions to a world-wide trend towards neo-liberalism that has shaped—and plagued—politics since the beginning of the 1980s. For example, as Janine Brodie writes:

> The emerging neo-liberal state rests on a radical redrawing of the boundaries among the public, the market and the domestic spheres. The new citizenship is based on a disembodied individualism, unattached to social structures, and is contingent upon participation in the waged economy . . . [and] is profoundly phallocentric. (Brodie 1997, 239)

If the times are simply neo-liberal, why did the federal Liberal government work long and hard before 2005 to establish agreements in principle with the provinces that provided funding for non-parental childcare and why did the Conservative government cancel the same agreements with great fanfare?

Neither of these accounts is satisfactory, therefore. The first account is too specific in its focus on persons and partisan ideology, and it provides little to account for some of the continuity visible at the federal level from the Liberals to the Harper government. The second account, however, focuses too much on continuity and does not explain the differences among federal governments, between the federal and Quebec governments, and across the policy domains of childcare and gender equality. The plunge in attention to gender equality occurred under the federal Liberals. When the Conservatives were replaced by the Liberals in 1993, the new government did not renew its ties to the women's movement and its organizations (Dobrowolsky 2004, 2008). The Liberal government quickly and without fanfare dismantled huge chunks of the 'women's state', dissolving the Canadian Advisory Council on the Status of Women, for example, and reducing the links between state institutions and civil-society organizations (Jenson and Phillips 1996). The same Liberal governments, however, developed and maintained ties to groups advocating social justice, including those advocating for affordable and accessible childcare, and often consulted with them (Laforest and Orsini 2005).

In order to understand both continuity and difference, it is helpful to turn to the institutional level of analysis. The institutional level allows partisan effects to be included in the analysis without their being made the sole explanatory factor. It also permits a better periodization of the last several decades. There is now consensus that neo-liberalism profoundly challenged and destabilized post-1945 political projects, policy arrangements, and practices of governing. Both in the global South, where the Washington Consensus reshaped economies and political institutions, and in the OECD world, there was a move away from the policies and practices of the three decades after 1945. In particular, there were concerted efforts to roll back existing guarantees—limited as they were—of social protection and practices of interest intermediation in the name of a larger role for the market, families, and communities.

In the mid-1990s, however, ideas about 'social investment' spread in Europe, Canada, and Latin America. Close observers began to identify positions they characterized as 'after–neo-liberalism' and policy interventions substantially different from those of neo-liberals (Larner and Craig 2005; Riesco 2007). There is little agreement about what these ideas mean, however. Two principal positions exist. One is that neo-liberalism is still hegemonic. Political projects that claim to offer something 'after neo-liberalism', such as those proposing 'a third way' or promising to 'modernize' social policy, are treated as little more than a slightly adjusted version of the basic form itself. A second position is that after two decades of hegemony, neo-liberalism hit an impasse in the mid-1990s as social problems multiplied. This position rests on documentation of waning enthusiasm for neo-liberalism and a search by policy communities for more generous alternatives, albeit without a return to past practices.

In large part, whether one sees no change or some change between neo-liberalism and after–neo-liberalism depends on the object of the analysis. This important epistemological point is often missed by those who see neo-liberalism everywhere. If the social relations of capitalism are the object of analysis, there is a tendency to gloss over policy differences in order to describe the deep structures, which do not change. In many ways, such formulations take us back to the all-encompassing structuralism, whether Marxist or sociological, of earlier decades.[11] They demonstrate little concern for comparative analysis and, therefore, for variation across time and space. They remain at a high level of generalization without systematic attention to policy objectives and instruments.

For those whose object of analysis is public policy, such high-level abstractions and structural analyses are of limited use and indeed seem to belie some of the observed patterns of policy development. Empirical findings raise difficult questions for broad-brush structuralism, whether Marxist or sociological. The failure of American and British neo-liberal projects to downsize significantly has been amply documented (for example, by Huber and Stephens 2001) and others have analyzed the variable consequences of even neo-liberal projects for social citizenship (see, for example, Jenson and Sineau 2001).

Policy analysts focus on the institutional level of analysis, therefore. They emphasize that since the second half of the 1990s, a number of countries in Latin America and Europe, as well as in the English-speaking world, international organizations, and the European Union have moved away from the cuts and constraints of neo-liberalism towards another response to new social risks.[12] Indeed 1997 was a watershed year around the world (Porter and Craig 2004, 391).[13] In Canada, it was the year that the Parti Québécois government announced its new family policy, redesigning family allowances and other income supports, as well as introducing universal and affordable childcare in order to fight poverty, encourage labour-market attachment, and provide quality preschool and out-of-school childcare (Jenson 2002). It was also the year of the National Child Benefit (NCB), whose introduction was meant to spark a pan-Canadian redesign of social policy and remake intergovernmental relations in the social domain. In particular, it was meant to encourage labour-force attachment by parents as well as removing the welfare wall and making 'wise and strategic investments', as the 1997 Speech from the Throne had promised (Dobrowolsky and Saint-Martin 2005, 9–10).[14] The Provincial/Territorial Council on Social Policy Renewal was established, and over the next years, until the Social Union Framework Agreement (SUFA) was signed in 1999, a number of important initiatives in the area of child and family benefits as well as a rethinking of policy perspectives on disability emerged from these processes of intergovernmental negotiations (Fortin, Noël, and St-Hilaire 2002).[15]

The convergence of ideas and policies for a social architecture of labour-force activation and investment to reduce the effects of child poverty has generated the three main principles of what we can term the 'social investment perspective'.[16] First, it defines 'security' less in terms of income security in the present than as the capacity to respond to new challenges throughout the life course. Life-long learning, as well as investments in human capital, are assumed to be the individual's best guarantee of having this capacity, and it is educational experiences in the early years which are the foundation of that capacity. Second, this perspective is future-oriented. What is happening to children and youth now is already creating the future, and future success will depend on what happens to them now. Therefore, investments must be targeted to their needs. Finally, successful social investment strategies benefit more than individuals: they enrich our common future. Activity in the present is beneficial for the community as a whole, now and into the future (Jenson and Saint-Martin 2006, 435). This social investment perspective informed federal policy actions after 1997, prompting attention to child development, health, and social care (Dobrowolsky and Saint-Martin 2005).

The child-centred social investment perspective was less influential in Quebec, however. Although the government was moving towards a major redesign of family policy at the same time as the federal government and some provinces, there was much less emphasis on 'investing in children'. Indeed, the government of Quebec systematically opted out of the child-focused policy initiatives of the late 1990s, in the name of respect for the constitutional division of powers and its own family policy initiatives. Then, when it did sign a childcare agreement with Ottawa in 2005, the accord was quite different from the other nine. It did not focus on the ideas of social investment but on Quebec's existing childcare system as well as the division of constitutional responsibilities.

This different route to similar policy goals (encouraging labour-force participation and healthy child development as well as reducing poverty) was followed for several reasons. First, Quebec has had a family policy since the 1980s, something the other provinces have never had. Therefore, the new program model could be inserted into pre-existing institutions rather than necessitating the creation of new institutions and arrangements. Second, those institutions were ones that had been under the influence of feminists for several years. The minister who brought forward the new family policy in 1997, Pauline Marois, was a feminist of long standing,[17] and her assistant deputy minister, Nicole Boily, was another long-time feminist. Although they represented the family policy reform of 1997 as having many objectives, a key one was the promotion of gender equality.[18] The needs of children were of course emphasized, but they did not have the priority they had in initiatives such as the National Child Benefit or the National Children's Agenda (NCA). The Quebec reform did not write gender out, and as seen above, there continued to be political space for women's groups of all kinds to defend gender-based and equality claims.

The rest of this chapter will trace the ways that the federal version of a social investment perspective, which, in contrast, focused on children, has resulted in gender being written out of the story such that excising the word 'equality' from Status of Women Canada's mandate could, as Judy Rebick put it, 'receive so little attention'.

## The Social Investment Perspective Is Taken Up in Canada

In 1997, the government of Canada consolidated its new approach to social policy.[19] Objectives as well as instruments were remodelled. Pressure for change came from the perception of new social risks, to be sure. But it also came from the government's goal of regaining some of the policy influence lost when Ottawa slew its deficit by off-loading to the provinces. In 1995 the minister of finance, Paul Martin, unilaterally sounded the death knell of the Canada Assistance Plan (CAP), which had shaped the relationship between the federal government and the provinces since 1966. He also announced unilaterally its replacement, the Canada Health and Social Transfer (CHST). In exchange for greater autonomy in how they could spend the money transferred from Ottawa into their coffers, the provinces would receive billions of dollars less in transfer payments. Not surprisingly this initiative generated huge objections from most provinces, which suddenly found their budgetary situation deteriorating as that of the federal government moved into the black. As it conquered its fiscal problems, the federal government found itself facing an intergovernmental crisis (Boismenu and Jenson 1998). The eventual result was a significant reform of the approach to social policy, a reform with a social investment perspective at its heart.

The post-1945 social policy paradigm had concentrated on the male breadwinner and his dependants. Thus, unemployment insurance, pensions, and social assistance were designed to provide some replacement income when that breadwinner could no longer earn enough. In that paradigm, women were assumed to be dependent on male breadwinners. Social assistance, for example, provided a replacement income for women without a male breadwinner to count on, such as widows or lone mothers. Indeed, well into the 1990s several provincial social-assistance regimes excused lone mothers with preschool children (and in Ontario under age 16) from the work requirements imposed on other social-assistance recipients. In keeping with long-standing notions of the gender division of labour, they were considered 'unavailable' for employment (Boychuk 1998, 34; Jenson 1999, 32–3).

After the federal, provincial, and territorial governments agreed to target child poverty, the National Child Benefit and National Children's Agenda both received high priority in the 1997 Speech from the Throne (Dobrowolsky and Saint-Martin 2005, 9–10). They were followed by later initiatives on early child development and childcare, all marking the institutionalization of the social investment focus on children. The NCB and the NCA were founded on a different policy logic than that of the male breadwinner and female caregiver. This 1998 description of the NCB clearly exposes its multiple objectives:

> Goals of the initiative are to: help prevent and reduce the depth of child poverty; promote attachment to the work force; and reduce overlap and duplication between Canadian and provincial/territorial programs. The National Child Benefit will begin to remove child benefits from welfare, assist parents with the cost of raising children, and make it easier for low income parents to support their families through employment without resorting to welfare.[20]

In other words, all parents were to be in the labour market, while governments targeted income support towards children so as to fight child poverty. Provinces redesigned their social assistance programs, reducing benefits to adults without children under 18, although, as we will see in more detail below, not all provinces did so with the same enthusiasm. In Ontario between 1995 and 2005, a single employable social-assistance recipient saw his or her income drop from $9,927 to $7,007 (29 per cent); in Quebec the drop was from $7,573 to $6,947 (8 per cent) (NCW 2006, Table 3.1, 44ff.). Governments also reworked their health programs to emphasize the early years and developmental milestones, which all children were expected to achieve in order to be ready for school (Stroick and Jenson 1999, 38ff.).

This logic of targeting children was embedded in a larger framework, that of the National Children's Agenda. It proceeded clearly from a social investment perspective:

> There is strong evidence, including scientific research, that what happens to children when they are very young shapes their health and well-being throughout their life-time. Science has proven what we have intrinsically known all along—healthy children grow into healthy, successful adults, who will shape our future. . . . Many people and levels of government already work every day to give Canada's children the best possible opportunity to develop their full potential as healthy, successful and contributing members of society.[21]

Here we see not only the focus on children, but also the future orientation and the notion that 'we all' benefit from investing in children now.

A third pillar of Canada's social investment perspective was the effort from 1997 through 2005 to revitalize the movement towards a pan-Canadian child-care system. The federal government offered funds to the provinces in several different packages in an attempt to entice them to make a strong commitment to early childhood education and care (Mahon and Phillips 2002). Often the advocates for a pan-Canadian system took Quebec as a model, arguing for a situation in which both childcare for preschoolers and out-of-school care would be widely available and affordable. This tendency to look to Quebec was given a boost when a major cross-national study, by the Organisation for Economic Co-operation and Development (OECD), of childcare in twenty countries found Canada to be lagging far behind the others and praised Quebec for its far-sightedness in establishing its childcare programs in 1997 and reforming parental insurance later (OECD 2006, 79, for example). Finally, in 2005, and just before its electoral defeat, the Liberal government managed to negotiate the agreements in principle, based on four principles accepted by the provinces: quality, universal inclusion, accessibility, and development. The following statement from the agreement in principle between Canada and Nova Scotia (signed on 16 May 2005) is typical of the agreements between the federal and nine of the provincial governments:[22]

> The early years of life are critically important for the development and future well-being of children. Research demonstrates that high quality early learning and child care (ELCC) can play an important role in promoting social, emotional and cognitive development of young children. Promotion of learning and development in early childhood supports the participation of parents in employment and education, and supports parents in their primary responsibility for the care and nurturing of their children by improving early learning and child care for families with young children.

In these documents, the governments (those of some of the provinces only reluctantly) described a vision of early learning and childcare that took it far beyond support for parents so that they could engage in paid work. The federal government and several provinces had wholeheartedly adopted the social investment perspective that was the underpinning of, for example, the OECD's focus on the early years as those in which the most productive investments in human capital and in learning are made (OECD 2006, 38). Other governments accepted that framing of the agreement in order to receive the funds.

The form and content of the agreement with Quebec (signed on 28 October 2005) was quite different, however. It did not frame the agreement in terms of child development or investment. Instead it focused on the quality of the existing system and the recognition of Quebec's constitutional powers over social policy. In essence, the agreement was one that would provide federal support for the existing practices of the province, and it was described as one that demonstrated the possibility of 'asymmetrical agreements to meet reciprocal objectives.'[23]

These social investment initiatives organized by the federal government were commitments to end Canada's status as laggard among developed countries in the area of child poverty and particularly early childhood education and care (ECEC), where it ranked dead last (OECD 2006, 214, 104, 105). This third pillar of the social investment perspective collapsed, of course, in 2006, when the newly elected Conservative government cancelled the agreements with the provinces and replaced that spending with the so-called Universal Child Care Benefit. The NCB, however, continues to be a growing source of income for families with children. Its design has not been altered by the Conservative government, and the amount of the benefit continues to rise. It is, in other words, a solidly institutionalized part of the social investment design, although it is unlikely ever to reach the level that would cover the costs of child raising, as its advocates had originally hoped.

At the same time that the federal Liberal governments swung the policy spotlight over to shine on children and their needs, they thrust adult poverty into the social policy background, even as the situation of many adults became more difficult. The treatment of joblessness was one clear sign of this shift. A flagship program of the post-1945 social policy regime had been significantly reformed in the first half of the 1990s. Unemployment Insurance became Employment

Insurance, with much stricter eligibility criteria (see MacDonald in this volume). The percentage of the unemployed receiving regular benefits fell between 1989 and 1997 from 87 per cent of the officially counted unemployed to 42 per cent. In other words, well over half of the unemployed received no insurance payments. In addition, between 1992 and 1997 there was a reduction in the amount of the average benefit from $272.05 to $249.72 (Battle 1997, 332). Even the decision to include part-time workers in the EI system did little to increase coverage because of the tight terms of eligibility.

Second, people receiving social assistance saw their incomes decline significantly. In the design of the NCB, parents who were not employed and receiving social assistance saw no increase in their income when the program came into effect (McKeen 2001b). As the official evaluation report of the NCB proudly put it in 2005:

> The truly innovative feature of the NCB Initiative was the agreement by provinces and territories to adjust the income support provided for children through their social assistance programs. Of particular importance was the provision that provinces and territories could deduct the NCB Supplement on a dollar-for-dollar basis from social assistance recipients' benefits (i.e., offsets). These adjustments were designed to help ensure that families are always better-off as a result of working—since families would not receive added financial assistance by remaining on social assistance, but are not penalized either by leaving. (FPT 2005, 6)

In all but two provinces a 'clawback' denied social-assistance recipients any increase when the National Child Benefit supplement was paid to them. This clawback was roundly criticized by everyone advocating for the poor.[24] As one quasi-public body put it:

> The National Council of Welfare has been opposed to the clawback of the National Child Benefit Supplement since it was first announced. Although the NCBS was lauded as a poverty reduction tool, its target was really low-income working families with children. And it has shown some success in reducing poverty for these families. However, there is a large group of families with children living in poverty—those on welfare—who have seen little or no benefit from the NCBS despite the substantial sums of new money provided by the federal government. (NCW 2006, 54)

One of the reasons for the dire situation of social-assistance recipients is the general reduction of benefits that has occurred in all provinces, whose governments are the level of government responsible for social assistance. In almost all provinces, benefits peaked somewhere in the 1980s or early 1990s and since then the declines have been, as described by the National Council of Welfare, 'staggering' (NCW 2006, x). Recipients of social assistance in all types of family situations have seen their real income decline, but not equally. The emphasis of the social investment approach on children and investing in the future have meant that although families receiving social assistance did experience cuts to their

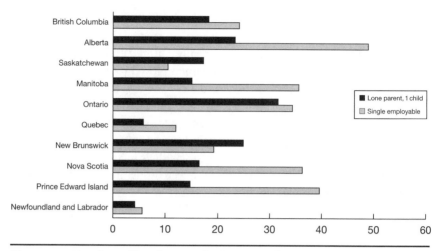

**Figure 1.1 Loss in welfare income between peak year and 2005**

Source: National Council of Welfare 2006.

income, in eight of ten provinces the losses have been even greater for single employable recipients of social assistance than for families with children. In some provinces the gap is very substantial. Figure 1.1 maps the difference between 2005 and the time in each province when social assistance rates were at their highest, for a lone-parent family with one child and for a single person without a disability.[25] The figure shows how much the provinces differed in their commitments to slashing social assistance. Quebec, for example, made the second-lowest cuts for lone-parent families and the third-lowest for single employables.

What these numbers tell us is that as the social investment perspective arrived, governments made few efforts to 'invest' in adults. They were meant to earn their own way. Adults without children saw their situation deteriorate significantly in comparison to earlier decades.

## What Does All This Mean for Attention to Gender Equality and Women?

As is evident from the quotations above, one way in which the social investment perspective writes women out of the story is by using the term 'parents' or 'families' and rarely if ever mentioning women. A second method of writing women out of the story is to take policy instruments that had previously been dedicated to achieving gender equality and to use them to achieve other objectives.

An example of the first method comes from the domain of income security. The income supplements, benefits, and services of the NCB are described exclusively in terms of their consequences for children and families with children. Even parents are less relevant actors than are children. Take, for example, the

*Evaluation of the National Child Benefit Initiative: Synthesis Report* (FPT 2005). In its 64 pages, children are mentioned 115 times, parents 30 times, mothers once, and women not at all.

This writing of women out of the income-support system is in sharp contrast to earlier times. For example, through the 1980s four major income-security programs were clearly understood to have gender-differentiated effects. Family allowances (created in 1944) provided a universal flat-rate payment to mothers of dependent children. Women were front and centre in the design, albeit defined exclusively in their maternal role. For Leonard Marsh in his important report, written during the Second World War for the federal government, about post-war reconstruction and proposals for the ways that Canadian governments should organize the post-war years, writing the cheque to mothers was 'a way of promoting motherhood and mothers' individual rights' (cited in Timpson 2001, 17). The second objective was particularly important because for many women at the time it would be the only money 'of their own' that they would ever have in their purse.

The public pension system was the second of these income-security programs. Since the mid-1960s it has consisted of a universal Old Age Security Pension (created in 1952), the contributory Canada and Quebec Pension Plans (C/QPP) (which depend on earnings), and a Guaranteed Income Supplement. The OAS and low-income supplements have been particularly important to women who have never been in the paid labour force or who have earned low wages, thereby contributing less to the C/QPP and private pension plans. These gender-differentiated effects were recognized and widely discussed in public debate about retirement income during the heyday of second-wave feminism. Freda Paltiel (one of the first and most influential femocrats in the federal government), writing of 'the feminising of the pension debate' that began in the early 1970s, noted that 'legislation passed on equal treatment for men and women under the Canada Pension Plan came into force on the first day of International Women's Year, 1975' (Paltiel 1982, 333–4).

Unemployment insurance was the third of these programs. Although the design of UI definitely favoured the male model of employment (full-time and regular), it was re-jigged in 1971 to provide a paid maternity allowance to new mothers who took time off from work at the birth of a child. The provinces followed suit by reforming their employment standards to provide the right to maternity leave and some rights with respect to the return to work. The paid benefits were then extended to include 'parental' leaves open to fathers as well as mothers, thereby providing some support for more equal practices in families' gender division of labour.

The fourth income support program is social assistance. Beginning in the inter-war years, the provinces provided the Mother's Allowance to women who could not rely on a male breadwinner because they were widowed or 'abandoned'.

These benefits were restructured in 1966 by the Canada Assistance Plan (CAP), which set out the terms under which the federal government would share the costs of social assistance with the provinces. From its beginnings in the Mother's Allowance through the 1970s, the design of social assistance was sensitive to gender differences, albeit also being a bulwark of the male breadwinner norm. Recipients of social assistance who were mothers of preschool and school-age children were excused from any requirement to seek work. They would be allowed to live according to prevailing social norms, that is, to devote themselves to full-time motherhood (Mahon 2000, 596). For lone mothers who chose employment, as for low-income couples, however, CAP and provincial social-assistance regimes provided means-tested subsidies for childcare. [26]

Now income security is discussed in very different terms than in those four programs. Family allowances paid to mothers were eliminated in 1993 (after years of declining value) and replaced by the Child Tax Credit. The needs of mothers and women are no longer discussed in the design of income-security programs (McKeen 2001b). When the new and most legitimate income-support initiative—that is, the NCB—is described, there is scarcely any mention of adults, let alone women:

> The NCB Initiative is an important undertaking developed with the aim of helping children to get the best possible start in life. Governments recognize that child poverty has long-term consequences, both for children and for society in general. Governments also support the position that families are better off when parents are supported in their efforts to obtain and maintain employment. (FPT 2005, 1)

'Society in general' appears even before parents do. As noted above, a simple word count shows that adults have been written out: women are completely absent and parents are present in only a limited way. An analysis of the content shows clearly that this key reform of the income-security system, which was meant to remake both social assistance and support for the working poor, now focuses on children, not adults, and not on adult women at all.

The second method of writing women out of the story is to take policy instruments previously identified with gender equality and assign them to other ends. This is the story of childcare. It used to be a means of promoting equality between women and men. Now it is an instrument for achieving better developmental outcomes for children and to promote parents' attachment to the labour force, no matter the quality of job or the income it generates.

As early as the 1970s, feminists understood that affordable childcare was essential if women were to achieve some measure of economic autonomy and equality in the labour market. This understanding of childcare was not the dominant one in Canada after the Second World War, but by the time the Royal Commission on the Status of Women reported in 1971, the women's movement had defined it as a fundamental goal. Rianne Mahon describes the Royal

Commission's childcare recommendations: 'The commission report endorsed the establishment of a national framework for a universal childcare program, and it did so in the name of women's equal opportunity with men' (2000, 602; see also Mahon in this volume). Throughout the 1970s, women's groups were advocates for a pan-Canadian childcare system.

In the 1980s, the federal government also accepted this definition of the issue domain. When it appointed the Task Force on Child Care in 1984, it named Dr Katie Cooke to chair it. Her claim to expertise was not in the childcare field at all. She told an interviewer 'she had "zilch" knowledge about childcare when she took this position.' (Dawes 2002, 5). She did, however, have expertise in women's rights and feminist analysis. She had been the first president of the Canadian Advisory Council on the Status of Women, from 1973 to 1976. The task force began its report with references to the Royal Commission on the Status of Women (Cooke Task Force 1986, xxv, 3). The Cooke Task Force would report, moreover, to the minister responsible for the status of women.

The Liberal government, which had appointed the task force just a few months before the 1984 election, clearly defined childcare as a gender issue, but so too did the Conservative government whose minister responsible for the status of women eventually received the report in 1986. He chose International Women's Day (8 March) for the press conference at which he released the recommendations, which were organized around the theme that a publicly supported system was needed (Friendly 2006, 1). A quarter century later the story was very different. Also released in March, but certainly not on the 8th, the 2003 Multilateral Framework on Early Learning and Child Care set down the logic of the intergovernmental childcare discourse this way:[27]

> Federal, Provincial and Territorial Ministers Responsible for Social Services agree to make additional investments in the specific area of early learning and child care. Ministers recognize that quality early learning and child care programs play an important role in promoting the social, emotional, physical and cognitive development of young children. This early learning and child care framework represents another important step in the development of early childhood development programs and services.

Although increasing the employment rates of parents was one objective, the other was promoting early childhood development. No mention was made of childcare as a support for women or their goal of quality employment. A similar silence is found in the agreements signed in 2005 between the Liberal government in Ottawa and each of the provinces. The number of times children are referred to far outstrips the mention of parents, and mothers or women are simply not present.

As the federal government (and some of the provinces) have institutionalized the social investment perspective, policy documents and institutions representing women have become silent on gender equality, and women are invisible actors folded into the genderless category of parent. Why does the social invest-ment perspective have this effect?

## Why the Social Investment Perspective Writes Women Out

The preceding analysis has shown a reorientation of social policy towards employability, investments, and the future. Outside of Quebec, it brought not only new policy goals but also greater attention to children and young people. In the process, women and gender equality have been written out of the story. As the emphasis on early childhood education, investments, and parental employment has risen, attention to inequalities of gender in work, in education, and at home has diminished.

Why should this be the case? Why would a revamped social model for the twenty-first century have these implications? One reason might be a change in political orientation. Certainly the Harper government has little interest in sup-porting feminists or their understanding of social policy directions. This is clear. However, as we saw in the first part of this chapter, Jean Charest's neo-liberals in Quebec have not written gender out in the same way as the neo-liberal fed-eral Conservatives. Political orientation alone then is an inadequate explana-tion. Moreover, the marginalization of feminists and of the discourse of gender equality disappeared under the Liberal governments of Jean Chrétien and Paul Martin. Things have not improved since the 2006 elections to be sure; but the silence was already deafening, even after 1997 and the Liberals' decision to rein-vest in the social policy domain.

A second account might focus on the strategy of the movements that demand for more progressive social policies. Between the mid-1980s and the second half of the 1990s, defeats in constitutional debates and the failed opposition to the Free Trade Agreement and the North American Free Trade Agreement by the National Action Committee on the Status of Women (NAC) had resulted in NAC's being pushed aside. It was vilified and labelled an illegitimate represent-ative of women (Dobrowolsky and Jenson 2004, 165ff.). This did not happen to the women's movement in Quebec, which retained its political legitimacy through the debates around the Meech Lake Accord, the 1993 referendum on the Charlottetown Accord, and the 1995 Quebec referendum on independence. The movement and its associations remain a strong presence both within state institutions and in civil society, in Quebec and transnationally (Quéniart and Jacques 2001; Dufour and Giraud 2007).

The positions of social movements in civil society are important to this story, as well. At the same time as the women's movement outside Quebec was being marginalized, advocates for childcare who had once framed their claims in terms of gender equality began to frame the problem as one of 'child poverty' and 'child development'.[28] This strategic adjustment away from gender equality and towards the needs of children did provide some support to the federal government as it moved away from a discourse of gender equality. Nonetheless, the shifting by advocacy groups with the political winds cannot account for the winds themselves. Here we must examine the content of a social investment perspective focused on children. It is the perspective itself that makes it impossible to sustain attention to gender inequalities among adults. There are several reasons for that.

First, unlike demands for gender equality, a child-centred social investment perspective diverts attention from the here and now. For decades, demands for gender equality have depended heavily on comparisons of women's present situation to that of men. The key indicators of gender disparities, whether these are rates of violence, earnings gaps, differences in access to higher education, the need for pay equity, or unequal participation in politics, leadership roles, or professions, have always been measured in the present. In contrast, an investment focus shifts attention to children or youth and to their futures. And a focus on children and youth leaves no room for gender comparison. Neither preschool nor school-age girls can be shown to be at a disadvantage in comparison to their male counterparts. They reach developmental milestones as soon as boys if not sooner, and they do as well in school if not better. Indeed, if there are gender-related problems in these age groups, they are found more among boys than girls. Therefore, an analysis in terms of gender loses analytic purchase as more attention goes to the early years or is geared towards preparing for the future. The key tool of cross-sectional comparison of women and men, used throughout the second wave of the women's movement, is no longer of use.

Second, the reliance on education and investment in human capital as a strategy for success in the new economy also narrows the space for gender-differentiated analysis. Women have already made significant strides in secondary and post-secondary education. In fact, they are now more likely than young men to graduate from post-secondary institutions. Again, if anyone is falling behind, it is boys and men. Therefore, the enthusiasm for improving school-readiness and children's educational outcomes offers little opportunity for a thorough-going gender analysis or for policy attention to the reasons why 'investments in human capital' pay off less for women than for men. Nowhere in the social investment perspective is there room for the query: why do female university graduates still earn less than men?

A last reason why the social investment perspective results in women being written out is that it is ultimately a supply-side analysis, focused on what individuals do. The emphasis is on preparing future workers for successful participation in the labour market. Yet, as decades of feminist analyses and whole libraries of publications have shown, gender inequalities are not the result of women's inadequate preparation, education, or lack of ambition. They are due to systemic and structural barriers to equal opportunities. There are glass ceilings and gatekeepers. Violence against women undermines equal participation. Human-rights legislation and commissions are needed to protect against systemic discrimination. So too are gender-based analysis and mainstreaming. These barriers are all 'demand-side' factors. They are the social structures and relations within which women must live and act. But they are rendered invisible when the spotlight shifts to the supply side and investments today for future returns. Supply-side analyses offer little opportunity for classic gender analyses to reveal inequalities in the here and now.

## Conclusion

Through this chapter we have seen that it has not been neo-liberalism per se that has resulted in gender and women being written out of political debate, as can be shown by a double comparison. A first comparison is between the neo-liberalism of the Liberal government of Quebec since 2003 and the Harper Conservatives since 2006. Although the Charest Liberals have all the necessary credentials to qualify as neo-liberal, there is little evidence that attention to gender has been sidelined in the institutional forms of representation. The presence of women in the cabinet and the main beachheads of feminism within the state remain strong. So something other than neo-liberalism must account for the Harper government's closing off in 2006 of more of the institutional spaces for representing women and the relatively minor opposition in the name of gender equality it provoked. More is needed to explain why the decision to renege on a pan-Canadian childcare system resulted in more opposition than did the abolition of several longstanding institutions that advanced feminist and women-friendly politics.

  This second comparison of policy fields—gender equality and childcare—points to the social investment perspective as the culprit that set in motion the social mechanism of writing women out of the story. The perspective has been implemented since the watershed year of 1997 in Canada as well as a large number of other countries. In the case of Canada it was used to organize the reinvestment strategy of the federal government after years of neo-liberal cutbacks. In doing so, it reoriented policy away from women and the goal of gender equality towards children and the goal of investing in their futures. Inherent in a child-centred social investment perspective are several elements that close down the space for attention to gender inequalities, as detailed in the second half of this chapter. In Quebec, this child-centred social investment perspective has been much less influential, thereby allowing women's groups and their allies to continue to struggle to keep their needs and futures on the political agenda.

## Notes

1. See the platform, *Stand Up for Canada*, at http://www.conservative.ca/EN/2590/. On neo-liberalism and the language of choice see Jenson and Sineau (2001).

2. See *REALity*, the group's newsletter at http://www.realwomenca.com/newsletter/2006_mar_apr/ma2006.html.

3. For the major documents relevant to this debate see http://sisyphe.org/rubrique.php3?id_rubrique=68.

4. See the press release 'Égalité au conseil des ministres : voici un message clair', http://www.cnw.ca/fr/releases/archive/April2007/18/c6835.html.

5. For a similar analysis, applied to gender equality in the European Union, see Jenson (2008a).

6. Wendy McKeen (2001a) also uses the metaphor of 'writing out', but she concentrates on an earlier period and attributes the change to neo-liberalism.

7. On its role and mandate (only in French), see http://www.scf.gouv.qc.ca/index.asp. For some publications in English, see http://www.scf.gouv.qc.ca/index_an.asp.

8. Of the 29 countries classified by the World Wide Guide to Women in Leadership as having a 'higher number' (more than 20 per cent) of women in government, Canada—with 21 per cent of women in Parliament—was fifth from the bottom. Quebec was not classified, but with its 50 per cent, it would have ranked fourth. http://www.guide2womenleaders.com/situation_in_2008.htm.

9. For the long story of these cutbacks and the responses of women's groups see Dobrowolsky (2008).

10. For example, CTV, 'Harper pressed to axe "Status of Women Canada"', 25 August 2006, and DAWN (Disabled Women's Network of Ontario), the *(un) REAL Women of Canada Watch*, at: http://dawn.thot.net/rwoc_watch.html (accessed 19 Mar. 2008).

11. Sociology also has a long tradition of analyzing modernization and of treating macro social changes as the drivers of policy design, especially changes in family structures and practices, labour-force restructuring, and modification of the demographic structure of society. John Myles and Jill Quadagno (2002, 36) recently summarized this tradition: 'The first generation of welfare state studies typically turned to theories of industrialism to account for the common trajectory of rising welfare state expenditures throughout the developed world. . . . The main themes . . . were echoed, albeit in different language, in early marxist accounts.'

12. On Latin America see Riesco (2007). On the European Union see Jenson (2008a), and on Europe in general see Jenson and Saint-Martin (2006) and Bonoli (2005).

13. That year 1997 was one in which 'a range of critics assailed neo-liberalism's legitimacy, many from within the headline international financial institutions' (Porter and Craig 2004, 391). It was the year of the Asian financial crisis and the year in which the *World Development Report* called for a more capable state, New Labour defeated the British Conservatives, the OECD worried that structural-adjustment policies were undermining social cohesion (Dobrowolsky and Jenson 2005), the Mexican government introduced its conditional cash transfers to support poor households with school-age children (Barrientos and DeJong 2006), and so on.

14. On the Speech from the Throne, see McLean's magazine, 6 Oct. 1997, available at: http://www.canadianencyclopedia.ca/index.cfm?PgNm=TCE&Params=M1ARTM0011414. Other areas in which investments were to be made were healthcare and research and innovation (Dobrowolsky and Saint-Martin 2005, 6).

15. In 2001 the federal government used the Early Childhood Development Agreement (ECDA) to make $2.2 billion (over five years) available to provinces and territories on the condition that they use the funds to promote healthy pregnancy, birth, and infancy; improve parenting and family supports; strengthen early childhood development, learning, and care; and/or strengthen community supports. In 2003 the Multilateral Framework on Early Learning and Care again allocated $1.05 billion over five years to promote regulated childcare for children under the age of six.

16    For another presentation of the social investment perspective, focused particularly on human-capital themes, see Banting (2006).

17    Pauline Marois, who was elected leader of the Parti Québécois in 2007, had been a political aide to the historic Quebec feminist Lise Payette in the late 1970s. In her first ministerial post she was responsible for the status of women from 1981 to 1983 and again in 1985. She was also for a time treasurer of the Fédération des femmes du Québec.

18    See the press release presenting the 1997 policy: http://www.mels.gouv.qc.ca/CPRESS/CPRSS97/c970123.htm (accessed 19 Mar. 2008).

19    This shift did not happen overnight, of course. The way had been prepared since the 1993 election. But it had been blocked by opposition to any new spending in general from the Department of Finance, which was headed by Paul Martin, and by opposition to the proposals unveiled in the Social Security Review led by Lloyd Axworthy in the mid-1990s (Dobrowolsky and Saint-Martin 2005, 7).

20    From the 1998 presentation of the new program, archived at http://www.nationalchildbenefit.ca/ncb/ncbfaq_e.shtml (accessed 19 Mar. 08).

21    From the backgrounder prepared for the 1997 Speech from the Throne. Available at http://www.socialunion.ca/nca/nca1_e.htm (accessed 19 Mar. 2008).

22    The agreements signed with the 10 provinces are available at http://www.hrsdc.gc.ca/en/cs/comm/sd/news/agreements_principle/index.shtml (accessed 19 Mar. 2008).

23    This agreement is available at http://www.hrsdc.gc.ca/en/cs/comm/sd/news/agreements_principle/index.shtml.

24    Initially only New Brunswick and Newfoundland and Labrador did not claw back, but now the situation is more complicated. Only 5 of the 13 provinces and territories have a full clawback and 3 have a partial one (NCW 2006).

25    There are differences between the losses experienced by lone-parent and couple families, but in only a few cases are these differences large (NCW 2006, 41ff.).

26    In the 1950s, in addition to a discourse about childcare for working women, there was one about the need for day care for disadvantaged children, who would benefit from being exposed to play and playthings in a structured environment away from their family (Mahon 2000, 592–3). This discourse was then marginalized in discussions of childcare until the 1990s, when it reappeared in proposals for head-start programs for disadvantaged and especially Aboriginal children.

27    This document is available at http://www.socialunion.ca/ecd-framework_e.htm (accessed 19 Mar. 2008).

28    This shift is described in detail in McKeen (2001a) and Dobrowolsky and Jenson (2004, 166ff.).

## References

Banting, Keith. 2006. 'Dis-embedding Liberalism? The New Social Policy Paradigm in Canada'. In David A. Green and Jonathan R. Kesselman, eds, *Dimensions of Inequality in Canada*, 417–52. Vancouver: UBC Press.

Barrientos, Armando, and Jocelyn DeJong. 2006. 'Reducing Child Poverty with Cash Transfers: A Sure Thing?', *Development Policy Review* 25 (5): 537–52.

Battle, Ken. 1997. 'Transformation: Canadian Social Policy Since 1985', *Social Policy and Administration* 32 (4): 321–40.

Boismenu, Gérard, Pascale Dufour, and Denis Saint-Martin. 2004. *La Déconstruction libérale du Québec: Réalisations et promesses du gouvernement Charest*. Outremont, Que.: Athéna.

———, and Jane Jenson. 1998. 'A Social Union or a Federal State? Intergovernmental Relations in the New Liberal Era'. In Leslie Pal, ed., *How Ottawa Spends 1998–99: Balancing Act: The Post-Deficit Mandate*, 57–80. Ottawa: Carleton University Press.

Bonoli, Giuliano. 2005. 'The Politics of the New Social Policies: Providing Coverage against New Social Risks in Mature Welfare States', *Policy & Politics* 33 (3): 431–49.

Boychuk, Gerard W. 1998. *Patchworks of Purpose: The Development of Provincial Social Assistance Regimes in Canada.* Montreal: McGill-Queen's University Press.

———. 2004. *The Canadian Social Model. The Logics of Policy Development.* Canadian Policy Research Networks (CPRN) research report F|36. Ottawa: CPRN. www.cprn.org.

Brodie, Janine. 1997. 'Meso-Discourses, State Forms and the Gendering of Liberal-Democratic Citizenship', *Citizenship Studies* 1 (2): 223–42.

Canet, Raphaël. 2007. 'Un autre Québec est-il possible ? L'imposition tranquille de la société néolibérale', *Le Devoir*, 17 Aug. http://www.ledevoir.com/2007/07/17/150548.html.

Cooke Task Force (Task Force on Child Care in Canada). 1986. *Report of the Task Force on Child Care.* Ottawa: Minister of Supply and Services.

Dawes, Caroline. 2002. 'Pioneers in Child Care: Katie Cooke, No Easy Answers', *Interaction* 15 (4): 5.

Dobrowolsky, Alexandra. 1998. ' "Of Special Interest": Interest, Identity and Feminist Representational Activism', *Canadian Journal of Political Science* 31 (4): 707–42.

———. 2004. 'The Chrétien Liberal Legacy and Women: Changing Policy Priorities with Little Cause for Celebration', *Review of Constitutional Studies* 9 (1&2): 171–98.

———. 2008. 'The Women's Movement in Flux: Feminism and Framing, Passion and Politics'. In Miriam Smith, ed., *Group Politics and Social Movements in Canada*, 159–80. Peterborough, Ont.: Broadview Press.

———, and Jane Jenson. 2004. 'Shifting Representations of Citizenship: Canadian Politics of "Women" and "Children" ', *Social Politics: International Studies in Gender, State and Society* 11 (2): 154–80.

———, and Jane Jenson. 2005. 'Social Investment Perspectives and Practices: A Decade in British Politics'. In Martin Powell, Linda Bauld, and Karen Clarke, eds, *Social Policy Review* #17. Bristol: Policy Press.

———, and Denis Saint-Martin. 2005. 'Agency, Actors and Change in a Child-Focused Future: "Path Dependency" Problematised', *Commonwealth and Comparative Politics* 43 (1): 1–33.

Dufour, Pascale, Alexandra Dobrowolsky, Jane Jenson, Denis Saint-Martin, and Deena White. 2008. 'Émergence d'un référentiel sous tension: l'Investissement social au Canada'. In Oliver Giraud and Philippe Warin, ed., *Politiques publiques et démocratie*, 257–83. Paris: La Découverte.

———, and Isabelle Giraud. 2007. 'Globalization and Political Change in the Women's Movement: The Politics of Scale and Political Empowerment in the World March of Women', *Social Science Quarterly* 88 (5): 1152–73.

Fortin, Sarah, Alain Noël, and France St-Hilaire, eds. 2002. *Forging the Canadian Social Union: SUFA and Beyond.* Montreal: Institute for Research on Public Policy.

FPT (Federal, Provincial and Territorial Ministers Responsible for Social Services). 2005. *Evaluation of the National Child Benefit Initiative: Synthesis Report.* http://www.hrsdc.gc.ca/en/cs/sp/sdc/evaluation/sp-ah215e/page00.shtml.

Friendly, Martha. 2006. 'It was twenty years ago today . . . March 8, 1986'. CRRU Child Care Briefing Notes.

Holly, Grant. 2009. 'Shifting Political Opportunities and Strategies: The Case of Child Care Advocacy in 2004–2006'. In Rachel Laforest, ed., *The New Federal Policy Agenda and the Voluntary Sector: On the Cutting Edge.* Montreal: McGill-Queen's University Press. Forthcoming.

Huber, Evelyne, and John D. Stephens. 2001. *Development and Crisis of the Welfare State: Parties and Policies in Global Markets.* Chicago: University of Chicago Press.

Jenson, Jane (with Sherry Thompson). 1999. *Comparative Family Policy: Six Provincial Stories.* Canadian Policy Research Networks (CPRN) research report F|08. Ottawa: CPRN. www.cprn.org.

———. 2002. 'Against the Tide. Childcare in Quebec'. In Sonya Michel and Rianne Mahon, eds, *Child Care Policy at the Crossroads: Gender and Welfare State Restructuring*, 309–32. New York: Routledge.

———. 2008a. 'Writing Women Out, Folding Gender In: The European Union "Modernises" Social Policy', *Social Politics: International Studies in Gender, State and Society* 15 (2): 1–23.

———. 2008b. 'Rolling Out or Backtracking on Quebec's Child Care System? Ideology Matters'. In Marjorie Cohen and Jane Pucklingham, eds, *Public Policy for Women: The State, Income Security, and Labour*, 52–69. Toronto: University of Toronto Press.

———, and Susan D. Phillips. 1996. 'Regime Shift: New Citizenship Practices in Canada'. *International Journal of Canadian Studies* 14 (Fall): 111–36.

———, and Denis Saint-Martin. 2006. 'Building Blocks for a New Social Architecture: The LEGO™ Paradigm of an Active Society', *Policy and Politics* 34 (3): 429–51.

———, and Mariette Sineau. 2001. *Who Cares? Women's Work, Childcare, and Welfare State Redesign*. Toronto: University of Toronto Press.

Laforest, Rachel, and Michael Orsini. 2005. 'Evidence-based Engagement in the Voluntary Sector: Lessons from Canada', *Social Policy and Administration* 39 (5): 481–97.

Larner, Wendy, and David Craig. 2005. 'After Neoliberalism? Community Activism and Local Partnerships in Aotearoa New Zealand', *Antipode* 37 (3): 402–24.

McKeen, Wendy. 2001a. 'Writing Women Out: Poverty Discourse and Feminist Agency in the 1990's National Social Welfare Policy Debate', *Canadian Review of Social Policy* 48: 19–33.

———. 2001b. 'Shifting Policy and Politics of Federal Child Benefits in Canada', *Social Politics: International Studies in Gender, State and Society* 8 (2): 186–90.

Mahon, Rianne. 2000. 'The Never Ending Story: The Struggle for Universal Child Care Policy in the 1970s', *Canadian Historical Review* 81 (4): 582–615.

———, and Susan D. Phillips. 2002. 'Dual-Earner Families Caught in a Liberal Welfare Regime? The Politics of Child Care Policy in Canada'. In Sonya Michel and Rianne Mahon, eds, *Child Care Policy at the Crossroads: Gender and Welfare State Restructuring*, 181–218. New York: Routledge.

Maillé, Chantal. 2002. *Cherchez la femme: trente ans de débats constitutionnels au Québec*. Montreal: Éditions du remue-ménage.

Myles, John, and Jill Quadagno. 2002. 'Political Theories of the Welfare State', *Social Service Review* 76: 34–57.

NCW (National Council of Welfare). 2006. *Welfare Incomes 2005*. Ottawa: NCW. http://www.ncwcnbes.net/en/research/welfare-bienetre.html.

OECD (Organisation for Economic Co-operation and Development). 2006. *Starting Strong II*. Paris: OECD.

Paltiel, Freda 1982. 'Women and Pensions in Canada', *International Social Security Review* 35 (3): 333–44.

Porter, Doug, and David Craig. 2004. 'The Third Way and the Third World: Poverty Reduction and Social Inclusion in the Rise of "Inclusive" Liberalism', *Review of International Political Economy* 11 (2): 387–423.

QLP (Quebec Liberal Party). 2008. *Le meilleur pour le Québec—Famille*. Report of the Working Group on the Family. Working paper.

Quéniart, Anne, and Julie Jacques. 2001. 'L'engagement politique des jeunes femmes au Québec: de la responsabilité au pouvoir d'agir pour un changement de société', *Lien social et Politiques* 46: 45–53.

Rebick, Judy. 2006. 'A Nail in the Coffin of Women's Equality?' *Rabble News*, 16 October. http://www.rabble.ca/politics.shtml?x=53346 (accessed 4 Jan. 2008).

Riesco, Manuel, ed. 2007. *Latin America: A New Developmental Welfare State Model in the Making*. Houndsmill, Basingstoke: Palgrave.

Rouillard, Christian, Alain-G. Gagnon, Isabelle Fortier, and Éric Montpetit. 2003. 'Réingénierie, rénovation et redéploiement de l'État québécois: Une démarche sous le joug du pragmatisme ou de l'idéologie?', *Le Devoir*, 18 November, A7.

Stroick, Sharon M., and Jane Jenson. 1999. *What Is the Best Policy Mix for Canada's Young Children?* Canadian Policy Research Networks (CPRN) report F|09. Ottawa: CPRN. at www.cprn.org.

Task Force on Child Care in Canada. *See* Cooke Task Force.

Timpson, Annis May. 2001. *Driven Apart: Women's Employment Equality and Child Care in Canadian Public Policy*. Vancouver: UBC Press.

## Further Reading

Esping-Andersen, Gøsta, Duncan Gallie, Anton Hemerijck, and John Myles. 2002. *Why We Need a New Welfare State*. Oxford: Oxford University Press.

Jenson, Jane. 2004. 'Changing the Paradigm: Family Responsibility or Investing in Children'. *Canadian Journal of Sociology* 29 (2): 169–92.

Canadian Policy Research Networks. www.cprn.org

Canada Research Chair in Citizenship and Governance. www.cccg.umontreal.ca

## Questions for Critical Thought

1. How significantly does the social investment perspective differ from previous policy paradigms, such as Keynesianism and neo-liberalism?
2. Is it possible to have a version of the social investment model that would promote gender equality?
3. To what extent have the Canadian provinces other than Quebec adopted the social investment perspective?

# CHAPTER 2

# Childcare and Varieties of Liberalism in Canada

Rianne Mahon

## Introduction

At the same time as neo-liberal discourse celebrates the principle of laissez-faire, changes to labour markets and families are putting pressure on states to meet the growing need to facilitate the 'reconciliation of work and family life' (OECD 2005). This chapter focuses on two potential ways of meeting the need for non-parental childcare, both of which draw from the well of liberal ideas but in quite different ways. One is clearly in line with the core ideas of neo-liberalism, while the other takes its inspiration from the same kind of liberalism that inspired the Keynesian welfare state in countries like Canada and Britain.[1] Some would see the latter as simply part of a broader process of 'neo-liberalization', aimed at re-embedding neo-liberal capitalism. I will argue that such a position glosses over significant differences, not only in the direct policy impact, but also in the broader political terrain.

I illustrate my argument with reference to Canadian childcare policy. The Canadian case is useful in that the need for non-parental childcare emerged before the ascendance of neo-liberalism. The Canadian state initially responded in ways consistent with its (social) liberal variant of the Keynesian welfare state (Mahon and Phillips 2002). Yet just when it seemed that a universal childcare policy would be adopted to promote equality of the sexes, Mulroney's Conservative government instigated a neo-liberal turn. As the Jenson chapter notes, this also marked the beginning of 'writing gender out'. For much of the 1990s, the Chrétien Liberal governments appeared to follow the neo-liberal line charted by its predecessor. By the end of the decade, however, growing acceptance of the importance of early-childhood development led to new initiatives—the Multilateral Framework Agreement on Early Learning and Child Care in 2003 and the bilateral agreements negotiated under the short-lived Martin government in 2005—that promised to establish the foundations for universal, high-quality childcare. As we shall see, the foundations were inadequately secured and hence were vulnerable to a Harper government determined to implement its neo-liberal vision.

## Social Reproduction in Neo-liberal Times?

The current concern with the reconciliation of work and family life needs to be seen as yet another expression of the long-standing problem of social reproduction—the daily and intergenerational reproduction of that 'fictitious commodity', labour—in capitalist societies. For Polanyi as for Marx before him, the attempt by nineteenth-century liberalism to establish a market society encountered limits imposed by the conditions needed to reproduce this fictitious commodity on a daily and intergenerational basis. States were thus forced to step in, regulating the working day, prohibiting the employment of children, and introducing protective legislation for female workers and other measures that met the needs of social reproduction. Often these measures supported the male-breadwinner–female-caregiver family form. This was also true of most versions of the Keynesian welfare state, at least in the first post-war decades.

Neo-liberalism has given rise anew to problems of social reproduction through its concerted attack on the Keynesian welfare state and its political underpinnings. On the one hand, the privatization advocated by neo-liberals involves not just the shift of services from the public sector to the market ('recommodification'), but also devolution of increased care work to households. As Clarke notes, 'this form of privatization assumes the existence of a stable nuclear family as the norm of household formation, and the persistence of a gendered division of domestic/caring labour'(2004, 33). On the other hand, labour-market deregulation, which has fuelled the growth of precarious work and cuts to the male breadwinners' wages and social-security net, has made a two-earner household an economic necessity for most. The drive by neoliberalism to cut social assistance rolls by propelling all who can work into the workforce has also come to include lone mothers. The turn toward the adult-earner family, of course, has deeper roots, among them the shift to post-industrial employment, which boosted the demand for female labour, and the agitation by second-wave feminism for equality of the sexes, which stressed the importance of paid work to economic equality of the sexes. In this sense, challenges to contemporary social reproduction arise even where neo-liberal ideas do not hold sway.

As I have argued elsewhere (Mahon 2006), there are four broad strategies for meeting the need for non-parental childcare: neo-familial, egalitarian, neo-liberal, and 'third-way' or developmental liberalism.[2] In this chapter, I focus on the last two; the other two strategies can be described briefly.

The neo-familial strategy holds on to traditional 'gender difference' assumptions, stressing women's right to choose between labour-force participation and domestic caregiving, but the latter is no longer seen as a lifetime option for most. Rather, women are encouraged to return to work (often part-time) when the child enters preschool. The hallmark of the neo-familialist model is thus three or four years of publicly supported childcare leave. Although there may be publicly funded preschool, it is offered part-time. To the extent that public policy encourages the provision of non-parental care for children under three (and out-of-school-hours care), there is a clear preference for types of child-care—nannies or family day care—that resemble maternal care. Dutch policy has approximated this model. In contrast, an egalitarian strategy challenges gender inequality at its roots and fits well in a broader program aimed at tack-ling intergenerational class inequality. It includes a parental-leave program, which is designed to foster an equitable sharing of domestic care between par-ents; universally accessible early childhood education and care by workers whose skills are recognized in the form of equitable wages and good working conditions; and democratic control by parents and community. Swedish policy is a good example of this model.

Before examining a possible neo-liberal response and the inclusive liberal alternative, we need to take a brief detour to discuss 'varieties of liberalism', because some would dispute the existence of significant differences between them. Peck and Tickell's neo-liberalization thesis (2002), which is described in the introduction to this volume, does draw attention to the potential for changes to the neo-liberal project in response to resistance encountered. Yet to see these as still part of neo-liberalism is to miss important differences within liberalism. As described by Craig and Porter (2004), inclusive liberalism high-lights important themes—'opportunity', 'empowerment' or the activation of capacities, and 'security'—that began to appear in social policy initiatives in OECD countries and the discourses of international organizations in the 1990s. Jenson calls this the 'social investment paradigm'. This misses, however, the ways in which the new social policy discourse, at least in Canada, shares certain assumptions with neo-liberalism, while drawing (albeit selectively) on the 'social-liberal' vein that underpinned the Keynesian welfare state.

In other words, there are 'varieties of liberalism' across space and over time. O'Connor, Orloff, and Shaver (1999) distinguished three historical phases: clas-sic; new, or social, liberalism; and neo-liberalism. All share an emphasis on the individual and, as Macpherson (1962) so cogently argued, all retain an alle-giance to a capitalist market economy. Yet these similarities should not be allowed to obscure important differences among them. Under classical liberal-ism, individual freedom was defined as the ability to pursue one's self-interest 'free from' the interference of others. In this imaginary, the role of the state was to be limited to the protection of individual property and the maintenance of orderly relations of exchange. Social policy was limited to assistance to the 'deserving' poor and was clearly designed to reinforce the work ethic. In the era of classic liberalism, moreover, the 'man' who was imagined to be worthy of freedom was indeed male. Women were seen as non-rational beings, 'idealised as the mistresses of the domestic haven, creatures of sentiment . . . united with their husbands in upholding the interests of household and family' (O'Connor, Orloff, and Shaver 1999, 48).

'New', or social, liberalism began to emerge in the nineteenth century through the work of theorists like John Stuart Mill, but it received its fullest policy expression in the Keynesian welfare state. In this version of the liberal imaginary, the human capacity for development held a prominent position:

> Man is a being capable of developing his powers or capacities. The human essence is to exert and develop them. Man is essentially not a consumer and appropriater . . . but an exerter and developer. . . . The good society is one which permits and encourages everyone to act as exerter, developer, and enjoyer of the exertion and development, of his or her own capacities. (Macpherson 1977, 48)

Here, the state had a positive role to play in creating the conditions for humans to develop to their full potential, even if this involved measures like union rights and unemployment insurance for mitigating the effects of the market. Although the social and economic policies associated with post-war social liberalism may thus have mitigated the impact of capitalism, it is important to remember that such 'decommodification' was never more than partial. Social policies might have the effect of 'class-abatement', but capitalism and the class inequalities to which it gives rise remained the foundation (Marshall 1963). In terms of gender, although J.S. Mill was one of the first liberal theorists to see women as fully human beings endowed with the same capacities as men, maternal feminists, who based their argument for women's political inclusion on gender difference, initially had a greater influence on the Keynesian welfare state. This only began to change with the emergence of second-wave feminism in the 1960s.

Neo-liberalism shares with classical liberalism a celebration of market individualism and minimal government. Instead of destroying feudal privilege and mercantilist monopolies, neo-liberalism aims to destroy the Keynesian welfare state, roll back the rights of unions, and limit the influence of 'special interests', including the women's movement. Contracting out, public–private partnerships, and the use of private finance for public purposes are all part of the neo-liberal toolkit. Neo-liberalism's position on gender is, however, ambivalent:

> In practice, neo-liberal opinion is usually allied with conservative political forces, diluting its market individualism with resurgent conservative doctrines about the need to safeguard traditional family life. . . . But neo-liberalism itself claims to be blind to ascribed characteristics of individuals such as age, sex and race. (O'Connor, Orloff, and Shaver 1999, 53)

When combined with social conservatism, neo-liberal solutions would reinvent the male-breadwinner–female-caregiver family indirectly through the privatization (to the family) of elements of care once assumed by public institutions. In addition, the new disciplinary techniques associated with the 'roll-out' of neo-liberalism often enlist the family, which becomes the target of therapeutic 'parenting' discourses.

In a pure neo-liberal discourse, women are to be treated like men. This includes the expectation of full-time participation in the labour market. The neo-liberal solution to the resulting need for care is to purchase it on the market. The cost of care can be kept down through labour-market deregulation, which creates a substantial pool of low-wage workers. Neo-liberals also favour the use of tax deductions for corporations as well as individuals. Individual tax deductions work in the favour of those with higher incomes, and corporate tax cuts encourage the extension of corporate welfare to 'reconcile work and family life'. There may also be some, albeit limited, room for remedial state action to save children from the 'cycle of poverty'.

Although neo- and inclusive liberalism have some elements in common, they draw on different elements of liberal tradition. Inclusive liberalism shares neo-liberalism's commitment to non-inflationary growth and balanced budgets. It is equally dedicated to the liberalization of the flow of goods, capital, and with some provisos, labour. Both stress the centrality of employment but reject a public responsibility to create the conditions for full employment, which characterized Keynesian economic policy. Both advocate the 'flexibilization' of labour and labour markets and accept that this means greater inequality 'in the here and now'. For both, therefore, systems of income support need to be reconfigured to encourage labour-market participation. In contrast to the coercive workfare policies of neo-liberalism, inclusive liberals see a role for the state in providing training and other forms of assistance to develop individual 'capacities' to participate in the labour market. Such policies may include government support for childcare.

The roots of inclusive liberalism in social liberalism are apparent in its emphasis on the activation of human capacities, which harks back to Mills's developmental conception of human nature. Now, however, state support for the development of human and social capital is harnessed to the broader project of competitiveness in the global economy. As in the Keynesian era, then, the state recognizes the need for social policies but argues that they need to be redesigned to meet the challenge of economic globalization. What is needed are 'productive' social policies, which will replace the 'passive' policies of the Keynesian era with measures that support and encourage the development and use of human capital. The new social policies are seen as a form of social investment where 'the family becomes a kind of social investment account' as government seeks to 'find the best ways to encourage and support parents in work and help them bring up the next generation' (Craig and Porter 2004, 406–7).

Inclusive liberalism embraces the adult-earner family. The normalization of that family makes possible the redesign of social-security systems initially geared to support the male breadwinner in his role. While the adult-earner family may reduce the impact of 'old risks' (sickness, unemployment, aging) on family income, it also gives rise to new needs. The adult-earner family is thus to be supported in its social-reproduction role through publicly financed and legislated parental or care leave. From this perspective, public investment in early childhood education can also be justified as the first step in a process of 'lifelong learning'. The state is not to play the role of provider but rather is limited to supporting the choices of consumer-citizens through demand-side subsidies, improvements to the flow of information, and regulation.

Inclusive liberalism's solutions to the contemporary problems of social repro-duction allow the state to play a more supportive role than that admitted by neo-liberals. At the same time, it is quite different from the egalitarian model. Whereas the egalitarian strategy involves the active promotion of an equitable sharing of domestic care, inclusive liberalism stresses the right of families to choose. Whereas the former intervenes on the supply side (by subsidizing cap-ital and operating costs, wage enhancements, and training opportunities), the latter emphasizes the demand side (through tax deductions or fee subsidies for parents and improved information for parents about childcare facilities). Whereas the former favours non-profit provision of childcare, the latter sees an important place for commercial providers. Whereas the egalitarian model works from a dynamic and democratic conception of quality through an insti-tutionalized dialogue between parents and providers, for inclusive liberals, who follow the nostrums of 'new public management', childcare providers are seen as a group prepared to use its 'monopoly on information' to pursue its own self-interest. They therefore look to market mechanisms, backed by regulation, for quality assurance.

Thus far, neo-liberalism and inclusive liberalism have been treated as if they were autonomous forces; yet ideas do not speak for themselves. To be trans-lated into policy, they need to be adopted by people who are in a position to implement them. It is therefore important to examine the politics surrounding the adoption and implementation of ideas, as it is shaped by national (and provincial and local) contexts.

## Canadian Childcare Policy: Contested Terrain

The labour-force participation rates of Canadian women began to rise in the 1960s, from 29.5 per cent in 1961 to 38.7 per cent in 1971 and reaching 51 per cent in 1981 (White 1993, 46, Table 2:1). By 2000, it had climbed to 76.3 per cent

(OECD 2005, 59). The increase coincided with an accelerating shift to post-industrial employment, the erosion of the male wage, a growing polarization of earnings, and the 'feminization of employment norms' (Fudge and Vosko 2003). Neo-liberal ideas played their part in structuring Canada's response to these shifts, but the change in women's labour-force participation started earlier. Although the need for non-parental childcare was placed on the national agenda by the Royal Commission on the Status of Women, the Canadian state had already introduced a mechanism for subsidizing childcare: childcare—for those 'in need'—had been included in the list of remedial services the cost of which the federal government was prepared to share (fifty-fifty) with the provinces through the Canada Assistance Plan (CAP) as part of Canada's 'war on poverty'.

CAP funding did not mark the beginning of a truly national childcare program, however, for the provinces were not obliged to develop childcare programs and they were left to determine the eligibility rules and levels of subsidy. This meant that the amount of regulated childcare varied substantially across the country. For provinces that decided to participate, CAP did provide some broad regulations, including a modest bias in favour of non-profit providers. Nevertheless, the regulations reinforced the liberal view that childcare was a 'welfare service', targeted at those in financial or 'moral' need. In other words, this childcare policy was a 'liberal' policy but liberalism with a Keynesian hue. The program therefore targeted low-income (or 'at-risk') families, on the assumption that most families would provide for themselves, either by having the mother stay at home or by purchasing childcare on the market.[3] It was not a workfare program; although CAP supported lone mothers' 'right to choose' employment, the federal government also recognized their 'right to care' since federal funds were now available for lone mothers on social assistance.

For a while, it looked as if the federal government would adopt a universal childcare policy more in the spirit of the Commission's recommendations. For the Commission, childcare was essential to women's equality with men, not just a service for those who needed to work to stay out of poverty. As such, it should be treated as a service available to all women to allow them to develop to their full potential. The Commission thus called for the establishment of a childcare act, removing it from the shadow of anti-poverty policy by making it a universal social service. Although no new act was passed, the terms offered under CAP were improved by creating the potential for the cost-shared subsidies to reach middle-class families[4] (Mahon 2000).

The Commission's report and the subsequent struggle for a national childcare policy came at a time of a deepening of social liberalism in Canada. Although an emphasis on poverty continued to mark Canadian social policy, there was a shift to less intrusive forms of income testing and to 'rehabilitative services' like training and counselling. 'Activation', in other words, was not introduced by, or in response to, neo-liberalism; rather, it formed part of the high-Keynesian policy toolkit. Graefe nicely captures the difference between these forms of action and their successors. The former was part of a broader program

> whereby the problem is the limitation of the citizenship rights of social assistance recipients and the solution is the expansion of their legitimate claims (to income, housing, procedural fairness, training, transportation, child care, etc.) to an employability programme where the problem is welfare dependency and economic inactivity and the solution is finding means to insert recipients into the formal labour market or quasi labour markets of subsidized employment and training placements. (2006, 2)

This was also a time of a real 'thickening' of the representational structure in civil society, with only tenuous ties to the party system. In true Millsian spirit, the Liberal government had adopted the principle of 'equitable access', establishing a variety of programs designed to mitigate the 'political poverty' of women, Aboriginal peoples, environmentalists, and the poor (Jenson and Phillips 1996). The formation of the National Action Committee on the Status of Women (NAC) in 1972 helped to consolidate a vibrant pan-Canadian women's movement. Although childcare was but one item on its agenda, in the early 1980s, a pan-Canadian childcare advocacy movement—the Canadian Day Care Advocacy Association (CDCAA, now the Child Care Advocacy Association of Canada)—was forged, giving voice to the demand for universal, comprehensive, high-quality childcare provided by public or non-profit organizations (Friendly 1994).

In the dying days of Keynesian social liberalism, childcare advocates and their allies seem to have had an influence. The Royal Commission on Equality in Employment (the Abella Commission) stated clearly that equality for women 'means acknowledging and accommodating the changing role of women in the care of the family by helping both them and their male partners to function effectively both as labour force participants and as parents' (Canada 1984, 4). On the eve of the 1984 election, the minister responsible for the status of women established the Task Force on Child Care (also known as the Cooke Task Force), which she charged with the development of 'complementary systems of childcare and parental leave that are as comprehensive, accessible and competent as our systems of health care and education' (cited in Friendly 1994, 153). The recommendations of the Cooke Task Force reflected the strong social liberalism of its origins. In addition to recommending the introduction of parental leave, it proposed the establishment of a high-quality, universally accessible childcare system under non-profit auspices to be funded by a new and substantially more generous intergovernmental cost-sharing arrangement.

Unfortunately the task force's recommendations were presented to quite a different government, one that aimed to follow a neo-liberal agenda laced with elements of social conservatism. The Conservative government headed by Brian

Mulroney eschewed the 'interventionist' and nationalist economic policies pursued by previous Liberal governments. In social policy terms, the Conservative government aimed to eliminate universal social programs, including the family allowance (as it succeeded in doing in 1992). The Mulroney government imposed a cap on CAP transfers to the three richest provinces: Ontario, Alberta, and British Columbia. Greater emphasis was placed on the 'employability' of social-assistance recipients through the conclusion of the Agreement on the Enhancement of Employment Opportunities for Social Assistance Recipients, which encouraged the provinces to experiment with workfare. In the process, 'provincial regulations gradually changed definitions of employability in such a way as to lower the age of the youngest child, and hence assigned more lone mothers to the category of "employable"' (Bashevkin 2002, 32). The Conservative government, recognizing the presence of social conservatives in the party, also promised to be more attentive to 'family values' (Teghtsoonian 1993). At the same time, it launched an effective attack on the 'special interests', like the women's movement, that had been such vocal critics of its policies (Jenson and Phillips 1996).

The Mulroney government's policies may be considered 'neo-liberalism lite', in comparison to those of the Thatcher and Reagan administrations. Nevertheless, its years in office did mark a clear turn in a neo-liberal direction, and this was reflected in its childcare policy. Without waiting for the report of the Cooke Task Force, the Conservative government organized its own cross-Canada hearings on childcare. Although the CDCAA and its allies in women's organizations, trade unions, and other popular movements managed to dominate the hearings, the government largely ignored their arguments. To be sure, the government did introduce childcare legislation, but its *Child Care Act* reflected a neo-liberal turn with an element of social-conservativism. For the first time, it planned to impose a ceiling on federal contributions to childcare. The Act would also have made funds available to commercial as well as non-profit operations, a move strongly opposed by childcare advocates and their allies. The government also bowed in the direction of 'family values' by establishing a refundable child tax credit, which was designed 'with the express intent of permitting . . . [families] to choose among different types of childcare options, including the choice of one parent remaining in the home' (Phillips 1989, 166). Facing strong opposition to the bill, the government allowed the childcare bill to die in the House and did not reintroduce it following its re-election, but it did pass the child tax credit.

The Liberal government that succeeded the Conservatives in 1993 was, in fact, more successful in redesigning the Canadian state. The Liberals introduced substantial cuts to public expenditures in a way that transformed the system of intergovernmental relations that had underpinned Canada's Keynesian welfare state.

A particularly important move in this respect was the abolition in 1995 of CAP and its replacement by a block funding mechanism, the Canada Health and Social Transfer (CHST), which substantially reduced intergovernmental transfers across the full range of social policies. In the 1996 Speech from the Throne, the government also promised not to use its spending power to create new social programs without the consent of the majority of provinces. This principle was later codified in the Social Union Framework Agreement (SUFA) of 1999.

In making these changes, the Chrétien government also began to draw on inclusive liberalism. In fact, 'inclusion' became the new catchword—inclusion (in the labour market) of social-assistance recipients (lone mothers too) and inclusion of poor children through early investment in their development, in preparation for the kind of 'lifelong learning' needed in the global economy. This line of thinking was already visible in the Social Security Review, established under the minister of human resources development, Lloyd Axworthy, but it was only in the late 1990s that the government began to implement it with the introduction of the National Child Benefit (NCB). The NCB was designed as a means to 'break down the welfare wall' by creating incentives for social-assistance recipients to work—or for the working poor to keep at it, even at low rates of pay. Through the NCB, the federal government provided a child tax credit aimed at low- and middle-income families, a low-income supplement for working families, and a third component for social-assistance recipients. The provinces were then invited to claw back all or part of the income supplement for social-assistance recipients, which funds could then be 'invested' in children's services, including childcare, or additional income supplements for low-income families. In this sense, there was a modest social investment dimension to the NCB. True to SUFA, the federal government left it to the provinces to decide whether and how to use the third component. Some provinces used the funds in a manner consistent with the federal government's inclusive liberalism, focused on positive inducements to work, whereas others, including the largest province (Ontario), made it part of a coercive workfare set of arrangements (Jenson and Stroick 2000).

The National Children's Agenda (NCA), which was established by the provinces in 1997 and joined by the federal government in 1999, reflected an even more pronounced inclusive liberal orientation. Thus the NCA committed the federal, provincial, and territorial governments to work together to develop a comprehensive, cross-sectoral, and long-term strategy to ensure that *all* Canada's children receive the best possible opportunity to develop to their full potential. There are important differences, however, between this and the social liberalism of the 1960s and 1970s. As Jenson argues in the previous chapter, women had been written out: during the heyday of high Keynesianism, the case for universal childcare had been made in the name of women's equality, but under the NCA, universal programs are justified in the name of early child development. In addition, early childhood development is to be promoted largely as an investment in future competitiveness ('lifelong learning in the new economy') and as a way of saving future public expenditures on remedial measures.

Under the NCA, successive Liberal governments negotiated three new transfer agreements, all of which targeted early child development. The Early Childhood Development initiative made a federal contribution to provincial and territorial coffers[5] of $2.2 billion over five years. Yet, in negotiating the deal, the federal government gave up its original intention of requiring the provinces to invest in all four areas: the promotion of healthy pregnancy, birth, and infancy; improving parent and family supports; early childhood development, learning, and care; and community supports. The provinces were thus free to use the funds to invest in whichever areas they chose. With no requirement to spend on childcare, only six of the thirteen governments initially invested any money in childcare and none of the largest—Ontario, Alberta, and British Columbia—did so. As a result, a considerable portion was invested in the other areas. Some of these programs involve a highly gendered moral re-regulation (McKeen 2007), but this is not inconsistent with inclusive liberalism (Craig and Porter 2004). Mexico's much vaunted poverty-reduction policy reflects a similar thrust (Molyneux 2006).

The 2003 Multilateral Framework Agreement on Early Childhood Learning and Care (MFA) can be seen as an example of inclusive liberalism with a stronger developmental dimension. Through this agreement, which involved the transfer of $1.05 billion over five years, the two levels of government began to stake out principles for a pan-Canadian childcare system based on the following principles: (1) availability and accessibility,[6] (2) affordability, (3) quality,[7] (4) inclusiveness,[8] and (5) parental choice. These principles reflect the emphasis of inclusive liberalism on child development, while supporting parents' participation in the labour market or their preparation for such participation. In keeping with the post-1995 trend in intergovernmental arrangements, however, the agreement allowed substantial provincial diversity. The provinces and territories were free to choose from a broad selection of options—from classic 'market-enhancing' measures like information provision, fee subsidies, and quality-assurance systems, to the kind of supply-side measures (capital and operating grants, training and professional development, and wage enhancements) needed to lay the basis for an egalitarian regime. Funding, moreover, could go to commercial as well as non-profit providers.

In the 2004 election, the Liberals promised to establish a truly pan-Canadian childcare system along the lines of Quebec's egalitarian model.[9] Childcare advocates hoped that early learning and childcare would gain the same status as healthcare: a right enshrined in federal legislation and monitored by a pan-Canadian council. The minority Liberal government was only able to implement something less than this, albeit more than any previous government had managed to do.

In February 2005, a new federal–provincial–territorial agreement on the vision of a pan-Canadian early childhood learning and care system was reached; the agreement reiterated the principles outlined in the MFA, now described as QUAD (quality, universally inclusive, accessible, and developmental). The federal government announced that it was prepared to commit more than $5 billion over five years towards its development. Between April and November 2005, it negotiated bilateral agreements with all 10 provinces. All agreements referred to the QUAD principles, though only eight of them made it clear that investments would be made exclusively in regulated childcare. That this stipulation was omitted from the Quebec agreement is perhaps understandable since Quebec had already laid the foundations for a comprehensive childcare system. Yet the agreement with Quebec set a precedent for the agreement with New Brunswick, a province that currently provides regulated spaces for only 11 per cent of children under the age of 13. There were other weaknesses. True to its social conservatism, Alberta reserved the right to subsidize the cost of participation in part-day nurseries or preschool by the children of stay-at-home mothers. Only two agreements—Saskatchewan's and Manitoba's—made explicit a commitment to invest exclusively in non-profit care, while the Alberta, British Columbia, and New Brunswick agreements clearly stated that commercial providers would be included. The most serious flaw was that the Liberal government made no attempt to enshrine the right to early learning and childcare in legislation. Moreover, all agreements allowed either party to withdraw from the agreement with one year's notice. It was this escape clause that allowed the newly elected Harper Conservatives to kill the policy.

Although the Martin Liberals delivered less than childcare advocates hoped, the contrast between their policy and that of the Harper Conservatives underscores the importance of distinguishing varieties of liberalism. Whereas the former was inspired by an increasingly social form of inclusive liberalism, the latter bears the hallmark of neo-liberalism with a pronounced element of social conservativism.

In fact, the Harper government chose childcare as one of the five areas that would define its distinct profile. One of its first acts was to announce its intention to withdraw from the bilateral agreements, thus clearing the way for the implementation of its flagship Universal Child Care Benefit (UCCB). Rather than invest in the development of an early-learning and childcare infrastructure that also supported adult-earner families, the Harper government's UCCB offered all families with children under six—including traditional male-breadwinner families—a hundred dollars a month to use as it saw fit. As Lynne Yelich, parliamentary secretary to the minister of human resources and social development, put it, the UCCB is a benefit they are free to use in the best interests of their own children. For example, they can apply the $1,200 a year toward the cost of formal day care, they can use the benefit to pay for occasional babysitting or for child care help from a grandparent or neighbour. If parents so choose, they can purchase educational resources, like an educational DVD, for their preschoolers, or they can use the benefit to pay for special outings.[10]

For working parents, the benefit represents a drop in the bucket compared to childcare costs 'that range between $6,000 and $12,000 for infants and $5,000 to $8,000 for preschoolers' (Torjman 2007, 7). Moreover, it is a taxable benefit. The Caledon Institute has done a calculation of who gains what from the UCCB:

> No family ends up with the full $1,200. Welfare families net $951, while working poor and modest-income families are in the $600–800 area. Two-earner couples in the middle-income range . . . $50,000–90,000—get about $900. In the upper-income $100,000-plus range, one-earner couples get $970, two-earner couples between $850–680, and the very small group of single parent families from $680 to $640. (Battle, Torjman, and Mendelson 2006, 2)

Thus it is upper-income families with a stay-at-home parent that gain the most.

As Battle, Torjman, and Mendelson note, the UCCB 'is not really a childcare program, but rather simply another form of child benefit' (2006, 4). There was, however, a second component of the Conservatives' childcare policy—the Child Care Spaces Initiative (CCSI). What the Conservatives wanted to do was in line with the neo-liberal elements of their philosophy—to give incentives to business to create new childcare spaces. Both then 'privatize' childcare—the UCCB to families and the CCSI to business. This is in stark contrast to the earlier inter-governmental arrangements that transferred federal funds to the provinces and territories. The agreements negotiated by the Liberals also specified the common QUAD principles that were to inform provincial and territorial expenditures.

The Conservatives have been less successful in implementing this part of their policy than the UCCB. Consultations undertaken by departmental officials during the summer and fall of 2006 made it clear that, on the whole, businesses were not interested in investing directly in the creation of childcare spaces. It was also clear that the issue was not simply one of increasing the number of spaces but also of ensuring the quality and sustainability of existing programs.[11] The report of the advisory committee established by the government agreed.[12] Nevertheless, the Conservatives proceeded to introduce a 25 per cent investment tax credit to businesses that create new childcare spaces, to a maximum of $10,000 per space. At the same time, they allocated $250 million a year to the provinces and territories.[13] They also honoured the previous government's promise to continue funding under the Early Childhood Development Initiative and the Multilateral Framework Agreement. In total then, $1 billion will be transferred to the provinces and territories through the Canada Social Transfer fund—substantially less ($950 million) than they would have received had the bilateral agreements been maintained. This is not surprising since the UCCB alone will cost $2.4 billion a year. In other words, the Conservatives put the lion's share of the money into the UCCB and persisted in their plan to offer incentives to business to create spaces, leaving much less for investment in the early-learning and childcare infrastructures maintained by the provinces.

As Jenson notes in the previous chapter, the childcare advocacy community has been strong enough to keep the idea of a universal early-learning and childcare policy alive, but in this case party politics does indeed matter. The Harper government has made it clear that it has no interest in the kind of 'social investment' model favoured by the Liberals, much less any measures to advance gender equality. The support of the opposition parties for private members' Bill C-303 'to establish criteria and conditions in respect of funding for early learning and childcare programs' may give some grounds for optimism, but it is not possible to predict whether such consensus would survive a change of government.

## Conclusions

Like 'globalization', in popular and scholarly discourse, neo-liberalism is often presented as a giant steamroller, flattening all remnants of the post-war order to clear the way for the resurgence of what Polanyi (1957) called a 'market society'. Peck and Tickell's concept of neo-liberalization is more sophisticated than most, but it too risks incorporating too much. Alternatives remain viable. Some—like the egalitarian model sketched in the first section of this chapter—involve a radical challenge to the neo-liberal project. Others, like inclusive liberalism, would but modify the neo-liberal design. Thus inclusive liberalism accepts the basic terms of neo-liberal globalization and actively supports the existence of an increasingly polarized labour market 'in the here and now'. At the same time, it also draws on the developmental liberalism associated with John Stuart Mill and his successors. Thus it is prepared to invest in early childhood learning. In this sense, it retains a commitment to promoting equal opportunity 'over the life course'.

More broadly, this chapter has argued the importance of recognizing 'varieties of liberalism' across time and space. It has used the case of Canadian childcare policy to illustrate some of these differences, from a program narrowly targeted at those 'in need' through to the inclusive liberalism of recent years—and now to a genuinely neo-liberal policy laced with social conservatism. The analysis of these varieties of liberalism serves as an important reminder of the limits of post-war social liberalism, which are often forgotten in the critique of neo-liberalism. It also allows one to be critical of inclusive liberal strategies, both for the assumptions it shares with neo-liberalism and for the few ways in which it departs from them. At the same time, inclusive liberal policies like the

MFA and bilateral agreements would have gone some way toward establishing a QUAD-based childcare system, thus addressing real needs.

Like the earlier variant of social liberalism, inclusive liberalism establishes a more favourable discursive terrain on which to fight for a genuinely egalitarian alternative. That is what happened in the 1970s and in the early 1980s, when the Canadian state seemed poised to adopt such a model. The Liberals' QUAD model had similar potential, creating a 'horizon of legitimate expectations' (Marshall 1963) and thus an opportunity for childcare advocates and their allies to push for an egalitarian alternative. Bill C-303 did not receive third reading. It did, however, show that childcare really has become an issue that divides the neo-liberal Conservatives from the other parties, which are inspired by inclusive liberalism with a markedly egalitarian twist.

## Notes

1  As Esping-Andersen (1990) has argued, in the post-war era, different forms of welfare regime evolved. In this paper, the emphasis is on the national and pan-Canadian scale, although the importance of federal–provincial arrangements to the implementation of childcare policies will be stressed throughout. See Jenson, Mahon, and Phillips (2003) for a discussion of provincial variations, one of which conformed to liberal ideas.

2  These are of course ideal types. Actual childcare policies are often hybrids, as new initiatives embodying one logic of care are layered on pre-existing programs that often reflect other logics.

3  Several years after the passage of CAP, the federal government did introduce a childcare tax deduction, the Child Care Expense Deduction. This too was a classically 'liberal' policy instrument since it worked to support a market for care rather than investing in the development of a public service.

4  No province exploited this to the full, although at various times social-democratic governments in British Columbia and Manitoba moved in this direction.

5  Like the NCB and the multilateral framework agreement, Quebec decided to remain outside the ECD.

6  For example, through increased spaces, support for extended or flexible hours, and information for parents.

7  For example, training and support, child-to-staff ratios, pay scales, and the physical environment.

8  That is, children with different abilities, Aboriginal children, and children from various cultural and linguistic backgrounds were included.

9  For more on the Quebec model, see Jenson (2002).

10  Again, for a discussion of provincial variations, see Jenson, Mahon, and Phillips (2003) as well as Parliament of Canada, First Session, 25 September 2006, 11:30 a.m. Hansard #052.

11  See Summary of Consultations on the CCSI at http://www.hrsdc.gc.ca/en/ public_consultations/child_care?report_summary.shtml.

12  It is worth reading the report, submitted to the Honourable Monte Solberg, minister for human resources and social development, January 2007, because it made some very interesting recommendations that, on the whole, have been ignored by the government.

13  This figure will rise by 3 per cent a year as of 2009/10.

## References

Bashevkin, Sylvia. 2002. *Welfare Hot Buttons: Women, Work and Social Policy Reform*. Toronto: University of Toronto Press.

Battle, Ken, Sherry Torjman, and Michael Mendelson. 2006. *More Than a Name Change: The Universal Child Care Benefit*. Ottawa: Caledon Institute of Social Policy.

Canada. 1984. Commission on Equality in Employment. *Report*. Ottawa: Minister of Supply and Services. Prepared by Rosalie Abella.

Clarke, J. 2004. 'Dissolving the Public Realm? The Logics and Limits of Neoliberalism', *Journal of Social Policy* 33 (1): 27–48.

Craig, David, and Doug Porter. 2004. 'The Third Way and the Third World: Poverty Reduction and Social Inclusion in the Rise of "Inclusive" Liberalism', *Review of International Political Economy* 11 (2): 387–423

Esping-Andersen, Gøsta. 1990. *The Three Worlds of Welfare Capitalism*. Princeton: Princeton University Press.

Friendly, Martha. 1994. *Child Care Policy in Canada: Putting the Pieces Together*. Don Mills, Ont.: Addison-Wesley.

Fudge, Judy, and Leah Vosko. 2003. 'Gender Paradoxes and the Rise of Contingent Work: Towards a Transformative Political Economy of the Labour Market'. In W. Clement and L. Vosko, eds, *Changing Canada: Political Economy as Transformation*. Montreal: McGill-Queen's University Press.

Graefe, Peter. 2006. 'Neoliberal Federalism and Social Democratic Approaches to Social Assistance in the Canadian Provinces in the 1990s'. Presented at the annual meeting Canadian Political Science Association, York University.

Jenson, Jane. 2002. 'Against the Current: Child Care and Family Policy in Quebec'. In Sonya Michel and Rianne Mahon, eds, *Child Care Policy at The Crossroads: Gender and Welfare State Restructuring*. New York: Routledge.

———, Rianne Mahon, and Susan D. Phillips. 2003. 'No Minor Matter: The Political Economy of Child Care in Canada'. In W. Clement and L. Vosko, eds, *Changing Canada: Political Economy as Transformation*. Montreal: McGill-Queen's University Press.

———, and Susan D. Phillips. 1996. 'Regime Shift: New Citizenship Practices in Canada', *International Journal of Canadian Studies* 14 (Fall): 111–36.

———, and Sharon Stroick. 2000. *What Is the Best Possible Mix for Canada's Children?* Ottawa: Canadian Policy Research Networks.

Macpherson, C.B. 1962. *The Political Theory f Possessive Individualism: Hobbes to Locke*. Oxford: Clarendon Press.

———. 1977. *The Life and Times of Liberal Democracy*. Oxford: Oxford University Press.

McKeen, Wendy. 2007. 'The National Children's Agenda: A Neoliberal Wolf in Lamb's Clothing', *Studies in Political Economy* 80: 151–73.

Mahon, Rianne. 2000. 'The Never-Ending Story: The Struggle for Universal Child Care Policy in the 1970s', *Canadian Historical Review* 81 (4): 582–615.

———. 2006. 'The OECD and the Work/Family Reconciliation Agenda: Competing Frames'. In Jane Lewis, ed., *Children in Context: Changing Families, Changing Welfare States*. Cheltenham, UK: Edward Elgar.

———, and Susan Phillips. 2002. 'Dual Earner Families Caught in a Liberal Welfare Regime? The Politics of Child Care in Canada'. In Sonya Michel and Rianne Mahon, eds, *Child Care Policy at the Crossroads: Gender and Welfare State Restructuring*, 191–218. New York: Routledge.

Marshall, T.H. 1963. 'Citizenship and Social Class', *Sociology at the Crossroads*. London: Heinemann.

Molyneux, Maxine. 2006. 'Mothers at the Service of the New Poverty Agenda: Progresa/Opportunidades, Mexico's Conditional Transfer Program', *Social Policy and Administration* 40: 425–49.

O'Connor, Julia, Ann Shola Orloff, and Sheila Shaver. 1999. *States, Markets, Families: Gender, Liberalism and Social Policy in Australia, Canada, Great Britain and the United States*. Cambridge: Cambridge University Press.

OECD. 2005. *Babies and Bosses: Reconciling Work and Family Life*. Volume 4: *Canada, Finland, Sweden and the United Kingdom*. Paris: OECD.

Peck, Jamie, and Adam Tickell. 2002. 'Neoliberalizing Space', *Antipode* 34 (3): 380–404.

Phillips, Susan. 1989. 'Rock a bye Brian: The National Strategy on Child Care'. In Katherine Graham, ed., *How Ottawa Spends, 1989–90*. Ottawa: Carleton University Press.

Polanyi, Karl. 1957. *The Great Transformation: The Economic and Political Origins of Our Times.* Boston: Beacon Press.

Teghtsoonian, Katherine. 1993. 'Neo-Conservative Ideology and Opposition to Federal Regulation of Child Care Services in the United States and Canada', *Canadian Journal of Political Science* 36 (1): 97–122.

Torjman, Sherri. 2007. *Repairing Canada's Social Safety Net.* Ottawa: Caledon Institute of Social Policy.

White, Julie. 1993. *Sisters and Solidarity: Women and Unions in Canada.* Toronto: Thompson Educational.

## Further Reading

Bezanson, Kate, and Meg Luxton, eds. 2006. *Social Reproduction: Feminist Political Economy Challenges Neo-Liberalism.* Montreal: McGill-Queen's University Press.

Craig, David, and Doug Porter. 2006. *Development beyond Neoliberalism? Governance, Poverty Reduction and Political Economy.* New York: Routledge.

Gornick, Janet C., and Marcia K. Meyers. 2003. *Families That Work: Policies for Reconciling Parenthood and Employment.* New York: Russell Sage Foundation.

Gray, John. 2000. *Two Faces of Liberalism.* New York: New Press.

Harvey, David. 2005. *A Brief History of Neoliberalism.* Oxford: Oxford University Press.

Jenson, Jane, and Mariette Sineau, eds. 2001. *Who Cares? Women's Work, Childcare, and Welfare State Redesign.* Toronto: University of Toronto Press.

Lewis, Jane, ed. 2006. *Children, Changing Families and Welfare States.* Cheltenham, UK: Edward Elgar.

Lister, Ruth, et al. 2007. *Gendering Citizenship in Western Europe: New Challenges for Citizenship Research in a Cross-National Context.* Bristol: Policy Press.

Michel, Sonya, and Rianne Mahon, eds. 2002. *Child Care Policy at the Crossroads: Gender and Welfare State Restructuring.* New York: Routledge.

Morgan, Kimberly J. 2006. *Working Mothers and the Welfare State: Religion and the Politics of Work-Family Policies in Western Europe and the United States.* Stanford: Stanford University Press.

## Questions for Critical Thought

1. How is neo-liberalism different from other varieties of liberalism past and present?
2. How have different liberalisms understood women's place in society?
3. How did the male-breadwinner–female-caregiver family contribute to social reproduction in the past?
4. What are the different ways contemporary states can contribute to social reproduction now that the adult-earner family has become the norm? What are the implications for women's equality associated with each solution?

# CHAPTER 3

# Women and EI in Canada:

## The First Decade

Martha MacDonald

## Introduction

The introduction of Employment Insurance (EI) in 1996 was seen as a pillar of neo-liberal reform in Canada. It was part of fighting the deficit and was cast in neo-liberal language of economic independence and minimal government interference in the market. The gendered impacts of the reform also received considerable attention, most studies showing that changes to eligibility rules and benefit formulas hurt women disproportionately (HRDC 1996b; Pulkingham 1998; MacDonald 1999; Porter 2003; Salhany 1998; CLC 1999, 2003). Although the initial reform was extensively analyzed, there have been many revisions to the *Employment Insurance* Act in the decade since its introduction. First, do these changes reflect a new direction for the welfare state in either discourse or substance? Specifically, is there evidence of an emerging social investment approach in relation to income security? Second, how has gender played out in the course of these changes? Have the gender issues identified been rectified? These questions are examined by considering the evolution of the program as a whole over the decade since its introduction.

In addition to providing Regular Benefits for spells of unemployment, EI includes Special Benefits for interruptions in employment caused by illness, childbirth, infant care, and end-of-life care. There are important gender differences between Regular and Special Benefits, women being the primary beneficiaries of the latter and men the primary beneficiaries of the former (see Pulkingham and van der Gaag 2004 on these contrasting trends). In addition to gendered outcomes, there are also different discourses around Regular and Special Benefits. Whereas caregiving responsibilities receive recognition under the latter, they are invisible in the former. In this chapter, a close and careful examination of the components of the program shows ongoing gendered outcomes and helps shed light on the underlying gender and welfare state models discussed in the first section. Each change is analyzed in terms of its rationale and the surrounding political discourse in the context of a decade of research on the program by the author and others, including the government's own EI Assessment and Monitoring Reports. A review of changes to Regular EI in the decade after the initial reform shows they were relatively modest, fine-tuning the incentive structure and massaging the discourse by putting a more positive spin on the purpose of the program. The changes to caregiving benefits, on the other hand, have been dramatic, as I demonstrate through a discussion of Parental Benefits and the new Compassionate Care Benefit. In combination, the changes reflect a social investment discourse and an adult-worker model that remains highly dependent on continued caregiving by women. The gender-differentiated effects of the program have yet to be addressed.

## Welfare State Restructuring and Gender

In 1994, the Liberal government's Social Security Review emphasized the changing context for social security policy in terms of demographics, labour markets, family structure, and political ideology. The reform to social policy that followed in the mid-1990s was largely cast in neo-liberal terms. The underlying premises included reduced state expenditures, targeted social security spending, and the primacy of employment for economic security. The reforms continued the shift towards a smaller role for the state and a larger role not only for the market but also for the family and community, than in the Keynesian model. Although the reforms represented the consolidation of the neo-liberal welfare state (McKeen and Porter 2003; MacDonald 1999; Bashevkin 2002; Porter 2003), they have also been interpreted as sowing the seeds in Canada of what has become known as the social investment perspective (Dobrowolsky 2002; Dobrowolsky and Jenson 2005; Jenson 2006; Lister 2004), a term used to characterize the recent direction of many liberal welfare regimes, including those of the UK, Australia, and New Zealand.

With social investment, the state portrays its role more positively than under neo-liberalism. The state claims a role in investing in human capital and social capital in order to enable individuals to support themselves through the market and the country to compete globally. As in any investment model, not all investments have equal expected value and children are obvious targets for future-oriented spending. This child-centred approach has been depicted favourably by some progressive social scientists (Esping-Anderson 2002) but has been critically evaluated by many (Wiegers 2002; McKeen 2001; Jenson 2006; Dobrowolsky 2002, 2004; Lister 2004; Fletcher 2006). For some, it represents a substantive change in direction, whereas others see the shift more as a rhetorical one that masks essentially unchanged neo-liberal policies. The form of spending differs from both the Keynesian and the social democratic state. Tax expenditures are used extensively so that 'consumers' can purchase their own social services in the market. The state plays a smaller role in service delivery and moves towards being a service broker rather than a direct provider. Private partnerships are also part of the model (Larner and Butler 2005). Targeted entitlement to income security is favoured in the social investment approach. In short, although social spending is back on the agenda, marketization and the material reality of eroded benefits associated with neo-liberalism remain.

The feminist welfare state literature provides an additional lens through which to view changes since the mid-1990s. While the welfare regimes literature emphasizes the changing roles of the state, family, and market in the provision of social security, the feminist analysis of the welfare state focuses on the relationship of production and reproduction and the underlying assumptions about gender roles implicit in state policies. The Keynesian welfare state characteristic of liberal welfare regimes was premised on a male breadwinner model. Adult men received social security entitlements, such as unemployment insurance, via their market activity while adult women, as caregivers, received social security entitlements through their connections with male earners, or, in their absence, through second-tier state benefits such as means-tested social assistance. While the male breadwinner model still permeates the institutional framework in the labour market and public policy, an 'adult worker', 'citizen worker', or 'universal worker' model is emerging, as can be seen in the major social policy reforms of the last decade. All adults are now expected to be self-supporting, whether or not they have caregiving responsibilities. Social policy is framed to promote labour market participation and economic self-sufficiency. As Lister notes (2004), children are valued as future 'worker citizens', not 'child citizens'. Though the adult earner model is cast as gender-neutral, both the labour market and caregiving domains remain profoundly gendered. Thus, gender-blind income support policies based on an adult earner model have deeply gendered impacts. Although men and women are subject to the same rules for programs such as EI, their actual benefits vary systematically.

In both the welfare regimes and feminist welfare state literature, attention is drawn to the implications for caregiving of women's increased labour force attachment, cuts to state funding, and an aging population (Fletcher 2006; Stark 2005; Esping-Anderson 2003; Lewis 2001, 2002, 2004). The adult earner model does not ensure social reproduction. The default is to rely on the double, triple (or more) days of women as they juggle paid work, child rearing, elder care, and community volunteer work (Baines 2004; Fletcher 2006; Williams 2004). The broader social and economic feedback effects of this are now being manifested in falling birth rates and stress-related productivity problems.

If we use the care of children as an example, policies support social reproduction include child benefits that put money into the hands of parents, state-provided or -subsidized childcare, and work–family balance policies (such as parental leave) that allow parents to combine employment and caregiving more easily. Of these, the Canadian state has put the most emphasis on child benefits, as is consistent with a social investment perspective. The benefits are means-tested, families are given money to help equalize opportunity, and the market takes it from there. Expanded parental leave benefits through EI are the second avenue of support, allowing parents (mainly mothers) to provide care in the first year without giving up their longer-term status of 'adult workers'. Support for childcare services has been woefully inadequate. Canada's immigration policy has helped support a low-wage private childcare market, most notably through the live-in caregiver program (Gabriel 2004). Outside of Quebec, the goal of a publicly provided, accessible, quality childcare system has remained elusive (Fletcher 2006; Timpson 2001; see Mahon and Jenson in this volume).[1]

The caregiving crisis is not limited to children, for the disabled, the ill, and the elderly are also left to fall back on unpaid family caregivers, who themselves are under pressure to be good citizen workers or risk their own current and future social security entitlements. And the family caregivers, like the low-wage paid caregivers, are mostly women. It is clear that whether one focuses on the move from a neo-liberal state to a social investment approach, or from a male breadwinner model to an adult-worker model, the central issue remains its reliance on women's work of social reproduction. We may have a universal (though by no means equal) breadwinner model, but we are far from having a universal caregiver model (Stark 2005; Fraser 1997). It is instructive to view EI through this lens, because women's roles as workers and caregivers are intricately interwoven into the program. Furthermore, there are implicit child benefits in EI through the Family Supplement.

Several themes common to recent restructuring of the welfare state are represented in the decade of EI changes. These include individual responsibility, primacy of employment for economic security, privatization (to the family and the market), use of means-testing based on family income, use of the tax system for targeting and delivery of benefits, and a focus on children. In addition, the EI changes highlight the gender issues in the adult-worker model. Is the prototypical work pattern supported by Regular Benefits implicitly 'male'? Is the generic caregiver for whom Special Benefits are designed implicitly female?

## Regular EI: A Decade of Tinkering

With the change from a system based on weeks (with minimum of 15 hours) to one based on hours, more women became contributors, but their eligibility actually decreased because fewer were able to qualify. A 35-hour work week, clearly a male norm, was used to translate the weeks required under UI (12 to 20) into hours under EI (420 to 700). This increased the amount of work needed to qualify for anyone working less than 35 hours a week (who disproportionately are women). The duration formula also reduced weeks of benefits for part-time workers. The government's own EI Monitoring and Assessment Reports showed that women lost eligibility more than men,[2] and a court challenge claimed discrimination based on gender, given the predominance of women in part-time work (Salhany 1998). Women were further affected by the tough new entrant and re-entrant (NERE) rules, since the hours this group needed to qualify jumped to 910,[3] penalizing those with irregular work patterns or care-related employment interruptions, who again are more likely to be women (Phipps and MacPhail 2000; HRDC 1999).

The goal was to encourage continuous labour force attachment and create incentives to take any and all available work. Several new features reflected this direction: the intensity rule penalized repeat users by gradually lowering the benefit rate from 55 per cent to 50 per cent; the high-income clawback rate was tied to past EI use; the benefit formula used a 'minimum divisor' to calculate average insurable earnings, lowering benefits for those who qualified with less than 14 to 22 weeks of work (depending on unemployment rates).[4] Part-time workers needed more work to qualify for EI, while multiple job holders fared better under EI than UI (HRDC 2001a), in keeping with the goal of encouraging people to take any available work. Seasonal workers with low earnings or fewer than 30 hours per week (who were disproportionately women) lost their eligibility (de Raaf, Kapsalis, and Vincent 2003), and seasonal workers with long hours (who were predominantly men) could qualify more easily but were hurt by the penalties for repeat users (HRDC 2001b, c). Self-employed workers, a growing percentage of whom are women, remained outside the system. A full-time worker who was rarely unemployed (the prototypical male breadwinner) would have noticed little difference. Thus, the adult-worker model that underpinned EI translated the inequalities of a gendered labour market into differential entitlements (Porter 2003).

These program parameters are consistent with both the emphasis of neo-liberalism and social investment on the market and its desire to discourage 'dependency' on the state for income support. 'Good' workers are rewarded and 'bad' ones are punished. The emphasis was on the supply side of the market, and the program assumed jobs were available. EI also continued the policy begun in 1977 of using UI and EI funds for 'employment benefits and support measures' as they are now called, such as counselling, skills development, and wage subsidies, now delivered through Labour Market Development Agreements with the provinces. In line with the social investment approach, the emphasis on human capital investment increased under EI, and access to training became tied almost exclusively to EI eligibility.[5] Furthermore, the delivery model changed to one of partnership and individual responsibility, with participants required to help fund their own training.[6] Thus, although there was more rhetoric about human capital investment, access was increasingly targeted.

The EI rules have been tinkered with over the last decade, mostly to remove unforeseen work disincentives. Thus, the tinkering serves the program's original intent of promoting labour force attachment. Although it was argued that EI supported a low-wage supply of labour for precarious jobs (Myles 1995), many such employers complained that the penalties for irregular earnings or repeat seasonal work made it more difficult to fill such jobs. For example, the benefit formula (which averaged the earnings over the last 26 weeks of work) discouraged workers from taking weeks of work with lower earnings that would reduce their average earnings and benefits. Both employers and employees complained about this, and after a series of pilot projects, EI was amended in 2001 so that 'small weeks' (earnings of less than $225) are ignored in the benefit calculation.[7] Also in late 2000, the intensity rule was dropped, as was the escalating high-income clawback for repeat users. These changes were seen as political, given the intense opposition in areas with high concentrations of seasonal work, such as the Atlantic region. They mainly benefited men, given that more repeat users and seasonal workers are male (Stratychuk 2001; de Raaf, Kapsalis, and Vincent 2003) and more men are affected by the high-earnings clawback. In 2005/06 there were twice as many male as female frequent claimants (HRSDC 2007).

These changes did not totally correct the work incentive problems with the benefit formula. The use of the last 26 weeks of work to calculate average earnings, subject to the minimum divisor, hurts precarious workers with irregular earnings and those who qualify with limited weeks of employment, including substitute teachers and casual and seasonal workers. Presentations to the Task Force on Seasonal Work called for the use of the best 12 weeks of earnings (FFAW 2004). A pilot project begun in October 2005 uses the best 14 weeks (out of 52) to calculate average earnings in high unemployment regions. Although this is a welcome change, it leaves the minimum divisor in place, something that is of particular concern to seasonal workers, and it also enhances the availability of a flexible work force. In the language of HRDC, it will 'promote labour force attachment'.

The NERE rules that inadvertently affected parents returning from child-related leaves were also modified in 2000. Parents who have received maternity or parental benefits in the five years before the qualifying period are now exempt from the higher NERE eligibility requirement. Note, however, that parents who do not qualify for Maternity or Parental Benefits, as discussed below, and people who take time out for other kinds of caregiving again, most of whom are women, are still considered re-entrants. The rules reward continuous labour force attachment, in keeping with the adult-worker model discussed above.

Workers with caregiving responsibilities or in precarious jobs (which often go hand in hand), have difficulties meeting this ideal. Seasonal workers have to stay on the work and EI treadmill, since finding 910 hours can be impossible.

The NERE rules also intentionally discourage young people from taking seasonal work, thereby contributing to the erosion of rural communities. In the Atlantic provinces, for example, rural communities are now scrambling to find workers for seasonal processing and tourism work as young people leave the area. In response to such concerns, a 2005 pilot project allows NEREs in high unemployment regions to qualify for EI with only 840 hours if they agree to participate in 'employment measures' to enhance their job prospects (such as counselling or career planning). This modest change is consistent with a social investment approach (it facilitates people's marketability). From the applicant's perspective, however, it will likely be seen as one more punitive hoop to jump through to get benefits.[8]

Another change since 1996/7 also focuses on work incentives in high-unemployment regions. A pilot project begun in 2005 increases the allowable earnings while on EI (to $75, or 40 per cent of benefits), encouraging people to work while on EI. This reduces the effective 'tax' on earnings for claimants and is an approach used to reduce the welfare-work wall. Note that maximum EI benefits have risen by only $10 a week in 11 years. Instead of raising the benefits, this rule encourages claimants to supplement their EI through marginal work.

A final change in high unemployment regions has to do with the duration of benefits, which was reduced to a maximum of 45 weeks under EI. The formula that was used to calculate benefit length also reduced the duration for those who worked less than 35 hours a week. A 2004 pilot project on extended benefits provides five extra weeks of EI for eligible workers in high unemployment regions (up to the 45-week maximum). According to the press release, 'some part-time, seasonal and workers with short employment periods, because of the very nature of their work, face situations where their EI benefits end before finding new employment' (Service Canada 2007). It should be noted that the problem is as much with the EI formulas as with the 'nature of their work'.

The testing ground for all such pilot programs has been high unemployment regions. Six of the nine economic regions in the Atlantic provinces are included in the twenty-three covered by the pilot projects. Most are predominantly rural. Employers in such areas depend on EI to maintain a flexible work force. UI and now EI not only maintain individual workers; they support employers and communities. In high unemployment areas it is also less reasonable to expect that workers can easily 'adjust' out of precarious work and into full-time stable employment. In this context EI is an income supplementation program as much as an income replacement program. Precarious workers in low unemployment regions remain bound by the original EI rules and face higher eligibility requirements (up to 700 hours), which severely limit their access to the program.

As noted earlier, the emphasis of the social investment perspective on children is manifested in EI through the Family Supplement (FS) for claimants in low-income families with children. In the early years of UI, workers with dependents were also differentiated from those without, in the context of a male breadwinner model. Claimants (mainly men) who had dependent spouses or who were the main supporter of dependent children got higher benefits (Porter 2003, 44). In 1975, as a cost-cutting measure, this provision was dropped. However, a version was reintroduced in 1994 to soften the blow when the benefit rate was cut from 57 per cent to 55 per cent. This used a 60 per cent rate for low-earning claimants with dependents under the age of 16. Note that spouses were no longer considered 'dependents', a change that reflected the erosion of the male breadwinner model. Support for dependents took another turn with EI, in that eligibility is based on *family* income, not individual earnings. Women's groups have long opposed the use of family income, which assumes resources are shared within families and denies women an independent entitlement based on their own earnings. Married women lost entitlement to a supplement with EI, while married men and single parents gained, reflecting gender differences in labour market earnings (Phipps, MacDonald, and MacPhail 2001). However, women remained the main recipients of the FS.[9]

Means-testing based on family income is associated with welfare. The Family Supplement—like social assistance—targets the neediest and provides extra money for children, as is consistent with social investment discourse. In fact, the FS, with a maximum benefit of 80 per cent, is dramatically more generous than earlier UI supports for dependents.[10] The FS is also fully integrated with the Child Tax Benefit. Again, the social investment state delivers benefits for children by putting extra money in the hands of parent consumers and letting the market deliver the goods and services needed to develop future 'citizen workers'. Furthermore, the unemployed are divided into more deserving (those with children) and less deserving (those without).

In summary, although the changes to Regular EI over the decade have addressed some of the concerns of workers and employers, especially in high unemployment regions—and all changes were certainly welcomed—the major gender concerns remain. These include the impact on part-time workers and the implications of NERE rules for caregivers. The changes have strengthened the incentives to engage in precarious work. However, women and men in some precarious jobs continue to be poorly served by the minimum divisor and the exclusion of the self-employed. The total number of claims dropped by over 25 per cent, and women's share of claims decreased over the decade (see Tables 3.3 and 3.1). Claimants in low-income families with children, mostly women, have benefited from the more generous FS, consistent with a social investment ideology. Thus, women's total Regular Benefits have declined less than men's (28 versus 33 per cent, see Table 3.4). Even so, women's share of Regular Benefit dollars remains under 35 per cent (see Table 3.2).

**Table 3.1   New EI Claims ('000) by type of benefit and gender**

|  | Regular | Parental (biological) | Compassionate | Total |
|---|---|---|---|---|
| **2005/6** | | | | |
| Men | 801 | 34.1 | 1.37 | 972 |
| Women | 548 | 185.4 | 3.81 | 855 |
|  | (40.6%)[a] | (84.5%) | (73.6%) | (46.8%) |
| **2000/1** | | | | |
| Men | 831 | 13 | – | 957 |
| Women | 541 | 165 | – | 797 |
|  | (39.4%) | (92.7%) | – | (45.4%) |
| **1997/8** | | | | |
| Men | 898 | 7.7 | – | 999 |
| Women | 605 | 156.8 | – | 834 |
|  | (40%) | (95.3%) | – | (45.5%) |
| **1995/6[b]** | | | | |
| Men | 1,066 | 8 | – | 1,161 |
| Women | 752 | 160 | – | 969 |
|  | (41.4%) | (95%) | – | (45.5%) |

a   Female share of total new claims, for each benefit and time period.
b   The 1995–6 year is the last year of UI and is used as the base comparison in all HRDC *EI Monitoring and Assessment* reports.

Source: Based on HRSDC (2007), Annex 2; HRDC (2002), Annex 2; HRDC (1999), Annex B.

# Maternity and Parental Benefits: A Decade of Significant Change

Porter (2003) has documented the rocky history of the treatment of mothers by UI. Viewed as potential abusers of the system, they were originally disqualified from receiving benefits for six weeks before and six weeks after their due dates. Maternity Benefits were introduced in 1971 but were harder to qualify for than Regular Benefits (20 insurable weeks of work were required as opposed to 10 to 14). Furthermore, 10 of those weeks had to have been before conception to prove that the woman had not entered the labour force just to obtain Maternity Benefits. Unlike with Regular EI, the eligibility requirement has never varied with regional unemployment rates. In 1981, the '10-week rule' was dropped and benefits were extended to adoptive mothers, broadening the rationale from a focus on the mother's health needs to caregiving (Phipps 2006). This opened the way for fathers to claim entitlement, and in 1990, 10 weeks of Parental Benefit that could be shared between parents were added to the 15 weeks of existing Maternity Benefits, with a 30-week maximum for combined Maternity, Parental, and Sickness Benefits (Perusse 2003).

As with UI, most provisions developed for Regular EI Benefits were also applied to Maternity and Parental Benefits. For example, the benefit rate calculation was

**Table 3.2  Average EI benefits (weekly) and total amount paid by type and gender (nominal dollars)**

| | Regular | | Parental (biological) | | Compassionate | | Total benefits | |
|---|---|---|---|---|---|---|---|---|
| | Weekly av. $ | Total $ (M) | Weekly av. $ | Total $ (M) | Weekly av. $ | Total $ (M) | Weekly av. $ | Total $ (M) |
| **2005/6** | | | | | | | | |
| Men | 351 | 5,251.0 | 376 | 193.2 | 361 | 2.45 | 351 | 6,328.7 |
| Women | 285 (81.2%)[a] | 2,794.3 (34.7%)[b] | 323 (85.9%) | 1,963.7 (91.0%) | 306 (84.8%) | 5.35 (68.6%) | 291 (82.9%) | 6,357.4 (50.1%) |
| **2000/1** | | | | | | | | |
| Men | 326 | 4,610.9 | 360 | 33.4 | — | — | 326 | 5,410.6 |
| Women | 252 (77.3%) | 2,223.2 (32.6%) | 292 (81.1%) | 447.4 (93.1%) | — | — | 259 (79.4%) | 3,897.3 (41.8%) |
| **1997/8** | | | | | | | | |
| Men | 309 | 5,125 | 350 | 21.0 | — | — | 309 | 5,866 |
| Women | 231 (74.8%) | 2,591 (33.5%) | 281 (80.3%) | 426.8 (95.3%) | — | — | 240 (77.7%) | 4,147 (41.4%) |
| **1995/6** | | | | | | | | |
| Men | 311 | 6,333.1 | 361 | 20.6 | — | — | 312 | 7,138.0 |
| Women | 226 (72.7%) | 3,148.8 (33.2%) | 288 (79.8%) | 436.5 (95.5%) | — | — | 237 (75.9%) | 4,798.8 (40.2%) |

a  Female average benefit as a percentage of male average benefit (for each benefit and time period).
b  Female share of total amount paid (for each benefit and time period).

Source: Based on HRSDC (2007), Annex 2; HRDC (2002), Annex 2; HRDC (1999), Annex B.

**Table 3.3    Percentage change in claims 1995/6–2005/6 by type and gender**

|  | Regular (%) | Parental (biological) (%) | Total (%) |
|---|---|---|---|
| Male | –24.9 | +326.3 | –16.3 |
| Female | –27.1 | + 15.9 | –13.3 |

Source: Based on HRSDC (2007), Annex 2; HRDC (2002), Annex 2; HRDC (1999), Annex B.

**Table 3.4    Total benefits in 1995 dollars (million)[a] and percentage change 1995/6–2005/6**

|  | Regular | Parental (biological) | Total |
|---|---|---|---|
| **Men** |  |  |  |
| 1995/6 | $ 6,331.1 | $    20.6 | $ 7,138.0 |
| 2005/6 | $ 4,253.1 | $   156.5 | $ 5,125.4 |
| Change | –32.8% | +660% | –28% |
| **Women** |  |  |  |
| 1995/6 | $ 3,148.8 | $   436.5 | $ 4,798.8 |
| 2005/6 | $ 2,263.3 | $ 1,590.2 | $ 5,149.3 |
| Change | –28.1% | +264% | +7.3% |

a    Calculated using the Bank of Canada Inflation Calculator, based on CPI (2002 = 100), http://www.bankofcanada.ca/en/rates/inflation_calc.html.

Source: Based on HRSDC (2007), Annex 2; HRDC (2002), Annex 2; HRDC (1999), Annex B.

the same (including the minimum divisor and the FS), the NERE rules and two-week waiting period applied, and the self-employed were not covered. The two main differences were the hours required to qualify (700, with no regional variation, up from a minimum of 300) and the duration (there was a set maximum with no relation to hours worked, unchanged from 1990). Beneficiaries are also exempt from the high-income clawback. Thus, the program parameters combine the logic of promoting labour force attachment (through eligibility requirements and benefit levels) with the logic of supporting caregiving needs, for example, by not tying the length of benefits to work experience.

The potential impact of the change from weeks to hours was dramatic, especially for part-time workers. However, an HRDC evaluation found that 90 per cent of those who left jobs for maternity-related reasons (as shown on their Record of Employment) had the 700 hours they needed (HRDC 2004a). Other research showed that although *overall* eligibility among employed women was not reduced, younger mothers, those in casual employment, and those who worked for smaller firms were less likely to qualify under either UI or EI rules (Phipps 2001). It should also be noted that in 2000 about 20 per cent of eligible mothers did not participate in the Parental Benefits program (HRDC 2004a, 20), perhaps for reasons related to benefit levels. Furthermore, many participants returned to work early, especially younger workers, single parents, those whose spouses did not work full-time, and those with post-secondary education (Phipps 2001). Clearly the program design did not meet the needs of many new mothers.

There was considerable objection to the 700-hour entrance requirement, including a court challenge (Salhany 1998). In addition, women who took their entitled leaves and subsequently had other children could find themselves classified as NEREs. In response to these concerns, in 2000 the required number of hours was decreased to 600 and those who had received Maternity or Parental Benefits in the five years before the qualifying period were exempted from the NERE rules. Furthermore, only one parent would have to serve the two-week waiting period. The government admitted that the logic of Regular Benefits should not have been applied to Maternity and Parental Benefits. The maximum number of weeks of parental leave were also increased dramatically, from 10 to 35, with a combined maximum of 50 (which was raised to 65 in 2004).

The reduction in required work hours resulted in a 4.4 per cent increase in the number of mothers qualifying for Maternity Benefits in 2002, compared with 2000 and a 4.3 per cent (2.3 per cent) increase in mothers (fathers) receiving Parental Benefits (Perusse 2003). In addition, the *total* benefits paid in these programs more than doubled from 2000 to 2002 (Perusse 2003). Marshall (2003) found that the proportion of all new mothers receiving benefits increased from 54 per cent in 2000 to 61 per cent in 2001. (Phipps 2006 reports similar findings with a different data set.) However, 12 per cent of new mothers were employees who did not meet the entrance requirements for benefits and another 5 per cent were self-employed and thus excluded from the program (Marshall 2003). Significant differences in the likelihood of receiving benefits also persist amongst women, for single parents, younger mothers, those with less education, and those with other children are still *less* likely to report benefits (Phipps 2006, 43). The length of leave increased, with 47 per cent of mothers returning to work within 9 to 12 months in 2001, compared to 8 per cent in 2000 (Marshall 2003, 6). The median length of time at home increased from 6 months to 10 months for women who received benefits (2003). However, lower earnings were associated with an earlier return to work and Marshall points out that the behaviour of *ineligible* new mothers did not change.

Although the 2000 changes addressed some (though not all) of the eligibility concerns, benefit levels remain tied to regular EI levels and did not increase for ten years. A 2005 study found that low benefit levels were the main complaint about the program and that average weekly benefits were unchanged at $295 per week (HRSDC 2005a). Women beneficiaries have fewer hours and lower insurable earnings (and therefore benefits) than men (Perusse 2003). In 2005/06, average Parental (biological) Benefits for women were $323 a week, compared with $376 for men (see Table 3.2). As with Regular EI, how parents fare depends on their type of work and also—because of the FS—their *family* income. Phipps (2006) shows changes over time in the entitlements of new parents. While *total* benefit entitlements of the 'typical' new mother have increased dramatically since 1971, *weekly* benefits have actually declined, including since 1997, as the real value of maximum benefits has decreased along with the benefit rate. The impacts of changes vary by work and family characteristics. For example, a woman working 30 hours a week for 20 weeks lost eligibility with EI and regained it with the 2000 changes, but she is worse off now than under UI in terms of benefits unless she qualifies for the FS. The effective weekly replacement rate for high-earning mothers has also decreased—as it has for a father with median earnings, given that maximum insurable earnings were frozen from 1996 to 2006 (all examples from Phipps 2006).

Overall, while key neo-liberal priorities persist, the changes clearly reflect the social investment themes. The dramatic increase in the length of leaves is consistent with the emphasis on investing in children. The Parental Benefits program is a core component of the National Children's Agenda. Using a social investment discourse, an HRSDC evaluation report notes that the 2000 program is designed to:

- promote child development;
- balance demands of work and very young children;
- make short-term investment for long-term economic gain;
- use EI as an effective instrument;
- promote gender equality; and
- allow businesses to retain valuable, experienced employees. (HRSDC 2005a, i)

The caregivers who are supported are parents, not daycare providers. Social reproduction remains in the private sphere. The state is not providing services but helping parents provide care. As is consistent with an adult earner model, stay-at-home parents do not benefit. Fairly continuous labour force attachment is needed to qualify; thus eligibility decreases with the number of children, as it becomes more difficult to meet this norm. Non-standard work is less well served than full-time, and the changes over the decade increase the incentive for workers to take on more precarious work.[11]

Though Parental Benefits are cast in gender-neutral terms, the interaction of the program parameters with gendered labour markets leaves women as the main recipients (85 per cent of Parental Benefit claims in 2005/06 were by women—see Table 3.1). The low benefit rate encourages the lower earner (usually the mother) to take the leave. The program does not promote a universal caregiver model. Parents are on their own to cope with work and family demands beyond the first year of the child's life. In fact, the lack of flexibility in how one can structure the time off is a key criticism of the program (Phipps 2006; Women's Network PEI 2004.).

Quebec opted out of the EI Maternity and Parental Benefits program and in 2006 established its own program that responds to some of these concerns (Phipps 2006).[12] The Quebec plan is more flexible, with one option that provides higher earnings replacement (75 per cent) for a shorter duration (15 weeks of maternity, 25 weeks' shared parental and 3 weeks' paternity benefits) and a second option of longer duration but a lower replacement rate (some weeks at 70 per cent and some at 55 per cent).[13] It also raises maximum insurable earnings (to $57,500, compared with $40,000 under EI), increasing the benefits under either plan. These provisions meet the criticism that the effective earnings-replacement rates under EI are too low, especially for higher earners. Furthermore, the eligibility requirement is $2,000, considerably lower than EI, and it includes self-employed workers.[14] The waiting period is also waived. These changes remove the questionable tie-in between the rules and incentives for Regular EI and Maternity and Parental Benefits. The Quebec program gives a concrete example of how the major weaknesses of Maternity and Parental Benefits—lack of access for many women in non-standard paid work, lack of coverage for self-employed, low replacement rates, and inflexibility in the structure of the leave—could be corrected even within EI (Phipps 2006).

The Quebec program, especially in combination with its seven-dollars-a-day childcare program (see Jenson in this volume), is more in line with the greater emphasis on social reproduction in social democratic welfare regimes. In contrast, in its ruling that Maternity and Parental Benefits are a coherent extension of traditional EI, the Supreme Court focused on income protection for employment interruptions, not on caregiving:

> The argument of the Attorney General of Quebec, that the purpose of maternity benefits is to support families and to enable women to care for their children at the time of birth, cannot be accepted. . . . Although support for families and the ability to care for children may be one of the effects of the measure, that is not its pith and substance. The fundamental objective of the maternity benefits plan is to protect the workers' incomes from the time when they lose or cease to hold their employment to the time when they return to the labour market. (Supreme Court of Canada 2005, par. 35)

This view reiterates the primacy of production over reproduction in the adult earner model, with its genderless 'worker'. The social investment perspective takes account of caregiving primarily within the context of promoting labour-force attachment and enhancing productivity.

# Compassionate Care Benefits: A New Direction

Bill C-28, which took effect in January 2004, added a Compassionate Care Benefit (CCB) to EI to provide income security to workers who take time off to care for dying family members. The decision to support family members as end-of-life caregivers should be seen in the context of the pressures on families created by the deinstitutionalization and cutbacks that characterized healthcare delivery in the neo-liberal period (Armstrong and Armstrong 2002; see also Armstrong in this volume). The social investment approach puts some money back into healthcare, but it still relies on both formal home care and informal caregivers.

HRDC described the program as part of a 'global movement toward more family-friendly labour legislation' (HRDC 2004b). It is firmly situated within an adult-worker model in which many care responsibilities reside with the family. The state's response is to provide some support to families to balance these work–family demands. Benefits go to workers to ease the burden somewhat— and then they can get back to work! Full-time family caregivers are *not* supported in this model. Nor does the state directly provide caregiving services. Rather, it facilitates the provision of care in the private sphere by adults (mainly women) who are also expected to be employees.

Eligibility for the CCB is based on the rules for other EI Special Benefits such as Maternity and Parental Benefits (as amended in 2000). Six hundred hours of insurable employment are needed to qualify for up to six weeks of Compassionate Care Benefits (with a two-week waiting period). As with Parental Benefits, the leave can be shared among family members, and now only one waiting period is served. The benefit formula is the same as for Regular EI and other Special Benefits. Claimants must also obtain a medical certificate stating that the family member is gravely ill and that the claimant could provide care and support; the six weeks of leave must be taken within a six-month period established by the medical certificate.

While HRDC consulted widely with stakeholders before implementing the CCB (Cummings 2001; Fast et al. 2002a, 2002b; Moore 2001), it was clear within the first year that the take-up rate was considerably lower than the 270,000 expected. In 2004/05 less than 4 per cent of the $190 million annual budget was spent on claims (Osborne and Margo 2005). An evaluation began in 2004 to understand the problems with the program (HRDC 2004b). Critical reaction to the program centred on key parameters that limit its effectiveness.[15] The definition of 'family member' was restricted to one's child, parent, parent-in-law, spouse, or common-law partner. The requirement for medical certification of a 'significant risk of death' also poses a barrier, certainly on an emotional level. Furthermore, many people provide care for very ill family members who do, in fact, have a reasonable chance of recovery. In addition, the length of the leave is short, given the unpredictability of terminal illness. The concept of care is also based on a narrow medical model—directly providing or participating in the care, arranging for care by a third party, or providing psychological or emotional support. The benefit ends upon death, even if the six weeks have not been exhausted. However, the time following death may demand at least as much caregiving, under a broader notion of care. Although many of these concerns have been acknowledged, only one change has so far been made (HRSDC 2005b). An amendment in June 2006 expanded the definition of family to include siblings, grandparents, grandchildren, other in-laws, aunts, uncles, nieces, nephews, foster parents, guardians, and wards and allowed the patient to certify an unrelated person as 'like family'.

Only a narrow set of end-of-life caregivers are supported by this program—those who are employed and can meet the EI eligibility requirements. As with other Special Benefits, the self-employed are omitted and workers in part-time, seasonal, and other non-standard jobs face particular difficulties in qualifying. Those who have been providing care full-time are not supported. The program enables worker-caregivers to maintain their labour market connection and it also enables employers to retain workers. Such work–life balance programs are consistent with a social investment state discourse, though the CCB is a very modest initiative. Not surprisingly, almost three-quarters of the claimants are women (see Table 3.1). EI fails to support the many caregiving challenges adult workers, especially women, face in between caring for infants and the terminally ill.

## Conclusion

As has been shown, EI has continued to evolve over the decade since the initial reform. Whereas changes to Regular Benefits have involved 'tinkering' to fine-tune the original incentives, more substantive changes have been made to Special Benefits. The main elements of the changes—and the related discourse—are consistent with the social investment model. The language has been softened, and the most punitive elements of the program, such as the intensity rule, have been withdrawn. The changes to Special Benefits and the increased generosity of the FS especially resonate with a child-centred model.

Some things have *not* changed, however. No change has been made in eligibility for Regular Benefits, and the NERE rules remain in force, despite widespread acknowledgment of the difficulties they pose for those in precarious employment. Benefits (for both Regular and Special Benefits) are still substantially lower than under UI. After being frozen for a decade, maximum insurable earnings were increased by only $1,000 for 2007, thereby raising maximum benefits by $10 per week (2.4 per cent), despite a 20 per cent rise in the consumer price index over the decade. Several changes to the benefit formula encourage people to take all available hours (ignoring 'small' weeks, increased allowable earnings while on claim, and the 'best 14 weeks' pilot project), in keeping with the intent of the original reform. Encouraging and rewarding labour force attachment remains the hallmark of EI, in line with both neo-liberal and social investment models. The cutbacks that were at the heart of the original design are essentially still in place, and great savings have been realized,[16] though nominal benefits have increased somewhat since 2000 as a result of the various changes.

With the introduction of EI, women lost in terms of both eligibility and duration of benefits. Women's share of Regular claims fell by 27 per cent over the decade, compared with a 25 per cent drop for men. The challenges for non-standard workers, which affect women more than men, remained in place a decade later. Whereas women made up 40.6 per cent of Regular EI claimants in 2005/06, they made up 45 per cent of the unemployed (HRSDC 2007, Annex 1.4), a higher gap in entitlement than in 1995.[17] The percentage of the unemployed who receive EI is lower for women and has fallen more since 1997 (Townson and Hayes 2007, 22). Gender inequalities in earnings and work patterns are reflected in women's lower *weekly* benefits in all programs as well as their lower *total* benefits in Regular EI, which are barely half those of men, because of fewer weeks of entitlement. Gender-based analysis can be one mechanism for identifying such gender-differentiated consequences of policies. Gender-based analysis of policies has been promoted throughout the federal government for well over a decade by Status of Women Canada. However, as a report by the House of Commons Standing Committee on the Status of Women indicates, this is done minimally and unevenly (2005).

Women's gains have been exclusively in Special Benefits related to caregiving—indeed so have men's (see Tables 3.3 and 3.4). The focus on care in EI reflects the emphasis on children in the social investment approach as well as its preferred method of spending (for example, facilitating parental caregiving rather than delivering public services). Although women now receive slightly more than half of all EI payments, this is almost totally due to the increased generosity of the caregiving benefits, especially Parental. The gender gap in weekly benefits, though still significant, has narrowed, partly because of the increased generosity of the Family Supplement.

With current social policy driven by an adult-worker model with an emphasis on human capital, the state is grappling with the caregiving tensions inherent in that approach; hence the enhanced role of EI in care-related employment interruptions. The social investment approach is to tie entitlements to labour-force attachment and to rely on families to provide the care. EI has been the main vehicle for this approach, which is not gender-neutral. As can be seen in Table 3.1, the caregivers are overwhelmingly women. Even so, gender inequalities in work patterns, which are themselves partly due to caregiving, restrict the entitlements of some women, such as part-time workers and those who take time out of the labour force. The low earnings-replacement rate reinforces women's continued responsibility for caregiving, because it makes sense for the lower-earning spouse (usually the woman) to take the leave.

The different trends in Regular and Special Benefits make sense in an adult-worker model. Regular EI is less generous now since everyone is expected to work, and individuals are expected to fall back on the earnings of other family members; families with children are given targeted consideration, means testing is based on family income via the tax system; and finally, Special Benefits provide modest income support to the individual worker-carer for some care-related work interruptions. However, at the same time as the social investment perspective provides more caregiving benefits for its 'adult workers', it relies on—and reinforces—women's responsibility for care. Gendered patterns of paid work and unpaid caregiving permeate both Regular and Special Benefits. Changes to both types of benefits are necessary to provide equitable income security to all adult worker-caregivers. Unfortunately, the emphasis of the social investment model on equality of opportunity, not outcomes, makes such changes unlikely (see Dobrowolsky in this volume).

## Notes

1  Even in Quebec there has been backsliding on the commitment to childcare (see Jenson in this volume).

2  The 1998 report showed a 20 per cent decrease in claims by women compared with a 16 per cent decrease for men between 1995/6 and 1997/8 (HRDC 1999). Various ways of calculating EI eligibility and unemployment rates also consistently show lower rates for women (HRSDC 2005c: 57; CLC 1999, 2003; Townson and Hayes 2007).

3  One is categorized as a NERE if one has fewer than 490 hours or equivalent EI benefit weeks in the year *preceding* the 52-week qualifying period (called the 'labour force attachment' year). Under UI, eligibility for NEREs was 20 weeks (minimum 15 hours a week), compared to 910 hours under EI.

4  For example, a seasonal worker who qualified with 10 weeks of work in a high unemployment area would have her earnings averaged over 14 weeks. She would receive 55 per cent of this average rather than 55 per cent of her actual average weekly earnings (subject to the maximum insurable earnings, MIE).

5  This chapter does not discuss changes to these measures over the decade. Implementation took many years.

6  Training purchases were gradually phased out, and extended UI benefits for those in training programs were ended.

7  Note that a person must have *more that the minimum divisor number of weeks* for this to apply, meaning many seasonal workers do not benefit from this provision.

8  A similar approach was taken by the TAGS program, where applicants had to participate in 'active' labour-market measures to get their income benefits. However, the measures were often viewed as demeaning and inappropriate (HRDC 1996a).

9  Women made up two-thirds of FS recipients in 1997/8, 15 per cent of women claimants receiving the benefit (HRDC 1999). In 2005/6 three-quarters of FS recipients were women and 13.6 per cent of female claimants received the benefit (HRSDC 2007, Annex 2, Table 2–13).

10  An early evaluation found that the average FS (for Regular Benefits) was $23 per week compared to $13 under the UI dependency rate (Phipps, MacDonald, and MacPhail 2001). By 2006 this was $43 (for all benefits), and the total amount paid was $169,387 compared

to $108,514 ten years earlier (HRSDC 2007, Annex 2, Table 2–13). However, the 2005 *EI Monitoring and Assessment Report* (HRSDC 2006, iii) notes that the percentage of people qualifying for the FS had declined since 1998/9 to 9 per cent, attributing this to the fact that the eligible income level (less than $25,921) has remained unchanged since EI began.

11 Many of the changes to Regular Benefits over the decade, including the pilot projects on using the 14 best weeks in the benefit formula and allowing more earnings while on EI, also apply to Maternity and Parental Benefits.

12 For details on the plan see the Quebec Parental Insurance Plan website at http://www.rqap. gouv.qc.ca/index_en.asp.

13 Note that the spouse in a female same-sex couple is eligible for the Paternity Benefits, but only the biological father can take them in a male same-sex couple. Adoption benefits can be taken by either adoptive parent, regardless of gender.

14 It should be noted that there is a precedent in EI for using an earnings criteria and insuring the self-employed, namely fishing benefits.

15 See the recent Health Council of Canada evaluation, for example, for a good summary of these issues (Osborne and Margo 2005).

16 The *2005 Monitoring and Assessment Report* estimated average annual savings of $1.4 billion per year from the 1996 reform (HRSDC 2006, 93).

17 In 1995, women made up 43.2 per cent of the unemployed (Statistics Canada 1995) and 41.4 per cent of beneficiaries (see Table 3.1).

## References

Armstrong, Pat, and Hugh Armstrong. 2002. *Wasting Away—The Undermining of Canadian Health Care*. 2nd edn. Oxford: Oxford University Press.

Baines, Donna. 2004. 'Seven Kinds of Work—Only One Paid: Raced, Gendered and Restructured Care Work in the Social Services Sector', *Atlantis* 28 (2): 19–28.

Bashevkin, Sylvia. 2002. *Welfare Hot Buttons: Women, Work, and Social Policy Reform*. Toronto: University of Toronto Press.

Canadian Labour Congress. 1999. *Left Out in the Cold—The End of UI for Canadian Workers*. Ottawa: Canadian Labour Congress.

———. 2003. *Falling Unemployment Insurance Protection for Canada's Unemployed*. Ottawa: Canadian Labour Congress.

Cummings, Joanne. 2001. *Report on Working Parents with Gravely Ill Children*. Canadian Alliance for Children's Healthcare. Submitted to Human Resources Development Canada. Toronto: Canadian Alliance for Children's Healthcare.

de Raaf, Shawn, Costa Kapsalis, and Carole Vincent. 2003. 'Seasonal Work and Employment Insurance Use', *Perspectives on Labour and Income* September 4 (9): 5–11.

Dobrowolsky, Alexandra. 2002. 'Rhetoric versus Reality: The Figure of the Child and New Labour's Strategic 'Social Investment State', *Studies in Political Economy* 69: 43–73.

———. 2004. 'The Chretien Liberal Legacy and Women: Changing Policy Priorities with Little Cause for Celebration'. In Lois Harder and Steve Patten, eds, *The Chrétien Legacy: Politics and Public Policy in Canada,* 181–210. Montreal: McGill-Queen's University Press.

———, and Jane Jenson. 2004. 'Shifting Representation of Citizenship: Canadian Politics of "Women" and "Children"', *Social Politics* 11 (2): 154–80.

———, and ———. 2005. 'Social Investment Perspectives and Practices: A Decade in British Politics', *Social Policy Review* 17: 203–30.

Esping-Andersen, Gøsta. 2002. 'A Child-Centred Social Investment Strategy'. In G. Esping-Andersen, D. Gallie, A. Hernerijck, and J. Myles, eds, *Why We Need a New Welfare State,* 26–67. Oxford: Oxford University Press.

———. 2003. 'Women in the New Welfare Equilibrium', *The European Legacy* 8 (5): 599–60.

Fast, Janet, and Norah Keating. 2000. *Family Caregiving and Consequences for Carers: Toward a Policy Research Agenda*. Canadian Policy Research Networks Discussion Paper No. F/10. Ottawa: CPRN.

————, Linda Niehaus, Jaquie Eales, and Norah Keating. 2002a. 'A Profile of Canadian Palliative Care Providers'. Prepared for Human Resources Development Canada.

————, ————, ————, and ————. 2002b. 'A Profile of Canadian Chronic Care Providers'. Prepared for Human Resources Development Canada.

Fish, Food and Allied Workers (FFAW). 2004. Presentation to the Task Force on Seasonal Work. 13 Apr. http://www.ffaw.nf.ca/BriefDetails.asp?ID=4.

Fletcher, Stephanie. 2006. *The Canadian Policy Response to the Crisis of Care: Opportunities and Consequences for Women*. MA thesis. Halifax: Saint Mary's University.

Fraser, Nancy. 1997. *Justice Interruptus: Critical Reflections on the 'Postsocialist' Condition*. New York: Routledge.

Gabriel, Christina. 2004. 'A Question of Skills: Gender, Migration Policy and the Global Political Economy'. In Kees van der Pijl, Libby Assassi, and Duncan Wigan, eds, *Global Regulation: Managing Crises after the Imperial Turn*. New York: Palgrave Macmillan: 162–76.

HRDC (Human Resources Development Canada). 1996a. *The Atlantic Groundfish Strategy*. Background Paper, TAGS Household Study SP-AH007E-BP1–01–96. Ottawa: HRDC.

————. 1996b. *Employment Insurance: Gender Impact Analysis*. Ottawa: HRDC.

————. 1999. *Employment Insurance 1998 Monitoring and Assessment Report*. Ottawa: HRDC.

————. 2001a. *EI Reform and Multiple Job Holding*. Ottawa: HRDC.

————. 2001b. *An Evaluation Overview of Seasonal Employment*. Ottawa: HRDC, Evaluation and Data Development, Strategic Policy.

————. 2001c. *EI Reform and Seasonal Workers That Earn Less than $12,000*. Final Report. SP-ML013-12-01E. Ottawa: HRDC, Evaluation and Data Development, Strategic Policy.

————. 2002. *Employment Insurance 2001 Monitoring and Assessment Report*. Ottawa: HRDC.

————. 2004a. *Evaluation of EI Parental Benefits*. Ottawa: HRDC, Evaluation and Data Development, Strategic Policy.

————. 2004b. *Evaluation Framework of the Evaluation of EI Compassionate Care Benefits*. Ottawa: HRDC, EI Evaluation, Program Evaluation.

HRSDC (Human Resources and Skill Development Canada). 2005a. *Summative Evaluation of EI Parental Benefits*. Program Evaluation, Strategic Policy and Planning, SP-AH-674-01-05E. http://www.hrsdc.gc.ca/en/publications_resources/evaluation/2007/sp_ah_674_01_05e/page00.shtml.

————. 2005b. *Government of Canada initiates regulatory changes to expand eligibility criteria for the Employment Insurance Compassionate Care Benefit*. Press release. 28 Nov. http://www.news.gc.ca/cfmx/view/en/index.jsp?articleid=186529&.

————. 2005c. *Employment Insurance 2004 Monitoring and Assessment Report*. SP-102-04-05E. Ottawa: HRSDC.

————. 2006. *Employment Insurance 2005 Monitoring and Assessment Report*. SP-102-04-06E. Ottawa: HRSDC.

————. 2007. *Employment Insurance 2006 Monitoring and Assessment Report*. SP-102-04-07E. Ottawa: HRSDC.

Jenson, Jane. 2006. 'Social Investment for New Social Risks: Consequences of the Lego Paradigm for Children'. In Jane Lewis, ed., *Children, Changing Families and Welfare States*, 27–50. Cheltenham, UK: Edward Elgar.

Larner, Wendy, and Maria Butler. 2005. 'Governmentalities of Local Partnerships: The Rise of a "Partnering State" in New Zealand', *Studies in Political Economy* 75: 79–102.

Lewis, Jane. 2001. 'The Decline of the Male Breadwinner Model: The Implications for Work and Care', *Social Politics* 8 (2): 152–69.

————. 2002. Gender and Welfare State Change, *European Societies* 4 (4): 331–57.

————. 2004. 'The Gender Settlement and Social Provision: The Work-Welfare Relationship at the Level of the Household'. In Robert Salais and Robert Villeneuve, eds, *Europe and the Politics of Capabilities*, 239–52. Cambridge: Cambridge University Press.

Lister, Ruth. 2004. 'The Third Way's Social Investment State'. In Jane Lewis and Rebecca Surender, eds, *Welfare State Change—Towards a Third Way?*, 157–81. New York: Oxford University Press.

MacDonald, Martha. 1998. 'Gender and Social Security Policy: Pitfalls and Possibilities',
    *Feminist Economics* 4 (1): 1–25.

———. 1999. 'Restructuring, Gender and Social Security Reform in Canada', *Journal of
    Canadian Studies* 34 (2): 57–88.

McKeen, Wendy. 2001. 'Shifting Policy and Politics of Federal Child Benefits in Canada', *Social
    Politics* 8 (2): 186–90.

———, and Ann Porter. 2003. 'Politics and Transformation: Welfare State Restructuring in
    Canada'. In Wally Clement and Leah Vosko, eds, *Changing Canada: Political Economy as
    Transformation*, 109–34. Montreal: McGill-Queen's University Press.

Marshall, Katherine. 2003. 'Benefitting from Extended Parental Leave', *Perspectives on Labour
    and Income* 4 (3): 5–11.

Moore, Celia. 2001. *Report on Working Parents with Gravely Ill Children*, Part Two. Submitted to
    HRDC by the Canadian Alliance for Children's Heathcare.

Myles, John. 1995. *When Markets Fail: Social Welfare in Canada and the United States*. United
    Nations Research Institute for Social Development Discussion Paper 68. Geneva: UNRISD.

Osborne, Kate, and Naomi Margo. 2005. *Analysis and Evaluation: Compassionate Care Benefit*.
    Toronto: Health Council of Canada.

Perusse, Dominique. 2003. 'New Maternity and Parental Benefits', *Perspectives on Labour and
    Income* 4 (3): 12–15.

Phipps, Shelley. 2001. *Unemployment Insurance—Employment Insurance Transition: An
    Evaluation of the Pre-2001 Maternity and Parental Benefits Program in Canada*. SP-AH133-
    03-00E. Ottawa: Human Resources Development Canada, Strategic Evaluation and
    Monitoring, Evaluation and Data Development.

———. 2006. *A Story of Maternity and Parental Benefits in Canada*. Toronto: C.D. Howe
    Institute.

———, Martha MacDonald, and Fiona MacPhail. 2001. 'Gender Equity within Families versus
    Better Targeting: An Assessment of the Family Income Supplement to Employment
    Insurance Benefits', *Canadian Public Policy* 27 (4): 423–46.

———, and Fiona MacPhail. 2000. *The Impact of Employment Insurance on New Entrants and
    Re-Entrants*. Final Report. Human Resources Development Canada, Strategic Evaluation and
    Monitoring, Evaluation and Data Development. SP-AH135-11-00E. Ottawa: HRDC.

Porter, Ann. 2003. *Gendered States: Women, Unemployment Insurance, and the Political Economy
    of the Welfare State in Canada, 1945–1997*. Toronto: University of Toronto Press.

Pulkingham, Jane. 1998. 'Remaking the Social Divisions of Welfare: Gender, Dependency and UI
    Reform', *Studies in Political Economy* 56: 7–48.

———, and Tanya van der Gaag. 2004. 'Maternity/Parental Leave Provisions in Canada: We've
    Come a Long Way but There Is Further to Go', *Canadian Women's Studies* 23 (3/4): 116–25.

Salhany, R.E. 1998. 'Reasons for Judgment in the Matter of the Employment Insurance Act and
    in the Matter of a Claim by Kelly Lesiuk' Ottawa, Ontario: Office of the Umpire,
    Employment Insurance Act.

Service Canada. 2007. 'Pilot Project on Increased Weeks of Employment Insurance (EI)
    Benefits'. http://www.hrsdc.gc.ca/en/ei/information/increased_weeks.shtml.

Standing Committee on the Status of Women. 2005. 'Gender-based Analysis: Building Blocks
    for Success'. http://cmte.parl.gc.ca/Content/HOC/committee/381/fewo/reports/rp1778246/
    feworp02/feworp02-e.pdf.

Stark, Agneta. 2005. 'Warm Hands in a Cold Age—On the Need of a New World Order of Care',
    *Feminist Economics* 11 (2): 7–36.

Statistics Canada. 1995. CANSIM. Labour Force Survey Data. http://www.statcan.ca/english/ads/
    cansimII/index.htm.

Stratychuk, Lori. 2001. 'Repeat Users of Employment Insurance', *Perspectives on Labour and
    Income* 2 (4): 5–12.

Supreme Court of Canada. 2005. Reference re *Employment Insurance Act* (Can.), ss. 22 and 23,
    [2005] 2 S.C.R. 669, 2005 S.C.C 56. October 20. http://scc.lexum.umontreal.ca/en/2005/
    2005scc56/2005scc56.html.

Timpson, Annis May. 2001. *Driven Apart: Women's Employment Equality and Child Care in Canadian Public Policy*. Vancouver: UBC Press.

Townson, Monica, and Kevin Hayes. 2007. *Women and the Employment Insurance Program: The Gender Impact of Current Rules on Eligibility and Earnings Replacement*. Ottawa: Status of Women Canada.

Wiegers, Wanda. 2002. *The Framing of Poverty as 'Child Poverty' and Its Implications for Women*. Ottawa: Status of Women Canada.

Williams, Cara. 2004. 'The Sandwich Generation', *Perspectives on Labour and Income* 5 (9): 5–12.

Women's Network PEI. 2004. *Looking beyond the Surface: An In-Depth Review of Parental Benefits*. Charlottetown: Women's Network PEI.

## Further Reading

HRSDC 2006. *Summative Evaluation of EI Part 1: Summary of Evaluation Knowledge to Date. Final Report*, EI Evaluation, Audit and Evaluation Directorate. http://www.hrsdc.gc.ca/en/publications_resources/evaluation/index.shtml (accessed 7 Oct. 2008).

International Network on Leave Policies. 2008. *International Review of Leave Policies and Research*. http://www.berr.gov.uk/files/file47247.pdf (accessed 7 Oct. 2008).

Gabrielle-Tremblay. 2007. 'Family Policies and Labour Market Participation: The Situation in Quebec and Canada'. Research Note No. 2007–01 of the Canada Research Chair on the Socio-Organizational Challenges of the New Economy. Tele-universite/Université du Québec à Montréal. http://www.teluq.uquebec.ca/chaireecosavoir/pdf/NRC07-01A.pdf (accessed 7 Oct. 2008).

*Feminist Economics*. http://www.tandf.co.uk/journals/titles/13545701.asp.

*Perspectives on Labour and Income*. http://www.statcan.ca/english/ads/75-001-XIE/index.htm.

Canadian Centre for Policy Alternatives. http://www.policyalternatives.ca.

## Questions for Critical Thought

1. What are the arguments for and against having care benefits as part of EI rather than as a separate program(s)?
2. What changes to EI would be needed to fully remove its implicit male breadwinner norms?
3. Is there a tension in the social investment approach between meeting the needs of women and those of children?

# CHAPTER 4

# Social Cohesion and the Neo-liberal Welfare State:

## The Healthcare Example

Pat Armstrong

In 1999, *The Economic Journal* published an article by Bruce Wydick (1999) entitled 'Can Social Cohesion Be Harnessed to Repair Market Failures?'. The question nicely summed up a critical development in neo-liberal discourse and strategy, a development that followed in the wake of emerging evidence demonstrating the dramatically growing income gaps and social dislocations that had resulted from the neo-liberal promotion of market strategies in all areas of social life. In the early stages of neo-liberalism, 'a powerful coalition of interests managed to convince all major political parties that government spending was the biggest danger facing Canada' (Walkom 2008, A11) and that the business of government was business (Murphy, Chodos, and Auf Der Maur 1985, 205). Social programs were slashed and new regulations applied to social entitlements while old regulations were removed from business, and market strategies were applied to the public sector. The result was not only increasing inequality in economic and social rights but also the undermining of many social relations in households, communities, and the formal economy. Individual, rather than collective, responsibility was emphasized and reinforced. The negative consequences have been felt particularly by women and by women in particular social economic and physical locations (Day and Brodsky 1998). This evidence of increasing social and economic disintegration grew at the same time as governments were enjoying the bulging coffers that accompanied economic recovery from recession and that removed the excuse of deficits for slashing social programs.

It was in this context that the World Bank published a book on social capital (Dasgupta and Serageldin 1999). In it, James Coleman (1999) talks about social capital as a resource that involves such mechanisms as group enforcement of norms, as a consequence such as privileged access to information, and as a social organization such as a community group that provides both support and control. Social capital was presented as both a contribution to and a substitute for human capital, one that could help smooth the edges of or facilitate access to the market. As Alejandro Portes (1998, 2) explains, this old sociological concept 'evolved into something of a cure-all for the maladies affecting society at home and abroad'. The concept was stretched, he says, by authors like Robert Putnam (1995) to mean 'features of social organizations, such as networks, norms, and trust that facilitate action and cooperation for mutual benefit' (cited in Portes 1998, 18). In this way, social capital is transformed into a particular notion of social cohesion with an emphasis on shared values and social controls that are created largely through individual efforts. Such a notion of social cohesion is promoted as a means of compensating for market failures while leaving most of the mechanisms and policies of neo-liberal marketization in place. In this approach, the emphasis tends to be on individuals working to create communities that are based on values rather than on social programs and social rights established by governments that would help create the conditions for equitable participation in communities and thus for some agreement on fundamental values and mutual respect. Much of the responsibility for this community creation is left to women. There is now more recognition of social relations and of communities, as well as some new investment in social programs in the wake of evident dislocations and government surpluses. But the emphasis remains on markets, the targeting of excluded populations, and individual responsibility for creating social cohesion and shared values.

In this chapter, which is based on a feminist political-economy approach, I argue that appropriately supportive communities and some shared values are fostered primarily by equitable and secure social programs and by social as well as political rights rather than supportive communities being created by shared values. Regulation of markets and employers is also critical. I stress 'appropriate', which is determined through informed, democratic public debate, because some forms of communities can be destructive, not only for individuals, but also for societies as a whole. Appropriately supportive communities require a strong welfare state to promote social cohesion that is based on an equitable distribution of resources and rights. It means, not a return to the post-war version of the welfare state, but rather the creation of one that is rendered both responsive to democratically determined methods and goals and transparent through strategies such as public budgeting. It means a state that intervenes actively both to regulate and limit markets in order to promote an equitable distribution of and access to resources. Such social cohesion means supporting diversity and equity, openness and debate through an active state. This means as well public policies, programs, and services that create the right conditions for social reproduction, by which I mean providing for the individual's daily needs and producing the next generation. Providing for our daily needs and for the next generation in ways that promote some shared basic values implies redressing marginalization, rather than merely compensating for or accommodating it through targeted programs, and it requires respect for differences in social locations. It means paying attention to the needs of women and to differences among women as well as those between women and men. And the idea of some shared values does not imply that all values are shared but rather that some fundamental ones, such as the right to healthcare and freedom of speech, are held in common.

I begin by framing the discussion in relation to the current literature on social cohesion and by setting out the main features of my critique. I then move on to use Canadian healthcare as an example of how appropriate forms of social cohesion have developed at least as much as a result of this universal public program as they have as a product of shared values. Women in particular have benefited, and inequities among women have declined. I provide some detail here in order to establish the case for how some shared values are created and to challenge the notion that positive forms of social cohesion result primarily from individuals' acting in their immediate communities or simply from shared values. I argue that more equitable access to healthcare promoted shared values and demonstrated the importance of both supportive communities and state involvement to strengthen those communities. I then move on to look at neo-liberal reforms, many of which have been undertaken in the name of the social. Neo-liberal leaders, such as former prime minister Brian Mulroney, declared that healthcare was a public trust but one that should be saved by the application of market principles (Murphy et al. 1985). Almost two decades later, Prime Minister Paul Martin restored some of the public health funding he had previously cut as minister of finance, once more in the name of saving the public system and of saving that trust but with no regulation to ensure that this would happen and no prohibition of market mechanisms. And he introduced a very limited national childcare program to support women, although it was replaced by an even more limited plan targeted directly at individual women in an explicit attempt to keep women in their communities. Such strategies largely serve to undermine both collective support for care and democratic control over it. At the same time, they further undermine women's access to and work in care. Healthcare once again provides the most trenchant example, in part because it has developed a faith in shared responsibility through state intervention and in the process has become a defining feature of being Canadian. Timely access to healthcare has become an issue that challenges this faith, because it is used to make a case for privately purchased and provided care based on the notion of individual choice. Finally, I argue that only an active, responsive state can support some shared values and supportive social relations.

# Social Cohesion

As the title of Bruce Wydick's article suggests, social cohesion is increasingly being offered as a means of solving the problems created by neo-liberal market strategies. But social cohesion, as Jane Jenson (1998) explains, has a host of meanings. In general, there is agreement that social cohesion is the glue that holds people together and that this glue has been weakening (Putnam 1995). According to Jenson (1998, v–vi) this glue consists of 'shared values and a commitment to a community', although it should be recognized that some forms of shared values and commitment to community can lead to exclusion and even violence. The important debates are about what promotes and maintains social cohesion, as well as about where and how social cohesion develops (Prakash and Selle 2004). Of course, this also raises the question of what kind of social cohesion is being promoted and for whom is it beneficial. Although there seems to be agreement that associations, institutions, relationships, and values are involved, there is little agreement about the relative influence they exert, at what scale, in what direction, through which mechanisms, for whom, and with what purpose.

For some, social cohesion is primarily the result of individual actions at the local level. In 'Bowling Alone', for example, Robert Putnam (1995) maintains that it is the face-to-face interactions of individuals through voluntary associations in their neighbourhood that combine to create general trust across society. The local-level analysis is often extended to families, which are defined as producers of health and social cohesion, and by families we mean mainly women (Bolin et al. 2003). In turn, these local relations are understood to lead to both social order and social institutions based on trust, as well as to health and prosperity. Such an analysis frequently promotes a small-government approach, given the emphasis on civic organizations and local responsibility. It can become a justification for reducing social programs and for shifting responsibilities to communities without providing them with the means to take up these responsibilities in ways that promote equity, as happens with the regionalization of health services. It can also be a way of shifting responsibility to women, as we will also see particularly in the case of healthcare. Thus social cohesion 'may function as a health policy alternative to large-scale government redistribution' (Muntaner, Lynch, and Smith 2001, 220). Indeed, the emphasis on civic engagement can be used as a means of blaming individuals for their own condition. Equally important, social networks can be defined as a substitute for welfare-state programs, with exclusion from state support justified on the grounds that there are lots of friends and family to compensate for the poverty of services and income. In addition, as Vincente Navarro (2002) points out, for those taking this approach there is a fundamental contradiction between the call for increased competition, especially through free trade, and the call for a greater togetherness cemented by shared values.

Sara Mackian dismisses the Putnam-type personal approach to social cohesion:

> It is no longer adequate to premise face-to-face meetings, rooted in the locality, as the cornerstone of social cohesion. Nonetheless, this conservative and paternalistic emphasis on the lay community persists in the public health literature. (2002, 205)

This paternalism is not only about the notion of the father telling others what to do. It is also about assigning responsibility for developing social cohesion mainly to women, given that they do the majority of interpersonal work in families and much of the work in voluntary communities. Indeed, Putnam (1995) identified women's rising labour-force participation as one of the factors contributing to social disintegration (Gidengil et al. 2003).

Others have integrated the notion of membership in organizations and trust with other factors that are understood to contribute to social cohesion. For example, in their report published by the World Bank, Jo Ritzen, William Easterly, and Michael Woolcock (2000) add income distribution and ethnic heterogeneity as determinants of social cohesion. Their report (2000, 21) concludes that there are 'two determinants of social cohesion and thus good institutions—initial inequality and ethnolinguistic fractionalization' and that 'more social cohesion leads to better institutions and that better institutions lead to higher growth' (2000, 22). Education, although not assessed in this report, is defined as an important contributor to social cohesion through the knowledge it provides of social contracts, appropriate behaviour, and the consequences of breaking social contracts. The report reflects a social investment association typical of the response to the growing inequalities and dislocations, and thus supports the need to invest in education to promote human capital and ultimately contribute to social cohesion. It also reflects the tendency that Portes (1998) identified of conflating social capital and social cohesion. Acknowledging that the state sets 'the context and climate within which civil society is organized', this expansion to include education, income inequality, and ethnic heterogeneity moves the authors beyond the local to argue that the state 'can, in some cases, also actively help create social cohesion' (Ritzen, Easterly, and Woolcock 2000, 26). At one and the same time, the report supports social investment in ways that depart from early neo-liberalism while still promoting markets and limited social investment by the state in individuals.

Today's greater income inequality is traced by these authors mainly to history; hence the emphasis on 'initial' inequality, with no reference to state intervention to redistribute income or to the consequences of marketization and free trade. The period between 1950 and 1974 is defined as one of general prosperity, when 'everyone did well' (Ritzen, Easterly, and Woolcock 2000, 16). Yet the reduction in income inequality within and between countries during those years had much to do with the development of strong welfare states and international as well as national limits on both capital and human-rights abuses (Armstrong 1997). At the same time, persistent inequalities related to gender, racialization, colonization, disabilities, and exploitation at paid work remained throughout the period of general prosperity, leaving many questions about the effectiveness of welfare states.

Structural inequalities, conditions and relations of work, and state social programs and interventions have not been ignored by all those exploring issues of social cohesion. Those who emphasize the social determinants of health link income inequality and working conditions, along with other factors, to social supports and thus social cohesion and health (Evans, Barer, and Marmor 1994; Marmot and Wilkinson 1999; Marmot 2004). Moreover, in the European Union, it is common to include both income distribution and social ties in assessments of social cohesion (Berger-Schmitt 2000). But there is little critique of markets, international capital expansion, or even of the overall economic conditions or working conditions that establish the context for these inequalities. There are few calls for redistribution through international taxes and public services, for limits on privatization, or for means to improve collective control. Instead, we see mainly the promotion of public–private partnerships, which frequently use public funds to pay for-profit companies to provide services or parts of services. In this case, public investment becomes a means of making private profit, often in ways that prevent the public from even knowing what is going on in these services, let alone in ways that allow collective social control over them. There is also some social reinvestment, largely through targeted programs and often combined with market mechanisms. Even though some individuals may be better off, without universality as a central principle these programs are unlikely to promote either social cohesion or equity.

Instead of collective efforts to create the conditions that would allow genuine participation in decision-making and promote social relations, there is often an emphasis on measurement as a method to ensure accountability (Policy Research Initiative, 2004). Participation becomes a private responsibility, to be carried out by individuals based primarily on values and their individual assessment of the reported measures. Democratic accountability is thus increasingly defined in terms of our personal assessment of the numbers created by the measurement of state services. Rather than promote collective strategies, an emphasis on social cohesion understood in this way can lead to a 'privatization of both economics and politics' (Muntaner, Lynch, and Smith 2001, 213). All these strategies are particularly evident in healthcare.

Social cohesion as an entry point for change strategies has gained widespread appeal in part because it means so many different things. It seems to offer an answer to current levels of tensions, alienation, and inequalities without threatening the further development of capitalism and other forms of privatization at home and abroad. It pays attention to local interactions and associations, to values, and to the social and cultural in ways economists seldom do. Although these factors and actors are important, appropriate social cohesion is more a consequence of decent paid employment, limits on and regulation of markets and marketization, social programs and services, responsive, transparent government, and social-reproduction policies than an alternative to or compensation for the lack of them. Indeed, the social networks and social supports at the local and family level can be undermined by the lack of such state interventions and the potentially harmful associations at the local level that may result. While I agree with those who see social cohesion as a complex construct, which is promoted at many interacting levels (Prakash and Per Selle 2004), I also see an active, democratic welfare state as a critical condition for appropriate forms of social cohesion, namely, those that support communities and equity.

## Developing Support for Public Care

The discussion of social cohesion immediately leads me to healthcare, as it would many Canadians. After listening to thousands of Canadians and examining the research, the Commission on the Future of Health Care in Canada (2002) (also known as the Romanow Commission) concluded that healthcare is one important form of the glue that holds Canadians together. Every poll has shown that the overwhelming majority of Canadians support their public healthcare system and see it as central to our identity as Canadians (Blendon et al. 2004). It is a fine example of shared values and commitment to community, representing as it does shared responsibility for healthcare, in other words, of social cohesion. Yet support for this public system has been declining in recent years, suggesting a move away from this commitment even in the face of some new public investment in the name of the social. Healthcare thus offers us a way of exploring that complex of factors and actors that promote and undermine social cohesion. Of course, there is space here only to highlight major factors and actors, and to explain how this kind of social cohesion developed.

The Second World War demonstrated that governments could finance and deliver programs and services in ways that supported large numbers of the population, not only in battle but also at home. Faith in government intervention increased significantly, along with a demand that governments intervene to ensure a better life for Canadians after the war. Health services also improved significantly during the war, although many were without the means to pay for them. In other words, the value attached to government intervention was, in part at least, the result of effective government intervention. Women's groups and church groups, professional organizations and unions, farm and urban community organizations—in short, many of Putnam's actors—pressured governments to act in their collective interest. The private non-profit organizations providing the services joined in making the demands, as did municipal and provincial governments. In general, employers supported government provision mainly because they were facing pressure from their employees to offer healthcare insurance and because they wanted a healthy workforce. So the struggle involved a wide range of actors, without strong resistance from those with the economic power although the result did not necessarily reflect shared values.

Conditions in the United States in terms of healthcare were similar, although the economy there was richer. Indeed, popular support for public health was stronger in the United States than in Canada after the war (Maioni 1998). Nevertheless, Canada ended up with a public insurance scheme and the United States did not. To understand why, we need to look at public healthcare itself. Of course, values were a factor. Tommy Douglas, the Saskatchewan premier who introduced the first universal public health-insurance system, was acting on the basis of his values. However, Emmet Hall, who led the Royal Commission that recommended a universal, public medical system, was not committed to such a concept when he began. Indeed, he favoured a program targeted at the most marginalized. What convinced him was the economic evidence, rather than values. It would be more expensive to sort the deserving from the undeserving than it would be to cover everyone. Certainly the criteria of universality, accessibility, comprehensiveness, and even portability set out in the *Canada Health Act*, the federal legislation that establishes the conditions for financial support, are about values and shared commitments. But there is little evidence that these initially came out of a pre-existing shared commitment.

Instead it was the success of this program that expanded the shared public support for healthcare. Saskatchewan demonstrated that a universal program could provide accessible, quality medical care. Experience with the system built support for the system because it worked. It significantly reduced inequalities in access without bankrupting the state or individuals, while providing many patients with choices about which services to use. Women in particular benefited from improved access to public care because they had a greater need for health services and less ability to pay for the care they required. Increased access to health services also helped relieve some of women's responsibility for unpaid care in the home. At the same time, the number of paid jobs in traditional female areas of work grew (Armstrong and Armstrong 2003). Once they were gathered together over longer periods in these jobs, women started to unionize and to experience some success in improving their pay and conditions. Many of these female workers were immigrants and/or women of colour, and union contracts in health services helped reduce the kinds of disparities they still faced in other sectors of the labour force (Armstrong and Laxer 2006). The growth in unionized public-sector jobs, combined with the decline in the manufacturing and primary extraction sectors where men dominated, helped give women more clout in unions (White 1993). As we have argued elsewhere (Armstrong and Armstrong 2006), the development of the welfare state during this period meant that clearer lines were drawn between the private sector and the public sector in the formal economy, public sector employment being subject to laws such as pay equity that helped make jobs there better for women. Similarly, women were successful in demanding that the state stay out of their private lives in areas such as birth control and abortion and in social programs such as inspections to determine welfare eligibility. The result in healthcare was declining inequality among women and between men and women in access both to services and to decent paid work. The rich and poor shared the same doctors and hospitals without obvious negative consequences for either class but in ways that promoted shared support for public care.

Many voluntary associations and community-based hospitals continued to deliver health services. It was essentially a centralized public payment and regulation scheme that left a great deal of control in local hands. There was little centralized, bureaucratic control of the sort denounced by those supporting small-government options. The non-profit nature of these hospitals meant they did not report to anonymous shareholders through the market and they could not claim the need for secrecy in order to remain competitive, as is often the case with for-profit firms.

Nevertheless, this was neither a perfect system, nor a perfectly accessible one. The method of payment for doctors and the power left in their hands reinforced both their control and the emphasis on medical intervention over prevention. Women in particular faced inappropriate treatment, especially when it came to their reproductive and mental-health needs. Institutionalization became more common and was often inappropriate as well. Because of the local nature of many hospitals and doctors' private practices, the system was not well integrated for care and male doctors still tended to make the major decisions. And there were other problems for both patients and providers. Some of these have been partially addressed through regulation, such as the patient's right to receive enough information to give informed consent to treatment, and some through union efforts around issues such as homophobia and racism. But inequities related to sex, race, age, sexual orientation, and class remained, and members of racialized groups still tended to be found in greater numbers at the bottom of the healthcare hierarchy. Moreover, the lack of other state support, such as universal public childcare, made it difficult for women to combine paid jobs with household responsibilities. Nevertheless, the system worked in ways that increased equitable access, built collective support, and helped women see the benefits of shared responsibility for shared risks. The commitment to the system grew with its success. This contrasts sharply with the United States, where public systems targeted at the poor, the elderly, and the severely disabled served to challenge values that had once supported a shared system. The US thus offers a natural experiment in building social cohesion, an experiment that demonstrates that targeted programs, even when they come out of shared values, can undermine those values so central to notions of social cohesion.

## Declining Support for Public Care

The fiscal crisis of the state, marked by growing deficits and debts in the 1980s, became the justification for an attack on the services provided by the state. One solution was cutbacks in social services, even though economists showed that the crisis was caused by tax reductions and a slowing economy rather than social programs (Mimoto and Cross 1991). But the overall solution offered by neo-liberals was an elimination of differences between the public and private sectors of the formal economy, with a call for a marketization of the state and a commitment to free trade. What could not be handed over to for-profit organizations could be done in partnership with them or on the basis of their techniques. State activity in general has become more narrowly defined, with the state increasingly policing households to make sure that they take over the services it no longer provides, either by paying for them or doing them without pay. Meanwhile, new technologies are making it possible to send paid work home, blurring the line both between public and private space and between paid and unpaid work, with negative consequences for equity, for solidarity, and for women. Although neo-liberalism has rediscovered the social in recent years as inequities and social disruption become increasingly obvious and Canadian government coffers grow, new investments in social programs and other efforts that were claimed to promote social cohesion have had little positive impact on shared values. Indeed, the reverse is too often the case. The federal government has restored most of the money it cut from healthcare, and the provincial governments have increased healthcare spending (Canadian Institute for Health Information 2008), but they have done so on the basis of older neo-liberal strategies that fail to build collective social support. All these processes are particularly evident in healthcare, as we shall see in this section.

In spite of the demonstrated success of shared responsibility, public support for public healthcare has started to decline. The decline has accompanied the neo-liberal restructuring of public health services. At the height of neo-liberal attack on deficits, governments reduced significantly the amount of money going to healthcare services while also reducing significantly the number of doctors being trained and the number of nurses practising. Hospitals were amalgamated into giant conglomerates, imitating corporate practices. Many of the community hospitals that were embedded in their localities have disappeared or been transformed. In most of these community hospitals, patients often knew the care providers, and neighbours as well as family members could drop in for a visit. The elderly, most of whom are women without access to cars, now find it particularly difficult to visit at the amalgamated hospitals. And the work of volunteers, which is central to the functioning of many hospitals, becomes more difficult as hospitals are bigger and more physically remote. Equally important, the hospital employees knew each other and often remained in the same jobs for years in ways that allowed them to construct thick and dense social relations there.

The new healthcare structures challenge these ties. In other words, neo-liberal strategies over the last two decades have helped undermine communities and their capacity to provide mutual support and to maintain shared values. More recent new investment primarily means more of the same, even when done in the name of the local and social. As Ricca Edmondson makes clear,

> The neo-liberal organizations which form work settings for large proportions of Western populations and which structure the delivery of their health care involve standards and conventions which demand radical modification if they are to promote central features of social capital such as trust. (2003, 1723)

The problems linked to being transported out of their community for care are not new for most Aboriginal peoples or for significant proportions of those living in remote regions. Now, however, the experience has spread to more of the population.

Regionalization of health services has been promoted as a means both of integrating care and of responding to local needs. However, regionalization has too often meant the replacement of local boards with members appointed by provincial governments and reporting to them. It can also promote the shift of service delivery to the for-profit sector, as each region seeks short-term financial gains. These gains tend to come from losses to women in terms of fewer jobs and worse jobs with private contractors (Armstrong et al. 2002). Moreover, it can mean that women are separated from each other, not only in terms of employers but also in terms of working conditions and pay, with public-sector jobs offering more to women. Huge regions, based on some technical calculation rather than community ties, often work to prevent responses to local needs, as do rules and budgets set at the provincial level (Ontario Health Coalition 2006). The voluntary organizations that initiated many of the services have little role to play, and patients have fewer choices about where to seek care. It is difficult to see how these new regional conglomerates can promote lasting social ties. In other words, the sort of players Putnam promotes can be undermined even when there is new social investment.

Neo-liberal strategies, even with new social investment, are characterized by market approaches to public health services. Managerial strategies adopted from the for-profit sector have been applied to the work and the workers. Just enough care by just enough people for just enough time, based on evidence linked to managerial practices rather than to the provider's judgment, has increasingly become the norm (Armstrong and Armstrong 2003; Rankin and Campbell 2006). More of the jobs are casual, part-time, and short-term, as are many of the assignments within the hospital. All this churning makes it difficult to form relations of trust, and so does the intensification of labour. The women who form the overwhelming majority of the healthcare labour force feel responsible and are held responsible for the gaps in care. In their effort to make up the difference for the sake of the patients, they are undermining their own health. They tell us they 'have no time to care' and no time to do the other things, like supporting each other after a death (Armstrong and Daly 2004). Not surprisingly perhaps, the healthcare sector now has by far the highest illness and injury rates of any industry. Such approaches can hardly be described as promoting trust and social cohesion among workers and with patients or a sense of solidarity among the public at large. And new social investment in health services has done little to change these conditions of work, although looming shortages in care providers may encourage some movement away from market approaches in care.

The contracting out of services to for-profit concerns has further undermined social relations at work and undermined quality of care. Before the neoliberal reforms, almost everyone working in a single institution had the same employer. Now many of those who are called ancillary or hotel workers are employed by a private contractor, and a growing number of the professionals are from temporary-help agencies. Different employers create different work relations, ones that often separate the groups from one another and, as British research shows, undermine morale (Sachdev 2001, 33). Canadian research on the consequences of contracting out reveals similar patterns. For example, women housekeepers report that because of contracting out, they no longer did the Christmas decorations or socialized with other staff, both because there was no time to talk and because they worked by different employer rules (Kahnamoui 2005). Here, too, women account for most of those whose work is contracted out and for even more of those who see their conditions of work and job security undermined (Cohen and Cohen 2004). Without permanent work, it is hard to develop strong social ties at work. Moreover, a disproportionate number of those whose work is contracted out are from racialized and/or immigrant groups. Unlike the unionization moves in the 1970s, which tended to bring workers together, the contracting out serves more to divide workers among multiple employers in ways that reinforce the divisions and inequalities linked to such social locations.

Rapid deinstitutionalization and rapid turnover in hospital beds also continue to be part of the neo-liberal reforms, even with new investment. So is the increase in out-patient care. Some of this reform reflects developments in technology that make it possible to move care out of hospitals and to do less invasive surgery. But some of it also reflects neo-liberal ideas about increasing individual and family responsibility characterized as moving care closer to home. Closer to home means more unpaid care work for women, who provide the bulk of personal care (Decima Research 2002), giving them less time for other social interaction and engagement. It also often means less care for women, both because more care must be purchased and because women receive less of the care provided by the public system (Grant et al. 2004). Less care is often linked to less social interaction. In addition, the paid home-care work that is provided through the public system is increasingly contracted out through competitive bidding, mainly to the for-profit sector. The result is that more of this work is precarious in ways that undermine the possibilities for beneficial social relations either with patients or with other providers.

All this restructuring has been combined with warnings about dangerous increases in healthcare costs and dangerous waiting times for care, even as government coffers are full and more taxes are cut. A moral panic has been created, suggesting that dramatic reforms are still necessary in order to save the system and to ensure that care will be there. The panic about costs has been perpetuated by governments and the media even though the evidence indicates that the costs of public care are not out of control, except in the case of the too often useless or dangerous drugs and technologies. Nor is there strong evidence that the growing numbers of elderly will bankrupt the system. The panic about waiting times has been perpetuated by bodies such as the Fraser Institute and the Supreme Court (Flood, Roach, and Sossin 2005), even though the evidence shows that waiting times have not been increasing, that close to 90 per cent of Canadians have family doctors, and that we have significantly increased the number of such surgeries as hip and knee replacements (Canadian Institute for Health Information 2006). All this talk about waiting times and costs serves to undermine trust in the public system and our shared commitment to care. In spite of the convincing evidence that public care is the cheapest, most efficient, and most effective care, and in spite of the claims that evidence-based decision making is being followed, the solutions offered to what is defined as a crisis are more for-profit care, more for-profit financing, and more for-profit managerial practices (Devereaux et al. 2004; Horwitz 2005). More public–private partnerships are created, even though such partnerships cost the public purse more and allow citizens less say in how public services are run, given that the private firms are accountable mainly to shareholders rather than to the public that pays them. And in spite of the growing evidence that market methods undermine beneficial social relations, these market methods are proposed along with proposals for policies promoting social cohesion.

In sum, social support for healthcare in Canada is at least as much a product of a system that works to share responsibility and support as it is a product of shared commitments. A public system still offers better jobs to women, jobs that are better in terms of pay, security, unionization, benefits, and equity among workers (Armstrong and Laxer 2006). It offers the possibility of influencing the structure and delivery of care through the political system and unions. It provides reasonable access to quality care for many of the most marginalized without draining their economic and social resources. Increasingly, however, the application of neo-liberal strategies to the public sector is undermining the possibilities for trust and for dense social relations among care providers and with those seeking care, even as governments invest more in health services. Inequalities among women in terms of both working conditions and access to care increase along with those between women and men. Inequalities seldom encourage strong social ties, and poverty or poor access to care seldom promotes social cohesion.

## Responsive Governments

The evidence from healthcare, then, suggests that states that are active in creating the conditions for equity are a necessary, though not necessarily a sufficient, condition for the development or maintenance of dense and rewarding social ties. This is the case not only for healthcare but for other life needs as well. Only an active state is in a position to monitor, regulate, and limit capital, marketization, and employers. Only an active state can develop universal programs and services that ensure that basic needs are met through collective resources. Of course, it cannot be assumed that states always act in the best interests of us all, or are responsive to diverse needs and demands, or are always good employers, as many feminists in Canada and in other countries have shown. Indeed, neo-liberal states have been active in supporting markets and have become more active in their investment in social programs recently, partly in an effort to promote social cohesion. But, as this section argues, the reliance on public–private partnerships and on accountability defined in accounting terms neither makes for a responsive state nor promotes social cohesion.

Neo-liberal strategies of privatization and regionalization have been sold not only as more efficient but also as a means of increasing choice and thus individual control or even participation. Yet private for-profit companies claim the need for confidentiality in order to compete, and they are responsible primarily to their shareholders. And regionalization often results in local responsibility without local control. Similarly, accountability is presented as a means of increasing efficiency as well as democratic input. However, this form of accountability has primarily been reduced to counting, equating accountability with the kinds of assessment done by accountants. We see governments requiring public data on hospital mortality rates, for example, data that are promoted as a means of allowing us choice and ensuring control. The elaborate reporting by voluntary organizations on measurable outcomes and the detailed counting of hours spent on care tasks, justified as ensuring accountability, too frequently mean less local control and less autonomy for the mainly female care providers, both paid and unpaid. But what is counted and by whom, and how it is reported, are determined with little public involvement, with little discussion of the choices and values involved in making these selections, and with little collective choice about what happens as a result. But transparency means more opportunity to influence decision making throughout the processes of governing, not just to receive more information about indicators that have been chosen for the public rather than with their input. It means being able to participate in making decisions about what is to be counted and why, and about what is to be done about what is found. Moreover, accountability defined as counting and reporting measurable factors or outcomes reinforces the notion of individual rather than collective choices.

Active, then, does not necessarily mean responsive. Jane Aronson and Sheila Neysmith (1997, 61) caution that 'an active state would always be formulating policy among unequal participants with conflicting interests' and that such policy making is always a 'huge challenge'. In that challenge, the weakest frequently lose. The weakest are most often women and too frequently women from racialized or immigrant groups. The strongest are those with economic power, who are pushing for states that support marketization while downsizing in other areas. And since the strongest often live outside our national boundaries, independent state action is made more difficult. Strategies that promote active states have to include strategies that ensure that the states are profoundly democratic. We need better mechanisms to ensure that states and managers are responsive to the needs of diverse groups within the population while supporting collective efforts to provide the conditions that allow equitable participation. This means greater transparency in the public and private realm so that we can together base our decisions on informed consent.

One mechanism for moving in this direction is public budgeting (see Bakker in this volume). Such budgeting begins with an explicit commitment to social justice and equity. The purpose would be to assess how well governments, economies, and employers are meeting the needs, not only of individuals, families, and local communities, but also of the country as a whole. In turn, this would require an assessment of both the short and long-term consequences for individuals, families, communities, and countries of the presence or absence of healthcare, education, income, transportation, housing, decent work and working conditions, and leisure time. It would also require assessments of the costs of marketization, the transaction cost of sorting the deserving from the undeserving, and the cost of incarcerating those who are simply struggling to survive. The costs would include measurable ones, such as labour and time lost from paid and unpaid work as a result of working conditions and employment relations. Poor health, injury and illness, family disintegration, and inequality would appear as costs and would be calculated as part of the budget. Less tangible costs that are more difficult to measure, such as lost opportunities, the disintegration of supportive social networks and social cohesion, and discrimination, would be estimated. And of course there would be a gender, race, and class analysis that recognized multiple social and physical locations. Such budgeting would be only one means of increasing transparency and the tools for democratic decision making. But it could be a critical one if it challenged the entire notion of budgeting with only profits in mind. In addition, it could expose the impact of global and national strategies that are so often ignored by the neo-liberal promotion of social cohesion.

Clearly many more mechanisms are necessary, not only to make costs and values hidden in current budgets transparent, but also to ensure that action is taken to alleviate the cost burden and the inequality. In addition to this kind of public budgeting to allow democratic control, we also need specific strategies to promote equity, especially between women and men. Let me suggest three that have long been on the agenda but have not yet been realized in democratic forms. First, there must be a basic public, universal infrastructure such as health and childcare, education and transportation, housing, and income. These would be decommodified in terms of service delivery but commodified in terms of labour. In other words, they would be paid for through public means, but people would be paid to provide the services. Second, there must be decent work and working conditions, which also means equitable ones. We do not want to reconcile women, or men, to bad jobs. This means state regulation of employment and corporate responsibility, as well as formal limits on capital and on marketization. Third, there must be transparent, participatory decision making at all levels, with efforts made to ensure that the most vulnerable are heard. All of these require initiatives at the international, regional, national, and local levels. And of course, these must be designed on the basis of not only a gender analysis, but also an analysis that takes context and other social locations into account in ways that would allow some targeting within these universal programs.

Some specific programs aimed at creating woman-friendly, equity-producing policies, such as pay and employment equity, and designed to address new employment relations are required; so are anti-violence and harassment policies; parental and other care leave; literacy, training, and re-entry programs, including prior-learning assessment; transparent, enforced criteria for hiring and promotion; and pensions, sick leave, and vacation benefits. Such programs would help women and men participate in paid and unpaid work and would promote social relations in and out of the labour force (Fudge, Tucker, and Vosco 2002).

All this would require social investment based on equity rather than on market principles, with responsibility defined in collective, transparent ways to promote supportive forms of social cohesion.

# Conclusion

As I write this conclusion, I am struck by the headlines of my daily newspapers. The *Globe and Mail* reports that 'Klein issues warning on sharing the wealth', going on to say that the Alberta premier (at the time) wants to pull out of the equalization program that gives poorer provinces money 'so they can give their residents services comparable to those of wealthier parts of the country' (Harding and Laghi 2006, A1). Meanwhile, the front page of the *Toronto Star* reports that a 'Teen flies to Calgary as blood machine sits idle' (Talaga 2006, A1), and notes that a 'Toronto hospital doesn't have funds to operate device'. An opinion piece in the *Star* comments on the scathing conclusions by the United Nations Committee on Economic, Social and Cultural Rights about Canada's failure to meet our international legal obligations. Together the stories reflect what is happening to social solidarity, social programs, and human rights in Canada in the wake of neo-liberal policies. They also show that our governments have failed to meet their obligations to equity under the law. They fail, however, to indicate the ways in which women in particular have suffered in their paid and unpaid work, their access to services, and their right to participate in decisions that affect their daily lives. Women have also suffered in their relations with other women, as inequities among women increase.

More than any other program, healthcare symbolizes our shared values, based on a system that has demonstrated we can provide relatively equitable access to quality services. In spite of all its flaws, it shows social justice in action. The healthcare example shows that social cohesion and equity are only possible if states take primary responsibility for social reproduction and for regulating, monitoring, and limiting capital. This requires mechanisms to ensure that states are responsive, transparent, and committed to social justice as well as to equity. It also requires states to act as model employers, employers who make decent work as well as decent services a priority. Recent restored investment in health services has served primarily to perpetuate earlier neo-liberal strategies, in the process reducing equity along with public support for public care. Public budgeting offers a better means than most neo-liberal accountability mechanisms to promote responsive governments. But such budgeting, like the accountability mechanisms, is effective only if it allows for collective involvement in the creation of the budgets and collective action on the results. We already know, even without such budgeting, that equity requires universal access to services that are provided with equity in mind and with the enforcement of legal commitments.

In part through their support for public healthcare, Canadians have shown that social cohesion can restrain the excesses of neo-liberalism by emphasizing equity and fairness. Public healthcare is, in some sense, the weakest point in neo-liberal reforms; that is one reason it has received so much attention from neo-liberals as well as reminding us all of what we can lose under neo-liberal reforms. What we need are reforms thought through in terms of both their relationship to other initiatives and their long-term capacity to fundamentally alter the structural, material, and symbolic outcomes. With such reforms as our goal, we need to act in concert across national boundaries while respecting local conditions and multiple social locations.

## References

Armstrong, Pat. 1997. 'The Welfare State as History'. In Raymond Blake, Penny Bryden, and J. Frank Strain, eds, *The Welfare State in Canada*, 52–71. Concord, Ont.: Irwin.

———, Carol Amaratunga, Jocelyne Bernier, Karen Grant, Ann Pederson, and Kay Willson. 2004. *Exposing Privatization: Women and Health Care Reform*. Aurora, Ont.: Garamond.

———, and Hugh Armstrong. 2003. *Wasting Away: The Undermining of Canadian Health Care.* 2nd edn. Toronto: Oxford University Press.

———, and ———. 2006. 'Public and Private: Implications for Care Work', *Sociological Review* 53 (2): 167–87.

———, and Tamara Daly. 2004. *'There Are Not Enough Hands': Conditions in Ontario's Long-term Care Facilities*. Toronto: Canadian Union of Public Employees.

———, and Kate Laxer. 2006. 'Precarious Work, Privatization, and the Health-Care Industry: The Case of Ancillary Workers'. In Leah Vosko, ed., *Precarious Employment: Understanding Labour Market Insecurity in Canada*, 115–38. Montreal: McGill-Queen's University Press.

Aronson, Jane, and Sheila M. Neysmith. 1997. 'The Retreat of the State and Long-Term Care Provision: Implications for Frail Elderly People, Unpaid Family Caregivers and Paid Home Care Workers', *Studies in Political Economy* 53 (Summer): 37–66.

Berger-Schmitt, Regina. 2000. 'Social Cohesion as an Aspect of the Quality of Societies: Concept and Measurement'. EuReporting Working Paper No. 14 for the European Commission Project 'Towards a European System Reporting and Welfare Measurement'. Mannheim: Centre for Survey Research and Methodology.

Blendon, Robert J., Cathy Schoen, Catherine M. DesRoches, Robin Osborn, Kings Zapert, and Elizabeth Raleigh. 2004. 'Confronting Competing Demands to Improve Quality: A Five Country Hospital Survey', *Health Affairs* 23 (3): 119–35.

Bolin, Kristian, Björn Lindgren, Martin Lindström, and Paul Nystedt. 2003. Investments in Social Capital—Implications of Social Interactions for the Production of Health. *Social Science and Medicine* 56 (12): 2379–90.

Canadian Institute for Health Information. 2006. *Waiting for Health Care in Canada: What We Know and What We Don't Know*. Ottawa: Canadian Institute for Health Information.

———. 2008. *Health Expenditures by Year, by Source of Finance, by Province/Territory, by Source 1975–2007*. www.cihi.ca.

Cohen, Marjorie Griffin, and Marcy Cohen. 2004. *A Return to Wage Discrimination: Pay Equity Losses through Privatization in Health Care*. Vancouver: Canadian Centre for Policy Alternatives.

Coleman, James S. (1999) 'Social Capital as the Creation of Human Capital'. In Partha Dasgupta and Ismail Serageldin, eds, *Social Capital: A Multi-faceted Perspective*, 13–39. Washington: World Bank.

Commission on the Future of Health Care in Canada [Romanow Commission]. 2002. *Building on Values: The Future of Health Care in Canada*. Ottawa: The Commission.

Dasgupta, Partha, and Ismail Serageldin, eds. 1999. *Social Capital: A Multi-faceted Perspective*. Washington: World Bank.

Day, Shelagh, and Gwen Brodsky. 1998. *Women and the Equality Deficit: The Impact of Restructuring Canada's Social Programs*. Ottawa: Status of Women Canada.

Decima Research. 2002. *National Profile of Family Caregivers in Canada 2002*. Ottawa: Health Canada.

Devereaux, P.J., Diane Heels-Ansdell, Christina Lacchetti, Ted Haines, Karen E.A. Burns, Deborah J. Cook, Nikila Ravindran, et al. 2004. 'Payments for Care at Private For-Profit and Private Not-For-Profit Hospitals: A Systematic Review and Meta-Analysis', *Canadian Medical Association Journal* 170 (12): 1817–24.

Edmondson, Ricca. 2003. 'Social Capital: A Strategy for Enhancing Health?', *Social Science and Medicine* 57: 1723–33.

Evans, Robert G., Morris L. Barer, and Theodore R. Marmor, eds. 1994. *Why Are Some People Healthy and Others Not? The Determinants of Population Health.* New York: Aldine De Gruyter.

Flood, Colleen M., Kent Roach, and Lorne Sossin. 2005. *Access to Care, Access to Justice: The Legal Debate over Private Health Insurance in Canada.* Toronto: University of Toronto Press.

Fudge, Judy, Eric Tucker, and Leah Vosko. 2002. *The Legal Concept of Employment: Marginalizing Workers.* Ottawa: Law Commission of Canada.

Gidengil, Elisabeth, Elizabeth Goodyear-Grant, Neil Nevitte, André Blais, Richard Nadeau. 2003. 'Gender, Knowledge and Social Capital'. Paper presented to the Gender and Social Capital Conference, University of Manitoba, May 2003.

Grant, Karen R., Pat Armstrong, Carol Amaratunga, Madeline Bosco, Ann Pederson, and Kay Willson. 2004. *Caring for/Caring about Women, Home Care and Unpaid Caregiving.* Aurora, Ont.: Garamond.

Harding, Katherine, and Brian Laghi. 2006. 'Klein issues warning on sharing the wealth'. *Globe and Mail*, 25 May, A1.

Horwitz, Jill R. 2005. 'Making Profits and Providing Care: Comparing Nonprofit, For-Profit, and Government Hospitals', *Health Affairs* 24 (3): 790–801.

Jenson, Jane. 1998. *Social Cohesion: The State of Canadian Research.* Ottawa: Canadian Policy Research Networks.

Kahnamoui, Niknaz. 2005. 'After Outsourcing: Working Collaboratively to Deliver Patient Care'. MA thesis, Simon Fraser University.

Mackian, Sara. 2002. 'Complex Cultures: Rereading the Story about Health and Social Capital', *Critical Social Policy* 22 (2): 203–25.

Maioni, Antonia. 1998. *Parting at the Crossroads: The Emergence of Health Insurance in the United States and Canada.* Princeton, NJ: Princeton University Press.

Marmot, Michael. 2004. *The Status Syndrome: How Social Standing Affects Our Health and Longevity.* London: Henry Holt.

———, and Richard C. Wilkinson. 1999. *Social Determinants of Health.* New York: Oxford University Press.

Mimoto, H., and P. Cross. 1991. 'The Growth of the Federal Debt', *Canadian Economic Observer* 3 (1): 1–17.

Muntaner, Carles, John Lynch, and George Davey Smith. 2001. 'Social Capital, Disorganized Communities, and the Third Way: Understanding the Retreat from Structural Inequalities in Epidemiology and Public Health', *International Journal of Health Services* 31 (2): 213–37.

Murphy, Rae, Robert Chodos, and Nick Auf Der Maur. 1985. *Brian Mulroney: The Boy from Baie-Comeau.* Halifax: Formac.

Navarro, Vincente. 2002. 'A Critique of Social Capital', *International Journal of Health Services* 32: 423–32.

Ontario Health Coalition. 2006. *Bill 36 LHINS Legislation Analysis.* www.ontariohealthcoalition.ca.

Petchesky, Rosalind Pollack. 2003. *Global Prescriptions: Gendering Health and Human Rights.* London: Zed.

Policy Research Initiative. 2004. *Synthesis Report of Expert Workshop on the Measurement of Social Capital for Public Policy.* Ottawa: Policy Research Initiative.

Portes, Alejandro. 1998. 'Social Capital: Its Origins and Applications in Modern Sociology', *Annual Review of Sociology* 24: 1–25.

Prakash, Sanjeev, and Per Selle, eds. 2004. *Investigating Social Capital: Comparative Perspectives on Civil Society, Participation and Governance.* London: Sage.

Putnam, Robert. 1995. 'Bowling Alone: America's Declining Social Capital', *Journal of Democracy* 6 (1): 65–78.

Rankin, Janet M., and Marie L. Campbell. 2006. *Managing to Nurse: Inside Canada's Health Care Reform*. Toronto: University of Toronto Press.

Ritzen, Jo, William Easterly, and Michael Woolcock. 2000. 'On "Good" Politicians and "Bad" Policies: Social Cohesion, Institutions, and Growth'. http://info/worldbank.org/etools/library.htm (accessed June 2008).

Romanow Commission. *See* Commission on the Future of Health Care in Canada.

Sachdev, S. 2001. *'Contracting Culture: From CCT to PPPs': The Private Provision of Public Services and Its Impact on Employment Relations*. London: UNISON.

Talaga, Tanya. 2006. 'Teen flies to Calgary as blood machine sits idle'. *Toronto Star*, 25 May, A1.

Taylor, Malcolm. 1987. *Health Insurance and Canadian Public Policy*. Montreal: McGill-Queen's University Press.

Walkom, Thomas. 2008. 'Deficits not always the work of the devil', *Toronto Star*, 22 Jan., A11.

White, Julie. 1993. *Sisters and Solidarity: Women and Unions in Canada*. Toronto: Thompson.

Wydick, Bruce. 1999. 'Can Social Cohesion be Harnessed to Repair Market Failures? Evidence from Group Lending in Guatemala', *Economic Journal* 109, issue 457 (July): 313–518.

## Further Reading

Muntaner, Carles, John Lynch, and George Davey Smith. 2001. 'Social Capital, Disorganized Communities, and the Third Way: Understanding the Retreat from Structural Inequalities in Epidemiology and Public Health', *International Journal of Health Services* 31 (2): 213–37.

Navarro, Vincente. 2002. 'A Critique of Social Capital', *International Journal of Health Services* 32: 423–32.

Prakash, Sanjeev, and Per Selle, eds. 2004. *Investigating Social Capital: Comparative Perspectives on Civil Society, Participation and Governance*. London: Sage.

## Questions for Critical Thought

1. Is social cohesion a useful concept in working for equity?
2. What is the difference between social solidarity and social cohesion, and are these distinctions useful in developing an analysis of progress?
3. Can terms such as social cohesion be used simultaneously for progressive and regressive ends?

# CHAPTER 5

# Women and Climate-Change Policy:

## Integrating Gender into the Agenda

Kathleen McNutt and Sara Hawryluk

## Introduction

Climate change has attracted a lot of attention in Canada over the past twenty years. It is high on both political and policy agendas and has garnered extensive coverage by the media. The increasing frequency of unpredictable weather, floods, and glacial retreat have heightened both scientists' and the public's sense of urgency. Whereas the problems associated with global warming were largely identified through biophysical research, solutions to the problem must move beyond the technical dimension to also address social, economic, and political consequences of climate change. Although governments recognize that climate change presents such social risks as health impacts, displacement, and food insecurity, little attention is given to how different Canadian communities and social groups will experience climatic variability.

Globally, gender plays a significant role in the adapting of behaviour to global warming and has also been correlated with greater vulnerability to climatic variability; however, in Canada, the implications of climate change on gender and gendered roles have largely been ignored. Despite Canada's international and national commitments to gender equality and the numerous promises to include women in decision making, discussions of gender continue to be excluded from the climate-change debate. In this chapter we examine how gender has, or has not, been included in the development of climate-change policy in Canada. International development organizations and women's groups have repeatedly demonstrated how women's roles in social reproduction and in food and energy production have been influenced by global warming; however, in Canada there has been very little discussion of how climate change might affect women and men differently. Although the differential gendered effects of climate change are not as extreme in Canada as in developing nations, there is evidence that women are particularly vulnerable to climatic variability and that women shoulder an unreasonably large share of the adaptation burden.

Canada's historic response to climate change was built around the principles of the United Nations Framework Convention on Climate Change (UNFCCC), an international treaty adopted at the Earth Summit in 1992. In the original treaty, compliance was voluntary; however, in 1997 the Convention was supplemented by the Kyoto Accord, which assigns mandatory emissions-reduction targets to the 38 signatory nations (Yamin 1998). The Kyoto Accord is predominately a strategy for mitigating global warming through the reduction of anthropogenic sources of greenhouse gas (GHG) emissions (Schipper 2006). The international pressures to adopt the Kyoto Accord and reduce greenhouse gas emissions have put pressure on national decision makers to produce new regulations that conform to the treaty on climate change. Policy development to date largely assumes that climate change will have universal impacts that require two macro-level responses to global climate change: mitigation and adaptation (Klein et al. 2005).

Mitigation limits or stabilizes GHG emissions to *postpone* the impacts of global climate change and thus is largely concerned with energy policy (Pielke 2005). Alternatively, adaptation requires changes in human behaviour and a reduction in greenhouse gas emissions to stop or at least *minimize* the effects of global warming. The UNFCCC and the Kyoto Protocol are concerned primarily with reducing greenhouse gas emissions (Schipper 2006); however, there is a growing recognition that human society must adapt to climate change because the predicted negative impacts on the economy, human health, and catastrophic weather patterns have demonstrated that carbon abatement is only part of the solution (Thompson 2006).

The differential experience of climate change across Canada threatens social cohesion and undermines commitments to social protection. The effects are uneven across communities with the southern regions experiencing droughts, floods, and deforestation (Milne 2005), while the northern communities have had to adjust to shorter winters, less ice coverage, and disruptions to traditional subsistence hunting (Fast and Berkes 2002).

The Canadian literature on gender and climate change is extremely limited, few studies having explored the social impacts of climatic variability on gendered roles and social reproduction. As Sally Kenney suggests, 'the transformation of conditions into problems' (2003, 191) is the first step in getting gender onto the climate-change agenda.

This chapter explores the opportunities for and constraints on women's participation in the climate-change policy debates, focusing on how the social risks arising from vulnerability to climate change threaten social cohesion. To begin, we briefly discuss social investment, locating climate change in this post–neo-liberal paradigm. Next we trace the history of various federal governments' responses to climatic variability and discuss how successive governments have offered solutions focused on environmental and economic risks, largely ignoring the social risks from global warming. We then ask whether gender really matters in the climate-change debate in Canada, offering some examples of how climate change may threaten social cohesion and affect women differently from men. In the final section we argue that the federal government's failure to use gender-based analysis as a horizontal policy tool across all sectors affected by climate change will increase women's vulnerability to climate change and adaptation strategies.

We thus recommend three actions that must be taken to improve climate-change policy analysis and recommendations. First, women must be included in the decision making. Second, gender-based analysis must be undertaken across all affected policy domains to identify the differential impacts of climate change and what this may mean in terms of reproduction, production, and social organization. Third, it is essential to mainstream gender throughout the implementation and evaluation of all climate-change policies and programs. As this chapter demonstrates, the failure to do so and the lack of 'investment' in women's equality have resulted in a flawed response to climate change and a failure to address the social threats posed by global warming.

## From Neo-liberal to Social Investment: Climate Change as a New Social Risk

Climate-change policy is designed to address changes in the earth's global climate and the human-induced causes of rising temperatures. To address this problem, governments must take a number of actions. First, they must develop a plan that is economically sound and able to address the adaptive capacity of various sectors. Second, they must mitigate risks by reducing the impact of human activity on the natural environment. Third, they must protect social cohesion in their responses to climate change. In Canada, policy responses have largely focused on the first two actions, adaptation and mitigation, and have paid very little attention to the effect of climate change on social cohesion. As a result, governments are unprepared for the possible social risks arising from vulnerability to climate change.

There is now a strong consensus that vulnerability to climate change and the actions necessary to adapt to a changing environment are largely social issues. The differential impacts of climate change across Canadian regions will affect methods of production, gender roles, and human health, the implications for social cohesion being largely unknown. While governments often refer to the importance of the social issues related to climate change, the current policies in Canada have little to say about levels of vulnerability and the implications for women. Concerns expressed by women's organizations and gender-based experts on the implications of climate change for women were largely ignored and, as a result, investment in mitigating the social risks of vulnerability to climate change and the attendant threats to social cohesion have been largely absent.

Social cohesion is a sense of belonging, acceptance, and worth in a community. The concept includes a number of issues focused on the valuing of diversity, equality, providing opportunities, and participation (Jenson and Saint-Martin 2003). After twenty years of neo-liberal policies, the social cohesion of Canada was severely threatened as the nation experienced income polarization, persistent poverty, and increasing inequality. This has led to a redesign of the welfare structure in recent times and has meant that women are being exposed to increased social risks. Social cohesion is a characteristic of the social unit; acting as a macro-level concept that refers to the overall state of social bonds within any society (Jenson and Saint-Martin 2003). In this macro context policy makers can operate only at the institutional level of analysis and focus only on how these institutions and actors influence the distribution of well-being (Alford and Friedland 1985). Thus, to protect and promote social cohesion, especially in the social investment model, the most efficient allocation of resources from the state is to those who are marginalized. The danger of this is that the allocation of programs and resources is to those who will return the highest payoff (usually young children), as opposed to those considered to have less potential (adult women, the disabled, and seniors) who are viewed as poor investments.

Over the past ten years the transition from a neo-liberal to a social investment perspective has produced new policy priorities as the federal government decides how to spend a growing surplus. The governing strategies of a social investment model are largely concerned with return on investment, a focus that can lead to the linking of social and economic policy goals. As Dobrowolsky explains, social investment is promoted 'to counterbalance *social* ills in part wreaked by pure, unfettered neo-liberalism. Yet, unlike the welfare state, the social investment state concentrates its spending in areas with perceived dividends and pay-back potential, such as promoting life-long learning, supporting activation, and innovation' (2006, 186, emphasis in original). Unlike the neo-liberal regime, which assumed that spending on social policies and programs was contrary to priorities associated with competition and economic prosperity, the social investment approach promotes macro-level social goals tied to social inclusion and social cohesion. In other words, spending is justified insofar as the investment produces future value (Saint-Martin 2004).

Under the leadership of Jean Chrétien, the federal government largely overlooked the significance of gender in its response to climate change. This is not surprising given that the Liberal government dramatically restructured the institutionalized relations of women and the state, beginning with the abolition of the Canadian Advisory Council on the Status of Women, which had operated as an autonomous agency that advised the federal government about women's specific policy considerations, produced gender-sensitive research and recommendations, and educated the general public about women's policy concerns and program needs (Burt 1998). The Liberals also cut state funding to organizations that advanced women's equality, thus undermining the influence of 'femocrats' and gender experts in policy development and curtailing women-specific advocacy (Burt 1999). One of the most serious blows to the women's policy agenda was the loss of core funding to the National Action Committee on the Status of Women, Canada's feminist umbrella organization. The governments' decision to disinvest in women's equality significantly impaired the policy capacity of women's organizations and gender experts to engage in the climate-change debate. As a result, policy analysis related to climate change has been largely gender-blind, resulting in the failure to address women's vulnerability to climatic variations.

Since taking office, the Harper government has further decreased the state's commitment to women's equality by reorganizing the Status of Women Canada, closing 12 regional offices, cutting the operating budget by 43 per cent, and removing the word 'equality' from its mandate. In addition, the Conservatives imposed new funding limits on women's advocacy groups, substantially decreasing funding for gender-based analysis and research. After these cuts a number of women's organizations, including the National Association of Women and the Law (NAWL), a once powerful advocacy group that promoted women's equality in Canada since 1974, were forced to close their doors. In addition, the Conservatives cancelled the national daycare program and the Court Challenges Program, while refusing to implement pay-equity legislation. Overall, the Harper government has been hostile to women's policy claims. In short, social investment in the equality of women is viewed as a bad investment lacking any identifiable return.

## The Canadian Climate-Change Agenda

Attention to climate-change policy in Canada began in earnest in 1988 when the Conservative prime minister, Brian Mulroney, hosted the Toronto Conference on the Changing Atmosphere, which laid the groundwork for the UN Framework Convention on Climate Change. In these early years of the debate, Canada was closely aligned with the European Union in advancing firm targets and producing a domestic commitment to stabilize greenhouse gas emissions to 1990 levels by 2000. After the 1992 Rio Earth Summit, the Mulroney government ratified the UNFCCC, which was a largely symbolic agreement that committed the 155 signatory nations to voluntary reduction targets.

Mulroney's approach to climate change dovetailed closely with his strong commitment to neo-liberalism. Although he was vocal about the importance of an international agreement to curb global warming, Mulroney never introduced legally binding targets, nor was he responsible for creating a substantive policy direction. As Heather Smith suggests, '[climate-change] policy post-1992 has been driven by concerns for potential negative economic impacts arising from reduction in greenhouse gas emission' (2002, 286). Mulroney's rhetorical stance on climate change never threatened his commitment to smaller government, market primacy, and deregulation.

When the Chrétien Liberal government came to power in 1993, the Liberals had campaigned on an aggressive pro-environment platform. The Liberals were in power in Canada from 1993 until 2006 and were always publicly committed to multilateral environmental agreements and upholding Canada's international reputation as a good global citizen (Lantis 2005). However, a substantive policy response to climate change was not forthcoming, as both the natural resource complex and the business lobby were strongly opposed to binding targets. In addition, the influence of the American government in both the energy sector and the climate-change field significantly influenced the actions the federal government was willing to take. Nonetheless the Chrétien Liberals in 2002 ratified the Kyoto Accord, which committed Canada to a 6 per cent reduction in greenhouse gas emissions.

Despite its pro-Kyoto stance, the federal government's ability to take decisive action was restrained by the institutions of federalism and by domestic and regional interests, both environmental and industrial. The environment is largely a provincial domain, and despite the creation of several intergovernmental mechanisms for developing national climate-change policy, there was a great deal of disparity among the provincial governments' priorities (Macdonald, VanNijnatten, and Bjorn 2004). Thus, the Liberal government's commitments to climate change were largely political and were considered economically unfeasible and environmentally ineffective (Böhringer and Vogt 2003; Page 2002; Van Kooten 2003). As Sears suggests, '[d]espite two separate Chrétien "Kyoto Action Plans" and a Martin promise of massive spending to cut emissions, it was foolishness like the "One Tonne Challenge" that was as close as the previous government came to actually implementing a policy' (2006, 7). The environmental priorities of the Liberals remained closely aligned with neo-liberal thinking throughout their tenure in government, with the state quite simply unwilling to risk Canada' economic competitiveness for environmental protection. Instead of mandatory reduction targets, the government continually opted for voluntary compliance and by the end of 2005 total greenhouse gas emissions in Canada were 25.3 per cent above 1990 levels and 32.7 per cent above the Kyoto target (Environment Canada 2007).

After the election in January 2006, the federal Conservative party, under Stephen Harper, replaced the Liberals and quickly realigned the climate-change policy agenda to focus on domestic and regional interests, moving away from the international consensus. Although Canada has not yet opted out of the Accord, the government has announced that Kyoto targets are unobtainable and thus a made-in-Canada solution is necessary for producing realistic initiatives to reduce greenhouse gases. As the Canadian government distances itself from its Kyoto commitment, it has also aligned Canada's climate-change priorities with the American agenda.

Under federal Conservative leadership, the approach to climate change in Canada shifted moderately in that the new government supports a compliance system based on domestic discretion, in which national decisions are left to Canada, and national co-operation between the federal government and the provinces. During the Liberal reign, industry had argued that the American government's withdrawal from Kyoto and the intensity of North American economic integration, combined with the two nations' geographic proximity, necessitated a harmonization of Canadian and American policy instruments (Barnsley 2006). The Canadian government has not yet, however, harmonized its programs with those of the United States. Rather, the Conservatives have sought to manage trade relations with the United States while serving various interests from the western provinces and accommodating the demands made by industry and business. The environmental portfolio has been governed as an increasingly domestic or continental affair, with the government focusing on sustainable economic development and the removal of trade obstacles, as opposed to environmental protection and adaptation to climate change.

At the UN climate conference in Bali in December 2007, the Canadian government agreed to a 2009 deadline to negotiate a new global climate-change treaty to combat climate change after 2012. The agreement obligates wealthy nations to make a 25 to 40 per cent reduction in greenhouse gas emissions. It is unclear how effective this successor to the Kyoto Protocol will be. It is equally unclear, given Canadian attempts to block negotiations at the conference, how committed the current government will be to such radical reductions in greenhouse gas emissions, for current domestic targets are not nearly as aggressive. Unlike the Kyoto Protocol, which committed Canada to cutting emissions 6 per cent below 1990 levels by 2012, the current Conservative government's made-in-Canada solution sets a 20 per cent reduction below 2006 levels by 2020. Some analysts predict that if the current policy is followed, Canada's greenhouse gas emission will have risen approximately 25 per cent above 1990 levels by 2020 (Jaccard and Rivers 2007).

The problem of climate change has been misrepresented as a scientific, technical, and economic problem leading to policy prescriptions that do not recognize or integrate differential social outcomes that put social cohesion and equality at risk. Despite the attention the climate-change portfolio has received, successive federal governing parties have failed to produce a consensus on how best to respond to global warming and the resulting climatic extremes. Using the precautionary principle to develop a holistic climate-change plan would suggest that in addition to macro-level responses, policies and implementation strategies must recognize the social impacts of climate change, including the fact that social risks are uneven across communities and social groups.

## Does Gender Matter in the Climate-Change Debate?

Climate-change strategies include both mitigation and adaptation. Mitigation measures are used to reduce or stabilize greenhouse gas emissions so as to limit global climate change. This will require nations, industries, and individuals to curb their consumption of commercial, residential, transportation, and industrial and manufacturing energy use. Adaptation measures, on the other hand, recognizing that the global climate has changed, are designed to alter human behaviour in order that individuals and communities can adapt to the earth's altered atmosphere. Although there is a tacit agreement among all Canadian policy actors that climate change must be addressed, there is wide disparity about how to regulate the emission of such greenhouse gases as energy-related carbon dioxide, methane, and nitrous oxides: some interests advocate cooperative compliance, while others demand strict enforcement of measurable targets.

While both mitigation and adaptation have gendered dimensions, there has been no concerted effort in Canada to integrate gender into climate-change policy measures. The gendered impacts of mitigation measures, for example, include the different consumption patterns of women and men and gender-specific resource use. Similarly, adaptation strategies do not fully account for the extent to which climate change affects the lives of women and men differently and the extent to which men and women are vulnerable to climate change. In Canada, the failure to take into account the different effects of climate change on women and men is impairing cross-domain policy co-ordination and impeding the successful implementation of climate-change policies. Instances of women's vulnerability to climate change, the differential impacts across regions, and limited capacity to adapt are not difficult to find in Canada. For example, northern environmental degradation has significant implications for the natural-resource base of Aboriginal communities. The Native Women's Association of Canada (NWAC) presented a number of underlying principles regarding the environment, including respect for social structures, vulnerable languages and cultures, indigenous plants and medicines, hunting, fishing and trapping grounds, and areas of spiritual significance. Furthermore, NWAC emphasized that there must be a willingness to understand the unique spiritual connection of Aboriginal women to the environment and to use this understanding to find a solution to global warming that benefits future generations. NWAC recommends that Aboriginal women must be engaged as full and effective partners with the ongoing implementation of policies that affect the environment. The spiritual significance of water to Aboriginal women requires policies for its protection and accessibility. In addition, Aboriginal peoples' and particularly women's—because of their primary care-giving roles—connection to the environment, their spiritual connection to the land, habitat, and species, and their dependence on the environment as a source of sustenance and income must be considered in decision making.

In highly urbanized areas, climate change may affect quality of life, disadvantage the urban poor, and increase health problems. As Hemmati argues, 'all economic consequences of climate change and response measures need to be analysed by gender to identify and effectively counter disproportionate disadvantages for women' (2005, 2). Gender-based analysis is particularly germane in urban centres, where women are increasingly vulnerable to the effects of climate change and where they constitute the majority of the poor (Skutsch 2002). In terms of health, Poumadère et al. (2005) found that older women with low incomes were far more vulnerable than the average citizen to health problems and death during the 2003 heat wave in France. In urban centres, high levels of pollution caused by transportation, residential, and industrial energy consumption degrade air quality and increase the rate of environmentally related illnesses (Grimmond 2007), increasing women's care-giving responsibilities and vulnerability to illness. These brief examples suggest that the intersection between gender, socio-economic status, and geography with climate-change policies will produce differential experiences of climatic vulnerability, which will only be addressed through gendered analysis and the integration of gender in all stages of decision making and policy development. The capacity to adapt to climate change varies markedly among and between women and men.

For example, the vulnerability of rural women to global warming will likely be directly associated with changing weather patterns—including drought, excessive rainfall, and intense heat or cold—and with pest infestations. Though it is clear that long-term gradual climate change will have an effect on agricultural lands and ecosystems, it is difficult to predict accurately the effects of natural disasters, environmental degradation, and long-term climate change on the sustainability of rural communities (Nelson et al. 2002). We can expect, however, that the changed environment will challenge gender roles and the rural population's ability to cope with climate variation in the long term. Women, who in many cases are the main users and managers of natural resources, are disproportionately affected by environmental degradation. Changing weather patterns and the loss of farm income, for example, are already altering the gendered relations of small producers. Similarly, natural disasters, whether it be forest fires, floods, or ice storms are increasing women's care-giving roles and leaving entire communities vulnerable to property loss, illness, and family disruption.

There is growing evidence that the differential experiences of climate change across Canada threaten social cohesion and undermine current policy commitments to social protection. In short, gender is both an important consideration in adaptation strategies and an important variable in measuring levels of vulnerability to climate change. Integrating gender into climate-change policy will require the inclusion of women's groups in the decisions and a commitment on the part of governments to treat gender as a critical variable in the design and implementation of climate-change policy. Although both the Conservative and Liberal responses to climate change recognize the threats to the environment and the economy, the threats to society are largely ignored. Investment has been largely focused on new science (biofuels for example) and the opportunities represented by a growing green-technologies market.

## Investing in Gender

Canada needs a gender-aware response to climate change. Neither the Liberal nor the Conservative governments mainstreamed gender throughout the analysis, design, and implementation processes of climate-change policy, nor were there any concerted efforts to include women's groups in consultations or decisions. The increasingly institutional absence of gender-based analysis and the infrequency with which governments consult women's groups in Canada have resulted in a serious analytical deficit in our ability to respond to climate change. This approach patently ignores the social risks of climate change and fails to recognize that vulnerability to changing weather patterns, droughts, floods, deforestation, and so on directly impacts gender roles since women are disproportionately affected by environmentally related health problems, food insecurity, availability of drinking water, and crisis management during natural disasters.

Although the last twenty years of climate-change policy has been deeply embedded in neo-liberal thinking, the shift to a social investment approach does provide opportunities for examining the gendered aspects of climate change. As yet, however, the failure of governments to treat women as a social investment and to support women's agencies and organizations has made a gendered analysis in this domain impossible. Focusing on the social dimensions of climate change, including who is vulnerable and who is expected to alter their behaviour, will provide a more holistic approach to developing climate-change solutions. In Canada, we do not know what the long-term implications of climate change on women will be and governments must thus invest in gender-based analysis to provide a fair balance of women's participation in the decision-making process. These two prerequisites will allow for an integrated policy response that can address the complexities of climate change while guarding against climatic vulnerability and protecting social cohesion.

First, women's inclusion in decision making is crucial. The Platform for Action adopted by the Fourth World Conference on Women: Action for Equality,

Development and Peace in Beijing on 15 September 1995 calls for all governments to ensure that women have opportunities to participate in the environmental decisions. Agendas taken up at the Platform for Action as well as at other UN conferences on the environment reflect an evolving understanding of the links between women, the environment, and sustainable development. The participation of organizations representing women's interests and gender experts in the Canadian climate-change debate has been nominal. To overcome this knowledge deficit the government will have to work with Status of Women Canada, women's organizations, non-governmental organizations, and international women's organizations. Facilitating women's active participation in climate-change negotiations will make for better decisions and produce gender-sensitive policies regarding climate change specifically, and the environment more generally. As Minu Hemmati has argued, '[w]omen must be involved in climate-protection negotiations at all levels and in all decisions on climate protection. Representation by numbers is not enough' (2005, 3). The inclusion of gender experts and women's organizations in the design, implementation, and evaluation of climate-change policies will ensure that the previous work done in related areas and on gender mainstreaming is incorporated into horizontal policy mechanisms.

The second necessary action will be to undertake gender-based analysis of the consequences of climate change. Gender-based analysis is a key component in a number of commitments that the government has made to advance gender equality. Recently in Canada, the federal government has put in place two five-year plans on gender equality: Setting the Stage (1995–2000) and the Agenda for Gender Equality (2005). Ten years ago at the Fourth United Nations World Conference on Women in Beijing, the participating nations developed an ambitious political declaration and platform for action, which outlined objectives and actions required of signatory countries to promote equality between men and women. By adopting the Beijing Platform for Action, governments throughout the world committed to integrate a gender perspective throughout their operations, policies, planning, and decision making. Governments also committed to carry out gender-impact assessments of the effects of government policy and political decisions on women and men across all sectors.

Although the use of gender-based analysis to assess policies, procedures, and programs is important, there are limitations, some of which are particularly germane to the social investment model and social inclusion. One such limitation is that the social investment perspective emphasizes equity in the future without considering how women have historically been discriminated against. Furthermore, in the social investment state, policies focus on investments for some groups that are considered likely to be more profitable than other groups (Jenson and Saint-Martin 2003). Significantly, those that are viewed as more profitable are young children and families with children. This approach lacks the integral focus of gender-based analysis because it focuses solely on children and families and excludes entire social groups from the analysis.

In Canada's 1995 action plan for implementing the Beijing Platform for Action, the Canadian government required federal departments and agencies to conduct gender-based analysis of all policies and legislation. However, the use of gender-based analysis across government departments has been uneven. While some departments have well-established gender-equality or gender-based-analysis units; others have none. Moreover, Status of Women Canada reports that the lack of any obligation to conduct gender-based analysis, internal resistance, and the lack of shared responsibility have led to a decreased interdepartmental capacity to ensure gender equality. Developing policy that responds to all dimensions of the climate-change problem will require investments in identifying differential levels of vulnerability between women and men, producing knowledge that can then be integrated into the design and implementation of climate-change policy. As is argued in the next section, the effects of climate change on non-environmental policy domains demand intersectoral policy co-ordination, with environmental policy integrated across all affected areas, including gender.

## Mainstreaming Gender into Climate-Change Integration

A significant collection of scientific research and policy analyses has been produced on the effects of climate change in Canada. Decision makers understand that the challenges surrounding climate-change policy are complex and are plagued by uncertainty, so that there are numerous spill-over effects into other policy fields and a diverse collection of policy actors are involved. Climate-change policy is inextricably linked to many policy domains, all of which play a role in terms of the domain's impact on climate change (that is, the effects of carbon emissions on policy development in the energy sectors, transportation, natural resources, and industry) or the effects of climate change on such domains as health, economic and social development, and the natural environment. Policy co-ordination across these domains is crucial if viable policy solutions are to be identified.

Environmental policy integration is defined by Lafferty and Hovden as the 'incorporation of environmental objectives into all stages of policy making in non-environmental policy sectors' and 'an attempt to aggregate presumed environmental consequences into an overall evaluation of policy, and a commitment to minimize contradictions between environmental and sectoral policies by giving principled priority to the former over the latter' (2003, 9). Numerous types of analysis have been undertaken, including risk assessment, social-impact analysis, cost-benefit analysis, environmental-impact assessments, and scientific research, all of which make recommendations on climate-change policy; however, these analyses usually fail to take gender into account. In Canada the differential effects of climate change on gender is impairing cross-domain policy co-ordination and impeding the successful implementation of policy instruments designed to solve the problems associated with climate change.

The establishment of an integrated climate-change policy framework must take gender into account if policy co-ordination across these domains is to be achieved. Policy integration, also called mainstreaming, refers to the inclusion of universal policy objectives across all policy domains. The explicit intent of policy integration is to implement one policy through the implementation of other policies (Mickwitz and Kivimaa 2007). To achieve policy co-ordination, complex policy problems must be solved by the use of an approach that not only combines specific program objectives, but also includes concerns for larger social, environmental, and economic issues. Determining the effects of gender on a policy or program is essential in analyzing how the organization of social life impacts on policy outcomes. As Charlotte Bretherton suggests, '[i]ts influence on the processes of production, reproduction and resource allocation ensures that gender plays an important role in mediating relationships between social and natural environments' (1998, 85). Addressing issues of gender and the intersections between race, class, ability, demography, language, and other such diversities is critical to achieving policy objectives and avoiding inequality, harm to human health, and environmental degradation. Indeed, if an integrated climate-change policy framework is to be successful, gender mainstreaming will be a significant component of a comprehensive strategy.

Status of Women Canada has not given much attention to climate-change policy; however, it is responsible for overseeing the integration of gender-based policy analysis in overall government decision making so as to ensure women's equality is not impaired by faulty programming. Status of Women Canada advocates gender mainstreaming, which refers to the inter-sectoral policy co-ordination around gender issues with the objective of improving gender equality. Gender-based analysis is the typical analytical approach used to identify differential gender impacts and outcomes. The global impetus for gender mainstreaming was a result of the UN Fourth World Conference on Women, where Canada was one of the 189 signatory countries (Hanson 2007). Status of Women Canada created the Gender-Based Analysis Unit to encourage gender mainstreaming; however, recent studies suggest that the extent of gender mainstreaming is limited. Status of Women Canada reports that the lack of binding obligations to conduct gender-based analysis has resulted in internal government resistance with a lack of shared responsibility leading to a decreased interdepartmental capacity to ensure gender equality (Status of Women Canada 2005).

Mainstreaming gender often includes gender-sensitive as well as women-specific policies and programs. As discussed previously, it is clear that climate change and the effects that it has on the environment require a gender-sensitive approach to ensure women's equality. Furthermore, gender mainstreaming acknowledges that gender does not operate in isolation but in relation to other factors such as income, geographic location, race, ability, and age (Hankivsky 2005). Gender mainstreaming will improve climate-change responses because it will help identify who is most vulnerable and who is most at risk. The extent to which women will be affected by climate change is an integral aspect of policy co-ordination.

## Conclusion

Climate change is one of the most significant policy problems facing governments in the new millennium. The climate-change debate is riddled with uncertainty as the complexity of problems associated with global warming produce numerous spill-over effects, where an action taken in one domain may affect program performance in another policy field either negatively or positively. The harm that climate change will have on the environment, human health, community well-being, and the economy are well documented; however, there is a critical shortage of analysis concerning the gendered impacts of climate change in Canada.

Women's equality is a social investment in that it produces social cohesion and inclusion through the assurance of shared citizenship rights and social justice. Gender has never been on the climate-change policy agenda; however, as the effects of climate change in Canada intensify, there is a growing body of evidence that suggests that there are gender-specific impacts of climate change on women. Government responses to climate change, whether they involve mitigation or adaptation, directly intersect with economic policy priorities and social policy regimes, both of which have numerous gendered dimensions that will be reproduced in the experience of climate change. Without gender-based analysis and a clear sense of the differential impacts of climate change on women and men, an integrated response to climate change will be flawed. Understanding the long-term consequences of climate change on gender roles and expectations will improve the policy co-ordination across domains and priorities. Under the Chrétien government, gender-based consideration of climate change was nominal; under the Harper government, however, all women's issues have been marginalized and thus the opportunities for gender-specific research and gender-based policy analysis have been dramatically reduced.

Using gender-based analysis, the government must be committed to mainstreaming gender in all policies and programs designed in response to climate change. This will enable the government to identify gender-specific vulnerabilities to climate change in Canada. It will also support the implementation of horizontal policy instruments and the goals of an integrated policy approach. As Bernard and Armstrong (1998) suggest, the goal 'of integrated policy development is to better understand the scope of the changes occurring and to create more democratic mechanisms to frame problems and reach consensus. The process can be seen as a cooperative search for a negotiated path to more sustainable, equitable, and inclusive governance of social, economic, and environmental systems' (1998). Using gender-based analysis in the design and implementation of climate-change policy responses is imperative if proposed solutions are to prove workable.

In addition, consultations must take place with both governmental and non-governmental women's organizations throughout the formulation and implementation of the recommended mitigation and adaptation policies. Providing substantive representation of women in decision making and policy formulation is critical in both program evaluation and policy-instrument adjustment because, as Weldon (2002) argues, women's institutionalized relations with the state are just as important in achieving substantive policy change as women's electoral representation, if not more so. The erosion of gender-based policy capacity, through the loss of state commitment and the damage done to women's advocacy groups and gender-based research organizations, has weakened the quality of the recommended responses to climate change. Gender-based analysis will enable decision makers to implement responses to climate change that recognize that the long-term investment in gender equality will be a necessary consideration in both mitigation and adaptation strategies.

The federal government's commitment to policy co-ordination across domains affected by climate change has been uneven, with a disproportionate focus on economic development and innovation and a scarcity of analysis considering gender. The harmful effects of global warming include extreme weather, deforestation, coastal erosion, drought, and increases in environmental illnesses. However, not only is climate change not simply a technical or scientific problem, but it also has social and economic consequences as communities adjust to changing environments. The gaps in knowledge concerning the gendered impacts of climate change have profound effects on policy design and program delivery. Although there are numerous practical observations concerning women's potential vulnerability to climatic variations, there is also a growing body of evidence that this vulnerability varies across region, age, socio-economic status, culture, and other diversities. Vulnerability to climate change and strategies of adaptation will have a significant influence on gender roles and social organization. The government's failure to conduct gender-based analysis, to mainstream gender and diversity across all policy fields affected by climate change, and to invest properly in women's equality have resulted in a flawed response to climate change. The ability to respond effectively will require policy analysts and decision makers to incorporate women's differential vulnerability to adaptation and the gendered aspects of climate-change adaptation across all policy fields and between regions.

## References

Alford, Robert, and Roger Friedland. 1985. *Powers of Theory: Capitalism, the State, and Democracy.* Cambridge: Cambridge University Press.

Barnsley, Ingrid. 2006. 'Dealing with Change: Australia, Canada and the Kyoto Protocol to the Framework Convention on Climate Change', *Round Table* 95 (385): 399–411.

Bernard, A.K., and G. Armstrong. 1998. 'Learning and Policy Integration'. In Jamie Schnurr and Susan Holtz, eds, *The Cornerstone of Development: Integrating Environmental, Social, and Economic Policies*, Chap. 2. Ottawa: International Development Research Centre. http://www.idrc.ca/en/ev-9406-201-1-DO_TOPIC.html (accessed 3 Nov. 2007).

Böhringer, Christoph, and Carsten Vogt. 2003. 'Economic and Environmental Impacts of the Kyoto Protocol', *Canadian Journal of Economics* 36 (2): 475–96.

Bretherton, Charlotte. 1998. 'Global Environmental Politics: Putting Gender on the Agenda?' *Review of International Studies* 24 (1): 85–100.

Burt, Sandra. 1998. 'The Canadian Advisory Council on the Status of Women: Possibilities and Limitations'. In Manon Tremblay and Caroline Andrew, eds, *Women and Political Representation in Canada*, 115–44. Ottawa: University of Ottawa Press.

———. 1999. 'Canadian Women's Movements: Revisiting Historical Patterns and Considering Present Developments', 393–411. In James Bickerton and Alain-G. Gagnon, eds, *Canadian Politics*. 3rd edn. Toronto: Broadview Press.

Dobrowolsky, Alexandra. 2006. 'The Chrétien Legacy and Women: Changing Policy Priorities with Little Cause for Celebration'. In Lois Harder and Steve Patten, eds, *The Chrétien Legacy: Politics and Public Policy in Canada*, 181–210. Montreal: McGill-Queen's University Press.

———, and Jane Jenson. 2004. 'Shifting Representations of Citizenship: Canadian Politics of "Women" and "Children" ', *Social Politics* 11 (2): 154–80.

Environment Canada. 2007. *National Inventory Report, 1990–2005: Greenhouse Gas Sources and Sinks in Canada.* The Canadian Government's Submission to the UN Framework Convention on Climate Change. Ottawa: Environment Canada.

Fast, Helen, and Fikret Berkes. 2002. 'Climate Change, Northern Subsistence and Land Based Economies'. In Nicola Mayer and Wendy Avis, eds, *The Canada Country Study: Climate Impacts and Adaptation*, 149–65. Ottawa: Environment Canada.

Grimmond, Sue. 2007. 'Urbanization and Global Environmental Change: Local Effects of Urban Warming', *Geographical Journal* 173 (1): 83–8.

Hankivsky, Olena. 2005. 'Gender vs. Diversity Mainstreaming: A PreliminaryExamination of the Role and Transformative Potential of Feminist Theory', *Canadian Journal of Political Science/Revue canadienne de science politique* 38 (4): 977–1001.

Hemmati, Minu. 2005. Abstract of the paper *Gender and Climate Change in the North: Issues, Entry Points and Strategies for the Post-Kyoto-Process*. Focal Point Gender Justice and Sustainability, Germany. http://p1737.typo3server.info/fileadmin/downloads/themen/Themen_en/Gender_Post-Kyoto_en_abstract.pdf (accessed 14 Nov. 2007).

Jaccard, Mark, and Nic Rivers. 2007. *Estimating the Effects of the Canadian Government's 2006–2007 Greenhouse Gas Policies.* C.D. Howe Institute Working Paper. Toronto: C.D. Howe Institute.

Jenson, Jane, and Denis Saint-Martin. 2003. 'New Routes to Social Cohesion? Citizenship and the Social Investment State', *Canadian Journal of Sociology* 28 (1): 77–99.

Kenney, Sally J. 2003. 'Where Is Gender in Agenda Setting?' *Women and Politics* 25 (1): 179–204.

Klein, Richard J.T., E. Lisa, F. Schipper, and Suraje Dessai. 2005. 'Integrating Mitigation and Adaptation into Climate and Development Policy: Three Research Questions', *Environmental Science and Policy* 8 (6): 579–88.

Lafferty, William M., and Eivind Hovden. 2003. 'Environmental Policy Integration: Towards an Analytical Framework', *Environmental Politics* 12 (3): 1–22.

Lantis, Jeffrey. 2005. 'Leadership Matters: International Treaty Ratification in Canada and the United States', *American Review of Canadian Studies* 35 (3): 383–422.

Macdonald, Douglas, Debora VanNijnatten, and Andrew Bjorn. 2004. 'Implementing Kyoto: When Spending Is Not Enough'. In G. Bruce Doern, ed., *How Ottawa Spends 2004–2005: Mandate Change in the Paul Martin Era*. Montreal: McGill-Queens' University Press.

Mickwitz, Per, and Paula Kivimaa. 2007. 'Evaluating Policy Integration: The Case of Policies for Environmentally Friendlier Technological Innovations', *Evaluation* 13 (1): 68–86.

Milne, Wendy. 2005. 'Changing Climate, Uncertain Future: Considering Rural Women in Climate Change Policies and Strategies', *Canadian Woman Studies* 24 (4): 49–55.

Nelson, Valerie, Kate Meadows, Terry Cannon, John Morton, and Adrienne Martin. 2002. 'Uncertain Predictions, Invisible Impacts, and the Need to Mainstream Gender in Climate Change Adaptations', *Gender and Development* 10 (2): 51–9.

Page, Bob. 2002. 'The Kyoto Protocol: The Origins of Our Dilemma', *Journal of Business Administration and Policy Analysis* 30–31 (1): 125–48.

Pielke, Roger A., Jr. 2005. 'Misdefining "Climate Change": Consequences for Science and Action', *Environmental Science and Policy* 8 (6): 548–61.

Poumadère, Marc, Claire Mays, Sophie Le Mer, and Russell Blong. 2005. 'The 2003 Heat Wave in France: Dangerous Climate Change Here and Now', *Risk Analysis* 25 (6): 1483–94.

Saint-Martin, Denis. 2004. *Building the New Managerialist State: Consultants and the Politics of Public Sector Reform in Comparative Perspective*. 2nd edn. New York: Oxford University Press.

Schipper, Lisa. 2006. 'Conceptual History of Adaptation in the UNFCCC Process', *Review of European Community and International Environmental Law* 15 (1): 82–92.

Sears, Robin. 2006. 'The Politics of Climate Change: From One Government to the Next', *Policy Options,* October: 6–11.

Skutsch, Margaret, M. 2002. 'Protocols, Treaties, and Action: The "Climate Change Process" Viewed through Gender Spectacles', *Gender and Development* 10 (2): 30–9.

Smith, Heather. 2002. 'Dollar Discourse: The Devaluation of Canada's Natural Capital in Canadian Climate Change Policy'. In Debora VanNijnatten and Robert Boardman, eds, *Canadian Environmental Policy: Context and Cases*. 2nd edn. New York: Oxford University Press.

Status of Women Canada. 2005. *Equality for Women: Beyond the Illusion*. Final report of the Expert Panel on Accountability Mechanisms for Gender Equality. Downloaded from HYPERLINK. http://www.swccfc.gc.ca/resources/panel/report/report_10_e.html.

Thompson, Alexander. 2006. 'Management under Anarchy: The International Politics of Climate Change', *Climatic Change* 78: 7–29.

Van Kooten, G. Cornelis. 2003. 'Smoke and Mirrors: The Kyoto Protocol and Beyond', *Canadian Public Policy* 29 (4): 397–415.

Weldon, Laurel S. 2002. *Protest, Policy, and the Problem of Violence against Women: A Cross-National Comparison*. Pittsburgh: University of Pittsburgh Press.

Yamin, Farhana. 1998. 'The Kyoto Protocol: Origins, Assessment and Future Challenges', *Review of European Community and International Environmental Law* 7 (2): 113–27.

## Further Reading

Bretherton, Charlotte. 1998. 'Global Environmental Politics: Putting Gender on the Agenda?' *Review of International Studies* 24 (1): 85–100.

Milne, Wendy. 2005. 'Changing Climate, Uncertain Future: Considering Rural Women in Climate Change Policies and Strategies', *Canadian Woman Studies* 24 (4): 49–55.

Nelson, Valerie, Kate Meadows, Terry Cannon, John Morton, and Adrienne Martin. 2002. 'Uncertain Predictions, Invisible Impacts, and the Need to Mainstream Gender in Climate Change Adaptations', *Gender and Development* 10 (2): 51–9.

Gender and Climate Change. www.gencc.interconnection.org/.
Gender CC—Women for Climate Justice. www.gendercc.net/.
*Women and Environnent International Magazine.* www.weimag.com/.
United Nations Commission on the Status of Women. www.un.org/womenwatch/daw/csw/.

## Questions for Critical Thought

1. What steps should be taken to mainstream gender in the Canadian climate-change debate?
2. Should governments be obliged to integrate gender into climate-change policy practices?
3. How could governments reduce women's vulnerability to climate change?
4. How can women's voices be more fully incorporated in the national climate-change policy development process?

# CHAPTER 6

# Neo-liberal and Social Investment Re-constructions of Women and Indigeneity

Isabel Altamirano-Jiménez

## Introduction

Over the past few decades, a large body of research has shown how gender relations shape state policies (and vice versa) and that qualitative differences characterize the trajectories of social policy in different countries, particularly under the neo-liberal agenda. However, less attention has been devoted to the connection between internal differences, the institutionalized race inequalities, and the perpetuation of the marginal subject. Generalizations about the constraints the state places on women as a group and the ways in which women have influenced the state ignore the diversity of women and their different political capacities to influence social policy.

This chapter traces changes in key Canadian policies vis-à-vis Indigenous peoples and the ways Indigenous women have been affected. The claim here is that while the gender dimension is crucial to understanding the nature of welfare states, race-biased policies are also embedded in the construction of citizenship, which has historically excluded Indigenous peoples. Consequently, both gender and race intersect and play out in different ways as state priorities change over time. Since its inception, the Canadian welfare state has produced uneven levels of support for Aboriginal women. For instance, discriminatory gender provisions included in the *Indian Act* were not removed until 1985. More recently, the turn from neo-liberalism to a social investment perspective reflects the fact that state policies are still immersed in the Euro-Canadian experience or 'white experience'. Indigenous policies also include new discourses and practices of Indigenous citizenship that serve both to empower Aboriginal women and, contradictorily, to discredit them as subjects. From this perspective, the constituted Indigenous gender identity becomes 'the site of liberation so that cultural identity becomes that which must be modified' (Newdick 2005, 74).

Alastair Bonnett (1999), Michael Eric Dyson (1999), and Ryan Walker (2006) have noted that racism remains a major challenge to building a culturally diverse society. Indigenous peoples' ability to negotiate citizenship is limited by the white experience or 'whiteness', which is a racial identity and social construction that is taught, learned, experienced, and identified in certain forms of knowledge, values, privileges, and dominance, and which has an impact on others (Moreton-Robinson 2000, 246). From this point of view, the redefinition of Indigenous citizenship continues to be embedded in neo-colonial relations of power and political and economic structures of domination that continue to marginalize Indigenous women. At the same time, however, as will become apparent in this chapter, new citizenship discourses and practices respond to current social conditions by constructing Indigenous women as both empowered citizens and victim-subjects.

This chapter elaborates on these contentions and looks at the continuities and changes to neo-liberalism and social investment priorities. The first section reviews the intersections between racialized gender, citizenship, and the welfare state. The second section traces and analyzes the connections between gender, Aboriginal policy, and the rise of neo-liberalism in the 1980s. The third and final section explores the emergence of the social investment perspective and its meaning for Indigenous women.

# Racialized Gender, Citizenship, and Welfare-State Architecture

The progressive realization of social rights as the primary goal of social citizenship was a pillar of many social-democratic welfare states for many years after the end of the Second World War (Kemeny 2001). Social citizenship included notions of equality, which allowed for the accommodation of some universal women's rights and women's movements claims in Canada, particularly in the 1960s and 1970s (Dobrowolsky and Jenson 2004, 155). However, marginalized groups, particularly Aboriginal women, have not been as successful in influencing the state, specifically with regards to enjoying full membership status. Questions of how the welfare state and 'difference' connect and the question of how equality with difference coexists when intersected with gender and race have not been resolved. Although race has been a central component of the definition of citizenship, men and women have different experiences. For example, justification for policies affecting women's reproductive rights fits pre-existing images of poor women as being sexually undisciplined. Equally revealing is the fact that women who challenge abuses within their communities are confronted with ostracism and other forms of disapproval for not being loyal to their communities. Thus, race is itself gendered and marks distinctions between men and women, and such differences become part of the rules and ideologies constructing women in specific ways (Brookes 2002).

As Eileen Boris has noted, race 'is an arena of power, deriving its meaning from political struggle and in turn offering a language through which politics operates and people comprehend their lives' (2003, 10). Colonial discourse and laws defined the status of Indigenous peoples by differentiating them from the white settlers, and dispossessing them of their lands. As a legacy of colonialism, bodies, particularly those of Indigenous women, were objectified. They not only took the form of property, but were also considered as being 'ugly', 'impure', 'savage', and 'sexual'. What results from this process is the all-inclusive and omnipresent division of the world into the familiar places of inside and outside, sacred and profane, public and private, economic and domestic, urban and rural, city and suburb, as well as specific places marked by race and gender. These attributes become the colonized group's experience of racial oppression and the place from which racialized gender is constructed (Tengan 2002).

Colonial governance and the *Indian Act*, the statute that concerns registered 'Indians', their bands, and the reserve system, was enacted in 1876; it gave the federal government exclusive authority to legislate in relation to these peoples and their lands. This legislation was amended numerous times, further limiting Indigenous peoples' mobility and expanding the federal government's control over them. Aboriginal women have experienced the harmful consequences of the *Indian Act*. In paternalistically defining who was and was not 'Indian', the government took away the birthrights of First Nations women and their children. Colonial definition and governance have affected the construction of social provision and the boundaries of inclusion and exclusion within Indigenous communities. From this perspective, the interaction of race and gender is essential to understanding the difference between formal and *de facto* citizenship and the discourses and strategies embedded in policy making and state structures, which have marked citizenship and the rights of people (Boris 1994). Denying citizenship and restricting political agency on the basis of race and gender are strategies that have produced contradictory discourses that both enable some social groups to have power over others and prevent other social groups from having that power.

The evolution of the welfare state and the contemporary transitions to a neo-liberal and social investment state and their impact on marginal groups cannot be fully understood if these racialized gender constructions are not made explicit. The assumption that the fundamental dimensions of Canadian citizenship that have been undermined by neo-liberalism affect everybody equally ignores the fact that, in practice, some groups never had full social rights. As a result, in contexts where discourses of equality and social rights have become more and more difficult to support, marginal groups such as Indigenous women have become even more vulnerable.

# Neo-liberalism and Indigenous Women

The changes Canadian social citizenship experienced in the 1980s were dramatic because they replaced the state–society relationship. Like many other western nations, Canada underwent a period of neo-liberal cuts, which were detrimental to the welfare state and the social fabric. Social policy was reoriented towards the goals of economic integration and privatization, which were seen as the key to domestic well-being (Banting 1996; McKeen and Porter 2003, 125). The neo-liberal transformation undermined universality in favour of major reductions in social programs and the transfer of social-welfare responsibilities from the federal government to the provinces. Moreover, the view that social support was an entitlement of citizenship was replaced by an emphasis on individual responsibility and economic independence, regardless of a person's status in society (Bashevkin 2002; Cohen 1997). This model exacerbated poverty, social and regional disparities, violence, and internal migration, and deepened the experience of racialized gender.

In the neo-liberal model, a new Indigenous citizenship was configured. Historically excluded Indigenous peoples were encouraged to integrate into the global market in order to realize their collective rights to self-government and cultural difference. Like social citizenship, Indigenous citizenship has evolved. As Patricia Wood notes, 'there is citizenship within the Aboriginal nation . . . and there is citizenship within the modern nation-state that has claimed jurisdiction over the former' (2003, 374). Aboriginal women's rights have not been fully protected in either level of citizenship. Indigenous peoples have historically been excluded and became citizens only in the 1960s. Aboriginal women, along with their children, were excluded from band membership and residence for legislative reasons until 1985, precisely the period when neo-liberal citizenship was redefined (see Dobrowolsky in this volume). However, the legislation that was intended to create equality in fact created different categories of people. Green (2001, 716) observes that the abrogation of Indigenous women's citizenship (both Canadian and First Nation) shows that citizenship in Canada has not been fully achieved and that questions about the connections between law and politics and between discourses and practices remain unanswered.

Moreover, as David Mercer (2003) points out, individual rights and universal applicability in liberal democracies are given precedence over the basic collective right of Indigenous political communities to self-determination. Neo-liberal discourse and the assumed neutrality of white Canadian values led to the implementation of modes of service delivery that, on the one hand, equated devolution with self-government and, on the other, praised efficiency. However, they were ineffective for the reality and aspirations of a diverse Aboriginal population (Henry et al. 2000, 388), particularly women.

While activists and scholars have identified the negative effects of neo-liberal policies on the social and economic well-being of women (Larner 2000; Bird Rose 1999; Teghtsoonian 2003), less attention has been given to the unevenness of substantive citizenship between Indigenous peoples and mainstream Canadians and between different groups of Indigenous women (First Nations, Métis and Inuit, and urban Indigenous women). These differences have had important implications for how individuals are defined as competent members and recipients of public resources. Moreover, the ubiquitous power of government policy to intrude into private lives, collective identity, and the self reflects common assumptions about citizenship and how it is constituted (Morrow 2003; Rutman et al. 2000).

## The 1980s

According to Abele, Graham, and Maslove (2000), over the past three decades Indigenous policy in Canada has been guided by four paradigms, each of them based on the identification of specific problems and solutions. Indigenous peoples have moved from being politically irrelevant to having a central role in the reformulation of the relationship between Indigenous peoples and the state. As part of the constitutional politics and economic uncertainty experienced in Canada in the early 1980s, Indigenous people re-emerged as political actors, both defending their treaty rights and pushing for constitutional recognition of Indigenous citizenship in the context of the patriation of the Constitution in 1982 (see Dobrowolsky in this volume). This process, however, resulted in few tangible changes. Indigenous treaty rights were recognized; a new umbrella term was created—'Aboriginal peoples', which included First Nations, Métis, and Inuit peoples; and the Canadian Charter of Rights and Freedoms was entrenched. Later, in 1985, Bill C-31 was passed to override the historical gender provisions of the *Indian Act* that Aboriginal women had been challenging since the 1970s.

These changes have had mixed consequences for First Nations women. The amendments to the *Indian Act* had two objectives: to remove sexist discrimination from regulations determining Indian status and to grant greater autonomy to band councils in determining membership. However, these amendments were challenged by both band leaders and women on different grounds. Band leaders argued that the rights of bands to determine membership were, in fact, being infringed upon. That is, the Act required the bands to restore membership to women who had been stripped of Indian status and band membership because they had married non-Indian men.

Bill C-31 also resulted in new policies that have continued to affect women. Since this bill was enacted, some bands have stopped providing services to non-status Indians and have refused to extend those same services to newly registered women and their children. In some cases, women have been denied fishing licences, and their children have not been admitted into reserve schools and have not received medical services (Holmes 1987, 19). In addition, Bill C-31 has created two classes of Indian status: section 6(1) refers to individuals who have two parents with Indian status, while section 6(2) lists individuals with only one registered parent. Women wanting to register their children must now disclose the father's identity and prove his Indian status. First Nation women have objected to this policy because it intrudes into their personal lives and does not eliminate sexist discrimination, but merely defers it from one generation of women to their descendants. Moreover, women have little legal recourse for redressing their situations because the *Human Rights Act* does not take precedence over the *Indian Act*. John Borrows (2002) has argued that Bill C-31 put limits on Indigenous citizenship on racialized grounds. Although the intentions behind these amendments may have been good, exclusions based on either blood or descent can too easily lead to racism.

A critical legal debate that has developed about Bill C-31 portrays the gender conflict as a conflict between collective and individual rights (AFN 1985; Bear 1991; Fiske 1999; Green 1985, 2001; Holmes 1987; Manyfingers 1986; MacDonald 1986; McIvor, 1995). Collective rights are considered to be threatened by the individual rights protected under the *Constitution Act*, 1982. Sections 15 and 28, which protect individuals' rights to equality, are seen by Indigenous male leaders as conflicting with Aboriginal and treaty rights as provided for in section 25, which explicitly protects against any abrogation or derogation that might arise through conflicting Charter provisions. This debate, which has positioned women's rights as being in conflict with the inherent and constitutional rights of First Nations peoples to self-determined citizenship, has important implications for other policies regarding traditional marital practices, housing, and justice (Bartlett 1986; Cornet 2002). Although the tension is framed as being between gender and self-government, the Canadian state has created and perpetuated the framework in which gender exclusion exists. Bands in Alberta such as the Sawbridge, Sturgeon Lake, Ermineskin, Enoch, Sarcee, and Blackfoot challenged Bill C-31 in the Federal Court of Canada, arguing that the bill was in conflict with the constitutional protection of existing Aboriginal and treaty rights. By forcing membership codes to conform to Canada's Bill of Rights, the bill denies bands the right to define their own self-governing laws (Holmes 1987, 21). These challenges illustrate that issues involving women's rights and membership are extremely divisive and can perpetuate the double marginality of Indigenous women.

The arguments against Bill C-31 have focused on limiting self-government because of the discriminatory practices against women. However, this conflict also reflects the lack of resources for dealing with the number of people that were regaining status. Right after the bill was passed, the Mulroney government made cutbacks to two programs of critical importance to the Indigenous people regaining status: the off-reserve housing program was reduced, and the funding for

Aboriginal post-secondary students was severely restricted. Although the housing crisis affects Aboriginal peoples in general, Aboriginal women are particularly vulnerable. The cuts in the budgets of government programs and organizations representing Aboriginal women have also severely damaged their ability to influence Aboriginal policy. Arguably, the challenges facing Indigenous women are the result of a complex system of oppression involving race, colonization, rules, institutions, and traditions. However, violence against women and gender discrimination are often cast as a cultural problem, a distinctive mark of otherness attributed to Aboriginal people. This construction of the woman-victim-subject conceals the multiple social markers and power relations that structure social, economic, and political systems and social policies.

In keeping with a neo-liberal approach, Aboriginal self-government was presented as a way of producing wealth and enabling 'Indians, Inuit, and Métis to play their full roles as active and important contributors to the national economy' (Mulroney 1985). Self-government was envisioned as promoting Aboriginal 'entrepreneurship' and 'productive', 'happy lives'. At the same time, the concept of self-government was translated into the transfer of some administrative responsibilities from the state to Indigenous institutions (Ekstedt 1999). Neo-liberal discourse, which emphasized self-government and control over locally delivered services and one's personal well-being, assumed that all communities are capable of self-government. However, Aboriginal peoples were not considered fully capable, so self-government provided some autonomy and devolution of some services, but preserved state and provincial control over the terms of Indigenous development (Alfred 1999). Tripartite action, or the active participation of the federal and provincial governments and Aboriginal leaders, became the major tenet of the government's Indigenous policies. This policy has undermined national Aboriginal policies and produced a complex infrastructure with many grey areas, where neither the federal nor the provincial government takes responsibility.

In the early 1990s, the Canadian government continued to emphasize Indigenous self-government. In this understanding of self-government, 'partnership' and 'decentralization' were crucial in order to deliver child and family services. The idea was to build Indigenous peoples' capacities for the future. However, as will be shown in the next section, these targets continued to be embedded in racialized gendered constructions of identity, moral assumptions, and discourses that empower Indigenous women as citizens while discrediting them as subjects.

## Social Investment

Critiques of neo-liberalism, along with the elimination of the federal deficit in 1998, brought new possibilities for social policy change, in particular targeted investment. In the late 1990s, the Liberal government began to invoke a new discourse aimed at seeking a balanced approach and addressing new priorities, arrangements, and agreements (Dobrowolsky and Saint-Martin 2005; Jenson and Saint-Martin 2003; McKeen and Porter 2003; Lister 2003). The 'social investment state', a term coined by Anthony Giddens (1998), was associated with the 'third way', or a middle ground, between neo-liberalism and the postwar welfare state. Among the elements Giddens emphasized were entrepreneurship, portability of achievements and entitlements, and public partnerships (1998, 124–7).

While the social investment model still positions the free market as the primary and most effective organizing principle in society, this market is no longer the so-called untamed market. Instead, it is recognized that government intervention is necessary to direct the market forces towards improving both economic and social outcomes. Like neo-liberalism, the social investment perspective also includes the redefinition of citizenship discourses and practices. As Dobrowolsky and Jenson (2004, 155) have shown, this shift moves away from a discourse of rights to a discourse of duties. Citizenship rights can only be achieved if partnerships are created between an investment state and an active and responsible civil society (Lister 2003, 437).

Under the social investment state, Indigenous citizenship is closely connected with Indigenous communities entering the market through a resource-extraction model of development, and with a commitment to human rights. Yet, as will be shown in the next section, this shift to a social investment state agenda is also embedded in values and notions of the victim-subject, which is deepening a contested Indigenous politics of rights, identity, property, and governance that focuses on collective versus individual rights and women's rights versus self-government. These values and notions not only obscure women's agency but also show the effectiveness of reproducing the victim-subject.

## The 1990s

In the early 1990s, the Chrétien government continued to emphasize self-government but moved away from constitutional recognition. Instead, neo-liberal individualism framed two important issues: land and resource development and authority over child welfare, which were perceived to have serious implications for power relations between Aboriginal peoples and non-Aboriginal peoples. The main purpose of the Chrétien Aboriginal policy was to fight poverty and discrimination by connecting self-government with economic development and investing in the future Aboriginal generations to help them get a fair start in life.

Although the emphasis was on self-government, Aboriginal peoples' capacity for self-government was constantly questioned in the mass media. Discourses of collective and personal control and the failure to reverse conditions of life became constructed as a 'lifestyle' issue rather than as failure to uphold federal policy (Harding 2005). Such failure was linked directly to public concerns about the cost of programs administered by First Nations and the public desire for First Nations accountability, which would become a major concern in the late 1990s. This situation shows the challenges Indigenous peoples face while negotiating Indigenous citizenship within a changing welfare architecture (Walker 2006, 395) and also of how whiteness undermines some groups' claims and gives precedence to others. Thus, the questioning of Aboriginal peoples' ability for self-government is used to justify government intervention in how this right is defined and exercised.

The federal government's goal was to implement a 'certainty policy', which connected self-government to economic development. However, only those Indigenous communities ready to negotiate modern treaties on the basis of their needs and interests rather than their rights were considered in this approach. The goal of this policy was to create stability and certainty for investors through the signing of modern treaties focusing on development. According to this approach, economic development would provide new opportunities and jobs for Aboriginal peoples, regardless of their gender, and would end Indigenous peoples' dependence on state programs (Ratner et al. 2003, 218). In other words, the self-sufficiency of Aboriginal peoples, as advanced through land-claim agreements, depends upon the commercial exploitation of natural resources (Slowey 2001, 118). In 1995, the Chrétien government approach was formalized with the 'Aboriginal Self-Government Policy', which recognized the inherent right to self-government in an abstract sense but did not recognize that any particular First Nation had the right on the ground. Though it aimed at fulfilling the Aboriginal policy goals commitment to recognize the inherent right of self-government, the government policy required individual First Nations peoples to negotiate with the federal government the terms under which such a right would be exercised and the areas that would fall under Aboriginal jurisdiction. Self-government power jurisdictions included law-making authority over marriage and property rights on reserves. However, Indigenous women were not represented at the land-claim negotiation table.

Many First Nations' leaders rejected this policy. It recognized the inherent right to self-government, but negotiation over this right made it a contingent right, a right dependent on reaching agreements with federal and provincial authorities. Moreover, the emphasis on individual negotiations has produced additional inequities among and between First Nations and other Aboriginal peoples such as the Inuit, and between on-reserve and off-reserve Aboriginals. Furthermore, beyond the political and financial arrangements of self-government, one of the most contentious issues is the connection between self-government, the Canadian Charter of Rights and Freedoms, and gender discrimination. Once again, the tensions among self-government, collective rights, women's rights, and individual rights are being interpreted as an internal Aboriginal problem.

According to Bird Rose (1999), this approach is completely embedded in a neo-liberal discourse that conceptualizes discrimination against women as cultural, and marginal and Indigenous peoples as dependent on welfare. This policy approach has not only been gender-blind but has been deeply embedded in inaccurate colonial representations of women as landless and domestically placed. Since gender is subsumed under the notion of collective rights, the female category is submerged under the male (Van Woudenberg 2004, 6). The institutional gendered consequences of this approach extend beyond land-claim negotiations. For instance, the entities mandated to hold and distribute the compensation funds provided through an agreement do not guarantee equal representation of women and men, nor ensure that women have equal access to these funds. As part of the Nunavut land claims agreement, the Tungavik Federation of Nunavut (TFN) negotiated wildlife income support with the Northwest Territories government and agreed 'to narrow the focus of the program from the "household" to the "hunter" ' (Archibald and Crnkovich 1999, 8). This agreement 'fit within an existing government initiative where hunters (primarily men) were provided with small amounts of funds to subsidize gas and repairs to machines used for harvesting' (1999, 8). The shift from the 'household' to the 'hunter' not only valued men's activities rather than women's but also provided men with more material compensation.

'Women's inequality is a likely outcome of a land claims policy that promotes large-scale resource development' (Archibald and Crnkovich 1999, 12), for employment opportunities are promoted mainly in male-dominated areas such as mining, forestry, and fishing. In addition, since most development projects take place outside of the communities, employees must work away from their communities and families for long periods. Because Aboriginal women are the main family caregivers, they seldom benefit from these employment opportunities (1999, 17). Thus, gender-blind development projects have only accentuated gender discrimination.

Besides land and economic development, the other issue in the debate about Indigenous self-government has to do with child welfare. While control over land and resources has direct economic implications for both Aboriginal and non-aboriginal peoples, child welfare can be seen as a symbolic battleground where the inherent right and ability of Aboriginal people to govern themselves and exercise control over their own lives is at stake (Harding 2005, 22). Since policy is ideologically constructed, it tends to perpetuate the dominant normative ideals regarding culture and gender (MacDonald 1986). In the mass media and legal discourses, Aboriginal women are often portrayed as victims of violence, a high-risk lifestyle, and substance addictions, who are necessarily 'marginalized' and 'welfare-dependent' and who lack parenting skills.

As a result, discourses, policies, and institutions that focus on the child as the centre of social investment become particularly challenging for Aboriginal women. This focus does not interfere with the market priorities of neo-liberalism and, though it does reflect a more communitarian ethos, it also conveniently prevents governments from addressing specific identities such as gender, race, and class, and ultimately it promotes greater individual freedom and choice (Dobrowolsky and Saint-Martin 2005, 8). By stereotyping Indigenous peoples, the dominant society is able to question Indigenous peoples' claims, aspirations, and capabilities and to justify government's intervention in Indigenous and family matters (Tait 2000, 95).

Indigenous communities have consistently rejected these representations of themselves and the *Child, Family and Community Services Act* for not recognizing the cultural, historical, and social circumstances of Aboriginal peoples. Childcare has been particularly symbolic for Indigenous peoples because of the negative effects of racist and colonial practices in childcare development, which continue to exist since Aboriginal children are still being placed outside the Aboriginal community.

In 1992, the Aboriginal Community Panel released a report entitled *Liberating Our Children, Liberating Our Nations*. This document recommended a radical new approach to child-welfare policy for Aboriginal peoples, one in which the distinctive Aboriginal historical experience would be recognized and an Aboriginal right to self-determination would be acknowledged. At a time when large-scale cuts had been made to health and welfare budgets, the chances of developing the preventative side of the child-welfare system seemed remote.

The Aboriginal approach associated self-government with history, and it underlined the connections between child, family, and community. The proposal emphasized the need to develop culturally appropriate ways of meeting the structural challenges facing Aboriginal children. A number of reports and studies, including the report of the Royal Commission on Aboriginal Peoples (RCAP 1996), have emphasized the need to consider women's perspectives and knowledge, the impact of colonization on gender roles, and the interconnectedness of women to family, community, and nation when defining Indigenous policies.

The Aboriginal Head Start Program was designed to invest in Aboriginal children. It was first implemented in urban and northern communities in 1995, and then was expanded in 1998 to include Aboriginals on reserve. The main target of this program was Aboriginal children and youth, and its main goal was to build a positive identity and empower parents and communities to foster the growth of every child in order to achieve 'positive outcomes' (Holland Stairs and Bernhard 2002). The assumption behind this program was that abilities, intelligence, wisdom, good care, and motherhood were universally defined across cultures. Therefore, whereas the report *Liberating Our Children, Liberating Our Nations* emphasized the need for a culturally appropriate, holistic approach that connects self-government and child welfare, some components of the Head Start program were aimed at developing Aboriginal women's parenting skills, such as those involving first aid, breast feeding, prenatal care, and early childhood development and nutrition. This focus shifts 'problems' back onto the Aboriginal subject's lifestyle and away from the racialized and gendered structures, processes, and relations of power. This disavowal of Indigenous women's capacity for agency and self-governance has profound implications for every aspect of Aboriginal policy.

The increase in poverty and disadvantage amongst Aboriginal people suggests that policies for Aboriginal children and youth have failed, not only because of the policies themselves, but also because of the uneven funding allocated to different Aboriginal peoples and non-Indigenous children. The National Council of Welfare's *Report on First Nations, Métis and Inuit Children and Youth* (NCW 2007a) found that, on average, First Nations children's and family-service agencies were receiving 22 per cent less funding per child than their provincial counterparts, despite the documented higher Aboriginal child-welfare needs. This report also documented the fact that Indigenous women are more likely to be single mothers and to live in poverty than women in any other social group.

The different government policies developed in the 1990s continued to erode the political, economic, and social significance of gender experience. The Gathering Strength Policy of 1998 was a government response to the Royal Commission Report (RCAP 1996), which emphasized the need to establish a more comprehensive approach and a nation-to-nation relationship with Aboriginal peoples. The government response focused instead on recognizing past mistakes and injustices; renewing partnerships among the federal, provincial and territorial governments, Aboriginal peoples, and the private sector; strengthening Aboriginal governance; developing a fiscal relationship; and supporting economic development. Although this policy recognized that the state itself had caused the current situation of Aboriginal peoples, the policy on self-government did not change. Indigenous women feared that Aboriginal self-government, as promoted by the government and envisioned by the male Aboriginal leadership, was nothing more than a continuation of gender discrimination and oppression.

To put an end to gender discrimination and further promote Indigenous development, the Chrétien government implemented a policy aimed at extending the property-rights regime. The *First Nations Land Management Act*, 1999, allowed participating First Nations to develop their own land codes for administering their reserve lands and matrimonial property rights. Like other previous Aboriginal policies during the Chrétien era, this act was implemented on a voluntary basis.

## The 2000s: A Third Way for Indigenous Peoples?

In his final years as prime minister, Chrétien moved further away from the agenda of the RCAP. Among his final projects was the *First Nations Governance*

*Act*, which focused on making Indigenous governance more accountable. Once again, the chiefs opposed this policy because it violated the Aboriginal right to self-government. This opposition was strong enough that Paul Martin, who became prime minister in 2003, was forced to withdraw the draft legislation. Instead he held high-profile meetings with Aboriginal organizations and provincial and territorial governments, which culminated in the Meeting of First Ministers and National Aboriginal Leaders in Kelowna in November 2005.

In the document entitled *First Ministers and National Aboriginal Leaders Strengthening Relationships and Closing the Gap*, also known as the Kelowna Accord, all the negotiating parties agreed on the need to close the socio-economic gaps between Aboriginal and non-Aboriginal Canadians and to end discrimination against Aboriginal women. These parties acknowledged that in Canadian cities, half of all Aboriginal children are members of lone-parent families living in poverty, and that some of the most devastating obstacles that have, for far too long, afflicted the lives of Aboriginal women, the lives of their children, and the health of their communities had to be removed. The historic Accord committed $5.1 billion dollars to Canada's Aboriginal population. The federal, provincial, and Aboriginal organizations agreed on targeting areas, such as education, health, housing, infrastructure, and economic opportunities, that are critical to Indigenous peoples. In general, the Accord envisioned a large-scale investment in education targeted at Indigenous peoples and tailored to their specific linguistic and cultural characteristics. The Accord's ultimate goal was to combat poverty by increasing investment in human and social capital and promoting Aboriginal peoples' productive success in both market and non-market activities (Library of Parliament 2005). Like the neo-liberal model, the social investment state still positions the free market as the primary and most effective organizing principle in society. However, the latter assumes that government intervention is necessary to direct market forces in order to improve both economic and social outcomes (Perkins et al. 2004, 2). Like neo-liberalism, the investment state also redefines citizenship discourses and practices to emphasize individual duties over rights.

During his campaign, Stephen Harper noted that Aboriginal issues would become a priority for his government. His approach has followed a different path than that of the Kelowna Accord. According to the Conservative government, the emphasis in the Kelowna Accord on on-reserve Indigenous peoples does not make sense because half of the one million Canadians identified as Aboriginal in the 2001 Census live in urban settings. The Harper government insists on the need to realign federal Aboriginal expenditures and development. Furthermore, it has moved away from gender and equality issues. However, the victim-subject continues to exist. The neo-liberal ideology and the discourse of human rights continue to perpetuate a hierarchy in which certain peoples and places fall into the margins. In this approach, the treatment of women signals either progress or failure toward democracy and development. Thus, the treatment of Aboriginal women and the gender discrimination they face is cast as a cultural problem, rather than as a consequence of the state's racialized gender policies. Within this scheme, the construction of the victim-subject elides the multiple social markers and power relations that structure social, economic, and political systems.

The election of the Conservative government in 2006 significantly shifted the terms of the Aboriginal policy debate in Canada. The Harper government represents not only a continuation of market-based neo-liberalism, but also a shift that will likely alter both the framework and nature of social policy discussions (Porter 2006). The Conservative agenda promotes a new type of social and economic order that implies not only the continuation of privatization and market-oriented solutions, but also the promotion of certain ways of intruding into the lives of families and women. In terms of the Aboriginal policy, the two pillars of the Conservative government are economic development and human rights, while self-government has a lower profile.

This Aboriginal policy focuses on strategies and programs to alleviate Aboriginal poverty that are grounded in common sense and the acceptance of everyone's responsibility. Under the Conservative policy, *everyone* involved must accept responsibility and get equally involved. Unlike other governments, the Harper government has stated that a new relationship between Aboriginal peoples and the government is unnecessary, for all that is needed is to make the existing relationship work. The government's commitment to Aboriginal peoples focuses on empowering Indigenous citizens while protecting the vulnerable (Harper 2007). To the Harper government, the extension of the *Human Rights Act* to the *Indian Act* would protect Indigenous Canadians, particularly women. However, extending the *Human Rights Act* to Indigenous peoples has been extremely controversial. While it has been acknowledged that the Act has a role to play in the advancement of the human rights of Aboriginal women, it should not be interpreted as abrogating Aboriginal collective rights (NWAC 2007).

Ironically, under the Harper government, the word 'equality' has become obsolete. This government decided that organizations would no longer be eligible for funding for advocacy, government lobbying, or research projects. As part of the new terms and conditions, the Status of Women Canada eliminated 'equality' from its mandate. These decisions have important implications for all women but particularly for Aboriginal women. Pay inequity is still the rule. Women still make only 71 cents for every dollar earned by a man, Aboriginal women only 46 cents. While 0.67 per cent of non-Aboriginal children need child welfare, 3.31 per cent of Métis children and 10.23 per cent of status Indian children receive welfare (National Welfare Council 2007b).

Government cuts to programs have also limited women's resources. For close to twenty years, First Nations women have fought to reverse the sexual discrimination in the *Indian Act* and to restore equal Indian status to First Nations women and their descendants. In 2007, in a case brought forward by Sharon McIvor dealing with gender discrimination, the Supreme Court ordered the federal government to remove any trace of gender discrimination from the *Indian Act*. The government decided to appeal this ruling; it also ended the Court Challenges Program, which would have assisted McIvor financially in taking her case to court once again. This government's actions seem to contradict the human-rights arguments used to advance the *Human Rights Act*. While one of the policies enables Aboriginal women to challenge Aboriginal governments, the other prevents these same women from challenging federal government legislation. In other words, the government promotes equality at the Indigenous-nation level but undermines citizenship at the national state level.

This situation not only exacerbates the challenges Indigenous women face within their communities, but also perpetuates the widespread mistreatment of Aboriginal women, who seek to secure the same rights as those of other women. Matrimonial property rights have been an important yet controversial issue in the 'cultural gender war' since 1986, when the Supreme Court of Canada ruled that provincial and territorial laws on matrimonial real property do not apply to reserve land. This decision created a gap in the law which has had serious consequences for Aboriginal women.

The report by the Native Women's Association of Canada (NWAC) on matrimonial property rights showed that women do experience greater disadvantages and are allocated fewer property certificates of possession than men. The study also showed that a greater percentage of Aboriginal women than men live off-reserve and that the differences between on- and off-reserve suggest that matrimonial real property has an uneven impact on where a child lives. While the report acknowledged that matrimonial property rights would greatly benefit women, the report was careful to emphasize a more holistic approach for dealing with women's rights (NWAC 2007). It also called for solutions that are based on Indigenous peoples' traditions, that accommodate human rights, and that acknowledge the traditionally strong role of First Nations women in their communities.

The federal government's goal of privatizing property on reserves so that valuable property can be sold, mortgaged, or used to fight poverty is implicitly linked to the issue of matrimonial property. Similarly, the government response to the Seventh Report of the Standing Committee on Aboriginal Affairs and Northern Development on Aboriginal Housing was that structural reforms are needed to address the housing needs of Aboriginal peoples through the promotion of market-based housing, including individual ownership and private rental housing (Canada, Parliament 2007).

This suggestion seems to take the *First Nations Land Management Act*, 1998, a step forward by transforming land into a commodity and questioning

Indigenous peoples' connections to the land in name of a better future. Battles for individual land ownership and matrimonial property rights are seen as strategies women have adopted to claim rights to land. Because Indigenous women's ties to land have been mediated by the Canadian state and women's relationship with men in a patriarchal society, women's attempts to assert their rights are often perceived by male Indigenous leaders as an attempt to disrupt gender relations. Ironically, these women's actions are regarded by non-Aboriginals as a liberating battle against the backwardness of their cultures. Thus, like race, culture can also be used to conceal the structural sources of discrimination against Aboriginal women.

The negotiation of Indigenous citizenship in the neo-liberal and social investment states cannot be fully understood if racialized gender constructions are not considered. The assumption that the fundamental dimensions of Canadian citizenship have been undermined by the neo-liberal state and that the redefinition of citizenship has consequences for women ignores the fact that, in practice, Indigenous women continue to fight for their citizenship rights. The constant tensions around collective rights, individual rights, women's rights, and self-government show that Aboriginal women's rights are still far from being realized and that gender discrimination within Indigenous communities is constructed by governments and the mass media as an anomaly that is inherent in Indigenous cultures. Therefore, human-rights discourses disguise the role that the state has played in creating and perpetuating the exclusion of Indigenous women from citizenship in both the national state and the Indigenous nation. Government policies aimed at reversing these discriminatory conditions justify interfering with self-government, on the grounds of rescuing women from their own culture. The transformation of this rhetoric conceals the colonial economic uncertainty of Aboriginal peoples, which continues to exist within economic structures that favour some social groups over others (Fiske and Browne 2006, 94).

Several studies (RCAP 1996; Amnesty International 2004) have shown that despite new, partial Aboriginal policies, the conditions of life in Indigenous communities have not changed and will not change without a long-term policy. Indigenous organizations have produced their own reports emphasizing the urgent need for action. The *Solving Poverty* report (NCW 2007b) advises the federal government on the cornerstones of a workable, national strategy for solving poverty, a strategy that should be connected to larger economic, social, and political issues. In particular, the report warns that factors such as racism and gender discrimination, which put Aboriginal women, men, and children, at greater risk than others, must be addressed. The elimination of the equality mandate and cuts to housing and healthcare have worsened the conditions of life of Aboriginal women overall. The First Nations campaign to make poverty history and to create new opportunities demands that the government act to remedy the disadvantages, discrimination, and poverty facing Aboriginal women beyond Indigenous communities.

This campaign also emphasized that Aboriginal peoples are very diverse, so policies for removing barriers must also be diverse. Despite racial prejudice, off-reserve Aboriginals have significantly higher employment rates, incomes, and education levels than on-reserve Aboriginals. The urban population is increasing and thus posing a challenge to social services. Aboriginal people are receiving services from three orders of governments—federal, provincial, and band-based. The tensions between the commitment to Aboriginal self-government and the ideal of constrained spending imply that Canadians perceive that culturally based Aboriginal services are beneficial but are also a financial burden, particularly since Aboriginal populations are growing at twice the rate of the Canadian population (Health Canada, First Nations and Inuit Health Branch 2002, quoted in Fiske and Browne 2006). These racialized constructions have shaped a contradictory dynamic where recognition of Aboriginal women's rights is problematized only at the level of the Indigenous nation while their citizenship rights at the level of the national state remain limited.

## Conclusions

Government policies are inextricably linked to the dominant ideology, and they serve to justify who is empowered and who is silenced. The discursive framing of Aboriginal women's rights and citizenship reveals itself as intricate intersections of racist assumptions, moral judgments, and government intervention that have been reproduced within the neo-liberal and social investment approaches. The development of the welfare state and the assumed neutrality of white Canadian values have led to Aboriginal policies and modes of service delivery that have praised efficiency and accountability, but have been of limited effectiveness for Aboriginal peoples, particularly women.

Aboriginal policies, which are intertwined with explicit resistance to Indigenous entitlements, construct Indigenous peoples as a policy issue, not as knowing subjects; Indigenous women as victim-subjects, not as agents of change; and their socio-economic, racial, and political conditions as social and cultural problems to be solved. From this perspective, Aboriginal policies reproduce racialized constructions of the victim-subject, who remains on the margins of citizenship and waits for the state to rescue her.

### References

Abele, Frances, Katherine Graham, and Allan Maslove. 2000. 'Negotiating Canada: Changes in Aboriginal Policy over the Last Thirty Years'. In Leslie Pal, ed., *How Ottawa Spends 1999–2000*. Toronto: Oxford University Press.

AFN. *See* Assembly of First Nations.

Alfred, Taiaiake. 1999. *Peace, Power, Righteousness: An Indigenous Manifesto*. Oxford: Oxford University Press.

Amnesty International. 2004. *Stolen Sisters: A Human Rights Response to Discrimination and Violence against Indigenous Women in Canada*. http://www.amnesty.ca/campaigns/sisters_overview.php.

Anthony, Giddens. 1998. *The Third Way: The Renewal of Social Democracy*. Cambridge: Polity Press.

Archibald, Linda, and Mary Crnkovich. 1999. 'If Gender Mattered: A Case Study of Inuit Women, Land Claims and the Voisey's Bay Nickel Project'. http://www.swc-cfc.gc.ca/pubs/pubspr/0662280024/199911_0662280024_e.html (accessed 15 Jan. 2008).

Assembly of First Nations (AFN). 1985. *Sexual Discrimination in the Indian Act and First Nations Jurisdiction*. Report to the Special Assembly of First Nations. Ottawa.

Banting, Keith. 1996. 'Social Policy'. In G. Bruce Doern, Leslie A. Pal, and Brian W. Tomlin, eds, *Border Crossings: The Internationalization of Canadian Public Policy*, 27–54. Don Mills, Ont.: Oxford University Press.

Bartlett, Richard. 1986. 'Indian Self-government, the Equality of the Sexes, and Application of Provincial Matrimonial Property Laws', *Canadian Journal of Family Law* 5 (1): 188–95.

Bashevkin, Sylvia. 2002. *Welfare Hot Buttons: Women, Work, and Social Policy Reform*. Toronto: University of Toronto Press.

Bear, Shirley. 1991. 'You Can't Change the *Indian Act*?' In Jeri Dawn Wine and Janice L. Ristock, eds, *Women and Social Change: Feminist Activism in Canada*. Toronto: Lorimer.

Bird Rose, Deborah. 1999. 'Land Rights and Deep Colonising: The Erasure of Women', *Aboriginal Law Journal* 3 (85): 6–14.

Bonnett, Alastair. 1999. 'Constructions of Whiteness in European and American Anti-Racism'. In R.D. Torres, L.F. Miron, and J.X. Inda, eds, *Race, Identity, and Citizenship: A Reader*. Malden, Mass.: Blackwell.

Boris, Eileen. 1994. 'Gender, Race, and Rights: Listening to Critical Race Theory'. *Journal of Women's History* 6 (2): 111–24.

———. 2003. 'From Gender to Racialized Gender: Laboring Bodies That Matter', *International Labor and Working-Class History* 63: 9–13.

Borrows, John. 2002. *Recovering Canada: The Resurgence of Indigenous Law*. Toronto: University of Toronto Press.

Brookes, Barbara. 2002 'Gender, Work and Fears of a 'Hybrid Race' in 1920s New Zealand', *Gender and History* 19 (3): 501–18.

Canada. Parliament. 2007. Standing Committee on Aboriginal Housing. Government response to the seventh report of the Standing Committee on Aboriginal Housing. http://www2.parl.gc.ca/HousePublications/Publication.aspx?DocId=3077327&Language=E&Mode=1&Parl=39&Ses=1.

Cohen, Marjorie. 1997. 'From the Welfare State to Vampire Capitalism'. In Gerde Wekerle and Patricia Evans, eds, *Women and the Canadian Welfare State*, 28–67. Toronto: University of Toronto Press.

Cornet, Wendy. 2002. *Discussion Paper: Matrimonial Real Property on Reserve*. Ottawa: Indian and Northern Affairs Canada.

Dobrowolsky, Alexandra, and Jane Jenson. 2004. 'Shifting Representations of Citizenship: Canadian Politics of "Women" and Children', *Social Policy* 11 (2): 154–80.

———, and Denis Saint-Martin. 2005. 'Agency, Actors and Change in a Child Focused Future: "Path Dependency" Problematised', *Commonwealth and Comparative Politics* 43 (1): 1–33.

Dyson, M.E. 1999. 'The Labor of Whiteness, the Whiteness of Labor, and the Perils of White-wishing'. In R.D. Torres, L.F. Miron, and J.X. Inda, eds, *Race, Identity, and Citizenship: A Reader*. Malden, Mass.: Blackwell.

Ekstedt, J.W. 1999. 'International Perspectives on Aboriginal Self-government'. In J.H. Hylton, ed., *Aboriginal Self-government in Canada: Current Trends and Issues*. 2nd edn. Saskatoon: Purich.

Fiske, Jo-Anne. 1999. 'The Womb Is to the Nation as the Heart Is to the Body: Ethnopolitical Discourses of the Canadian Indigenous Women's Movement'. In Pat Armstrong and M. Patricia Connelly, eds, *Feminism, Political Economy and the State: Contested Terrain*. Toronto: Canadian Scholars Press.

———, and Annette J. Browne. 2006. 'Aboriginal Citizen, Discredited Medical Subject: Paradoxical Constructions of Aboriginal Women's Subjectivity in Canadian Health Care Policies', *Policy Sciences* 39 (1): 91–111.

Giddens, Anthony. 1998. *The Third Way: The Renewal of Social Democracy*. Cambridge: Polity Press.

Green, Joyce. 1985. 'Sexual Equality and Indian Government: An Analysis of Bill C-31 Amendments to the Indian Act', *Native Studies Review* 1 (2): 81–95.

———. 2001. 'Canaries in the Mines of Citizenship: Indian Women in Canada', *Canadian Journal of Political Science* 34 (4): 715–38.

Harding, Robert. 2005. 'The Media, Aboriginal People and Common Sense', *Canadian Journal of Native Studies* 25 (1): 311–35.

Harper, Stephen. 2007. Speech on the Government Achievements for Aboriginal Peoples. Halifax, 2 November. http://www.pm.gc.ca/eng/media.asp?id=1885.

Health Canada. 2002. First Nations and Inuit Health Branch. *Mandate and Priorities*. http://www.hc-sc.gc.ca.fnihb/mandate_priorities.htm. Quoted in Fiske and Brown, 2006.

Henry, Frances, C. Tator, W. Mattis, and T. Rees. 2000. *The Colour of Democracy: Racism in Canadian Society*. 2nd edn. Toronto: Harcourt Brace Canada.

Holland Stairs, Arlene, and Judith K. Bernhard. 2002. 'Considerations for Evaluating 'Good Care' in Canadian Aboriginal Early Childhood Settings', *McGill Journal of Education* 37 (3): 309–30.

Holmes, Joan. 1987. *Bill C-31: Equality or Disparity? The Effects of the New Indian Act on Native Women*. Ottawa: Canadian Advisory Council on the Status of Women. Available at http://www.ainc-inac.gc.ca/pr/pub/matri/iob_e.html.

Jenson, Jane, and Denis Saint-Martin. 2003. 'New Routes to Social Cohesion? Citizenship and the Social Investment State', *Canadian Journal of Sociology* 28 (1): 77–99.

Kemeny, Jim. 2001. 'Comparative Housing and Welfare: Theorising the Relationship', *Journal of Housing and the Built Environment* 16: 53–70.

Larner, Wendy. 2000. 'Neo-liberalism: Policy, Ideology, Governmentality', *Studies in Political Economy* 63: 5–25.

Lister, Ruth. 2003. 'Investing in the Citizen-Workers of the Future: Transformations in Citizenship and the State under New Labour', *Social Policy and Administration* 37 (5): 427–43.

Library of Parliament. 2005. *Aboriginal Roundtable to Kelowna Accord: Aboriginal Policy Negotiations, 2004–2005*. http://www.parl.gc.ca/information/library.prbpubs/prb0604-e.html.

MacDonald, Christine. 2003. 'The Value of Discourse Analysis as a Methodological Tool for Understanding a Land Reform Program', *Policy Sciences* 36 (2): 151–73.

MacDonald, Michael. 1986. 'Indian Status: Colonialism or Sexism?' *Canadian Community Law Journal* 9: 23–48.

McIvor, Sharon. 1995. 'Aboriginal Women's Rights as "Existing Rights"', *Canadian Woman Studies/Les Cahiers de la Femme* 15 (2&3): 34–8.

McKeen, Wendy, and Ann Porter. 2003. 'Politics and Transformation: Welfare State Restructuring in Canada'. In Wallace Clement and Leah Vosko, eds, *Changing Canada: Political Economy as Transformation*. Montreal: McGill-Queens University Press.

Manyfingers, Martha. 1986. 'Determination of Indian Band Membership: An Examination of Political Will', *Canadian Journal of Native Studies* 6 (1): 63–75.

Mercer, David. 2003. '"Citizen Minus"? Indigenous Australians and the Citizenship Question', *Citizenship Studies* 7 (4): 421–45.

Moreton-Robinson, Aileen. 2000. 'Duggaibah, or "Place of Whiteness": Australian Feminists and Race'. In Jonh Docker and Gerhard Fischer, eds, *Race, Colour and Identity in Australia and New Zealand*. Sydney: UNSW Press.

Morrow, M. 2003. *Mainstreaming Women's Mental Health: Building a Canadian Strategy*. Vancouver: British Columbia Centre of Excellence for Women's Health.

Mulroney, Brian. 1985. Notes for an Opening Statement to the Conference of First Ministers on the Rights of Aboriginal Peoples. Cited in Menno Boldt and J. Anthony Long, eds, *The Quest for Justice: Aboriginal Peoples and Aboriginal Rights*. Toronto: University of Toronto Press.

National Council of Welfare (NCW). 2007a. *First Nations, Métis and Inuit Children and Youth: Time to Act*. http://www.ncwcnbes.net/en/research/TimeToAct-AgissonsMaintenant.html.

———. 2007b. *Solving Poverty: Four Cornerstones of a Workable National Strategy for Canada*. http://www.ncwcnbes.net/en/publications/pub-126.html.

Native Women Association of Canada (NWAC). 2007. *Reclaiming Our Way of Being: Matrimonial Real Property Solutions*. Ottawa: NWAC.

NCW. *See* National Council of Welfare.

Newdick, Vivian. 2005. 'The Indigenous Woman as Victim of Her Own Culture in Neoliberal Mexico', *Cultural Dynamics* 17 (1): 73–92.

NWAC. *See* Native Women Association of Canada.

Perkins, Daniel, Lucy Nelms, and Paul Smyth. 2004. 'Beyond Neo-liberalism: The Social Investment State?' Social Policy Working Paper 3. Melbourne: Centre for Public Policy, University of Melbourne, and the Brotherhood of St Laurence.

Porter, Ann. 2006. 'The Harper Government: Towards a New Social Order?' Socialist Project E-Bulletin 21. http://www.socialistproject.ca/bullet/bullet021.html.

Ratner, R.S., William K. Carroll, and Andrew Woolford. 2003. 'Wealth of Nations: Aboriginal Treaty Making in the Era of Globalization'. In John Torpey, ed., *Politics and the Past: On Reparing Historical Injustices*. Lanham, Md.: Rowman and Littlefield.

RCAP. *See* Royal Commission on Aboriginal Peoples.

Royal Commission on Aboriginal Peoples. 1996. *Report*. Volume 4, *Perspectives and Realities*, Chap. 2, 'Women's Perspective'. Ottawa: Minister of Supply and Services.

Rutman, D., M. Callahan, A. Lundquist, S. Jackson, and B. Field. 2000. *Substance Use and Pregnancy: Conceiving Women in the Policy-Making Process*. Ottawa: Status of Women Canada.

Slowey, Gabrielle A. 2001. 'Globalization and Self-government: Impacts and Implications for First Nations in Canada', *American Review of Canadian Studies*, Spring/Summer: 265–81.

Smyth, M. 2003. 'Cruel to Pass the Buck on Kids', *Vancouver Province*, 15 June, A4.

Tait, C. 2000. 'Aboriginal Identity and the Construction of Fetal Alcohol Syndrome'. In L.J. Kirmayer, M.E. MacDonald, and G.M. Brass, eds, *The Mental Health of Indigenous Peoples*, 95–111. Culture and Mental Health Research Unit Report No. 10. Montreal: McGill-Queen's University Press.

Teghtsoonian, Katherine. 2003. 'W(h)ither Women's Equality? Neoliberalism, Institutional Change and Public Policy in British Columbia'. *Policy and Society* 22 (1): 26–47.

Tengan, Ty Kawika. 2002. '(En)gendering Colonialism: Masculinities in Hawai'i and Aotearoa', *Cultural Values* 6 (3): 239–56.

Van Woudenberg, Gerdine. 2004. 'Placing Gender in the Mediation of Aboriginal Resource Claims and Conflicts', *Recherches amérindiennes au Québec*. 34 (3): 75–86.

Walker, Ryan. 2006. 'Interweaving Aboriginal/Indigenous Rights with Urban Citizenship: A View from the Winnipeg Low-Cost Housing Sector', *Canada Citizenship Studies* 10 (4): 391–411.

White, L., and E. Jacobs. 1992. *Liberating Our Children: Liberating Our Nations*. Report of the Aboriginal Community Panel Family and Children's Services, Legislative Review in British Columbia, Victoria, BC: Queen's Printer.

Wood, Patricia K. 2003. 'Aboriginal/Indigenous Citizenship: An Introduction', *Citizenship Studies* 7 (4): 371–8.

## Further Reading

Bumiller, Kristin. 2008. *In an Abusive State: How Neoliberalism Appropriated the Feminist Movement against Sexual Violence*. Durham, NC: Duke University Press.

Agnew, Vijay. 2007. *Interrogating Race and Racism*. Toronto: University of Toronto Press.

Kuokkanen, Rauna. 2008. 'Globalization as Racialized Sexualized Violence: The Case of Indigenous Women', *International Feminist Journal of Politics* 10 (2): 216–33.

Native Women's Association. 2007. *Aboriginal Women and Self-Determination*. An issue paper prepared for the National Aboriginal Women's Summit, 20–2 June.

First Indigenous Summit of the Americas. http://www.dfait-maeci.gc.ca/aboriginalplanet/750/ archives/march2003/art4_main-en.asp.

Human Security and Aboriginal Women in Canada. http://www.swc-cfc.gc.ca/cgi-bin/ printview.pl?file=/pubs/pubspr/0662424263/200512_0662424263_10_e.html.

Women's Rights and Gender Issues. http://www.twnside.org.sg/women.htm.

The Canadian Women's Health Network. http://www.rcsf.ca/network-reseau/9-34/9-34pg2.html.

Sisters in Spirit Initiative. http://www.nwac-hq.org/en/documents/nwac.sis.jun1807.pdf.

## Questions for Critical Thought

1. Is the marginalization of Aboriginal women a result of racialized gender or of public policies that marginalize these women?
2. What historical conditions continue to disadvantage Aboriginal women?
3. How do gender and race create borders of inclusion and exclusion within Canadian citizenship?
4. How do race and gender shape decolonization efforts?

# CHAPTER 7

# The Welfare State Under Siege?:

## Neo-liberalism, Immigration, and Multiculturalism

Yasmeen Abu-Laban

The contemporary politics of 'welfare reform' take place on a ground where established
conceptions of people, nation and state have become unsettled and contested.

John Clarke (2003, 208)

## Introduction

The historic development of the welfare state has been implicated directly in the
evolution of the meaning of citizen rights in liberal democracies. Consequently,
understanding the shifting nature of social policy formation in light of neo-
liberalism (or possibly post–neo-liberalism) has a direct bearing on the issue of
equality between citizens in all their diversity. This is because neo-liberalism has
been seen to exacerbate social inequalities, particularly those based on gender,
race or ethnicity, and class. While there has been a spate of (contradictory)
writings in the past decade about the extent to which the welfare state is under
siege as a result of guiding rationales and discourses informed by neo-liberalism,
it is also important to note that neo-liberalism has not been the only purported
threat to the welfare state and its promised security.

The purpose of this chapter is to survey and assess the implications of three
distinct and much-debated propositions that appear in both empirically based
and theoretical scholarly writings about contemporary liberal democracies:
(1) immigration is a threat to the welfare state; (2) multiculturalism is a threat
to the welfare state; and (3) neo-liberalism is a threat to the welfare state. Since
neo-liberalism, with its emphasis on cost cutting, carries clear implications for
social spending, this aspect of the welfare-state debate is likely to be familiar discussion to many readers. However, the discussions concerning immigration and
multiculturalism are of special interest because they illustrate dramatically how
much current commentary blames immigrants and ethnic, racial, and cultural
diversity for social insecurity. This underscores the continued salience of
'foreigners' as a danger to the national community, which in turn takes on

decidedly gendered dimensions. For example, in some strands of the discussion, immigrants are portrayed as a potential drain on society and social programs, but it is female immigrants in particular who are portrayed as 'non-productive' and thus likely to overload the fragile welfare system (Abu-Laban 1998b). Similarly, the debate on multiculturalism and the welfare state features an argument that cultural diversity weakens the solidarity needed to sustain robust welfare programs and existing citizenship rights; however, it is female immigrants from the global South who have come to be cast as the unique victims of patriarchal cultures, whose status in the private sphere threatens the gains made by 'Western' women as rights-bearing citizens (Okin 1998; Abu-Laban 2002). In short then, the 'nation' is important to the unfolding debates about the welfare state and welfare reform, and attention to constructed lines of national belonging (or unbelonging) may illuminate a number of social divides, including gender, race, and ethnicity.

In the case of contemporary Canada, it is argued that a major impediment to social equality stems from the continued practical and discursive shifts in social policy away from universalism towards a focus on those perceived to increase risk. When universalism is de-emphasized, the opportunity to challenge inequities based on gender, as well as on race, ethnicity, country of birth, and citizenship status, is more circumscribed. Moreover, in the specific realm of immigration policy, any focus on 'risk' tends to exacerbate the fears associated with 'foreigners'. Indeed, since 11 September 2001, the perceived threat posed by 'the foreigner' has become more tightly enmeshed within security discourses and policies.

In making this argument, this chapter proceeds in three parts. First, the literature on the welfare state, citizenship, and rights is reviewed, with an eye towards the interconnection with 'nation'. Second, the contemporary literature dealing with challenges to the welfare state is analyzed with respect to its contradictory tenets. While the case of Canada demonstrates that the assumptions made in linking immigration and/or multiculturalism polices to the decline of the welfare state are faulty, these assumptions speak to an implicit resurrection of the nation-state as an imagined site where territory, identity, and citizenship define a 'people'. Finally, the actual changes to Canadian immigration and multiculturalism policy since 1990 are reviewed to show how both of these policies have been affected by neo-liberal rationales, as well as rationales laying stress on national attachment and national security.

## The Welfare State, Citizenship, and Rights

T.H. Marshall's classic account of citizenship and the welfare state portrays rights as developing in an evolutionary fashion, with civil rights characterizing the eighteenth century, political and voting rights characterizing the nineteenth century, and the social rights associated with the welfare state characterizing the mid-twentieth century (1965, 71–134). Much has been said about the limits of Marshall's account in light of the different experience of women in relation to citizenship in Britain, which was the country of his focus (Walby 1994), as well as differences among women (see Altamirano-Jiménez in this volume). Much has also been said of the complications introduced by a consideration of immigration, since certain citizenship rights have been extended to long-term migrants living in liberal democracies (Layton-Henry 1990; Soysal 1994).

Yet another difficulty in the work of Marshall is his equivocal use of the idea of 'nation' (Yuval-Davis 1991). Although Marshall himself avoided the term, instead emphasizing that 'citizenship is a status bestowed on those who are full members of a *community*' (1965, 92, my emphasis), he nonetheless suggested that 'citizenship requires a bond of a different kind, a direct sense of community membership based on loyalty to a *civilization* which is a common possession' (1965, 101, my emphasis). What I maintain, however, as Marshall suggests indirectly, is that citizenship serves simultaneously to animate *both* the welfare state *and* the nation-state in the popular imagination (see also Clarke 2003). Thus, contestations in the welfare state either implicitly or explicitly signal contestations in the nation-state and vice versa, and this becomes more visible in considering citizenship. Just as feminist scholars have demonstrated the manner in which citizenship rights have been experienced differently by women and men, they have also highlighted the manner in which different nations and expressions of nationalism can carry diverse constructions of masculinity and femininity (Abu-Laban 2008).

The term 'welfare state' is used in a very broad sense to characterize all Western capitalist interventionist states that emerged after the Second World War. As is well known, the work of the economist John Maynard Keynes provided some of the guiding assumptions of the welfare state in arguing that states could use their taxing and spending powers to actively intervene in the economy in order to promote full (male) employment and economic growth. In theory, the deficits that accumulated during economic downturns would not only keep the economy afloat, but would be paid for by funds generated during periods of economic growth.

These ideas were applied variously by policy makers in Canada and elsewhere in the industrialized world, with the result that a series of redistributive programs relating to unemployment, social assistance, healthcare, family support, education, and the like were introduced. Such programs reflected the idea of what Nikolas Rose (1999) has called the 'mutuality' of social risk. Put differently, these social policy measures were premised on the idea that the risks associated with a competitive market economy (namely economic insecurity and inequality) would be minimized by social rights that permitted citizens to meet their basic needs (Bakker and Scott 1997).

Of course, the exact nature of programs and consequently the relationships between state, market, and family (as well as the voluntary sector), varied between countries (Esping-Andersen 1990). Because of its comparatively weaker emphasis on universal programs and heavier emphasis on needs and means-tested programs, Canada's welfare state was never very generous, so that it is misleading to speak of a 'golden age' of welfare (Siltanen 2002). In addition, the consolidation of programs associated with the Canadian welfare state did not happen until the late 1960s (whereas in many other countries it happened earlier). This Lois Harder attributes to the fact that Canada is a federal state (and social policy is technically a provincial competency), that Canadians may be more suspicious of the state than people in continental Europe, and that the Canadian economy was dependent on resource exports (2003, 177). Nonetheless, by the late 1960s Canada's welfare state came to include Unemployment Insurance, the Family Allowance, the *Medical Care Act* (1966), the Canada Pension Plan and Quebec Pension Plan, and not least the Canada Assistance Plan, which facilitated joint, equivalent, and uncapped federal and provincial funding of programs.

The post-war welfare state was not simply about these programs, for it also symbolized that there was a role for the state as a champion of social justice (Jenson 1997, 634). In addition to funding women's and Indigenous groups, from the 1970s new public policies like multiculturalism and official bilingualism entailed the funding of ethnic and linguistic minorities to enable them to engage in the policy process and helped to legitimize the recognition and demands of less powerful groups in the name of citizen equality (Breton 1986; Jenson and Phillips 1996). In addition, in 1967 the overt racial exclusion that had historically governed Canada's immigration policy was removed; thus 'potential Canadian citizens' were put on a more equal footing, at least formally, and the way was paved for greater demographic diversity.[1] In combination, these developments spoke to an egalitarian and culturally pluralist ethos of citizenship, and thus of an egalitarian and culturally pluralist nation-state. This same vision also found its way into the 1982 Charter of Rights and Freedoms in its promotion of individual and, to a lesser extent, group rights (see Dobrowolsky in this volume). Yet the last two decades have introduced new complexities in politics.

## The Welfare State, Its Challengers, and the Case of Canada

Today, as the academic literature attests, understandings of the post-war Keynesian welfare state are being challenged. As a result, the meaning of citizenship and of nation-state is also being challenged. The welfare state is being reconfigured in complex and uneven ways, which are leading to debates about the extent to which welfare-state policies and practices are eroded, the degree of convergence between changing national economies, the nature and scope of the state's withdrawal from the public realm, and the ways in which the changing international political economy is implicated in various reconfigurations (Abu-Laban and Gabriel 2002, 21). A spate of labels—lean, competitive, liberal, neo-liberal, post-Keynesian, social investment, post–neo-liberal—have also emerged to distinguish current state configurations from the post-war welfare state. There remains little agreement about the right way to label the form (or forms) of state we see today. This is arguably a reflection of the fact that there are national variations in responses (Cameron and Stein 2000, S26), as well as sub-national variations in responses (see Collier, Jenson, and MacDonald in this volume). In addition, the plethora of labels may be related to the fact that 'the state' (whether in social spending or other areas) is not a unitary or unified actor. Since it is beyond the scope of this chapter to consider all of the nuances implied by the many adjectives attached to the state today, I will focus on neo-liberalism and the question of its continued prominence as symbolized by the idea of post–neo-liberalism.

The term 'neo-liberal' captures certain assumptions that frame much of the public debate and the policy environment, both in Canada and internationally. These assumptions include a more limited role for the state and consequently an emphasis on cutting back state policies and programs, and a greater stress on individual self-sufficiency and a belief that free markets are efficient allocators of goods and services (Abu-Laban and Gabriel 2002, 21).

Despite alternative visions (see Held 2004) and despite their failure to deliver greater equality (Page 2004), neo-liberal assumptions, which view publicly financed welfare programs as an impediment to economic growth, still reign supreme at the international level. Thus, as Page (2004) notes, such powerful global institutions as the International Monetary Fund, the World Bank, and the World Trade Organization, in their adherence to the 'Washington Consensus', act to restrict greater social welfare, and equality between states, at the global level. The influence of neo-liberalism has also been evident in certain regional arrangements, such as the North American Free Trade Agreement between Canada, the United States, and Mexico (Grinspun and Cameron 1993).

Neo-liberal assumptions, as the chapters in this volume attest, have also had an influence on the core programs that marked the consolidation of the Canadian welfare state (for example, both Family Allowance and the Canada Assistance Plan were dismantled). Thus the nature of Canadian social citizenship was transformed dramatically in the mid-1990s. Some analysts, like Janine Brodie (2002a), called attention to the 'disenfranchisement' of the social citizen and in its wake a 'neo-liberal state' presiding over growing inequalities based on gender, race, and class.

Yet, the details of the Canadian budgetary and social policy climate have not been static: by 1998 the focus shifted to 'post-deficit budgets' and there was some injection of monies into new areas of social spending—for instance, the number of families eligible for the Child Tax Benefit was increased, and in 2006 a universal but taxable $1,200 Child Care Benefit for parents of children under six was introduced. How this is interpreted varies, and in doing so it captures one major component of the debate surrounding neo-liberalism versus post–neo-liberalism in Canada and other industrialized countries. Thus for example, Janine Brodie's analysis of current patterns of spending in Canada, while acknowledging these shifts, holds that neo-liberalism has actually become re-embedded through these practices (Brodie 2006). On the other hand, there is also a growing international body of literature which suggests that in certain areas, particularly funding directed at children and child poverty, the welfare state is being transformed into a 'social investment state' which is attentive to the idea of 'risk' and of minimizing 'future risk'. The focus on the child and its emergence as the model citizen is discussed in Alexandra Dobrowolsky and Jane Jenson's (2004) work on social policy in Canada, V. Elizabeth and W. Larner's (2003) work on social policy in Aotearoa/New Zealand,[2] and the work of Ruth Lister (2003) on social policy in the United Kingdom. The discourse associated with the 'social investment state' seemingly bypasses the economism of neo-liberalism (Elizabeth and Larner 2003), both by justifying spending in certain areas and by weakening a strict reliance on the market (or alternatively family) by forging 'partnerships' that included the voluntary sector.

Yet, despite the debate on whether to characterize the state in relation to neo-liberalism or social investment (or post–neo-liberalism), the two visions both suggest that the Keynesian welfare state, with the male-breadwinner model citizen at its helm, is a thing of the past. They are united in suggesting that gender and specifically the poverty of women and the claims-making of women in all their diversity are not central in contemporary policy formulations; that the nature of 'universal' programs associated with the post-war welfare state is undergoing transformation; and that 'risk' has emerged as an important factor in policy formulations. I will return to these points in considering immigration and multiculturalism policies more closely in the third section.

At this point, I want to focus more closely on the idea that the opportunity for minoritized groups to make claims has contracted in Canada. For example, as Jenson and Phillips (1996) show, the re-making of social policy in the mid-1990s clearly lent support to an ideological attack on groups such as women, racial minorities, and the poor, for these groups came to be depicted as 'special interests' whose demands and issues contrasted with those of 'ordinary Canadians'. Brodie, similarly, speaks of how 'group-based claims making on the state in the name of citizen equality' has been 'delegitimized' (2002a, 378). In this same climate, the 1990s populist discourses attacking the recognition and funding of official bilingualism, multiculturalism, and Indigenous peoples were further invigorated by the rising prominence of the Reform Party and its successor, the

Alliance Party. As I have suggested, since citizenship is simultaneously about the welfare state and the nation-state, this is in fact not surprising. In this particular case, it speaks to the contestation over a culturally pluralist nation-state that was supported in the policies and social-justice role of the post-war welfare state.

The way in which citizenship connects with both the welfare state and the nation-state can be seen further if consideration is given to a growing scholarly literature that does not directly engage the debate over neo-liberalism and post–neo-liberalism. Specifically, over the past five years there has been a Canadian and international body of academic work that debates the implications of immigration, as well as multiculturalism, for the welfare state. Put simply, this literature seeks to answer the question whether immigrants take more resources than they contribute to the welfare state and whether the presence of an ethnically and racially diverse population or policies recognizing diversity like multiculturalism weaken the solidarity necessary to support or sustain generous welfare practices.

There is much to be said about the relationship between immigration and the welfare state, for emerging research brings to light the distinctly exclusionary tendencies of the Nordic or social-democratic model in relation to immigrants (Forsander 2004). More broadly, EU member-states have worked in tandem with the EU to prevent the entry of refugees and forced migrants, and EU states have also attempted to restrict the welfare rights of asylum seekers crossing their borders (Dwyer 2005). Not least, the issue of 'protecting' the welfare state (and generous programs) from immigrants has been of great interest in Europe (Engelen 2003). To quote from the introduction of one recent volume, 'immigration to a country that espouses equal treatment and has an extensive welfare state challenges the population's generosity in the first instance, and *may* in the longer term affect the sustainability of the system itself if the bulk of the newcomers are unable to support themselves' (Brochmann 2003, 6; italics in the original). In the Canadian context, the debate on the relationship between immigration and the welfare state has for some years included the question of the 'tax burden' versus 'tax contribution' made by immigrants, as witnessed in studies dating back to the 1980s by economists and sociologists (Li 2003, 86–8).

The issue of the burden or contribution of immigrants remains on the agenda in Canadian research. Consider, for example, Grubel's 2005 paper, published by the Fraser Institute, in which he argues that since recent immigrants to Canada have lower incomes than those of the Canadian-born, the result is 'substantial transfers from other Canadians to these immigrants' (2005, 3). In order to 'reduce the burden on Canadian taxpayers' (2005, 3) Grubel's proposed solution is a new, more restrictive immigrant-selection system, which is far from neutral in its preference for paid employment—an arena that has traditionally been central to differentiating the 'public', paid labour of men from the 'private', unpaid labour of women. This is because the system Grubel envisions would make simple entry contingent on an offer of employment, would make loss of employment actual grounds for deportation, and would make landed-immigrant status (that is, permanent residence) contingent on successfully completing four years of Canadian employment (Grubel 2005, 4).

Moreover, the sole focus on recent immigrants, upon which the apparent need for Grubel's new immigration system is based, does not and can not reveal what happens to immigrants over the long run. As Li notes, the few available studies that take in a wider period show that 'over the course of their life, immigrants contribute taxes that exceed the costs of social assistance and social benefits they receive through transfer payments' (2003, 95). More broadly, a systematic review of all available studies makes it 'fair to conclude that immigrants have created a saving and not a burden for Canada's transfer payment program, and that the potential adverse economic effect of expanding immigration is nil or small while the predicted economic benefit of increased immigration is modest' (Li 2003, 88). Thus, despite the ongoing debate, the available evidence does not support the idea that in Canada immigrants are threats to the welfare state. This view has also been supported by assessments which suggest that immigration can offset two key challenges to the welfare state: population decline and to a lesser extent the aging of the population (Reitz 2004, 105).

Like immigration, Canada's official policy of multiculturalism from 1971 has triggered scholarly discussions. These discussions have included addressing what the policy means, given the existence of Indigenous and linguistic minorities who base their claims on the state on different legal and constitutional premises, the unrelenting class and gender inequities that the policy has not alleviated, and the ongoing questions about the future of Canadian national unity (Abu-Laban and Stasiulis 1992). Canada's experience has also contributed to an international philosophical debate concerning the limits of liberalism in light of ethnic diversity and the limits of ethnic diversity in light of liberalism (Abu-Laban 2002). A specific aspect of this international debate has been the view, argued most forcefully by the late Susan Moller Okin, that in liberal democracies multiculturalism serves to reinforce the illiberal treatment of minority women in their communities and homes. Okin's position generated a number of criticisms, not least for her stereotyped assumptions that non-Western cultures are more patriarchal than Western ones (Cohen et al. 1999; Abu-Laban 2002). The debate about minority rights and gender equality has had popular reverberations in Canada in recent years. This was seen, for example, in the controversy in Ontario in 2005 over faith-based arbitration in family disputes (and specifically the possible use of Shari'a law). The same debate can be seen in the creation by the government of Quebec of the Bouchard–Taylor Commission[3] which was given the task of studying the issue of 'reasonable accommodation' after the Quebec town of Herouxville passed a controversial 2007 code of conduct for immigrants that, amongst other things, banned the *hijab* and stressed that men and women have equal rights. It is in reference to such discussions that Sherene Razack (2008) argues that in the post–September 11 period Muslim men are stereotyped as 'dangerous' and Muslim women are stereotyped as 'imperiled' at their hands. Indeed, since September 11 the ideal of gender equality has at times been appropriated in civilizational (and national) discourses.

Unlike the philosophical discussion about gender equality and minority rights that has hit the front pages of Canadian newspapers in recent years, the view that multiculturalism—with its purported emphasis on difference—erodes the solidarity necessary for the welfare state is not one that has had wide circulation in Canada, nor did it emerge in Canadian scholarly writing. Its clearest expression can be found in Wolfe and Klausen's (2000) discussion of Britain's historic adoption of welfare policies, though it also finds some resonance in the communitarian perspective of such American theorists as Michael Walzer.

The philosophical charge has been extended in the growing empirical literature, by both Canadian and international scholars, devoted to the question of multiculturalism and the welfare state. One example would be the volume, edited by Frank Salter (2004), that is devoted to testing, and ultimately in most cases defending, the proposition that ethnically and racially diverse societies are prone to be hostile to, and less redistributive in, welfare policies. In Salter's words, 'the decline in welfare rights observed in multi-ethnic states is due to a decline in public altruism; the willingness to help strangers. Public altruism declines . . . when fellow citizens are perceived to belong to different ethnic groups, so that the society at large is no longer identified with one's own ethnic group' (2004, 3). Notably, in this volume the Canadian federal government's transfer payments to Quebec, with its majority French-speaking population, emerge as an anomaly that is 'explained' by Salter as an attempt to 'buy territorial unity' (2004, 15). Conversely, Keith Banting and Will Kymlicka focus on nine multiculturalism policies (MCPs). For Banting and Kymlicka, these include not only official multiculturalism, but policies like affirmative action and dual citizenship. They find that in OECD countries 'there is no evidence of a systematic relationship between the adoption of MCPs and the erosion of the welfare state' (2004, 262). In a separate intervention, Banting also finds that for Canada specifically, 'immigration, multiculturalism policies and social redistribution can represent a stable political equilibrium' (2005, 112). Thus, while the debate is growing over the relationship between multiculturalism and the welfare state, there is no evidence that in Canada multiculturalism or ethnic diversity weakens the welfare state (see also Banting and Kymlicka 2006).

Nevertheless, the fact that these questions are being asked here and elsewhere—continually and even more often—is significant. In particular, it should not escape notice here that these very questions take up a concern that is at the heart of movements and parties of the radical right, especially, though not exclusively, in Europe. As Hans-Georg Betz argues, the radical right is today united by a common doctrine:

> The core of this ideological platform has variously been described as 'reactionary tribalism', 'ethnocratic liberalism', 'holistic nationalism', 'exclusionary welfarism', or 'exclusionary populism'. Its main characteristic is a restrictive notion of citizenship, which holds that genuine democracy is based on a culturally, if not ethnically, homogeneous community; that only long-standing citizens count as full members of civil society; and that society's benefits should be restricted to those members of society who, either as citizens or taxpayers, have made a substantial contribution to society. (2002, 194–5)

I do not wish at all to imply that those analysts who discuss these questions adhere to the radical right—far from it. More to the point, the answers being given to these questions may actually undermine the agenda of far right parties and movements today. To illustrate, the contradictory findings just reviewed are re-stated schematically in Table 7.1, to highlight how responses may lend support to 'exclusionary welfarism' or its obverse, which I term 'inclusionary welfarism'.

Thinking about the implicit policy prescriptions of 'exclusionary welfarism' is a reminder of the relevance of ethno-nationalist discourses of entitlement, even if these discourses assume a misleading 'golden age' of population homogeneity. More broadly the tension between inclusionary and exclusionary welfarist findings is a reminder that the current debates about welfare contain

**Table 7.1  Summary of findings from scholarly literature**

|  | Immigration | Multiculturalism |
|---|---|---|
| Exclusionary welfarist findings and implicit policy prescription | Immigrants use or take more state resources than they contribute and, as a consequence, put strains on the welfare state. Therefore, immigrants need to be barred from entering or barred from social citizenship. | Multiculturalism, by emphasizing difference, weakens the social solidarity needed to support the welfare state. Therefore, multiculturalism should not be endorsed by the state. |
| Inclusionary welfarist findings and implicit policy prescription | Immigration sustains the welfare state by combating the decline and aging of the population and by contributing to the tax base. Immigration policy can and should be open. | Multiculturalism is the outgrowth of a number of policies. There is no evidence that it weakens overall social spending or solidarity. Therefore, multiculturalism policies do no harm and bring benefits. |

disagreements about people, nations, and states that should therefore also alert us to gender differences.

With the relevance of nation and gender in mind, the next section will return to the debate over neo-liberalism and post–neo-liberalism to assess whether the actual changes in Canadian immigration and multiculturalism policy reflect a neo-liberal or post–neo-liberal ethos.

## Immigration and Multiculturalism Policies in Canada

As we have seen, the new emphasis on the child in Canadian social spending has led to a discussion of the social investment state, with this state form having some characteristics that are distinct from the discourse and emphases associated with neo-liberalism and the idea of the neo-liberal state. Rather than assert the value of one state vision over the other to explain the emphasis on the child in contemporary welfare reform, we can draw from some of the shared features of these two perspectives to trace what I see as their implications for the imagined nation-state particularly in an immigrant-receiving country like Canada.

In the neo-liberal and especially the social investment perspective attention is given to the relevance of the language of risk. Notably however, the stress on risk is given a distinctive spin in the realm of immigration. Rather than investment, here the emphasis on risk has come to signal enforcement and control. As Anna Pratt notes in her examination of immigration and refugee practices, beginning in the late 1980s and escalating since 11 September 2001, there has been an ever growing concern with security, crime, and fraud (including, significantly, welfare fraud), with the result that immigrants and refugees are cast as 'actually or potentially "risky" individuals' (2005, 18). In fact, she demonstrates that between 1990 and 2003 the use of detention and deportation by the Canadian state increased significantly (2005, 23–52). While control is not a new theme in immigration (Canadian or otherwise), the implications of its increased use are poignant in light of the post-war international human-rights regime. As Pratt notes, 'the humanitarian objective and the international legal obligation to protect refugees have come to be represented as a residual effect that is contingent in the first instance on the identification and exclusion of those who pose risks' (2005, 218).

With risk identified in relation to enforcement and control, the blunt economism of neo-liberalism not only remains, but operates in tandem with the blunt violence of state security. Likewise, while neither 'risk' nor 'investment' is a word being used in relation with multiculturalism, the major shifts in that policy reflect the impact of one of neo-liberalism's key premises: cuts to social spending. For ease of illustration, Table 7.2 shows the major policy shifts that have characterized Canadian immigration and multiculturalism policies from 1990 to 2008. In 1991 the Quebec–Canada Accord gave Quebec sole

**Table 7.2 Major policy changes in immigration and multiculturalism policies**

| Immigration 1990–2008 | Multiculturalism 1990–2008 |
|---|---|
| Quebec–Canada Accord signed (1991) and aspects extended to most other provinces and territories through the nominee programs | Greater emphasis on multiculturalism and business (1990–) |
| | Separate multiculturalism department dismantled (1993) |
| Greater emphasis on economic immigration (1994) | Cuts to multiculturalism spending (1993–) |
| Right of Landing Fee (1995) repealed for refugees in 2000; cut for incoming immigrants by 50% in 2006 Budget | Re-evaluation of multiculturalism program (1995–7) with emphasis on fostering attachment to Canada (1997–) |
| Greater emphasis on researching integration through Metropolis Project (1996) and, in its Third Phase (2007), issues of security | Re-orientation of multiculturalism spending guidelines (1997–) |
| Settlement renewal accords with provinces other than Quebec (1996) | |
| *Immigration Act* (1976) replaced with *Immigration and Refugee Protection Act* (2001) | |
| Canada–US Smart Border Accords (2001) | |
| Canada–US Safe Third Country Agreement (2004) | |

responsibility for selecting all immigrants and refugees abroad who are destined for Quebec and allows the province to offer its own settlement and integration services to immigrants, with compensation from the federal government. The passage of the Accord relates to the fact that immigration is a constitutionally concurrent area of jurisdiction, that Quebec from the 1960s was at the forefront of asserting greater provincial control in the area of immigration, and that the proposed Meech Lake constitutional amendments, which would have covered immigration, failed. Although these factors are not directly related to neo-liberalism, as will be discussed further, the 1991 Quebec Accord is relevant because it laid a basis for further devolution of control to other provinces in the context of 'settlement renewal'.

In 1994 the federal government embarked on public consultations on immigration. Following these there came to be a new emphasis on attracting self-sufficient immigrants who could pay the costs of their own 'integration' into Canadian society (Abu-Laban 1998b, 205). The first way in which this neo-liberal emphasis on self-sufficiency became visible was through the reordering of the relative mix of immigrants away from the family and humanitarian and refugee classes towards the economic class. As Sunera Thobani notes, throughout the 1994 immigration consultation period and its aftermath, the independent category was masculinized and valorized in state discourse, while the family category was feminized and treated as a problem (2001, 59). Specifically, independent immigrants were assumed to be male economic actors who would contribute to the nation, whereas family-class immigrants were treated as non-contributory persons ('wives and children') who would drain social services. However erroneous this representation and this measuring of worth are (see Abu-Laban and Gabriel 2002, 37–60), by 1994 the government planned to give more priority to independent immigrants for the rest of the century for a distinctly neo-liberal rationale: they would be more likely to earn a high income and generate economic growth and less likely to use social welfare (Abu-Laban 1998a, 79). The effects of this shift, inspired by neo-liberalism with its emphasis on reducing social expenditures and promoting self-sufficiency, linger. In 2006, close to 55 per cent of new immigrants came in under either the economic or the independent category. This percentage is projected to increase to close to 58 per cent under the 2008 Levels Plan (Citizenship and Immigration Canada 2007). This can be contrasted with the decade of the 1980s, when the independent category tended to be smaller than the family category (Abu-Laban 1998a, 76). It can also be noted in this regard that the preference for economic immigrants effectively favours male applicants. For example, reflecting the trend over many years, in 2006 there were proportionately more men in the economic class and proportionately more women in the family class (even though the federal government's purported 'gender-based analysis' of 2006 arrivals fails to acknowledge this in the discussion of the statistics) (Citizenship and Immigration Canada 2007).

Since the 1991 Quebec–Canada Accord, and in keeping with the forging of new partnerships endemic in social investment as well as the emphasis on economic immigrants in the early 1990s, the federal government began to sign much less comprehensive agreements with other provinces and jurisdictions (see Papillon 2002). The jurisdictions that were part of these agreements, known as the 'Provincial Nominee Programs', now include British Columbia, Alberta, Saskatchewan, Manitoba, New Brunswick, Nova Scotia, Newfoundland, Yukon, and Prince Edward Island. These programs aim to foster an exchange of information when policies are being developed and to allow provinces to nominate potential immigrants (more likely male immigrants) 'who will contribute to the economic growth of their province' (Citizenship and Immigration Canada 2002).

The 1995 introduction of a Right of Landing Fee also reflected this neo-liberal emphasis on attracting self-sufficient individuals. As originally conceived, the Right of Landing Fee was a $975 fee levied on all adult immigrants, including refugees, entering Canada. In 2000, the federal government repealed this fee for refugees only (arguably this had much to do with the bad impression that was made by the levying of a charge against those fleeing persecution). Revenues generated by the Right of Landing Fee, according to the federal government, were to offset the cost of settlement programs and social services used by immigrants, even though incoming immigrants immediately pay taxes and even though settlement services were subject to cuts over the 1990s (Abu-Laban and Gabriel 2002, 68–9). Nonetheless, even in the 'post-deficit budget years' between 1997 and 2001, the amount spent by incoming immigrants on processing fees was higher than the amount spent by the federal government on settlement programs for refugees and immigrants (Li 2003, 168). In the 2006 Budget, the Conservative government of Prime Minister Harper cut the Right of Landing Fee in half and injected $307 million more into settlement services, thereby undoubtedly affecting the imbalance in fees and services. The Harper Conservatives also chose to re-name the fee as the 'Right of Permanent Residence Fee'. Despite name changes and reduction, the retention of this fee speaks to the continued emphasis on attracting self-sufficient immigrants.

A hallmark feature of the federal government's immigration policy in the 1990s was the growing focus on integration. The 'investment in knowledge about integration' is perhaps most striking in the national component of the Metropolis project (Pratt 2005, 177).[4] Nationally, the Metropolis project began with a joint effort by Citizenship and Immigration Canada (CIC) and the Social Sciences and Humanities Research Council of Canada (SSHRC) to establish four university-based centres of research excellence in the study of immigrant integration in 1996. These centres are in Vancouver, Edmonton, Toronto, and Montreal (with Halifax added to these four during the project's second phase from 2002 to 2007). The Metropolis project brings together academics, policy makers, and non-governmental organizations with the aim of improving 'policy and program development through scientific research' (SSHRC and Citizenship and Immigration Canada 2002, 2). The government-initiated Metropolis project has been described as a 'distinctly neo-liberal technology of government' (Pratt 2005, 176), though the particular emphasis Metropolis places on 'partnerships' between government, academics, and NGOs highlights a major tenet of social investment theory. In addition, reflecting themes covered in the popular press and emphasized by the Conservatives (and its predecessors the Reform and Alliance parties) since September 11, the third phase of Metropolis (2007–12) contains a new emphasis on 'enclaves', 'terrorism', 'domestic security', and 'radicalization' (Metropolis Phase III n.d.: 33–4).

In keeping with the neo-liberal principle that the state should assume a less prominent role, the year 1996 also saw the beginning of a process of 'settlement renewal' in which the federal government devolved the direct administration and funding of settlement services for immigrants to lower levels (see Citizenship and Immigration Canada 1996). As Joseph Garcea suggests, 'the result is an integration system in which the provincial governments will perform the key planning and administrative roles and the federal government will be limited to setting and enforcing national principles and standards and providing funding for settlement and integration programs' (Garcea 1998, 165).

Although changes to the 1976 *Immigration Act* were well under way before 11 September 2001, the 2001 *Immigration and Refugee Protection Act* was passed after September 11. The *Immigration and Refugee Protection Act* lays heavy stress on themes of security. This is in keeping with the way in which risk in the immigration sphere was translated into enforcement and control. Specific post–September 11 changes, including the Canada–US Smart Border Accords of 2001 and the 2004 Safe Third Country Agreement, serve to integrate the two countries' border policies and refugee-determination systems. The legal scholar Audrey Macklin (2003) suggests the Safe Third Country Agreement weakens Canada's ability to meet its international obligations towards refugees and to respond in a humanitarian way towards refugees who are claiming gender-based persecution. The growing integration of border control and immigration policy between Canada and the United States in the post–September 11 period highlights the impact of the (neo-liberal) NAFTA arrangement in further integrating the economies of the two countries; the period from September 11 has also raised new issues concerning the human and civil rights of both Canadian citizens and non-citizens by state immigration and security personnel (especially minorities since terrorism is a racialized discourse) (Abu-Laban 2004).

Reflecting the relevance of citizenship to both the nation-state and the welfare state, immigration policy over the past decade and a half has evolved in a way that simultaneously embraces the ideal of the self-sufficient (male) immigrant who will not make use of the welfare state and treats the (male) immigrant as a threat to the (national) community. The emphasis on national community is also to be found in the evolution of multiculturalism policy since 1990, where there came to be greater force placed on fostering Canadian identity in the context of neo-liberal program redesign. Reinforcing the idea that Canada's official policy of multiculturalism is largely symbolic, since it has never had great state resources attached to it, the changes in this area are less numerous than what has happened in the area of immigration. Nonetheless, it can be noted that in keeping with the valorization of markets within neo-liberalism, there has been a greater stress on the idea that multiculturalism is good for business and trade (Abu-Laban and Gabriel 2002, 105–28). Thus, in the words of the Conservative minister of Canadian heritage, Beverley Oda, 'Canada benefits from the exceptional, and growing, diversity of its population. This diversity is a powerful factor in our country's economic productivity' (as cited in Department of Canadian Heritage, 2007, 35).

In keeping with the neo-liberal emphasis on less state and less state spending, in 1993 the separate department of multiculturalism was dismantled and incorporated into the Department of Canadian Heritage and funding to the program was reduced. It should also be noted that again, despite post-deficit budgets, the funding given to multiculturalism has never returned to its pre-1993 'height' of about $27 million a year and under the Harper Conservatives funding has further decreased. Indeed, in April 2007, the Liberal MP Colleen Beaumier charged that that the 'Conservative government is dismantling Canada's multiculturalism program' (Beaumier 2007).

Between 1995 and 1997 there was a program review of multiculturalism, of which the central goal was to respond to criticism that the policy was weakening Canadian unity. In response, Canadian Heritage issued new guidelines. The multiculturalism program now stresses that the policy aims to 'foster a society that recognizes, respects and reflects a diversity of cultures such that people of all backgrounds feel a sense of belonging and attachment to Canada' (Department of Canadian Heritage 1997, 1). In addition, in 1997 a re-orientation of multiculturalism spending guidelines moved away from granting core funding to ethno-cultural groups (perceived as 'special interests'), towards project funding for a wider range of actors, including, notably, private-sector companies (Abu-Laban and Gabriel 2002, 114).

In partisan and parliamentary debates following 11 September 2001, proposals for policy changes were not primarily directed at multiculturalism—in part a reflection of the significant evolution of multicultural policy during the 1990s. Rather, policy debates came to focus more squarely on citizenship legislation. While Canada's 1977 *Citizenship Act* is still in force, various attempts since 2001 to change it have given rise to new controversies about proposals to have immigrants swear an oath of loyalty to Canada and to make terrorism a new ground for the Canadian state to actually revoke Canadian citizenship (Garcea 2003). However, multiculturalism remains an important symbolic area for contestation. Thus, under the Harper government, Jason Kenney was not simply named 'Secretary of State for Multiculturalism' as in Liberal governments over the 1990s, but rather 'Secretary of State for Multiculturalism and Canadian Identity'. This wording also conveys Kenney's emphasis on 'both openness and cohesion' (Kenney in Department of Canadian Heritage 2007, 3) (see also Armstrong in this volume).

In sum, the story of multiculturalism policy suggests that its fate is primarily explained by reference to the broad retreat of the Canadian state from social and cultural spending, as well as by struggles over the meaning of nation. Taken together, the evolution of immigration and multiculturalism policies reveals that these policies have been, and continue to be, shaped by neo-liberal rationales, as well as by notions of national attachment, national unity, and increasingly national security. Within this neo-liberal shift, there are ways in which an emphasis on partnerships and certain discourses pertaining to social investment (like social cohesion) have also come into play, but the overarching narrative has been neo-liberalism.

# Conclusion

The post-war welfare state, inspired by the ideas of Keynes, is clearly not a static entity. As this chapter has noted, the past couple of decades have brought about shifts that necessitate a way of describing the post-war welfare state and social policy that captures change. One term for referring to those changes is neo-liberalism; others are social investment and post–neo-liberalism. The reading given to immigration and multiculturalism policies in Canada suggests that the tenets of neo-liberalism explain much. While aspects of the emphasis on new state partnerships (with provinces or NGOs and the voluntary sector) stressed in the social investment perspective are also evident, it is notable that in immigration policy, a discourse of 'risk' plays out in a way that is distinct from other policy fields. Risk in immigration is at the heart of the growing enforcement and control practices that characterize immigration and border policies.

As this chapter has also shown, the politics of welfare reform have gone hand in hand with contestations over nation. Ethno-nationalist discourses of welfare entitlement ('they' are taking 'our' resources) and their echo in some academic work are a reminder of this. At the same time, inequities based on gender, race, class, and citizenship status linger, and the turning of social policy away from universalism towards a focus on 'the risky' has reduced the opportunity to challenge these inequities in the Canadian context. Since citizenship, welfare state, and nation-state are inter-related and not static, this may evolve. In the meantime, there remains much to say about how 'foreigners' have (re)emerged as a danger to the (national) community and about the gendered consequences of the focus on 'foreigners' and other features of the evolving politics of welfare reform in Canada.

## Notes

For helpful comments on this chapter I thank Alexandra Dobrowolsky, Jane Jenson, and the anonymous reviewers of this volume.

1  Of course, informally biases still operate. See Abu-Laban (1998a).
2  Aotearoa is the name given to New Zealand by the indigenous Maori; it is used by Maori and non-Maori alike.
3  This commission was jointly headed by historian Gérard Bouchard and the political philosopher Charles Taylor.
4  The international Metropolis project, of which Canada is also a part, is an international forum that brings together policy makers, academics, and non-governmental organizations in the immigration field. By 2000, 20 other governments, including the US, Argentina, Austria, Denmark, France, and the United Kingdom, were involved in this project. The Commission of the European Union and UNESCO were also involved (Abu-Laban and Gabriel 2002, 94–5).

## References

Abu-Laban, Yasmeen. 1998a. 'Keeping 'em Out: Gender, Race and Class Biases in Canadian Immigration Policy'. In Joan Anderson, Avigail Eisenberg, Sherrill Grace, and Veronica Strong-Boag, eds, *Painting the Maple: Essays on Race, Gender and the Construction of Canada*, 69–82. Vancouver: UBC Press.

————. 1998b. 'Welcome/STAY OUT: The Contradiction of Canadian Integration and Immigration Policies at the Millennium', *Canadian Ethnic Studies* 30 (3): 190–211.

————. 2002. 'Liberalism, Multiculturalism and the Problem of Essentialism', *Citizenship Studies* 6 (4): 459–82.

————. 2004. 'The New North America and the Segmentation of Canadian Citizenship', *International Journal of Canadian Studies* 29: 17–40.

————. 2008. 'Gendering the Nation-State: An Introduction'. In Yasmeen Abu-Laban, ed., *Gendering the Nation-State: Canadian and Comparative Perspectives*, 1–18. Vancouver: UBC Press.

————, and Christina Gabriel. 2002. *Selling Diversity: Immigration, Multiculturalism, Employment Equity and Globalization*. Peterborough, Ont.: Broadview Press.

————, and Daiva Stasiulis. 1992. 'Ethnic Pluralism under Siege: Popular and Partisan Opposition to Multiculturalism', *Canadian Public Policy* 18 (4): 365–86.

Bakker, Isabella, and Katherine Scott. 1997. 'From the Postwar to the Post-Liberal Keynesian Welfare State'. In Wallace Clement, ed., *Understanding Canada: Building on the New Canadian Political Economy*, 286–310. Kingston: McGill-Queens University Press.

Banting, Keith. 2005. 'The Multicultural Welfare State: International Experience and North American Narratives', *Social Policy and Administration* 39 (2): 98–115.

————, and Will Kymlicka. 2004. 'Do Multiculturalism Policies Erode the Welfare State?' In Philippe van Parijs, ed., *Cultural Diversity versus Economic Solidarity*, 227–84. Brussels: Deboeck University Press.

————, and ————, eds. 2006. *Multiculturalism and the Welfare State: Recognition and Redistribution in Contemporary Democracies*. Oxford: Oxford University Press.

Beaumier, Colleen. 2007. 'Conservative Government Dismantling Multiculturalism Program'. http://www.colleenbeaumier.parl.gc.ca/detail.asp?lang=e&type=med&sid=2298 (accessed 1 Jan. 2008).

Betz, Hans-Georg. 2002. 'Xenophobia, Identity Politics and Exclusionary Populism in Western Europe'. In Leo Panitch and Colin Leys, eds, *Fighting Identities: Race, Religion and Ethno-Nationalism (Socialist Register 2003)*, 193–210. London: Merlin Press.

Breton, Raymond. 1986. 'Multiculturalism and Canadian Nation-Building'. In Alan Cairns and Cynthia Williams, eds, *The Politics of Gender, Ethnicity and Language in Canada*, 27–66. Toronto: University of Toronto Press in co-operation with the Royal Commission on the Economic Union and Development Prospects for Canada.

Brochmann, Grete, ed. 2003. *Comparative Social Research*. Vol. 22, *The Multicultural Challenge*. Oxford: JAI Press.

Brodie, Janine. 2002. 'Citizenship and Solidarity: Reflections on the Canadian Way', *Citizenship Studies* 6 (4): 377–94.

————. 2006. 'Gender and the New Social "isms": Re-embedding Social Governance in Canada'. Paper prepared for workshop, Women, Public Policy, Post Neoliberalism, annual meetings of the Canadian Political Science Association, June, in Toronto.

Cameron, David, and Janice Gross Stein. 2000. 'Globalization, Culture and Society: The State as Place Amidst Shifting Spaces', *Canadian Public Policy* 26 (August): S15–S24.

Citizenship and Immigration Canada. 1996. *Change and the Management of Settlement Programs for Newcomers*. Ottawa: Department of Citizenship and Immigration.

————. 2002. 'Fact Sheet 11: Canada–Québec Accord'. Ottawa.

————. 2007. *Annual Report to Parliament on Immigration 2007*. Ottawa: Minister of Public Works and Government Services Canada. Available: http://www.cic.gc.ca/english/resources/publications/annual-report2007 (accessed 3 Jan. 2008).

Clarke, John. 2003. 'Turning Inside Out? Globalization, Neoliberalism and Welfare States', *Anthropologica* 45 (2): 201–14.

Cohen, Joshua, Matthew Howard, and Martha C. Nussbaum, eds. 1999. *Is Multiculturalism Bad for Women? Susan Moller Okin with Respondents*. Princeton: Princeton University Press.

Department of Canadian Heritage. 1997. *Multiculturalism: Program Guidelines*. April. Ottawa: Department of Canadian Heritage.

———. 2007. *Annual Report on the Operation of the Canadian Multiculturalism Act 2005–2006.* Ottawa: Department of Canadian Heritage. http://www.pch.gc.ca/progs/multi/reports/ann2005-2006/index_e.cfm.

Dobrowolsky, Alexandra, and Jane Jenson. 2004. 'Shifting Representations of Citizenship: Canadian Politics of "Women" and "Children"', *Social Politics* 11 (2): 154–80.

Dwyer, Peter. 2005. 'Governance, Forced Migration and Welfare', *Social Policy and Administration* 39 (6): 622–39.

Elizabeth, V., and W. Larner. 2003. 'Children, Families/Whanau and Communities: Gender and Ethnicity in New Forms of Social Governance in Aotearoa/New Zealand'. Research Paper Number 9, Local Partnerships and Governance Research Groups, University of Auckland, New Zealand.

Engelen, Ewald. 2003. 'How to Combine Openness and Protection? Citizenship, Migration, and Welfare Regimes', *Politics and Society* 31 (4): 503–36.

Esping-Andersen, Gøsta. 1990. *The Three Worlds of Welfare Capitalism.* Princeton: Princeton University Press.

Forsander, Annika. 2004. 'Social Capital in the Context of Immigration and Diversity: Economic Participation in the Nordic Welfare States', *Journal of International Migration and Integration* 5 (2): 207–27.

Garcea, Joseph. 1998. 'Bicommunalism and the Bifurcation of the Immigration System', *Canadian Ethnic Studies* 30 (3): 149–72.

———. 2003. 'The Canadian Citizenship Reform Project: In Search of the Holy Grail?' Paper presented at the annual meetings of the Canadian Political Science Association, June, in Halifax.

Grinspun, Ricardo, and Maxwell A. Cameron, eds. 1993. *The Political Economy of North American Free Trade.* Montreal: McGill-Queen's University Press.

Grubel, Herbert. 2005. *Immigration and the Welfare State in Canada: Growing Conflicts, Constructive Solutions.* Fraser Institute Occasional Paper 84. Vancouver: Fraser Institute.

Harder, Lois. 2003. 'Whither the Social Citizen'. In Janine Brodie and Linda Trimble, eds, *Reinventing Canada: Politics of the 21st Century,* 175–88. Toronto: Pearson.

Held, David. 2004. *Global Covenant: The Social Democratic Alternative to the Washington Consensus.* Cambridge: Polity Press.

Jenson, Jane. 1997. 'Fated to Live in Interesting Times: Canada's Changing Citizenship Regimes', *Canadian Journal of Political Science* 30 (4): 627–44.

———, and Susan D. Phillips. 1996. 'Regime Shift: New Citizenship Practices in Canada', *International Journal of Canadian Studies* 14 (Autumn): 111–35.

Layton-Henry, Zig, ed. 1990. *The Political Rights of Migrant Workers in Western Europe.* London: Sage.

Li, Peter S. 2003. *Destination Canada: Immigration Debates and Issues.* Don Mills, Ont.: Oxford University Press.

Lister, Ruth. 2003. 'Investing in the Citizen-workers of the Future: Transformations in Citizenship and the State and New Labour', *Social Policy and Administration* 37 (5): 427–43.

Macklin, Audrey. 2003. 'The Values of the Canada–US Safe Third Country Agreement'. Paper prepared for the Caledon Institute of Social Policy. http://www.maytree.com (accessed 3 Jan. 2008).

Marshall, T.H. 1965. *Class, Citizenship and Social Development.* Garden City, NY: Doubleday.

Metropolis Phase III. 2007–2012. *Annexes A-L Memorandum of Understanding between the Social Sciences and Humanities Research Council and Citizenship and Immigration Canada.* http://canada.metropolis.net/pdfs/Annexes%20A-L%20Eng.pdf (accessed 3 Jan. 2008).

Okin, Susan Moller. 1998. 'Feminism and Multiculturalism: Some Tensions', *Ethics* 108 (July): 661–84.

Page, Robert M. 2004. 'Globalization and Social Welfare'. In Vic George and Robert M. Page, eds, *Global Social Problems,* 29–44. Cambridge, UK: Polity Press.

Papillon, Martin. 2002. 'Immigration, Sustainable Diversity and Social Inclusion in Canadian Cities'. In Leslie Seidle, ed., *The Federal Role of Cities: Four Policy Perspectives.* CPRN Discussion Paper F/XX. Ottawa: Canadian Policy Research Networks.

Pratt, Anna. 2005. *Securing Borders: Detention and Deportation in Canada*. Vancouver: UBC Press.

Razack, Sherene H. 2008. *Casting Out: The Eviction of Muslims from Western Law and Politics*. Toronto: University of Toronto Press.

Reitz, Jeffrey G. 2004. 'Canada: Immigration and Nation-Building in the Transition to a Knowledge Economy'. In Wayne A. Cornelius, ed., *Controlling Immigration: A Global Perspective*, 97–133. 2nd edn. Stanford: Stanford University Press.

Rose, Nikolas. 1999. *Powers of Freedom: Reframing Political Thought*. Cambridge: Cambridge University Press.

Salter, Frank. 2004. 'Introduction'. In Frank Salter, ed., *Welfare, Ethnicity and Altruism: New Findings and Evolutionary Theory*, 97–133. London: Frank Cass.

Siltanen, Janet. 2002. 'Paradise Paved? Reflections on the Fate of Social Citizenship in Canada', *Citizenship Studies* 6 (4): 395–414.

Social Sciences and Humanities Research Council of Canada (SSHRSC) and the Department of Citizenship and Immigration. 2002. 'Revised Program Description: Immigration and the Metropolis'. Photocopy. February.

Soysal, Yasemin N. 1994. *Limits of Citizenship: Migrants and Postnational Membership in Europe*. Chicago: University of Chicago Press.

Thobani, Sunera. 2001. 'Closing the Nation's Ranks: Racism, Sexism and the Abuse of Power in Canadian Immigration Policy'. In Susan C. Boyd, Dorothy E. Chunn, and Robert Menzies, eds, *[Ab]Using Power: The Canadian Experience*, 49–64. Halifax: Fernwood Press.

Walby, Sylvia. 1994. 'Is Citizenship Gendered?' *Sociology* 28 (2): 379–95.

Wolfe, Alan, and Jyette Klausen. 2000. 'Other Peoples', *Prospect* (December): 28–33.

Yuval-Davis, Nira. 1991. 'The Citizenship Debate: Women, Ethnic Processes and the State', *Feminist Review* 39 (Autumn): 58–68.

## Further Reading

Abu-Laban, Yasmeen, ed. 2008. *Gendering the Nation-State: Canadian and Comparative Perspectives*. Vancouver: UBC Press.

Abu-Laban, Yasmeen, and Christina Gabriel. 2002. *Selling Diversity: Immigration, Multiculturalism, Employment Equity and Globalization*. Peterborough, Ont.: Broadview Press.

Banting, Keith, and Will Kymlicka, eds. 2006. *Multiculturalism and the Welfare State: Recognition and Redistribution in Contemporary Democracies*. Toronto: Oxford University Press.

Tastsoglou, Evangelia, and Alexandra Dobrowolsky, eds. 2002. *Women, Migration, and Citizenship: Making Local, National, and Transnational Connections*. London: Ashgate.

Thobani, Sunera. 2007. *Exalted Subjects: Studies in the Making of Race and Nation in Canada*. Toronto: University of Toronto Press.

Citizenship and Immigration Canada. http://www.cic.gc.ca/english/index.asp

Department of Canadian Heritage (Multiculturalism). http://www.canadianheritage.gc.ca/progs/multi/index_e.cfm

Metropolis (Canada). http://canada.metropolis.net/.

Canadian Council For Refugees. http://www.ccrweb.ca/eng/engfront/frontpage.htm.

## Questions for Critical Thought

1. Is the existing system of immigrant and refugee selection fair when it comes to gender? If so, why? If not, what would make the system fairer?

2. Do Canadians fear immigrants? What evidence supports the position you take? What evidence challenges the position you take?

3. What do you think the future of the welfare state in Canada is? How might this future impact Canadians in light of gender, ethnic, racial, class, and other differences?

# CHAPTER 8

# Violence against Women or Violence against 'People'?:

## Neo-liberalism, 'Post–neo-liberalism', and Anti-violence Policy in Ontario and British Columbia

Cheryl N. Collier

## Introduction

Many feminist political scientists have argued convincingly that neo-liberal approaches to governing, which have increasingly been adopted in Canada and other Western democracies since the mid-1980s, have had devastating impacts on women's lives. These approaches, which encourage less state involvement and reduced public spending in order 'to put an end to a perceived culture of welfare dependence', have often resulted in decreased investments in welfare-state programs in a variety of jurisdictions (Kendall 2003, 6). Since women are more often employed by the state than men are and are more reliant on welfare-state programs, they have borne the brunt of the negative consequences of neo-liberalism (Brodie 1996; Bashevkin 1998). Even though many authors have noted a softening of the neo-liberal approach in some states (including Canada and Britain) under what has been called 'after neo-liberalism', 'post–neo-liberalism', or the 'social investment state',[1] the tendency of governments to continue to embrace the managerial, market-driven agendas of neo-liberalism has increasingly delegitimized gendered analyses of public policy.[2]

At the same time, some have questioned whether neo-liberalism has negatively affected state willingness to address the women-focused policy area of violence against women. According to S. Laurel Weldon, some see violence-against-women policies as 'mainly symbolic measures that involve little redistribution. For this reason, they present an opportunity for right-wing or neo-liberal governments to mollify women's organizations without spending any money' (2002, 58). Yet Weldon herself questions this position, noting examples of neo-liberal regimes that have refused to address the anti-violence issue because they saw it as a political 'hot potato' or a private instead of a public matter. Still other right-wing administrations, particularly the Republican-controlled Congress in the

United States, authorized nearly a billion dollars in anti-violence expenditures in 1998 in an era of budget cutting and deficit reduction (2002, 59).

Since anti-violence measures generally cost less than other welfare-state programs,[3] is it possible that anti-violence policies are more likely to be promoted and protected and therefore are virtually immune from the cuts associated with neo-liberalism? At the same time, neo-conservative and right-wing regimes have embraced law and order and victims' rights agendas, providing opportunities to act on violence against women from inside gender-neutral frameworks (Lakeman 1999; Pilot 1993).[4] Have these gender-neutral policy frameworks expanded under neo-liberal and post–neo-liberal regimes? How have governments responded to women's-movement claims in the area of violence against women since the mid-1990s? Has neo-liberalism affected women's anti-violence policy positively or negatively? Have changes in anti-violence policy followed a generally linear path from neo-liberalism to post–neo-liberalism, or have different governments responded in different ways to these external forces?

This chapter seeks to answer these questions in the Canadian context, focusing specifically at the provincial level and drawing comparisons to the federal level where appropriate. I have chosen to focus on the sub-state level because fiscal responsibility for social-program delivery has been steadily downloaded from the federal to the provincial level—a reflection of neo-liberal trends. This was evident in the 1990 cap on Canada Assistance Plan (CAP) payments to the three 'have' provinces (Alberta, Ontario, and British Columbia) and the reduction of transfer payments through the introduction of the amalgamated Canada Health and Social Transfer, which replaced CAP in 1996–7.[5] Thus the provinces have assumed more and more responsibility for welfare-state programs of particular interest to women, including those addressing violence against women. Although criminal laws that target the problem of violence against women fall under federal jurisdiction, the provision of anti-violence shelter services, public education programs, directives to police forces, legal aid funding, and other anti-violence services fall directly under provincial control. Many of these services have also been funded through the shared-cost CAP program.

Even though anti-violence services and advocacy in Canada and elsewhere began at the local grassroots level, less scholarly attention has been paid to provincial violence-against-women policy. This chapter aims to shed light on this important level of women's-movement activity and to add to our wider understanding of the effect of neo-liberalism and post–neo-liberalism in the provinces and how this directly affects women's lives. To do this, I have chosen to compare provincial anti-violence policy expenditures and program changes between 1994 and 2007 in Ontario and British Columbia. I will argue that although aggregate expenditure statistics show that most governments have, over time, increased their funding for anti-violence programs, there has been much more variation in how responsive this spending has been to feminist anti-violence advocates. Thus some governments have been more neo-liberal in their policy responses, while others have aligned themselves more closely to post–neo-liberal or social investment positions. The former have pursued cuts to anti-violence programs and have delegitimized feminist anti-violence advocacy groups, whereas the latter have either resisted program cuts or re-invested money in anti-violence programs, restoring some of the funding initially cut under other neo-liberal regimes. Although all governments have been more willing to approach anti-violence policy from a gender-neutral position, some have made small moves at different times to recognize feminist anti-violence positions, although none to an extent that could be said to meet advocacy demands completely. Even so, these differences show that there are important variations in neo-liberalism given changing political contexts and political actors.

The partisan theory of public policy argues that diversity in public-policy directions is explained by ideological differences between governments formed by different parties (Castles 1982; Hicks and Swank 1992; Schmidt 1996). Furthermore, the argument is made that although party differences have been somewhat muted during neo-liberal times, significant differences in left- and right-wing approaches to violence against women are still present. These differences suggest that the influence of, particularly, neo-liberalism on anti-violence policy is worse under right-wing regimes than left-wing ones. Thus, the influence of neo-liberalism and post–neo-liberalism on policy cannot be fully determined outside of the partisan framework, since governments of different parties could diverge in their responses to anti-violence movements and were not necessarily beholden to the negative pressure associated with neo-liberal approaches to the welfare state.

## Neo-liberalism, Post–neo-liberalism, Women's Policy, and Partisan Choice

Sylvia Bashevkin's comparative study of women's policy in the US, the UK, and Canada concluded that cuts to women's programs and policies continued past their origins under the neo-conservative regimes of the 1980s well into the 1990s and 2000, even though supposedly more 'moderate' governments held power during these years.[6] She argues that some of the cuts actually deepened in later years and had quite damaging effects, particularly on poor single mothers (Bashevkin 2002, 14). Katherine Teghtsoonian, while recognizing diversity in government approaches, argues that the prominence of neo-liberal ideology created tension for left-of-centre NDP governments in British Columbia during the 1990s and likely modified their social-justice commitments (2003, 35).[7] These studies suggest that even though partisan differences were not erased during neo-liberal times, they were more muted and relatively insignificant, for governments seemed collectively to embrace neo-liberal managerialism at the expense of protecting social programs.

Over time, however, many researchers noticed that governments in a variety of jurisdictions began to back away from a strict neo-liberal agenda of cost-cutting and to demonstrate a willingness to re-invest in social programs after years of downsizing and cuts. Ruth Lister refers to this phenomenon in Britain under Tony Blair's 'New Labour' government as 'the social investment state'— 'a hybrid welfare regime, combining elements of liberal and social-democratic welfare regimes' (Lister 2004 quoted in 2006, 1). This social investment state continued to be informed by neo-liberalism in that it aimed to integrate citizens into the market as opposed to protecting them from it. Thus it was different from the Keynesian social-democratic welfare state that preceded it but was not as opposed to social programs as neo-liberalism had been. This investment, therefore, continued to uphold market values such as managerialism and program efficiency, and it was measured by how well it improved state competitiveness, particularly by promoting increased labour-market productivity (Jenson and Saint-Martin 2003). Associated with these goals was an emphasis on gender-neutral frames to justify new social investment policy. Thus, for example, post–neo-liberal childcare investments were framed as 'children's' issues instead of 'women's' issues, and they emphasized the benefits of investing in children instead of in working toward feminist goals of gender equality (Dobrowolsky and Jenson 2004).

Underlining both views of neo-liberal and post–neo-liberal approaches is the notion that different governments would generally follow a similar path from neo-liberalism in the mid-1980s to the mid-1990s through to post–neo-liberalism from the mid-1990s into the late 2000s. However, I argue that instead of assuming that all governments will follow this trajectory, it is essential to use the lens of partisan difference. Under partisan theory, there is an assumption that different parties will differ in their approaches to neo-liberal governing practices, which will likely be informed by their left- and right-wing ideological predispositions. The partisan approach helps explain the shift from neo-liberalism to post–neo-liberalism in the literature as well. For example, Lister (2006) identifies neo-liberalism with the right-wing Thatcher and Major Conservative governments in the UK. By contrast, she notes the move to a softer 'post–neo-liberalism' that occurred under the centre-left New Labour Party which replaced the Conservatives. Thus, post–neo-liberalism was clearly informed by a more centre-left ideology present under New Labour that was absent during Thatcher Conservatism. Others have similarly used the neo-liberal/post–neo-liberal dichotomy to describe differences between the policies of the federal right-wing Conservative government in Canada to those of its successor, the more centrist Liberals.[8] The problem with assuming a more linear neo-liberal/post–neo-liberal path, however, arises in jurisdictions where right-wing regimes resume office after 'post–neo-liberal' regimes are defeated.[9] The tendency for those right-wing governments to revert to neo-liberal practices suggests that partisan difference and choice has much to do with whether or not states are neo-liberal or post–neo-liberal in their approaches to the welfare state.[10] In the provincial cases discussed below, the fact that neo-liberalism occurred at two very different time points in Ontario and British Columbia supports the partisan theoretical approach.

Differences in government approaches to women's policy are particularly evident when researchers pay close attention to the finer details of policies, not just to establish whether program spending increased or decreased, but to determine how well the policy met long-standing demands of the women's movement in the particular policy arena.[11] This can be even more important in the area of violence against women because the way the issue is framed speaks directly to whether the state is willing to act on feminist critiques of women's structural inequality—which feminists have consistently identified as one of the main causes, if not *the* main cause, of violence. Bashevkin argues that if the state is successful in casting anti-violence policy in gender-neutral terms, it means essentially that 'women's movements are likely losing control of the issue' (1998, 243).

By comparing the development of anti-violence policy between 1994 and 2007 in Ontario and British Columbia, we can test whether ideologically different governments responded in different ways to feminist anti-violence demands. This will help clarify what influence neo-liberalism and post–neo-liberalism have had on anti-violence policy.

## Comparing Ontario and British Columbia

To uncover these influences, this chapter will compare aggregate changes in provincial-government anti-violence expenditures and the qualitative progression of anti-violence policies and programs[12] between 1994 and 2007 in Ontario and British Columbia. Ontario and BC were chosen for this study because they were both 'have' provinces in the federation and had both been greatly affected by social policy downloading, particularly since 1990, while at the same time being in generally better fiscal positions to support welfare-state services autonomously.[13] As well, both provinces also saw variety in government over the years, as centrist, left-, and right-wing parties held office (see Tables 8.1 and 8.3). I begin the study in 1994 to catch some of the left-wing NDP years while focusing the study more on the later years of neo-liberalism and the shift into post–neo-liberalism identified in the literature and in the other chapters in this volume.

In this chapter, anti-violence policy is measured in two ways. First, the chapter measures anti-violence expenditures as a percentage of overall program spending for each province, where possible.[14] However, it recognizes that positive and negative changes in programs and policies can often be hidden behind aggregate spending statistics. Therefore, this study measures qualitatively the significant changes in policy during these years to ascertain how closely the policy mirrors the demands of provincial anti-violence advocates.

Drawing on anti-violence advocacy interview data and internal anti-violence-movement documents collected between 2000 and 2007, I classify government anti-violence policy and program initiatives as either significant or secondary announcements.[15] Then using these same sets of data, I assess whether these significant policy or program responses were positive, negative, or mixed when compared to recent and past advocacy demands. Each assessment is made in reference to the specific policy in question, but more generally I determine whether the policy closely mirrors advocacy demands, whether it is reflective of consultation with feminist anti-violence groups, whether it is an appropriate response to the specific anti-violence issue in question and whether or not it is pro- or anti-feminist. If the majority or all of these criteria are met, the policy is classified as positive. If the policy response meets about half of these criteria, it is classified as mixed. Finally, if the majority or all of these criteria are not met, the policy is classified as negative.

## Anti-violence Expenditure and Policy in Ontario

Figure 8.1 illustrates the changes in Ontario government expenditures for anti-violence programs as a percentage of overall program expenditures between 1994 and 2006.[16] These data are weighed against significant changes in anti-violence policy in Ontario over those years, determined through confidential interviews with advocates and state actors.[17] On the basis of the interviews, these changes are rated as positive toward anti-violence advocates, negative, or mixed.

The qualitative policy data show considerable variation in significant anti-violence program and policy announcements.[18] Of nine significant policy

**Table 8.1   Ontario governments**

| Year | Party | Leader | Dominant ideology | Popular vote (%) | Seats |
|------|-------|--------|-------------------|------------------|-------|
| 1990 | NDP | Bob Rae | Centre-left | 38 | 74/130 |
| 1995 | Progressive Conservative | Mike Harris | Right | 45 | 82/130 |
| 1999 | Progressive Conservative | Mike Harris | Right | 45 | 59/103 |
| 2002 | Progressive Conservative | Ernie Eves | Centre-right | 45 | 59/103 |
| 2003 | Liberal | Dalton McGuinty | Centre | 46 | 72/103 |
| 2007 | Liberal | Dalton McGuinty | Centre | 42 | 71/107 |

Sources: Based on Collier 2006; Drummond and MacDermid 1997; Dunn 1996; Dyck 1996; www.electionsontario.on.ca; www.canoe.ca/CNEWSOntarioElection/home.

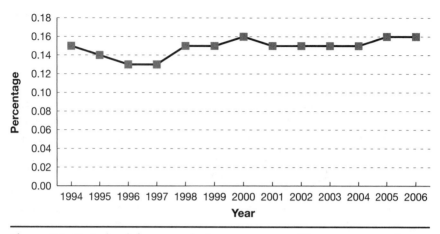

**Figure 8.1  Ontario violence-against-women expenditure as a percentage of total program spending**

Sources: Calculations made by the author from data drawn from Ontario Public Accounts 1994/95–2006/07.

**Table 8.2  Ontario's significant anti-violence policies, 1994–2007**

| Year | Party | Policy or program | +/– rating |
|------|-------|-------------------|------------|
| 1995 | PC | Funding for interval houses and women's shelters cut 2.5 per cent | – |
| 1996 | PC | Additional 5 per cent cut to funding for interval houses and women's shelters | – |
| 1996 | PC | Framework for action on the prevention of violence against women in Ontario (the McGuire Report) | – |
| 1997 | PC | Prevention of Violence against Women: An Agenda for Action released with $27 million in new funding for Violence Prevention Initiatives | +/– |
| 2000 | PC | Bill 117 (Domestic Violence Protection Act) introduced | +/– |
| 2000 | PC | Funding to Ontario Women's Centres cut | – |
| 2001 | PC | $4.5 million over five years for province-wide crisis help line | + |
| 2004 | Liberal | $60 million Domestic Violence Action Plan announced; included $56 million over five years to improve functioning of existing shelters, increase capacity, train workers, etc. | +/– |
| 2007 | Liberal | 3 per cent increase in annual sexual-assault-program funding | + |

Note: +, –, +/– ratings established by the author, based on elite interviews with anti-violence advocates and government actors and historical analyses.

Sources: Cairns 2000; Canada NewsWire 2001, 2002; Canadian Press NewsWire 2000; Community Action 2001; Crosby 2004; The Daily Press 2001; Della-Mattia 2004; Internal party documents; Leslie 2004; Lightman and Baines 1996; Livingston 2004; OAITH 1997; OWJN 2000a; Collier 2006; Whitnall 2001.

responses recorded, two (22 per cent) were positive, three (33 per cent) were mixed, and four (44 per cent) were negative. There is less variation in the expenditure graph, indicating that much of the differences within and between parties on the anti-violence issue was hidden behind the expenditure percentages.

Before 1994, the Ontario NDP had made significant improvements to anti-violence policy despite having entered a severe provincial recession in 1990. Up until that time, previous provincial governments had done little more than study the problem of violence against women. Some support for shelters and transition houses was made available under the Liberals in the later 1980s, but advocates consistently identified the NDP years as the most positive as far as movement gains were concerned. These included large increases in sexual-assault and wife-assault prevention and funding for shelters in 1991 and 1992. Even though the NDP put forward a largely gender-neutral law-and-order approach to fighting the problem of violence against women, they were at times persuaded by advocates to temper this approach, which represented a departure from other provincial regimes. For example, in 1991 the NDP attorney general directed crown attorneys to make every effort to fight attempts to refer to a victim's sexual history during sexual-assault trials (Women's Movement Archives). NDP attention to anti-violence issues cooled somewhat during the party's final years in office, when economic concerns took precedence. There were no new anti-violence policy announcements in 1994, yet provincial anti-violence expenditures reached their highest levels to date in that year and remained so until 2000, in contrast to federal social-spending cuts that had begun at that time (see Figure 8.1).

When the right-wing Conservatives under Mike Harris took power in 1995, government responses turned negative, as was more in line with the federal trend. All four negative responses recorded were for this period; they included the first recorded provincial cuts to anti-violence funding (Collier 2006). These included significant cuts in 1995 to the entire Ministry of Community and Social Services budget for second-stage housing, education and prevention services, counselling programs for male batterers, and culturally specific anti-violence services. The Conservatives cut funding for interval houses and women's shelters by 2.5 per cent in 1995 and another 5 per cent in 1996.

Anti-violence expenditures as a percentage of all program spending decreased slightly for the first time between 1995 and 1997. Even though the economy was nearing the end of a severe recession, the targeting of anti-violence programs did not save the province much money because the programs had not cost much in the first place. Cuts to anti-violence expenditures accounted for only 0.002 per cent of total government program spending between 1995 and 1997 (see Figure 8.1). This suggests that the cuts were largely ideological and aimed against the anti-violence movement, particularly since they involved feminist anti-violence services (OAITH 1997). This echoed the 'special interest' discourse that had been adopted at the federal level and often aimed squarely at women's groups.

In 1996, the Conservatives decided to re-examine anti-violence policy and drew up terms of reference for what they called the Framework for Action on the Prevention of Violence against Women in Ontario (the McGuire Report). Increased publicity surrounding the issue of violence against women put it into sharper focus for the Conservative government, but the movement was not invited to comment on the framework. Advocates were particularly worried about the Report's view that women's shelters and rape crisis centres helped to create a victim-centred dependence on services instead of empowering women (OAITH 1997, 2–3) and about its implied support for further cuts to services (OAITH 1997, 3).

In 1998, the Chief Coroner of Ontario launched an inquest into the high-profile murder of Arlene May by her male partner.[19] Advocates were pleased with the 213 recommendations released by the inquest later that year, many of which echoed their demands, but the Conservative government largely ignored the report, stating that it was already implementing most of the coroner's recommendations.[20] The report of the inquest in 1998 and three high-profile murders of women in the Toronto area in just over a week's time in 2000 heightened media attention and public pressure between 1998 and 2000.[21]

Although the restoration of and increases in funding, particularly in 2000, were significant, the corresponding policy responses were not. Money was not directed to feminist anti-violence services, but instead to gender-neutral law-and-order and victims-rights programs. Thus feminist activists were still struggling to provide front-line anti-violence services, despite increased government commitments to anti-violence spending.[22] Bill 117, the *Domestic Violence Protection Act*, which was introduced late in 2000, continued a law-and-order focus. At first, however, the movement was pleased with the fact that the Act appeared to accept some of the recommendations made by the May Inquest. Yet despite a speedy passage of the bill through the legislature, the Conservatives did not proclaim and implement the law until well into 2002 (OWJN, 2002). At the same time, the Conservatives cut funding to five women's centres because they were offering second-stage services to women who had already escaped violent homes (Canadian Press NewsWire, 2 Oct. 2000). Ostensibly, the Conservatives did not believe that government should be supporting these types of services.[23]

Although the Conservatives continued to spend new money on anti-violence programs, expenditure percentages actually shrank after 2000 to the end of the PC mandate in 2003. The only significant positive response during these years was a much needed increase of $4.5 million to expand a province-wide 24 hour crisis help line (Leslie 2004). The new money was welcomed by advocates, but the lack of attention to feminist demands continued. And, while that was an all too familiar experience, now it occurred at a time when women had 'disappeared' in a variety of policy areas (see Jenson in this volume).

When the Liberals replaced the Conservatives in 2003, there was room for improvement in the government's responsiveness to anti-violence movements, particularly in recognizing feminist expertise on the issue. However, even though the Liberals continued to increase spending and maintain the expenditure percentage, they at first failed to make any dramatic improvement to the state's receptiveness to advocate demands. After a small increase in sexual-assault program and shelter funding in 2004, the Liberals announced a major $60 million Domestic Violence Action Plan at the end of 2004. Although the funding increase was welcomed, a continued use of the gender-neutral term 'domestic' violence instead of violence against 'women' disappointed advocates and, again, reflected wider trends that were making women more and more invisibile. More disturbing were comments made by Premier Dalton McGuinty and Sandra Pupatello, the minister responsible for women's issues, that shelters would receive one-time funding and then were expected to become 'financially independent'—an untenable situation for shelters that were already struggling to raise funds to offset inadequate government support (OWJN 2005a).

By the end of 2005, some advocates were asking where the 'action' was in the Domestic Violence Action Plan, since much of the spending announced over the first year was not new and the Liberals had not moved forward on a plan to increase collaboration with anti-violence front-line workers (OWJN 2005b). In the lead-up to the provincial election, the Liberals released an action plan update in January 2007 (Ontario, Ministry of Citizenship and Immigration 2007) to highlight over $20 million in additional funding above its original four-year commitment. In the summer of 2007, the Liberals also announced a 3 per cent increase in yearly funding to 38 provincial sexual-assault centres (Ontario, Ministry of the Attorney General 2007) on top of the much-criticized one-time grants originally announced in the action plan. As a response to lobbying from the provincial anti-violence advocacy coalition headed by OAITH, titled 'Step-It-Up', the government also pledged that during its second term of office it would implement a more co-ordinated Sexual Violence Action Plan.[24] The attention to sexual assault was welcomed by anti-violence advocates, especially since it was largely invisible in the 2004 action plan, but the movement remained skeptical and vowed to keep track of Liberal promises by using an anti-violence 'scorecard program' (LaFleche 2007).

In the end, we can see much diversity in responses by the Ontario government to anti-violence advocates between 1994 and 2007. Although there was evidence of first-time cuts to anti-violence programs during the Harris Conservative years, all governments appeared willing to increase anti-violence expenditures over time, thereby keeping expenditures consistently between 0.13 and 0.16 per cent of overall program expenditure between 1994 and 2006/07. Yet most of the positive significant announcements occurred before 1994 under the left-of-centre NDP, which was the only party willing to adopt a more feminist approach to anti-violence issues. By contrast, the Conservatives had four negative and two mixed significant policy announcements and only one that was rated positive. The Liberals were mixed in two out of three of their significant responses to the movement, but seemed to be open to a more positive approach after the 2007 election. Thus, the evidence for Ontario did not show consistent neo-liberal or post–neo-liberal approaches to anti-violence policy by governments formed by different parties. On the contrary, the variation in state responsiveness, seems for the most part to indicate that centre-left governments were more open to feminist demands than right-wing regimes, with centrist governments falling somewhere in between.

## Anti-violence Expenditure and Policy in British Columbia

Anti-violence policies and program expenditure levels in Figure 8.2 demonstrate some similarities to data recorded for Ontario in Figure 8.1. In particular, expenditure percentages did not fluctuate dramatically, as was the case in Ontario. However, specific anti-violence expenditure data were left off the provincial public accounts in British Columbia after the Liberals took office in 2001.[25] The data listed between 2001 and 2004 instead reflect expenditure percentages for all 'women's services' in the Ministry of Community, Aboriginal and Women's Services (the only indication available in the public accounts). In 2004 it was renamed the Ministry of Community Services and included a Department of Women's and Senior's Issues. Expenditure percentages since 2004 reflect expenditures on all women's *and* seniors' programs (again the only information available in the public accounts). The fact that the percentage since 2001 has often represented a decreased amount when compared to specifically 'anti-violence' expenditure percentages in 2000 is very significant. The obvious cuts to anti-violence (and other women's) programs are also supported by the qualitative policy evidence in Table 8.4.

Qualitative policy data show variations in anti-violence program and policy announcements, as in Ontario. Of five significant policy responses, two (40 per cent) were positive, none (0 per cent) was mixed, and three (60 per cent) were negative.

### Table 8.3    British Columbia governments

| Year | Party | Leader | Dominant ideology | Popular vote (%) | Seats |
|------|-------|--------|-------------------|------------------|-------|
| 1991 | NDP | Mike Harcourt | Centre-left | 40 | 51/75 |
| 1996 | NDP | Glen Clark | Left | 39 | 39/75 |
| 2000 | NDP | Ujjal Dosanjh | Centre-left | 39 | 39/75 |
| 2001 | Liberal | Gordon Campbell | Right | 57 | 77/79 |
| 2005 | Liberal | Gordon Campbell | Right | 46 | 46/79 |

Sources: Blake 1996; Collier 2006; Dunn 1996; Dyck 1996; www.elections.bc.ca/elections.

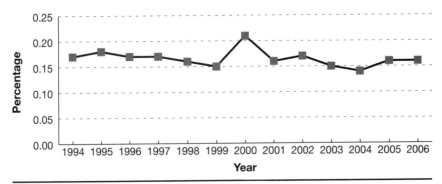

**Figure 8.2  British Columbia violence-against-women expenditure as percentage of total program spending**

Sources: Calculations made by the author from data drawn from British Columbia Public Accounts 1994/05–2006/07.

Just before the study period in 1994, anti-violence policies gained prominence under Bill Vander Zalm's right-wing Social Credit regime, which reached out to women voters by, among other things, establishing a Task Force on Family Violence.[26] After the NDP took power in 1991, it responded well to the recommendations in the task force report. The movement particularly welcomed increases in 1992 in funding of $10 million per year over the next four years under the Stopping the Violence Initiative, core-funding announcements for the BC/Yukon Society of Transition Houses and a reinstatement of core funding for the Vancouver Transition House. As in Ontario, the NDP made efforts to feminize its law-and-order approach to violence against women by revising the Wife Assault Policy in 1993. The resulting Violence against Women in

**Table 8.4  British Columbia's significant anti-violence policies, 1994–2007**

| Year | Party | Policy or program | +/– rating |
|------|-------|-------------------|------------|
| 1994 | NDP | 2 per cent wage increase for transition-house staff and anti-violence counselling agencies | + |
| 2001 | Liberal | Ministry of Women's Equality eliminated and incorporated into Ministry of Community, Aboriginal and Women's Services (later Ministry of Community Services–2005) | – |
| 2002 | Liberal | 50 per cent cut to abusive-men treatment programs | – |
| 2002 | Liberal | Core funding cut from women's centres | – |
| 2005 | Liberal | $12.5 million funding increase for anti-violence services including $5.1 million for transition houses, $2 million to expand Stopping the Violence and Children Who Witness Abuse programs, $1.6 million for outreach and prevention programs, and $2 million for new anti-violence measures | + |

Note: +, –, +/– ratings established by the author.

Sources: BCCWC 2005; BCIFV 2002, 2005; Canada NewsWire 2003; Creese and Strong-Boag 2005; Kachuk 1998; Leavitt 2002; Provincial government documents; Sigurdson 1996.

Relationships (VAWIR) Policy, recognized that domestic violence is not exclusive to marriage. This recognition was reflected in the pro-feminist change in name alongside a change in focus from 'wife assault' to 'violence against women in relationships'.[27]

The NDP continued its pro–feminist-movement announcements in 1994 by increasing the wages of front-line anti-violence workers (Women's Movement Archives). Yet, as in Ontario, the pace of anti-violence policy improvements slowed down under the NDP during its last years in office. Although the majority of the NDP government's program and policy responses (nine) were positive, none of these was considered very significant by movement actors.[28] Despite the lack of significant new programs, however, it is important to note that the free-standing BC Ministry of Women's Equality (MWE), created by the NDP, continued the pro-movement violence-against-women programs established in the early 1990s. The protection of the femocratic MWE alongside a resistance to cut anti-violence spending significantly was in stark contrast to the dismantling of women's policy agencies and cuts to social spending that occurred federally during this same period.

Figure 8.2 shows that anti-violence expenditure percentages decreased marginally between 1996 and 1999 under the Glen Clark NDP. However, in 2000, the NDP government of Ujjal Dosanjh increased expenditures to their highest levels since 1995. The increased expenditure does not, however, coincide with significant new policies or programs, as noted above. Moreover, even at its height in 2000, anti-violence expenditure only made up slightly more than 0.2 per cent of overall program spending, which was only 0.03 per cent higher than in 1995. It is likely that fiscal pressures, including the fact that BC became a have-not province in 2000, had an impact on the NDP agenda and tempered its progressive tendencies.[29]

Yet, advocates saw the provincial government become much more negative in its approach to anti-violence policy after the election of the right-wing Gordon Campbell Liberals in 2001. This regime was responsible for all of the significant negative policy announcements in Table 8.4, including the first substantial neo-liberal cuts to anti-violence services in women's centres and a 50 per cent cut to male-batterer counselling programs in 2002. This represented a departure from social investment trends that had already begun under the federal Liberal regime. The extent of the BC cuts[30] prompted criticism from the United Nation's Committee on the Elimination of Discrimination against Women (CEDAW) in a submission entitled 'British Columbia Moves Backward on Women's Equality' (BCCWC, 2003). The cuts were severely criticized by anti-violence advocates across the province and also led to separate protests by the Victoria Status of Women Action Group and the BC Coalition of Women's Centres in 2001 and 2004, respectively (*Brantford Expositor* 2001; BCCWC 2004).

This lack of commitment to women's anti-violence policy is evident in Figure 8.2 in the decreased expenditure percentages recorded between 2001 and 2004 for all women's services. It was not until 2005 that the Liberals began to reinvest in anti-violence policy, again falling behind federal investments that had begun earlier in the decade in other social policy areas. Moreover, the BC Liberals' reinvestment constituted only a modest increase in expenditure of $12.5 million, including $5.1 million for transition houses, $2 million for the existing 'Stopping the Violence' and the 'Children Who Witness Abuse' counselling programs, and $1.6 million to expand outreach and violence prevention (MCAW 2005). Although the expenditures were welcomed by provincial advocates and are rated positively, they were not enough to restore much of what had previously been cut, including core funding for women's centres. While the short-fall in social re-investment was typical of post–neo-liberalism, an unwillingness to reverse the previous cuts in core funding was much more in line with neo-liberal trends.

Between 2005 and 2007, the Liberals were largely silent on anti-violence issues. With women's services, including anti-violence programs, buried inside the Ministry of Community Services, which made no mention of 'women's equality' in its mandate, the anti-violence issue was all but guaranteed to be viewed inside of a gender-neutral law-and-order framework, if at all. In 2007, Gordon Campbell held the first Premier's Congress on Violence against Women, but he failed to invite any anti-violence organizations (a few individual advocates were invited) to speak alongside law enforcement and health 'experts', thus missing an opportunity to re-position the issue inside a gendered framework (BCASVCP 2007) and redress the marginalized status of critical actors, such as feminist representatives.

As with the Ontario example above, then, significant anti-violence policy diversity in BC between different party governments is apparent. Specifically, the evidence shows negative responses under the right-wing Liberals, who embraced neo-liberal ideology and cuts to programs along with a gender-neutral approach to anti-violence issues. The latter position was typified by a suggestion made in 2001 by Liberal Attorney General Geoff Plant to rename the Violence against Women in Relationships Policy the 'Violence against *People* in Relationships Policy', ostensibly in order to recognize that 'women, too, can initiate violence' (O'Neill 2002, 33). All of the significant negative policy announcements were made under the Campbell Liberals, with only one modest positive announcement near the end of the study period. Even this weak attempt at post–neo-liberal reinvestment was notable in its gender-neutral framing of violence against women and for failures to consult with feminist advocates. In contrast, the centre-left NDP was more open to feminist anti-violence approaches before and during 1994, and it resisted neo-liberal pressure to cut or eliminate programs into 2000, even during a severe provincial recession.

# Conclusion

In the end, the policy evidence presented above for both Ontario and BC raises more questions about the supposed linear influence of neo-liberalism and post–neo-liberalism on anti-violence policy. While governments have appeared to embrace neo-liberal cuts to anti-violence programs at certain time points, overall they do not seem to be following the same chronology in their policy approaches. Therefore it is difficult to pronounce definitively on the overall impact of neo-liberalism and post–neo-liberalism on anti-violence policy in Ontario and BC because of this obvious variation in the extents to which each party government adopted or rejected neo-liberal and post–neo-liberal practices between 1994 and 2007. Diversity was even present when we compare governments of similar parties at the same time in Ontario and BC. For example, between 2001 and 2002, the right-wing Harris Conservatives in Ontario were increasing their anti-violence expenditures and enacting new programs to combat violence against women, measures that were more in line with post–neo-liberal trends. Although these initiatives were prompted in part by media attention surrounding a number of high-profile murders and were not very responsive to feminist demands, they stood in stark contrast to the significant neo-liberal cuts to anti-violence services that were made by the right-wing Campbell Liberals in BC at the same time. Clearly, both right-wing regimes did not follow the same neo-liberal to post–neo-liberal path. Nor was provincial anti-violence policy immune to neo-liberal program cuts in either case, even if overall spending levels were small and changed little over time.

The comparative examples of the Harris Conservatives and the Campbell Liberals suggest that party differences are in fact more nuanced than they appeared earlier in this analysis—that is, the left is not always positive in its anti-violence policies and the right is not always negative.[31] However, the overall evidence from these two provincial cases generally demonstrates that left-wing regimes were consistently more responsive to feminist movements and were more willing to accept feminist critiques and solutions to violence against women. In contrast, right-wing regimes were consistently less open to feminist approaches to anti-violence policy, even when these regimes demonstrated a willingness to re-invest modestly in anti-violence services. This difference between partisan approaches to neo-liberalism and post–neo-liberalism was evident federally with the shift from the centrist Martin Liberals to the more right-wing Harper Conservatives, and it also demonstrates the non-linear progression of neo-liberalism to post–neo-liberalism (see Mahon, Jenson, and Dobrowolsky in this volume). Even though no left-wing regimes held provincial office past 2000 in these two cases, we can assume that they would have been more open to gendered approaches to anti-violence policy than right-wing regimes, particularly since they were able to emphasize the feminist nature of the issue in the less-forgiving cost-cutting era of earlier neo-liberalism. Therefore, while the evidence above supports the notion raised by Teghtsoonian that neo-liberalism has the potential to mute social-democratic tendencies of left-wing governments, we also see that this is not always the case.[32]

We also saw differences between centrist governments and right-wing regimes in the later 2000s. Even though both the right-wing Campbell Liberals in BC and the centrist McGuinty Liberals in Ontario made reinvestments in anti-violence spending after substantial cuts, the McGuinty Liberals made later efforts to improve their Domestic Violence Action Plan in response to anti-violence advocacy demands. The Campbell Liberals instead ignored advocates' calls to go further in restoring the funding and services cut previously. Although neither party was feminist in their anti-violence program approach, the centrist Ontario Liberals appeared more open to this feminist framework as they entered their second mandate.

In conclusion, this study raises important questions about how variations in partisan factors, political contexts, and actors influence the impact of neo-liberalism and post–neo-liberalism on feminist anti-violence policy. The evidence above suggests that neo-liberalism and post–neo-liberalism have the potential to manifest themselves differently, depending on the political context. And although there are some common examples of governments being unwilling to support feminist anti-violence expertise, it is not clear whether the problem of violence against women in some ways falls outside of the core social investment themes. These points deserve further research to help us understand better the relationship between neo-liberalism, post–neo-liberalism, and women's policy.

## Notes

Excerpts from this article have appeared in 'Neoliberalism and Violence against Women: Can Retrenchment Convergence Explain the Path of Provincial Anti-violence Policy, 1985–2005?' *Canadian Journal of Political Science* 41 (1) (March 2008).

1  For more on this discussion see Jenson (this volume), Lister (2006), Dobrowolsky and Jenson (2004), and Jenson and Saint-Martin (2003).

2  See Dobrowolsky and Jenson (2004, 155) and McDonald (2005).

3  This is particularly true with respect to state childcare expenditures. See Collier (2006).

4  Lakeman argues that both of these approaches individualize the issue and remove the 'women' from violence-against-women policy and therefore solutions are not aimed at more societal structural causes of inequality. She also argues that deference to law-enforcement agencies perpetuates the 'patriarchal order' in society—a main structural cause of violence against women (Lakeman 1999, 28).

5  Note the CHST was split into the Canada Health Transfer and the Canada Social Transfer in 2004.

6  Bashevkin's study recognizes diversity in government approaches, but still affirms the existence of broader, more negative neo-liberalism despite these differences.

7  See also Teghtsoonian and Chappell (2008).

8  See Jenson and Saint-Martin (2003), who also refer to New Labour in Britain, and Mahon (this volume), who uses a 'varieties of liberalism' framework and what she refers to as 'inclusive liberalism' versus neo-liberalism to contrast the Mulroney (and later the Harper) Conservatives to the Chrétien and Martin Liberals.

9   This occurred federally when the Harper Conservatives replaced the Martin Liberals in 2006. See also the Quebec example in Jenson (this volume).

10  See Jenson and Mahon (both this volume) for examples of this in Quebec and federally in Canada.

11  Elsewhere I argue that a measurement of steady increases in welfare-state expenditures over a significant period will not give a nuanced enough picture of what policy decisions are being made: for example, a government may increase its welfare spending overall while decreasing spending on unemployment insurance and simultaneously increasing its healthcare budget (Collier 2006). Similarly for anti-violence policy, a focus on aggregate expenditure statistics alone will not illuminate whether or not any of the responses are feminist or anti-feminist in nature or how well they respond to advocacy demands. In order to avoid false assumptions that all increases in expenditures on anti-violence policy are positive and similarly that all decreases in expenditures are negative, I use both quantitative expenditure statistics and qualitative program and policy analysis to get the full picture of anti-violence decision making.

12  For the purposes of the qualitative analysis of policies and programs, only provincial-government initiatives directed specifically at violence against women have been included and rated. Although I recognize and briefly mention the impact that broader welfare-state cuts can have on victims of violence, these broader policy initiatives are not included in the more detailed analysis because of time and space limitations. Those other initiatives that purport to be gender-neutral are indeed important to the anti-violence issue (as are more gendered policies including availability of childcare, for example), but they do not necessarily speak directly to state decisions about violence against women, which are the major focus of this particular study.

13  In 2000, BC became a 'have-not' province for the first time in its history but regained its 'have' status shortly thereafter.

14  For both provinces, anti-violence expenditures were identified in the provincial Public Accounts only from the 1990s, on. In BC, those statistics were available only until 2001.

15  Significant policies could be classified as positive, negative, or mixed, but to be included in this study, a policy or program needed to be (1) a significant amount of new or reduced spending depending on the program in question; (2) a major move in a new area that had not been acted on previously by the provincial government; (3) identified as significant by anti-violence advocates interviewed for this study, or as a long-standing movement demand in historic advocacy documents. Therefore, this study chooses to focus more on policy action by government than on policy inaction (which, depending on the circumstances, could also be considered 'significant'.)

16  I include the Ontario Public Accounts listing for violence-against-women expenditures made within the Ministry of Community and Social Services. Between 1995 and 1999, I add expenditure on Sexual Assault Initiatives within the Attorney General's Office, as well as expenditures on women's anti-violence services and women's centres in the Ontario Women's Directorate.

17  I also used historical advocacy and government data to compare demands over time, recognizing that advocates can be overly critical of state responses in order to maintain a strategic lobbying position vis-à-vis the state.

18  For more detailed discussion see Collier (2006).

19  In 1996 Arlene May was murdered by her former boyfriend, who then committed suicide. Before she was murdered, May had suffered years of abuse, which had been repeatedly reported to police. At the time of the murder, May's former partner was out on bail under an order prohibiting him from contacting her (OWJN archives http://www.owjn.org/archive/arlene.htm, accessed 19 Jan.19 2008).

20  This statement was made even when the prominent judge who had conducted the inquest stated publicly that this was not the case (Canadian Press NewsWire, 4 April 2002).

21  This prompted the Chief Coroner of Ontario to announce yet another inquest into one of the spousal murders—that of Gillian Hadley in 2000 (OWJN 2000b). In March 2006, another inquest was called into the death of Lori Dupont, who was stabbed at work by her estranged husband (Laucious 2006).

22  This follows the federal trend of cuts to core funding for women's groups.
23  Three Conservative cabinet ministers met with members of the Cross Sectoral Violence against Women Strategy Group in 2000 and made it clear that second-stage housing was off the table and 'would not come back onto the table for as long as this government is in power' (OWJN 2000b, 2).
24  See www.stepitupontario.ca.
25  In BC, expenditure data from the Stopping the Violence initiative of the Ministry of Women's Equality are included with any other identifiable anti-violence program spending.
26  See Collier (2006).
27  See Kachuk (1998) for more on the VAWIR policy, including movement critiques.
28  Because the responses were rated as not significant, they are not included in Table 8.4.
29  For more on the state of the economy in BC in 2000, see Spector (2002) and Collier (2006).
30  These included cuts in legal aid in 2001 and cuts to welfare rates in 2002, which advocates argued would particularly hurt women victims of violence. See BCIFV (2002).
31  I discuss this nuanced impact of the partisan variable in Collier (2006). It is also raised by Teghtsoonian and Chappell's 2008 comparative study of women's policy agencies in BC and Australia.
32  My argument here differs from the conclusion reached by Teghtsoonian and Chappell (2008) that neo-liberal tendencies 'increasingly' led the BC NDP to 'displace those of feminism and social justice' (2008, 43). However, my analysis agrees with their assertion of 'the importance of considering variability among parties of the right' (and I would add the left here as well) together with 'the particular political and ideological commitments of individual leaders' (Teghsoonian and Chappell 2008, 43). For more on this argument, see Collier (2006).

# References

Bashevkin, Sylvia. 1998. *Women on the Defensive: Living through Conservative Times*. Toronto: University of Toronto Press.

———. 2000. 'Rethinking Retrenchment: North American Social Policy during the Early Clinton and Chrétien Years'. *Canadian Journal of Political Science* 33 (1): 3–36.

———. 2002. *"Welfare Hot Buttons: Women Work and Social Policy Reform"*. Toronto: University of Toronto Press.

BC Association of Specialized Victim's Assistance and Counselling Programs (BCASVACP) 2007. *Summer 2007 Newsletter*. www.endingviolence.org (accessed 15 Nov. 2007).

BC Department of Finance. 1994/95–2006/07 inclusive. *Public Accounts of British Columbia*. Victoria: Department of Finance.

BC Task Force on Family Violence. 1992. *Report*. Victoria.

Blake, Donald. 1996. 'The Politics of Polarization: Parties and Elections in British Columbia'. In R.K. Carty, ed., *Politics, Policy and Government in British Columbia*. Vancouver: UBC Press.

*Brantford Expositor*. 2001. 'Women's group boycotts B.C. memorial'. 7 Dec., final edition, A10.

Brodie, Janine. 1996. 'Canadian Women, Changing State Forms, and Public Policy'. In Janine Brodie, ed., *Women and Canadian Public Policy*. Toronto: Harcourt Brace.

British Columbia Coalition of Women's Centres (BCCWC). 2003. 'BC Singled Out for Criticism by UN Committee'. 4 Mar. http://www3.telus.net/bcwomen/archives/ BCCEDAW_UNsubmission_jan_03_pressrel.html (accessed 15 May 2006).

———. 2005. 'BC Liberals Ensure Women's Voices are Silenced'. 27 Jan. http://www3.telus.net. bcwomen/archives/liberals_silence_women_jan_05.html (accessed 15 May 2006).

British Columbia Institute against Family Violence (BCIFV). 2002. 'BC Government Cuts Hurt Victims of Violence against Women'. Media release. 24 June 2002. http://www.bcifv.org/ hottopics/media/june24.shtml (accessed 6 May 2006).

———. 2005. 'Extensive Funding Cut Leads to Reduced, Restructured BC Institute against Family Violence'. Media release. 31 Jan. http://www.bcifv.org/hottopics/media/jan3105.shtml (accessed 6 May 2006).

Cairns, Alan. 2000. '$50M boost for victims of crime. Cell phones for women at risk'. *Toronto Sun*, 28 June 2000.

Canada NewsWire. 2001. 'Ontario government continues to combat domestic violence'. Ottawa, 1 Nov. http://proquest.umi.com.proxy.library.carleton.ca/pqdweb?index+45&did+87448352&Sr (accessed 6 May 2006).

———. 2002. 'Ernie Eves government announces funding to assist victims of domestic violence'. Ottawa, 2 Oct. http://proquest.umi.com.proxy.library.carleton.ca/pqdweb?index+20&did+202230741&S (accessed 6 May 2006).

———. 2003. 'Dark day for women, equity groups in wake of program and office closures'. Ottawa, 31 Mar. http://proquest.umi.com.proxy.library.carleton.ca/pqdweb?index+2&did+319984251&Sr (accessed 6 May 2006).

Canadian Press NewsWire. 2000. 'Ontario funding cuts to women's centres called blatant hypocrisy'. Toronto, 2 Oct. http://proquest.umi.com.proxy.library.carleton.ca/pqdweb?index+120&did+376949111 (accessed 6 May 2006).

———. 2000. 'Ontario judge under review for letter sent to Flaherty on abused women'. 4 Apr. http://proquest.umi.com.proxy.library.carleton.ca/pqdweb?index+25&did+348336151&S (accessed 6 May 2006).

Canoe—CNews. http://www.canoe.ca/CNEWSOntarioElection/home (accessed 5 May 2006).

Castles, Francis, ed. 1982. *The Impact of Parties, Politics and Policies in Democratic Capitalist States*. Beverly Hills: Sage.

Collier, Cheryl N. 2006. 'Governments and Women's Movements: Explaining Child Care and Anti-violence Policy in Ontario and British Columbia, 1970–2000'. Doctoral dissertation, University of Toronto.

Community Action. 2001. 'Ontario funds 436 shelter beds', *Community Action*, 20 Aug. Don Mills.

Creese, Gillian, and Veronica Strong-Boag. 2005. *Losing Ground: The Effects of Government Cutbacks on Women in British Columbia, 2001–2005*. http://www3.telus.net/bcwomen/archives/losinggroundexecsumm.html (accessed 2 May 2006).

Crosby, Don. 2004. 'Less emphasis on women's shelters, minister says', *Owen Sound Sun Times*, 26 Nov., A1.

Daily Press. 2001. 'Northern projects get $330,000 boost', *Timmins Daily Press*, 2 Feb. 2, 2.

Della-Mattia, Elaine. 2004. 'Women in crisis pleased with new funding plan', *Sault Star*, 15 Dec., A3.

Dobrowolsky, Alexandra, and Jane Jenson. 2004. 'Shifting Representations of Citizenship: Canadian Politics of "Women" and "Children" ', *Social Politics* 11 (2): 154–80.

Drummond, Robert, and Robert MacDermid. 1997. 'Elections and Campaigning: They Blew Our Doors Off on the Buy'. In Graham White, ed., *The Government and Politics of Ontario*. Toronto: University of Toronto Press.

Dunn, Christopher, ed. 1996. *Provinces: Canadian Provincial Politics*. Toronto: Broadview Press.

Dyck, Rand. 1996. *Provincial Politics in Canada*. Scarborough: Prentice-Hall Canada.

Elections BC. 2000. *Election Results*. http://www.elections.bc.ca/elections (accessed 25 July 2002).

Elections Ontario. 1999. *Election Results*. http://www.electionsontario.on.ca/results (accessed 25 July 2002).

———. 2007. *Election Results (unofficial)*. http://www.electionsontario.on.ca (accessed 15 Nov. 2007).

Gotell, Lise. 1998. 'A Critical Look at State Discourse on Violence against Women: Some Implications for Feminist Politics and Women's Citizenship'. In Manon Tremblay and Caroline Andrew, eds, *Women and Political Representation in Canada*. Ottawa: University of Ottawa Press.

Hicks, Alexander M., and Duane H. Swank. 1992. 'Politics, Institutions, and Welfare Spending in Industrialized Democracies, 1960–82', *American Political Science Review* 86 (3): 658–74.

Jenson, Jane. 'Writing Gender Out: The Continuing Effects of the Social Investment Perspective', this volume.

———, and Denis Saint-Martin. 2003. 'New Routes to Social Cohesion? Citizenship and the Social Investment State', *Canadian Journal of Sociology* 28 (1): 77–99.

Kachuk, Patricia. 1998. *Violence against Women in Relationships: An Analysis of Policies and Actions.* FREDA Centre for Research on Violence against Women and Children. http://www.harbour.sfu.ca/freda (accessed 25 July 2002).

Kendall, Gavin. 2003. 'From Liberalism to Neoliberalism'. Paper presented to the Social Change in the 21st Century Conference, Centre for Social Change Research, Queensland University of Technology. http://eprints.qut.edu.au/archive/00000134/.

LaFleche, Grant. 2007. 'Women's groups keeping track of Liberal's record'. *St. Catharines Standard.* http://www.stcatharinesstandard.ca/Article Display.aspx?e=749546&auth= GRANT+LaFLECHE (accessed 19 Nov. 2007).

Lakeman, Lee. 1999. 'Why "Law and Order" Cannot End Violence against Women; and Why the Development of Women's (Social, Economic and Political and Civil) Rights Might', *Canadian Women's Studies* 20 (3): 24–33.

Laucius, Joanne. 2006. 'We should be outraged these deaths are continuing unabated', *Ottawa Citizen*, 8 Apr., E1.

Leavitt, Sarah. 2002. 'Provincial Government Cutbacks: The Impact on Survivors of Abuse', *BC Association of Specialized Victim Assistance and Counselling Programs Newsletter*, Spring.

Leslie, Keith. 2004. 'Domestic violence plan rapped slammed', *Sarnia Observer*, 14 Dec. 2002, A7.

Lightman, Ernie, and Donna Baines. 1996. 'White Men in Blue Suits: Women's Policy in Conservative Ontario', *Canadian Journal of Social Policy* 38: 145–52.

Lister, Ruth. 2004. 'The Third Way's Social Investment State'. In J. Lewis and R. Surender, eds, *Welfare State Change: Towards a Third Way*, 157–82. Oxford: Oxford University Press.

———. 2006. 'Women and Public Policy, Post-neoliberalism? A UK Perspective'. Paper presented at the annual meeting of the Canadian Political Science Association, Toronto, May–June 2006.

Livingston, Gillan. 2004. 'Ontario giving $1.6M to aid sexual assault, violence victims', *St. Catharines Standard*, 31 May, A7.

MacDermid, Robert, and Gregory Albo. 2001. 'Divided Province, Growing Protests: Ontario Moves Right'. In Keith Brownsey and Michael Howlett, eds, *The Provincial State in Canada: Politics in the Provinces and Territories.* Peterborough, Ont.: Broadview Press.

McDonald, John. 2005. 'Neo-liberalism and the Pathologising of Public Issues: The Displacement of Feminist Service Models in Domestic Violence Support Services', *Australian Social Work* 58 (3): 275–84.

MCAW ([British Columbia] Ministry of Community, Aboriginal and Women's Services). 2005. 'Province Announces New Women's Transition House Funding'. News release. Victoria, 26 Jan. http://www2.news.gov.bc.ca/archive/2001-2005/2005MCAWs0003-000066.htm (accessed 17 May 2006).

O'Neill, Terry. 2002. 'Lady justice gets back her blindfold: The B.C. government prepares to dump anti-male spousal-abuse policies', *Report Newsmagazine* 8 July (national edition), 32.

Ontario Advisory Council on Women's Issues. 1992. *Untitled document.* Ontario Advisory Council on Women's Issues File, Women's Movement Archives, Box 86.

Ontario Association of Interval and Transition Houses (OAITH). 1997. *OAITH Response to the Framework for Action on the Prevention of Violence against Women in Ontario.* Toronto: OAITH. http://www.schliferclinic.com/oaith.htm (accessed 28 June 2002).

Ontario. Ministry of Citizenship and Immigration. 2007. *Domestic Violence Action Plan Update.* Toronto: Ministry of Citizenship and Immigration.

Ontario. Ministry of the Attorney General. 2007. *McGuinty Government Increases Funding to Sexual Assault Centres.* Press release. Toronto: Ministry of the Attorney General.

Ontario. Ministry of Treasury, Economics and Intergovernmental Affairs. 1992–2004. *Public Accounts.* Toronto: Ministry of Treasury, Economics and Intergovernmental Affairs.

Ontario Women's Justice Network (OWJN). 2000a. 'A Call for All-Party Cooperation in the Ontario Legislature in Support of Emergency Measures for Women and Children'. http://www.owjn.org/vaw/ (accessed 28 June 2002).

———. 2000b. 'Provincial Government Not Prepared to Make Meaningful Commitment to End Violence against Women'. http://www.owjn.org/vanov22.htm (accessed 25 Nov. 2002).

————. 2002. 'What's Happening with the Domestic Violence Protection Act?' http://www.owjn.org/issues/w-abuse/domup.htm (accessed 10 Mar. 2005).

————. 2005a. 'Government Announces "Domestic Violence Action Plan"'. http://www.owjn.org/issues/w-abuse/actionplan.htm (accessed 10 Mar. 2005).

————. 2005b. 'Where Is the Action in Ontario's Domestic Violence Action Plan?' http://www.owjn.org/issues/w-abuse/actionplanupdate.htm (accessed 11 Nov. 2007).

Pilot, Johannah. 1993. '"Stopping the Violence" and Sexual Assault Centres: Co-opting Centres', Kinesis, June: 15–16.

Schmidt, Manfred. 1996. 'When Parties Matter: A Review of the Possibilities and Limits of Partisan Influence on Public Policy', European Journal of Political Research 30: 155–83.

Sigurdson, Richard. 1996. 'The British Columbia New Democratic Party: Does It Make a Difference?' In R.K. Carty, ed., Politics, Policy and Government in British Columbia. Vancouver: UBC Press.

Spector, Norman. 2002. 'You're a mean one, Mr Campbell'. Globe and Mail, 21 Jan., A11.

Teghtsoonian, Katherine. 2003. 'W(h)ither Women's Equality? Neoliberalism, Institutional Change and Public Policy in British Columbia'. Policy, Organisation and Society 22 (1): 26–47.

————, and Louise Chappell. 2008. 'The Rise and Decline of Women's Policy Machinery in British Columbia and New South Wales: A Cautionary Tale', International Political Science Review 29 (1): 29–51.

Weldon, S. Laurel. 2002. Protest, Policy and the Problem of Violence against Women: A Cross-National Comparison. Pittsburgh: University of Pittsburgh Press.

Whitnall, Catherine. 2001. 'Women's shelter gets cash injection'. Lindsay Daily Post (Ont.), 9 Aug., 1.

Women's Movement Archives. 1970–2001 inclusive. Boxes 1–148. Ottawa: University of Ottawa.

## Further Reading

Lakeman, Lee. 1999. 'Why "Law and Order" Cannot End Violence against Women; and Why the Development of Women's (Social, Economic and Political and Civil) Rights Might', Canadian Women's Studies 20 (3): 24–33.

Lister, Ruth. 2006. 'Women and Public Policy, Post-neoliberalism? A UK Perspective'. Paper presented at the annual meeting of the Canadian Political Science Association, Toronto, May/June 2006.

McDonald, John. 2005. 'Neo-liberalism and the Pathologising of Public Issues: The Displacement of Feminist Service Models in Domestic Violence Support Services', Australian Social Work 58 (3): 275–84.

Weldon, S. Laurel. 2002. Protest, Policy and the Problem of Violence against Women: A Cross-National Comparison. Pittsburgh: University of Pittsburgh Press. www.stepitupontario.ca

## Questions for Critical Thought

1. Is the left–right political spectrum, routinely used to explain ideological partisan differences, adequate to account for different partisan approaches to women's policy arenas, particularly violence against women, or is there a better way to account for these differences?

2. Has Canada entered fully into a post–neo-liberal era, or can right-wing regimes still pursue mainly neo-liberal agendas in the 21st century?

3. What are the long-term impacts of a gender-neutral portrayal of the problem of violence against women?

# CHAPTER 9

# Intimate Relationships and the Canadian State

Lois Harder

## Introduction

In 1967, Justice Minister Pierre Trudeau declared, 'There's no place for the state in the bedrooms of the nation' (CBC 1967). He made this remark in reference to newly introduced legislation that legalized abortion and decriminalized private sexual activity between two people of the same sex over age 21. But Trudeau overstated his case. In fact, the Canadian state, like all nation-states, is deeply invested in regulating the sexual lives and identities of its citizens, especially through the regulation of marriage and 'marriage-like' relationships. These relationships are important to the state for several reasons. First, intimate relationships organize kinship and in so doing they are integral in determining membership in the state (Stevens 1999). For example, one of the most common avenues to Canadian citizenship is to be born to Canadian parents. As well, state-recognized relationships are a key site for the provision of care and for sharing private resources. The determination of membership through the organization of kinship as well as the provision of care and the distribution of resources are also infused with regulatory ideals concerning gender, race, class, and the national identity. Thus the laws that define and regulate intimate life constitute our identities. We may perceive our 'bedroom lives' as private and freely chosen, but that perception is itself an accomplishment of governance.

In this chapter, I examine Canadian court cases, legislation, and policy in order to show how ideas about the properly constituted family have changed and to argue that the regulation of intimate life is directly related to the regulation of identities. For the purposes of this volume, I will focus particularly on gendered identities. Canada, as one of only a few countries to recognize marriage between same-sex partners and to grant relatively equal status to marriage and common-law relationships, is generally held to be a global leader in advancing sexual-equality rights for its citizens and residents. At least two consequences may emerge from this relatively liberal acceptance of relationship diversity. First, the power of marriage to confer status, entitlement, and special privileges through the assumption of defined identities is diminished when other two-person monogamous relationships are recognized legally and socially. This development may, in turn, rework established rules of kinship and, by extension, political membership. By expanding the types of relationships that can claim legal status, the question of why some forms of intimate life and associated identities confer special privileges, while others do not, becomes a matter for public deliberation. As a society we may agree that certain forms of intimate relationship should be protected and supported, but in recognizing that the decision to do so is a political choice, we simultaneously disrupt claims that marriage, 'the family', and the identities of the people who compose these social forms are constituted through nature. The second result of Canada's comparatively expansive regime of relationship recognition, in particular, marriage and common-law partnerships for same-sex couples, may be to weaken the extent to which these relationships rely on and reinforce gendered identities in the figures of husband and wife. Whether or not same-sex relationships will have a demonstration effect for different-sex relationships, whether, by contrast, the power of heterosexual norms will impose themselves in same-sex relationships, or whether the relentless demands of capitalism for more production, more consumption, and more workers will finally disrupt gendered norms of participation in paid and unpaid labour and the gendered roles of family members, are open questions.

It is certainly plausible to assert that Canada's recognition of new family forms is in keeping with the governing ethos of the social investment state, an ethos which I understand in terms of an entrenchment, or normalization, of neo-liberalism (Peck and Tickell 2002; Harder forthcoming). As we will see, part of the rationale for extending recognition to common-law relationships was to compel people in interdependent but non-marital relationships to provide support for each other rather than relying on the state. Furthermore, as federal, provincial, and territorial governments have moved to confer relationship status, private support obligations can be imposed, whether or not the people participating in those relationships actually want those obligations. This legitimation of diverse family forms can be seen as a key component of the social investment state (Jenson and Saint-Martin 2003, 80). As Jane Jenson and Denis Saint-Martin argue, contemporary liberal democracies deliver social programs through what they term the 'welfare diamond,' composed of the state, the market, the family, and the voluntary sector (2003, 80). As the logic of neo-liberalism and social investment have advocated a shift away from the provision of social goods by the state, other areas of the diamond, including the family, variously defined, have had to take on both old and new obligations. Increasing the range of legitimated relationships thus contributes to this governing project.

This chapter, which draws on historical examples to set the stage for contemporary developments, begins with a review of two key rationales for regulating intimate life, political membership and economic efficiency. Legal scholars have argued that since the Supreme Court rendered its judgment in *Miron v. Trudel* in 1995, the significance of marriage, as distinct from other conjugal relationships, has diminished (Holland 2000; Law Commission of Canada 2001, 2). Indeed, the very meaning of conjugality and its relevance in triggering state recognition has become a subject of debate. As state agencies rethink the necessity of linking marriage, procreation, and regulation, we also see shifts in the meanings of gendered identities. The ensuing legal and legislative debates concerning the purposes of intimate relationships for the operation and identity of the state have been fascinating. The question whether sex *should* matter to the state then returns us to Trudeau's claim, though with a new set of considerations through which to assess its persuasiveness.

## Theorizing State Interests in Intimate Life

In her book *Reproducing the State,* Jacqueline Stevens (1999) advances the provocative and persuasive argument that political societies are membership organizations and that 'the paradigmatic membership structure for all political societies derives from invocations of birth and ancestry' (51). Since membership is one of the key features of the state, it makes sense that the rules of belonging would be a central public concern. Of course, the claim that birth and ancestry lie at the root of citizenship in contemporary democracies seems rather perplexing. After all, the basis for the authority of the liberal-democratic state, as the social contract theorists tell us, is supposed to be the consent of the governed. We think of our citizenship as a function of our agreement to accept the legitimacy of the democratic process. Yet, with the exception of immigrants (see Abu-Laban in this volume), the vast majority of Canadians belong to Canadian political society by virtue of being born on Canadian territory or born to citizen parents. A member of the Canadian polity may exercise her right to vote or not and belong to a political party or not, all without affecting her claim to citizenship in Canada.

Stevens proceeds to argue that in the absence of political authority, neither marriage nor kinship exists. In the case of marriage, for example, two (or more) people might commit themselves to each other, but this commitment has no legal weight or authority unless it is recognized by the state. With regard to broader kinship structures, we must also look to the political authority to determine who counts in a legally constituted family. Canadian family law, for example, asserts that when a child is born to a married couple, the husband is the father, regardless of whether or not he made a biological contribution to the creation of that child (Mykitiuk 2001, 780). In a case where the husband is not the biological father, the mother's husband can disavow the child, but the biological father cannot legally contest the husband's claim to fatherhood. Who constitutes a father is thus a function of law rather than 'nature'. We can also see the machinations of the state in the designation of 'legitimacy' to children. Historically, a child born 'out-of-wedlock' was *filius nullius*, or 'child of no one' (Mykitiuk 2001, 781). Not only does such a status tell us a great deal about the legal standing of the mother (no one), but it also rendered the child stateless, since the then-existing rules of membership granted citizenship only to men and to their family members and solely by virtue of marriage and the husband's status as head of the household. And with regard to the intersection of race, gender, and membership, until the coming into force of the Canadian Charter of Rights and Freedoms in 1985, women would lose their status as Indians if they married someone without status, whereas men could convey Indian status on their wives. Under current law, a child with a parent and a grandparent who both married non-status Indians will lose her status. In all of these cases we see very clearly that the relationships that constitute a recognizable family exist by virtue of political practices. Moreover, those same political practices articulate the membership criteria in that political society. The criteria may change over time; hence how one comes to be a Canadian may be altered (as in the demise of the category of illegitimacy), but the state's interest in articulating rules of belonging—a task it does primarily through rules of kinship—is enduring.

The state is also interested in the regulation of intimate life because of the central role that relationships and families play in sustaining the economy. Feminist political economists have been especially interested in explaining how the productive (surplus-generating) and reproductive (rejuvenating) tasks of capitalist economies are divided among the domestic sphere, the market, the voluntary sector, and the state (Folbre 2006; Jenson 2004; Waring 2003). In liberal theory, the home was identified as a site of extreme privacy, where shelter from the state, freedom from the expectations of rational action, and a suspension of the demands of commercial enterprise might be enjoyed. The extent to which such a vision obscured all of the work conducted within the domestic sphere, the power relations that were established through the separation of production and reproduction, and the gendering of these respective forms of work were obvious targets for feminist interrogation.

In the contemporary period, in which long struggles for equality rights have manifested themselves in unprecedented levels of workforce participation, it might be tempting to suggest that gender and racial divisions in productive and reproductive labour are vestigial remnants of an earlier era and are destined for the dustbin of history. Moreover, we might also observe that family law has become attuned to the gendered dynamics of heterosexual relationships and has established regimes of custody and support that recognize that disparities in income may arise from women's greater likelihood of having withdrawn from paid employment, either in whole or in part, in order to address the reproductive needs of their families. Clearly this recognition represents an important accomplishment for feminist activism. But to the extent that the courts are prepared to recognize that income inequality may exist in heterosexual marriages and common-law relationships, they may also be participating in the reinforcement of a heterosexual, racial, and class-based norm that renders other means of dividing responsibilities of production and reproduction as deviant and potentially less worthy of judicial redress. In terms of gender, an acknowledgement that women do shoulder a disproportionate share of responsibility for reproductive tasks creates a situation in which the courts, and by extension the state, might also be presuming that women *should* shoulder these responsibilities (Kershaw 2005). On the other hand, as the social investment model increasingly insists that adults, regardless of their care responsibilities, should be engaged in paid labour, feminists are less likely to succeed in making the case that divorce settlements should redress the care obligations shouldered by women.

It is important to note that support and maintenance decisions are highly privatized mechanisms for ensuring the economic well-being of families after the primary relationship has been severed. No additional funds are provided by the state to facilitate the operation of two residences or to offset the increase in reproductive costs that occur when the chief provider of those services is absent. Rather, the state sees its role as articulating the rules through which the privacy of the family can be sustained. When relationships end, the state oversees the redistribution of the family finances, particularly from fathers to children and in increasingly punitive ways. But the overriding expectation of the social investment state is the advocacy of a 'universal worker model' of citizenship through which all adults, regardless of their caring responsibilities, are expected to meet the needs of their dependents through participation in paid work. This thrust is especially apparent in social-assistance rules that compel single mothers with very young children to search for work, in mandatory participation in maintenance-enforcement programs to compel non-custodial parents to meet their support obligations, and in policies such as the National Child Benefit that provide greater financial support to low-income working families than to families receiving social assistance. The state is thus deeply invested in maintaining 'the family' as an institution of economic provision even, or perhaps especially, when families have shifted away from the normative, two-adult form.

The private quality of the family has been a foundational assumption of liberal modernity, but the character of that privacy has changed over time. In Canada, the rise of public education, public healthcare, and the contemplation of public childcare are examples of activities in which state services have breached the alleged boundary of the family's private, reproductive functions. Under the contemporary terms of neo-liberal or social investment governance, this relationship between the state and the organization and activities of intimate life is again being re-negotiated, with a notable decrease in the provision of public services and a related expectation that the market, voluntary sector, and the family will fill the void (Armstrong and Kits 2001; Brock 2006; Fudge and Cossman 2002; Jenson and Saint-Martin 2003; others in this volume). One important feature of this re-negotiation is the extent to which the neo-liberal state's efforts to reduce public expenditures both recognize and forget the necessity and costs of reproductive labour. On the one hand, social services are identified as a major component of state spending and thus a logical target for budget cuts. But the fact that a reduction in public spending and service provision shifts the costs to the private sphere, particularly families, with ensuing demands on unpaid labour and personal finances, is either disregarded or presented as an opportunity for greater consumer choice (Clarke 2004).

In Canada, neo-liberal privatization efforts have been harnessed to the recognition of increasingly diverse family forms. Since the mid-1990s, Canada's courts, and subsequently legislatures, have steadily extended legal recognition beyond marriage to 'marriage-like' relationships. This recognition is justified, at least in part, on the grounds that the legitimacy of more kinds of families offers more opportunities for the neo-liberal state to offload public responsibility for well-being onto the private sphere (Cossman 2002; Harder 2007). For example, in their judicial opinion in support of equating different- and same-sex common-law relationships (*M. v. H.* 1999), Supreme Court justices Cory and Iacobucci concluded, with regard to the *Ontario Family Law Act*, that the objectives of the statute were to provide for 'the equitable resolution of economic disputes when intimate relationships between financially interdependent individuals break down, and alleviating the burden on the public purse to provide for dependent spouses' (*M. v. H.* 1999, par. 4). Including same-sex partners within the law would, in fact, further these legislative objectives (*M. v. H.* 1999, par. 4). Thus, while *M. v. H.* was a watershed decision in extending relationship equality to common-law same-sex couples, it is significant that the rationale for that decision rested on an economic calculation, as well as a concern for fundamental justice (see also Dobrowolsky in this volume).

The state's interests in governing intimate relationships are fundamentally tied to concerns over its existence, both in terms of how membership is established and perpetuated and in the generation of resources, goods, and services to sustain the economic well-being of its population. And while it may not be *necessary* for state membership to be determined through kinship or for the reproductive functions of capital to be undertaken by families, it is nonetheless true that intimate relationships and families have been the key sites for this activity in all political societies. Moreover, it is also important to recognize that the rules of kinship vary across states and over time. Indeed, Jacqueline Stevens (1999) argues that because membership criteria are also kinship rules, it is precisely the rules of kinship that give specificity to any particular nation-state.

With that observation in mind, we will now examine how the Canadian nation-state governs intimate relationships and, in particular, how that task of governance has created gendered and sexual identities.

## Marriage, Privilege, and Gender

Marriage is the most important institution through which the state regulates the family and, as we have seen, it also plays an important role in defining, regulating, and reinforcing social identities. Being married also entitles the participants to a range of benefits. Among these is the ability to pass on social standing (citizenship) and property, preferential tax treatment, the authority to make healthcare decisions, and employer-provided benefits. Because marriage confers a range of benefits that are not available to people simply as individuals, or to people who have established intimate relationships outside of marriage, the privileges and exclusions that marriage establishes have subjected the institution to critiques for creating a hierarchy of modes of living, thus inspiring subsequent calls for its abolition, as well as the converse demand to extend its privileges to other forms of relationship.

Marriage, as feminist theorists have persuasively demonstrated, also plays a crucial role in defining gender. In addition to the rules that bring men into legal relation with children that we have already noted, the husband's position as the head of the household has also been integral to the gendering effects of marriage. Until the late 19th century in Canada, laws of coverture collapsed women's legal identities into those of their husbands and ceded control of any property a woman might have held before her marriage, or received as an inheritance during her marriage, to her husband (Arnup 2001). Under marriage two people became one, and that one was the husband (Brook 2000, 193). Moreover, the abolition of coverture, in 1884, had little effect on legal rulings since judges resisted giving women greater autonomy over their own affairs, fearing the implications that such control would have on the family (Arnup 2001, 15–16). Even when a marriage does not include children then, statuses of 'husband' and 'wife' have had, and continue to have, explicitly gendered meanings.

Today, the Canadian state's interests in the bedrooms of the nation are becoming more complex. Just as genetic testing and artificial reproductive technologies complicate our assumptions about who constitutes a parent, the growing social legitimacy of non-marital relationships among both different- and same-sex couples has inspired increased critical reflection on which relationships should matter politically and why. As part of this reflection and the ensuing legal and legislative reform, shifts are occurring on the terrains of kinship and national membership, economic efficiencies, and the gendering effects of intimate relationships. As I argue in the next section, the extent to which the recognition of more forms of relationship might disrupt all three of these elements depends crucially on whether 'conjugality' remains the trigger for state regulation of intimate life.

## Which Bedrooms Now?

Although marriage in Canada continues to command preferred social and legal standing among adult domestic relationships, and indeed, continues to be the most popular mode of forming an intimate partnership (in 2006, 81 per cent of all co-habitating couples were married), this status and popularity have been steadily declining (Statistics Canada 2007). Between 1996 and 2006, for example, the proportion of married family households declined from 55 per cent to 49 per cent of all Canadian households (Statistics Canada 2007, 1997). As Canadians have devised alternative household forms, courts and legislatures have had to contend with the question of their legitimacy. If, for example, a couple chooses not to marry, should this choice be respected? Or, in the interests of protecting people from exploitation within their personal relationships, should the state create some regulations to safeguard individuals' well-being, especially when the relationship ends? If the argument is that choice *should* matter, then on what grounds, if any, can marriage be a choice for some people (two people of different sexes) and denied to others (people of the same sex, or people involved in polyamorous relationships)? We might also step back from examining the meaning of marriage and the extent to which other forms of intimate life can be said to be 'marriage-like', to ask the prior question of why certain forms of intimacy, often presumed to include a sexual relationship, are more privileged than those that do not bear such a presumption.

One of the first catalysts for contemporary changes in the regulation of intimate life was the Canadian Supreme Court's decision in *Miron v. Trudel* (1995). In this case, the Court found that marital status should be considered an 'analogous ground' and thus protected under the equality-rights provision of the *Canadian Charter of Rights and Freedoms*. The facts of the case were as follows. John Miron was injured in a car accident while he was a passenger. Since neither of the drivers involved was insured, Miron attempted to submit an insurance claim under the policy of his common-law partner, Jocelyne Valliere. This remedy would have been available to Miron had he and Valliere been married, but the insurance company denied Miron's claim because Valliere was not a 'spouse' under the *Ontario Insurance Act* or the terms of the insurance policy (*Miron v. Trudel* 1995). Lower courts upheld the definition of spouse as married, but the Supreme Court overturned these decisions. Justices Gonthier, Lamer, La Forest, and Major dissented from this decision.

The rationales of the various justices are highly instructive regarding the stakes involved in reducing the privileged position of marriage in law. As the author of the dissenting position, Justice Gonthier's spirited defence of marriage as a 'fundamental social institution' is especially revealing. Gonthier cited an 1888 US case, *Maynard v. Hill*, to establish that marriage 'is an institution, in the maintenance of which in its purity the public is deeply interested, for it is the foundation of the family and of society, without which there would be neither civilization nor progress' (cited in *Miron v. Trudel* 1995, par. 48). In his assessment, and that of three of his colleagues, distinctions based on marital status were not discriminatory, since marriage was both a choice and a contract. People who chose not to marry were not expected to assume mutual obligations of support and may or may not be committed to permanence (par. 71). Gonthier argued that unmarried couples were not a 'disadvantaged group' and did not 'constitute a "discrete and insular minority" which had suffered "social, political and legal disadvantage in our society" ' (par. 58). People had a choice to marry or not, and marriage, as a distinctive social institution, was not to be diminished by including unmarried couples within its definition. In the minority opinion of the Supreme Court, then, marriage *should* be privileged, since it is the foundation of society and the basis of civilization. Moreover, because people have a choice as to whether or not to marry, that choice must be respected and the duties that the marriage contract imposes (including mutual support) should be limited to those people who willingly and publicly accept them by marrying.

As noted above, the majority of the Supreme Court justices felt differently. The majority decision made no mention of a fundamental connection between marriage and civilization, nor did it countenance the claim that marriage was a fundamental social institution. Instead, the argument was that people should have the freedom to organize their intimate lives as they see fit and that their choices should be respected. As Justice McLachlin argued,

> Discrimination on the basis of marital status touches the essential dignity and worth of the individual in the same way as other recognized grounds of discrimination violative of fundamental human rights norms. Specifically, it touches the individual's freedom to live life with the mate of one's choice in the fashion of one's choice. (*Miron v. Trudel* 1995, par. 145)

One might observe that both the dissenting and concurring judgments mobilize the language of choice and freedom to make their respective cases and both sides assert that those choices need to be respected. The decisions differ, however, on the issue of the consequences of that respect. For the dissenting judges, the choice not to marry results in a couple's freedom from mutual obligation and, concomitantly, their freedom from mutual benefit. For the concurring judges, the facts of mutual support are evident from the conditions of Miron and Trudel's lives, including the presence of children and a relationship of some permanence. Because their lives are, in fact, intertwined and 'marriage-like', their choice not to marry should not prevent them from enjoying the benefits that accrue through marriage.

Justice L'Heureux-Dubé concurred with the majority decision, but she also wanted to highlight the gendered consequences of inequality in relationship forms. L'Heureux-Dubé observed that the Ontario government had already extended benefits to common-law couples in more than 30 statutes and that much of the impetus for this extension resulted from the observation that dependent spouses—most often women—would be disadvantaged by the failure to recognize these relationships (*Miron v. Trudel* 1995, par. 100). She noted that the financial consequences of a failure to legitimate common-law relationships would be especially severe if the injured party was the primary or sole income earner (*Miron v. Trudel* 1995, par. 107). L'Heureux-Dubé also suggested that the choice to marry was infused by complicated dynamics and hence could not be understood as simply as it was portrayed in the dissenting judgment. One member of the couple might want to marry while the other was less inclined, and thus a common-law relationship provided a compromise (*Miron v. Trudel* 1995, pars 97–102). For L'Heureux-Dubé, the exercise of choice should be through the voluntary use of a domestic contract to 'opt out' of mutual obligations, rather than the mandatory use of a marriage contract or other form of domestic partnership for those who wish to 'opt in'. In this way, rather than having to persuade one's partner to commit to the relationship, the task is to persuade one's partner not to do so.

An economic rationale for equating heterosexual common-law and heterosexual married partners also appeared in the Miron decision. For Justice L'Heureux-Dubé, one of the benefits of relationship equality, with respect to obliging the insurance company to provide disability benefits to Miron, was that this private means of provision 'would not impose any additional burden upon the public purse' (*Miron v. Trudel* 1995 par. 121). Thus, despite her progressive views on gender equality, Justice L'Heureux-Dubé invoked the discourse of neo-liberalism that was especially thunderous at this time and maintained a distinctly liberal conception of the division between the public and the private and the importance of minimizing public costs. The question whether marriage should entitle people to specific state benefits was very much alive in the Miron decision, but ultimately the court diluted the privilege of marriage by asserting the functional equivalence of marriage and 'marriage-like' relationships. This decision might be viewed as a revision to kinship forms that entitle people to state benefits—in this case, Charter protection against discrimination. The ruling also expressed the gendered identities associated with marriage and marriage-like relationships. While the dissenting judgment appeared to defend the heterosexual gendered identities implied by the connection between marriage and the on-going existence of civilization, Justice L'Heureux-Dubé, by contrast, drew attention to the negative consequences of gendered dynamics in marriage and 'marriage-like' relationships. Finally, the importance of maintaining the capacity for the private sphere to attend to the demands of mutual support—and thus to prevent demands on public resources—was also evident in this consideration of the state's role in married and unmarried heterosexual bedrooms.

The Supreme Court's decision in *M. v. H.* (1999) further challenged the assumptions underpinning the married, heterosexual, nuclear family, in this case by extending legal status to a common-law relationship between same-sex partners. This decision involved a claim for support under the terms of the *Ontario Family Law Act* between former partners in a lesbian relationship. The outcome of the Court's decision was to equate different and same-sex common-law relationships, the majority of the justices arguing that not to do so would violate the dignity and respect that should be afforded relationships of mutual commitment, regardless of the sexuality of the participants and, as already noted, that extending mutual support obligations to same-sex spouses would realize the purpose of the Act in reducing demands on public welfare.

The place of gender and sexuality in this decision is complex. In seeking to uphold the heterosexual definition of common-law relationships, the Ontario government intervened in the case, arguing that the support provisions were designed to mitigate the economic effects of dependence created in heterosexual relationships by the partial or complete withdrawal of women from paid labour (*M. v. H.* par. 86). Because same-sex relationships were not marked by systemic gender inequality, the argument ran, they should not be included in the terms of the support obligations. To put it another way, different- and same-sex couples should not be considered equally unequal. This argument was also advanced by Justice Gonthier in his dissenting opinion. The problem with this line of argument, however, was that the *Ontario Family Law Act* was explicitly written in gender-neutral language. That is, the Act envisioned that men who were dependent on their female partners would have the same protection under the Act as women did. Even if women were the primary benefactors of the support provisions, prevailing gender inequalities did not preclude men from also gaining the protection of the law. Thus, if men in heterosexual relationships could receive support, despite the fact that such a situation would run counter to systemic patterns of discrimination, then income disparities within same-sex couples, which were also claimed to be non-systemic, would have to be covered by the terms of the Act. Neither the Ontario government nor Justice Gonthier was willing to concede this point, however. For Justice Gonthier, marriage and now the recognition of heterosexual common-law relationships were, again, about maintaining a fundamental institution of society:

> The definition of 'spouse' . . . is an extension of marriage. . . . Spousehood is a social and cultural institution, not merely an instrument of economic policy. . . . In Western

history, . . . the concept of 'spouse' has always referred to a member of a cohabiting opposite-sex couple. . . . That well-recognized definition does not discriminate on the basis of sexual orientation. . . . [M]arriage is a fundamental social institution because it is the crucible of human procreation and the usual forum for the raising of children. . . . [Section] 29's definition of 'spouse' corresponds with an accurate account of the actual needs, capacity and circumstances of opposite-sex couples as compared to others. . . . It is both legitimate and reasonable for the Legislative Assembly to extend special treatment to an important social institution. (*M. v. H.*, pars 227–8, 232, 240)

The question of gender that arises from this decision then, is whether there are fundamental differences between the gendered inequality of heterosexual relationships and same-sex relationships that require state regulation and the protection of heterosexual marriage and common-law relationships, or whether the purpose of all long-term, committed, monogamous relationships is sufficiently similar that they should be considered equal under the law. In *M. v. H.*, the Supreme Court struck a delicate balance. Although the *Ontario Family Law Act* was written in gender-neutral language, that neutrality belied the recognition of systemic gender inequality between men and women with regard to earnings and the division of paid and unpaid labour. Gender neutrality also allowed for access to the law in individual circumstances where the prevailing gender dynamics were reversed. By allowing for that possibility, the law effectively shifted the focus from the gendering of certain forms of activity within relationships to the condition of inequality in and of itself. The law thus applies in situations in which one partner is financially dependent on the other. It is the condition of dependence rather than the identity that matters. Once the condition of inequality becomes the trigger for state regulation, the gender and the sexuality of the participants cease to matter—at least in the law.

## Contesting Conjugality

What is less recognized but potentially more radical than its finding of legal equality between different- and same-sex common-law relationships is that the Supreme Court's ruling in *M. v. H.* also reflected on the meaning of conjugality and its significance for legitimating relationships. A dissenting judge in a lower court had asserted that same-sex couples did not constitute a 'conjugal relationship' for the purposes of the *Ontario Family Law Act* because they could not represent themselves as 'husband and wife' to the community (*M. v. H.* 1999, par. 42). The Supreme Court's ruling interpreted conjugality more broadly. Drawing on the functional definition of conjugality outlined in *Molodowich v. Penttinen* (1980), a definition which includes some undetermined combination of shared residence, sexual and personal behaviour, reproductive labour, social activities, economic support, and children, as well as the societal perception of the couple, the Supreme Court argued that same-sex couples clearly did meet the definition (*M. v. H.* 1999, par. 59). The Court asserted that conjugality necessarily required a flexible application, noting that a heterosexual couple 'may, after many years together, be considered to be in a conjugal relationship although they have neither children nor sexual relations' (*M. v. H.* 1999, par. 60). The Supreme Court was not prepared to take this analysis to its logical next step to consider whether friends and siblings might also be considered 'conjugal', or, alternatively, to challenge the usefulness of conjugality as a marker of relationships bearing rights and obligations. The Court insisted that its task was to address the case at hand, where the issue was the legal entitlement of same-sex partners to the support provisions of the *Ontario Family Law Act* (*M v. H* 1999, par. 135). Yet the ever more apparent difficulties in defining conjugality, especially once a sexual relationship was no longer an essential feature of definition, inspired further debate and critical reflection.

In response to the Supreme Court's findings in *Miron v. Trudel* and *M. v. H.*, the federal government passed the *Modernization of Benefits Act* in 2000. This statute deems couples (both same- and different-sex) to be common-law partners if they have been in a conjugal relationship for at least a year. 'Common-law partners' are included with 'spouses' (a term now reserved for legally married couples) throughout the federal statute book (Cossman and Ryder 2001, 277). It should be noted that while the federal government is constitutionally responsible for laws governing who can marry, provinces establish their own legislation surrounding the marriage ceremony (that is, solemnization) and are also responsible for governing domestic relationships outside of marriage. The *Modernization of Benefits Act* recognized common-law relationships for the purposes of federal laws, but provincial governments were obliged to formulate their own distinct responses to the Supreme Court's findings of relationship equality. A variety of responses to this requirement have thus emerged. But with the exception of Quebec, where couples must register in order to be considered common-law, all other provinces ascribe status, or deem common-law status to exist, after a couple has co-habited for two to five years and immediately if there are children of the relationship.

When the *Modernization of Benefits Act* was passed, the Liberal government made it clear that marriage would continue to be defined as 'the union of one man and one woman to the exclusion of all others' (Ayed 2000, A3). This view would prove to be unsustainable. As court rulings in Ontario, British Columbia, and Quebec extended marriage rights to same-sex partners, the Liberal government of Paul Martin was eventually obliged to pass the *Civil Marriage Act* in 2005. Conservative resistance to same-sex marriage continued for a time. The Alberta government of Ralph Klein advanced the hollow threat to invoke the notwithstanding clause of the Constitution, which allows legislatures to override sections 2 and 7–15 of the Charter of Rights and Freedoms. However, the notwithstanding clause does not apply to marriage law, since federal authority to make laws governing marriage is not derived from the Charter. In addition, the federal Conservative party promised to re-open the same-sex marriage debate as part of its election platform in 2005–06. A very truncated debate was held in Parliament in December 2006 on the question whether Parliament should re-open the issue. One hundred and seventy-five out of 308 MPs voted to maintain the Act (Riley 2006, B7). Canada's commitment to marriage between same-sex partners thus seems relatively secure.[1]

One might note that these legislative developments persisted in privileging conjugality as the characteristic required to ensure the state's protection and recognition. But in the debate surrounding the *Modernization of Benefits Act,* the Reform/Alliance party departed somewhat from this view. Motivated primarily by a desire to protect the privileged status of heterosexual marriage, members of the Reform/Alliance argued that if all that mattered to the state was interdependence, then close relationships between siblings and friends also merited state recognition (Canada 2000). This act was really a subterfuge. Rather than dignifying same-sex relationships through political recognition, the Reform/Alliance urged a de-privileging of non-marital relationships. Yet questioning the legitimacy of conjugality for state purposes is not an inherently conservative position. Indeed, the Law Commission of Canada, recognizing that conjugality was becoming an increasingly slippery basis from which to incur state legitimacy, hired several of Canada's most progressive legal scholars to consider the relevance of conjugality in a range of legal procedures and social policies (Law Commission of Canada 2001). Although these scholars disagreed on some counts, their work constitutes a profound and progressive challenge to the centrality of conjugality in determining benefits and obligations in close personal relationships. Indeed, the influence of their insights can be seen in revisions to the federal Care Giver Leave program, which allows people who are gravely ill to designate a friend who is 'like family' to provide care and to obtain benefits under the Employment Insurance program to finance this undertaking. It should be noted, however, that the Law Commission's report did not consider issues of kinship or political membership. As I argued above, this rationale, while often absent from the debate over family diversity, is nonetheless central to considerations of which relationships matter to the state.

In addition to these federal initiatives, the provinces were obliged to reform relevant provincial legislation in order to comply with the Supreme Court's decisions. Although all provinces now recognize common-law different- and same-sex relationships, they differ with regard to the length of time required before common-law status is established. And Quebec, with its distinctive civil-law tradition, does not impose status on relationships without the stated intent of the participants. Instead, couples must register with the state in order to be considered common-law partners. Alberta has also taken a distinctive approach. Echoing the Reform/Alliance proposal, Alberta chose to comply with the Supreme

Court's decisions by establishing adult interdependent partnerships through the *Adult Interdependent Relationships Act* (AIRA). These partnerships apply to both different- and same-sex conjugal partners as well as two people involved in a non-conjugal relationship. Technically, it is possible for two people who are not romantically involved but are dependent on each other to be deemed to have formed an adult interdependent partnership. An explicit contract is required only when these two people are blood relations. As yet, this is the only legislation in Canada that extends relationship status to non-conjugal partners.

Because Alberta's law works on the basis of private contracts, and adult interdependent partnerships are not registered, there are no statistics that show how many adult interdependent relationships that do not fit the conjugal-couple model have been formed. In my own brief survey of judicial proceedings, I have found the AIRA referred to only in reference to support obligations between former common-law spouses. Nonetheless, the Act (in sec. 2, 3(1)) extends recognition and ascription to any two adults who have lived together for at least three years, share each other's lives, are emotionally committed to one another, and function as an economic and domestic unit. Although the government provided assurances during the debate about this legislation that long-time roommates, for example, would not find themselves legally obliged to each other, the legislation is, arguably, less clear on this point.

Responding to concerns regarding the coverage of the AIRA in the debate surrounding the bill, Alberta's justice minister attempted to clarify the intention of the law by stating that it was designed to address the dependence created by people in close, personal relationships, regardless of whether or not those relationships had a sexual component. He insisted that such dependence was of a different order than that arising from a 'normal family relationship where family members routinely assist each other, where an adult child moves in with a parent or where a parent moves in with a child' (Alberta, Legislative Assembly 2002, 1388). In sum, the justice minister insisted, an adult interdependent relationship is constituted by a couple that

> ha[s] the type of relationship where if they ought to have gotten married or they could have gotten married, they should have got married, as some would put it. That's what you're talking about in this situation. It's not about casual, platonic relationships. It's not about two college roommates. It's about those people who have engaged in a close, intense, personal relationship that we now know as marriage or as a common-law relationship and also ought to include other relationships, because it's not up to us to determine what type of relationship you live in. (Alberta, Legislative Assembly 2002, 1604)

Of course, if the Alberta government had *actually* begun its legislative drafting from the position that conjugality should not be of interest to the state, the contortions of the justice minister's explanation would not have been required since, presumably, the legislation would not have used the heterosexual marital form as its point of departure. Nonetheless, in its effort to obscure and diffuse the recognition of same-sex partnerships, the AIRA does manage to diversify the realm of legitimated relationships, thus expanding access to benefits and obligations. But it also offers the potential to implement a radical privatization of care by imposing obligations of support on people whose willingness to accept those obligations is undeclared. In the case of the Alberta government then, the progressiveness of recognizing non-conjugal relationships is potentially overwhelmed by a widely cast net of ascription, creating the potential for a radically neo-liberal regime of personal obligation.

It is clear that a far-reaching reconsideration of who constitutes family is only in its initial stages. But if we take the challenge to conjugality seriously, we are forced to grapple with the questions of what relationships do and when and whether those functions merit state regulation or protection. Judith Butler has recently argued that contemporary modes of living create 'relations of kinship [that] cross the boundaries between community and family and sometimes redefine the meaning of friendship as well. When these modes of intimate association produce sustaining webs of relationships, they constitute a "breakdown" of traditional kinship that displaces the presumption that biological and sexual relations structure kinship centrally' (2004, 26). As Canadian courts and legislatures increasingly define relationships that carry benefits and obligations on the basis of what those relationships do, rather than the specific form they take, new forms of kinship and new ways of thinking about how we might organize our domestic lives are open to contemplation. Moreover, as these forms of intimate life become more flexible, the possibility of ridding ourselves of standard gender identities also arises. Of course, biological reproduction is still a crucial element in the process, but as it becomes possible to recognize that a child might have three parents, as was decided by a 2007 Ontario Court of Appeal decision, and we become aware that biology itself is imbued with social meaning, the established attachments to marriage and to the meanings of masculinity and femininity are increasingly difficult to sustain.

Nonetheless, it is clear that sex still matters to the state. The radical potential that a challenge to conjugality represents has yet to be realized. Indeed, it has been embraced in law only in order to diminish the status of relationships between same-sex partners. Moreover, there is evidence that Canada's willingness to recognize relationship diversity has as much to do with reducing costs to the state as it does with giving its citizens the freedom to form their intimate lives according to their own terms. And it is also evident that even as more kinds of relationships are recognized, legitimated relationships still look a lot like an idealized marital form—two people engaged in a monogamous, long-term commitment. There is a great deal of dynamism and tension in the recognition and operation of our intimate lives, but even as more opportunities to define those relationships emerge, the state maintains a steady presence.

## Note

1  It should be noted that in addition to Conservatives, many GLBTQ activists also oppose marriage between same-sex partners. The argument here is that marriage acts to normalize and regulate sexuality rather than to liberate it from the strictures of heterosexual norms. Moreover, there is a deep concern among GLBTQ activists that with the end of the marriage fight, their issues are considered 'resolved', making it very difficult to maintain matters pertaining to sexuality on the political agenda.

## References

Alberta. Legislative Assembly. 2002. *Debates and Proceedings*. 19 Nov. Afternoon and 27 Nov. Evening. http://www.assembly.ab.ca/net/index.aspx?p=han&section=doc&fid=1.

Armstrong, Pat, and Olga Kits. 2001. *One Hundred Years of Caregiving*. Ottawa: Law Commission of Canada.

Arnup, Katharine. 2001. *Close Personal Relationships between Adults: One Hundred Years of Marriage in Canada*. Ottawa: Law Commission of Canada.

Ayed, Nahlah. 2000. 'Liberals define marriage as part of same sex law'. *Kitchener Waterloo Record*, 23 Mar., A3.

Brock, Kathy. 2006. 'The Devil Is in the Details: The Chrétien Legacy for the Third Sector'. In Lois Harder and Steve Patten, eds, *The Chretien Legacy: Politics and Public Policy in Canada*, 255–75. Montreal: McGill-Queen's University Press.

Brook, Heather. 2000. 'How to Do Things with Sex'. In Carl Stychin and Didi Herman, eds, *Sexuality in the Legal Arena*, 132–50. London: Athlone Press.

Butler, Judith. 2004. *Undoing Gender*. New York: Routledge.

Canada. 2000. *Debates*. 36th Parliament, 2nd Session. Nos. 53 (3790–3819) and 77 (5558–5578).

CBC (Canadian Broadcasting Corporation). 1967. 'There's no place for the state in the bedrooms of the nation'. Online. http://archives.cbc.ca/400d.asp?id=1-73-538-2671.

Clarke, John. 2004. *Changing Welfare, Changing States: New Directions in Social Policy*. London: Sage.

Cossman, Brenda. 2002. 'Sexing Citizenship: Privatizing Sex', *Citizenship Studies* 6 (4): 483–506.

———, and Bruce Ryder. 2001. 'What Is Marriage-Like Like? The Irrelevance of Conjugality', *Canadian Journal of Family Law* 18: 269–326.

Folbre, Nancy. 2006. 'Measuring Care: Gender, Empowerment and the Care Economy', *Journal of Human Development* 7 (2): 183–99.

Fudge, Judy, and Brenda Cossman. 2002. 'Introduction: Privatization, Law and the Challenge to Feminism'. In Brenda Cossman and Judy Fudge, eds, *Privatization, Law and the Challenge to Feminism*, 3–37. Toronto: University of Toronto Press.

Harder, Lois. 2007. 'The Rights of Love: The State and Intimate Relationships in Canada and the United States', *Social Politics* 14 (2): 155–81.

———. Forthcoming. 'State Fantasies and Intimate Relationships: Family Forms and Functions in Canada and the United States'. In Laura Macdonald and Arne Ruckert, eds, *Inclusive Liberalism in the Americas*. London: Palgrave.

Holland, Winnifred. 2000. 'Intimate Relationships in the New Millenium: The Assimilation of Marriage and Cohabitation?' *Canadian Journal of Family Law* 17 (1): 114–68.

Jenson, Jane. 2004. 'Changing the Paradigm: Family Responsibility or Investing in Children', *Canadian Journal of Sociology* 29 (2): 169–92.

———, and Denis Saint-Martin. 2003. 'New Routes to Social Cohesion?' *Canadian Journal of Sociology* 28 (1): 77–99.

Kershaw, Paul. 2005. *Carefair: Rethinking the Responsibilities and Rights of Citizenship*. Vancouver: UBC Press.

Law Commission of Canada. 2001. *Beyond Conjugality: Recognizing and Supporting Close Personal Adult Relationships*. Ottawa. http://epe.lac-bac.gc.ca/100/206/301/law_commission_of_canada-ef/2006-12-06/www.lcc.gc.ca/about/conjugality_toc-en.asp.

Mykitiuk, Roxanne. 2001. 'Beyond Conception: Legal Determinations of Filiation in the Context of Assisted Reproductive Technologies', *Osgoode Hall Law Journal* 39 (4): 771–815.

Peck, Jamie, and Adam Tickell. 2002. 'Neoliberalizing Space', *Antipode* 34 (3): 380–404.

Riley, Susan. 2006. 'MPs finally put gay marriage to bed: Thursday's vote was a day to feel pride in our fair-minded country.' *Montreal Gazette*, 9 Dec., B7.

Statistics Canada. 1997. '1996 Census: Marital Status, Common Law Unions and Families', *The Daily*, 14 Oct.

———. 2007. 'Couple Families by Presence of Children of All Ages in Private Households: 2006 Counts'. http://www12.statcan.ca/english/census06/data/highlights/households/pages/Page.cfm?Lang=E&Geo=PR&Code=01&Table=1&Data=Count&Age=1&StartRec=1&Sort=2&Display=Page.

Stevens, Jacqueline. 1999. *Reproducing the State*. Princeton: Princeton University Press.

Waring, Marilyn. 2003. 'Counting for Something! Recognising Women's Contribution to the Global Economy through Alternative Accounting Systems', *Gender and Development* 11 (1): 35–44.

## Cases

*M. v. H.* [1999] 2 S.C.R. 3.

*Miron v. Trudel* [1995] 2 S.C.R. 418.

*Molodowich v. Pentinnen* [1980] O.J. No. 1904 (Ont. Dist. Ct.).

## Further Reading

Dua, Enakshi. 1999. 'Beyond Diversity: Exploring the Ways in Which the Discourse of Race has Shaped the Institution of the Nuclear Family'. In Enakshi Dua and Angela Robertson, eds, *Scratching the Surface: Canadian Anti-racist Feminist Thought*, 237–59. Toronto: Women's Press.

Roseneil, Sasha, and Shelley Budgeon. 2004. 'Cultures of Intimacy and Care Beyond "the Family": Personal Life and Social Change in the Early 21st Century', *Current Sociology* 52 (2): 135–59.

Weston, Kath. 1995. 'Forever is a Long Time: Romancing the Real in Gay Kinship Ideologies'. In Sylvia Junko Yanagisako and Carol Delaney, eds, *Naturalizing Power: Essays in Feminist Cultural Analysis*, 87–110. New York: Routledge.

## Questions for Critical Thought

1. Should intimate relationships between adults have a special legal status distinct from the status of the individual? Why or why not?
2. Why has the state used conjugality as the basis for defining relationships that merit regulation and status?
3. How does marriage define gender?
4. Will the recognition of same-sex marriage and non-marital relationships undermine or reinforce heteronormative gender identities? Why or why not?

# CHAPTER 10

# Charter Champions?
# Equality Backsliding, the
# Charter, and the Courts

Alexandra Dobrowolsky

## Introduction

With the patriation of Canada's constitution and the drafting of a homegrown Charter of Rights and Freedoms in the early 1980s, advocates for women, among other equality seekers, ensured that the Charter contained more than individual rights and a commitment to more than mere formal equality (Dobrowolsky 2000; Abu-Laban and Nieguth 2000; James 2004). Women's groups, in particular, were celebrated for both tightening up the wording and broadening the intent of section 15, as well as for adding an entirely new equality provision, section 28 (Kome 1983). Section 15 was extended further when gay and lesbian activism prompted the Supreme Court to interpret sexual orientation as a prohibited ground for discrimination (Smith 1999). In the words of Alan Cairns, constitutional 'outsiders' became 'insiders' as they lobbied successfully to have their interests and identities recognized. And then, having carved out their constitutional 'niches', these 'Charter Canadians' went on to strenuously protect their hard-won equality rights at the expense of ratifying new constitutional amendment packages, first the Meech Lake Accord (in 1987) and then the Charlottetown Agreement (in 1992) (Cairns 1991, 1992). The struggle has continued into the present, as Aboriginal women, for instance, have spurred the courts to resolve long-standing disputes over discrimination based on sex and racialization, which had only been partially addressed in 1985 (in a challenge to the *Indian Act* led by Sharon McIvor; see also Harder and Altamirano-Jiménez in this volume).

Yet, these so-called 'successes' came alongside the rise and consolidation of neo-liberalism in the 1980s and 1990s and then amidst the prevailing social investment discourses. And so, the developments discussed here do not necessarily coincide with the patterns outlined in many of the other chapters in this volume. When it comes to the Charter and the Supreme Court, we see somewhat of a lag when it comes to the effects of neo-liberalism. What does this tell us about the neo-liberal trajectory? Has it played out in the same ways, and has neo-liberalism had the same kind of impact on women at the level of the Charter and the courts as it has in other policy areas? Has neo-liberalism 'rolled out' in these realms? The answers to these questions are not clear cut, as the story here is a contentious one, with competing assessments.

This chapter evaluates whether women are winners or losers when it comes to the Charter, and in so doing outlines the more complex and debated consequences of neo-liberalism and interest mediation vis-à-vis the constitution and the courts. As we shall see, it depends when you ask, and in what context. It also depends upon who asks, who answers, on behalf of whom, and for what reasons. In other words, the answer is contingent and always political. What will become apparent, however, is that the objective reality is much more mixed: gains and losses, steps forward and steps back are subject to the strength and legitimacy of the political actors involved (whether they be women's groups, political officials, or judges), the ideas they embrace, and the actions they take.

The first section is a brief overview of how perspectives on women, Charter equality, and the courts have shifted. These views are counterposed by the socio-economic and political realities of women and the impact that these realities have on women's equality, and their search for equality. The second section considers the role of the courts, and reviews a number of illustrative court cases to show how presumed equality successes and defeats are never straightforward. The third section examines changes in institutions, ideas, interests, and identity politics to explain the current status of Canadian women's equality. Finally, the implications of the current dearth of Charter champions are considered in the conclusion.

## The Backdrop

After successfully entrenching various rights in the Constitution, equality seekers began using the Charter and courts as a strategy for making political inroads, especially because of the intransigence of the legislatures. Since the charge was led by prominent feminist organizations, many analysts, including right-wing critics, identified women as champions of the Charter. Whereas the left commended these efforts (Dobrowolsky 1997; Smith 2002), the right condemned them. Conservative scholars worried that anti-oppression activists had gained too much political ground. They pinpointed women's efforts, and groups such as the Women's Legal Education and Action Fund (LEAF), as epitomizing the work of an anti-democratic 'Court Party' (Morton and Knopff 2000). The impression given here was that feminists had overtaken the courts and the hearts and minds of judges. For example, when Madam Justice Rosalie

Abella, a renowned equality advocate, was appointed to the Supreme Court, right-wing condemnations came fast and furious.

Whereas the right exaggerated the influence of women, the left tended to minimize women's gains (Bakan and Smith 1997). For the latter, women were, more often than not, considered to be 'losers' not 'winners' in the courts and in the game of Charter chess (Majury 2003b). As socio-economic equality deteriorated, and despite diametrically opposed broader public perceptions of women's gains, the left, and even liberals, grew disillusioned. The first woman Supreme Court justice, the late Bertha Wilson, posed the question before a diverse group of feminist equality advocates, academics, and activists: 'Why . . . are so many dissatisfied with the way things have worked out? Why do they feel that they expended a great deal of effort and cherished such high expectations to so little avail?' (Wilson 1993, 1).

At the same time, the efforts of equality seekers were denounced and added to a list of problematic 'special interests' (Dobrowolsky 1998). This de-legitimizing discourse was useful to the promoters of neo-liberalism who wanted to streamline the state and silence voices that called for political and constitutional equality, since such redress would require the kind of political and legal activism staunchly opposed by the right. Nonetheless, because of a more conducive climate for equality seeking at the court level, as well as a more charitable assessment of the courts by the public, there was a lag in neo-liberal consolidation and the right-wing critique did not immediately take hold, nor did it have the intended blanket effect. Consider the work of women's groups that highlighted potential threats to equality in the Meech Lake Accord proposals of the late 1980s. While their stance was, no doubt, oppositional—that is, many women's organizations outside of Quebec opposed the Meech deal—women's mobilization against Meech still served to galvanize numerous equality seekers of various stripes and attracted considerable public support (outside of Quebec).

As time went on, and as we shall see, discourses and dictates that served to delegitimize equality seekers (Morton and Knopff 2000; Morton and Allen 2001; Brodie 2002a, 2002b) began to resonate more widely, moving beyond academic circles and into the broader political realm (and public consciousness). Neo-liberal justifications also crept into court decisions, in cases that considered, for example, the meaning and scope of conjugality, (Harder in this volume) as well as unemployment insurance (MacDonald in this volume).

Today, Conservative Prime Minister Stephen Harper, as well his top advisers, are advocates of the 'Calgary school' (represented by Rainer Morton and F.L. Knopff), who not only bolster the view that women's equality is a given, but that the judiciary needs to be reined in, as well as distanced from left-liberal interests and identities.[1] This explains why the Harper government drastically scaled back Status of Women Canada and shut down both the Court Challenges Program and the Law Commission in the fall of 2006.

There is, however, substantial evidence that challenges the government's view that Canadian women's equality is a given. As the various chapters in this collection detail, neo-liberal streamlining had the effect of rolling back women's equality in multiple ways. When the Canada Assistance Plan (CAP) was replaced by the Canada Health and Social Transfer (CHST), Day and Brodsky wrote:

> This . . . is no less significant than . . . the constitutionalizing of equality guarantees in the 1980s. At stake now is not just the repeal of the general entitlement to social assistance, further cuts to federal funding, the loss of national standards, and the threat of a race to the bottom in social programs—all of which will affect Canadian women, and especially Canada's poorest women. Also at stake is the ability of women's human rights to be a vital, responding, alternative discourse in a time of global and national restructuring. (1998, 6)

Given the dramatic nature of the cuts and the devastation they caused, this period was then followed by a return to strategic social spending in the late 1990s and early 2000s. However, Canadian women's concerns were sidelined (Dobrowolsky and Jenson 2004; see also Jenson in this volume). For all these reasons, the economic situation is a difficult one for many Canadian women and dire for others, including lone mothers, senior women, Aboriginal and other racialized women, women with disabilities, immigrant women, and so on.

Bruce Porter outlines the stark reality that exists, despite so-called Charter equality 'gains':

> Since the Supreme Court issued its first [equality] decisions under section 15 in *Andrews*, half a million more households have fallen into poverty. The number of single mothers living in poverty has increased by more than 50 per cent and their poverty has, in many cases, deepened to the point of extreme destitution. Food banks, a rare phenomenon in the early 1980's and unheard of when the Charter was first being debated are now a critical means of survival for three quarters of a million people and fail to come close to meeting the needs of an estimated 2.4 million hungry adults and children. Women and children have been most dramatically affected by the epidemic of homelessness. (2006, 42)

Let us now turn to an assessment of *Andrews,* and other prominent cases, to problematize further the nature and forms of equality for Canadian women.

## Courts and Cases: More Ambiguity Than Achievement

We have seen laudable changes to the composition of Canada's highest court, from the first woman Supreme Court justice (Bertha Wilson) to the first woman chief justice (Beverley McLachlin), and the number of women justices on average is about one-third of the Court. However, we cannot forget how long these judicial appointments were in coming (recall that it was the Supreme Court which ruled that women were not even persons and were not eligible for Senate or judicial appointments, a ruling which culminated in the 1929 *Persons* case) and that the makeup of the courts can change with different political mandates. Moreover, the number of women and the racial diversity in the lower courts are still not high (see Devlin, MacKay, and Kim 2000) and may be slipping.[2]

At the same time, women judges will not necessarily be more progressive in their approach to the Charter and sex equality. As research on women and politics reveals, numerical representation of women does not automatically translate into their substantive representation (Gotell and Brodie 1996; Trimble 1997; Trimble and Arscott 2003). Still, legal studies do suggest that women judges on the Supreme Court, up to early 2000 at least, 'have been more open and courageous in their equality analysis than their male colleagues' (Majury 2002a, 313).

Moreover, despite the Supreme Court's initial, more expansive interpretation of substantive equality, it is not hard to find examples of sexist (and racist) commentary, particularly from Canada's lower courts, and sometimes even directed at progressive women Supreme Court justices. Recall the infamous *Ewanchuk* case. An Alberta trial judge, Mr Justice McClung, acquitted Steven Ewanchuk of sexually assaulting a 17-year-old who had come to look for work. The judge resorted to rape myths and engaged in blatant sexual stereotyping when he quipped that the young woman was not exactly wearing a 'bonnet and crinolines'. Later, when the Supreme Court heard the case and McClung was taken to task for his judgment (in both senses of the word), McClung lashed out in the media with a vindictive and insulting retort directed at Madam Justice L'Heureux Dubé. While *Ewanchuk* is touted as a feminist victory, for the Supreme Court ultimately ruled that 'no means no', one could also claim that the positive ramifications may have been lost in the negative publicity.

In more ways than one, this case casts a shadow of doubt on the nature and effects of such 'successes'. Christopher Manfredi uses *Ewanchuk* as a prime illustration of the uncertain outcome of feminist activism:

> The increasingly narrow circumstances under which women can be said to have consented to sexual activity is to some extent inconsistent with the stated purpose of sexual assault law to promote the equal dignity and autonomy of women. Implicitly in LEAF's approach, in other words, is the idea that women have so little autonomy under current conditions that true consent is quite rare. (2004, 124)

Indeed, Diana Majury identifies this danger of 'over-protection' as one of the pitfalls of women's equality struggles (2002a, 335). This makes the *Ewanchuk* outcome less than clear. The waters become murkier in light of the issues raised in the cases that follow.

## Charter Winners and Losers? Contestation and Contingency in a Context of Political Change

Are women 'winners' or 'losers' when it comes to pivotal equality cases?[3] Here, it is important to ask who is asking the question, when, and why. For example, on the one hand, the right identifies LEAF as a powerful 'Court Party' intervenor that exerts undue influence on the courts and shapes public policy in ways that respond to its feminist, minoritarian agenda (Morton and Knopff 2000; Brodie 2002a).[4] On the other hand, feminist analysts have tended to be more skeptical or pragmatic with views that can be summed up by the title of an early report on women's equality outcomes: 'one step forward, or two steps back?' (Brodksy and Day 1989). After ten years of feminist advocacy around the Charter, LEAF's aims and influence were reviewed, and the conclusion was drawn that its

> proactive vision was severely tested by early equality cases that often involved male litigants who sought to undermine benefits achieved by feminist law reform. For example, men challenged the criminalization of sexual assaults, previously viewed as consensual, between older men and underage girls. Men also lost no time challenging evidentiary rules designed to ensure fair, non-sexist treatment of complainants during sexual assault trials. On other fronts, men challenged laws such as those providing economic assistance to single mothers, which were enacted to address the severe hardship of the most impoverished women. (LEAF 1996)

Let us review the implications of some classic equality 'wins'. In the 1989 *Andrews* case, Mark Andrews (and his co-claimant Elizabeth Kinersley) 'successfully' used section 15 to challenge the requirement of Canadian citizenship for admission to the British Columbia bar. Here the Supreme Court not only applied section 15 for the first time (seven years after the Charter and four years after section 15 came into force), but also moved away from the rigid formalism of the Bill of Rights that had preceded the Charter. *Andrews* was an accomplishment in that a more purposive approach to section 15 was taken. It also, no doubt, reflected the broader political context of women's equality mobilization.

Yet, while LEAF is often 'credited (or blamed)' for the approach taken in *Andrews*, and while a cursory analysis might lead one to assume that it had an impact on the Supreme Court's decision, after a close and careful study of LEAF's factum vis-à-vis the majority view, Heather MacIvor concludes that LEAF's intervention 'made little or no difference to the outcome of the case' (2006, 208–9).

The Supreme Court's unanimity in its support of substantive equality in that case nonetheless raised the hopes of equality advocates (Majury 2002a, 305). The flip side, however, is that because of abandoning the restrictive formalism of the past, 'equality under the Charter has become an even more amorphous and uncertain concept' (Majury 2002b, 123). This observation is certainly borne out when we see how understandings of equality can not only expand, but also contract with a shifting political and socio-economic context. Indeed, it was not long before the Supreme Court's 1989 unanimity in *Andrews* 'broke down in a trilogy of cases—*Egan, Miron*, and *Thibaudeau*—in 1995' (Faraday, Denike, and Stephenson 2006, 13).

Even the 'success' of cases considered to be equality milestones (for example, those that recognized minority rights for gays and lesbians in *Vriend v. Alberta*, or that required the British Columbia government to provide sign-language interpreters for deaf persons requiring medical services in *Eldridge*) become tempered over time. In Sheila McIntyre's assessment, and in hindsight, *Vriend* and *Eldridge* were ultimately 'easy' cases that displayed 'failures of nerve' and, in the case of *Vriend*, 'undue defensiveness' (2006, 111). And yet, these cases sparked a significant anti-court backlash against the nature and extent of judicial activism.

Fuel has been added to the fire by cases identified as banner feminist 'victories', such as the 1988 *Morgentaler* decision that struck down Canada's abortion law, or the *Butler* decision, where the Supreme Court viewed pornography through the lens of 'harm' and therefore considered it justifiable to limit the *Charter* right to freedom of expression. In both, LEAF played an instrumental role, and this fact was not lost on right-wing court watchers (Morton and Knopff 2000; Brodie 2002a). Yet these two cases also serve to highlight a much more convoluted political reality.

The *Morgentaler* decision has been described as 'a huge step forward for women' (Majury 2002a, 317) and as the epitome of how 'advocacy lobbying, grounded in the Charter, had changed the balance of power in the legislative process' (Pal 1993,152). LEAF's efforts 'had an impact on social condition' in that the data are 'relatively unambiguous that the rate of legal abortions increased after 1988, and that increase is almost entirely attributable to the removal of legal barriers to the establishment of private clinics' (Manfredi 2004,195). *Morgentaler* also had 'symbolic purchase' in that it was widely fêted as a feminist Charter and court win.

While Sheilah Martin recognized these contributions, she also points out the 'noteworthy limits to this decision that derive from the nature of litigation, the constraints of judicial reasoning, and the limiting narratives of law' (2002, 344). In *Morgentaler*, the Court drew mostly on section 7 in its decision, rather than sections 15 and 28, despite LEAF's best efforts to make the connections to women's equality explicit. Therefore, in this case and other related ones that arose in the next decade, such as *Tremblay v. Daigle, Winnipeg*, and *Dobson*, the Supreme Court persistently refused 'to actively consider the implications for women's equality' despite the fact that 'reproductive rights are a key location of women's social inequality' (Rodgers 2006, 281).

After the perceived feminist 'successes' of *Morgentaler* and *Daigle*, anti-choice forces grew more vocal and even violent (with fire bombings of clinics and the shooting of abortion-service providers). Anti-abortion activists' actions, and their discourses, for example, the 'unborn child', also started to have an effect on the courts and beyond (see also Brodie, Gavigan, and Jenson 1992). Consequently, 'ideological opponents of provision of such services have raised the issue of whether abortion services are truly a medically necessary service and have successfully persuaded some politicians to soft-pedal the issue' (Palley 2006, 568).

This anti-choice activism combined with the repercussions of neo-liberal policies (cost cutting, offloading, and privatization) explains access shortfalls. A 2003 report highlights the gaps: only 18 per cent of all Canadian general hospitals were providing abortions and, in a couple of instances there were no abortion services whatsoever (in Prince Edward Island and Nunavut) (CARAL 2003). The absence of a Canadian abortion law persists, and today 'the federal government lacks the coercive and monetary mechanisms to secure the policy goal of broad availability of abortion services and equal access to such services' (Palley 2006, 568). Canadian women remain, and arguably are more, circumscribed in their abortion options, despite the *Morgantaler* 'win'.

The *Butler* case rocked the feminist community and resulted in huge divisions among women over LEAF's anti-pornography position (Gotell 1997). This case highlights another potential downfall of equality struggles: the need for oversimplified categorization and the propensity for essentialism. LEAF's strategy in *Butler* required it to oversimplify sexuality and boil down pornography to male power and male domination. LEAF advanced the claims of an 'uncomplicated and unified legal subject', suggesting that '*all* pornography is harmful to *all* women' (Karaian 2005, 17). Yet not only were there women who were anti-censorship (Burstyn 1985), but there were also radical liberals and lesbians, among others (Cossman et al. 1997), who took issue with that argument, illustrating that 'a victory for LEAF may be a defeat for feminists (and nonfeminist women) who do not share the experiences and approaches of white, heterosexual female lawyers' (MacIvor 2006, 210).

Indeed, diverse women (lesbians, women of colour, Aboriginal women, women with disabilities, and so on), increasingly challenged not only LEAF, but many leading national women's organizations (for example, the National Association of Women and the Law (NAWL), NAC, and so on) for their mainstream personnel and their assumptions and strategies. The fallout from narrowly based equality struggles became more apparent, not only with cases like *Butler*, but also with the challenges raised by the mobilization by women around the Meech Lake and Charlottetown Accords in 1987 and 1992, respectively (Dobrowolsky 2000; Green 2001, 2003). These experiences contributed greatly to analyses that highlighted the limitations of legal strategies when it came to addressing complex, intersecting forms of discrimination (Jhappan 2002).

As a result of shifts in identity politics mobilization and ideas, the discourses and tactics of equality advocates were compelled to change. For example, LEAF's strategy moved from one of essentialism to 'particularity' (Gotell 2002, 147). LEAF nuanced its response after *Butler* and in the subsequent *Little Sisters* case, even though its efforts in the latter were still not without critics (Ryder 2001). Although LEAF begins with a more complicated construction of the category sexual minority in *Little Sisters*, one that is 'diverse and intersecting',

> it then proceeds to group lesbians, gay men, bisexuals, and transgendered persons together so that throughout the remainder of the factum this diverse group's experiences are combined and their differences elided. . . . Recognition of the intersecting understanding of identity is adopted and then relegated to the sidelines in order to present a 'unified' argument. (Karaian 2005, 129)

Again, LEAF is faced with the limitation of having to categorize, using the blunt instrument of law, in order to advance more finely tuned equality struggles.

In general, LEAF's position, along with other women's groups over this period (Dobrowolsky 2008), can be described as growing more defensive and reactive, rather than offensive and pro-active. One senior member of LEAF suggested that this reflects the fact that section 15 was getting 'a far more vigorous workout as a shield than as a sword' (quoted in MacIvor 2006, 207).

The larger point being made here is that so-called feminist 'wins' can easily be called into question by both critics and supporters. Moreover, it is also important to keep in mind that neither women nor the feminist community are a monolithic or unified group, but such homogenization is typically the outcome of categorical portrayals depicting 'women's' 'gains', or their 'losses'.

## Equality Losses?

Beverley Baines reviews sex-equality 'failures' in a variety of cases. Some, such as *Symes* (which challenged the *Income Tax Act*), were litigated by women. Others, litigated by men, included *Trociuk*, where the Court ruled that section 1 would not apply when it came to a provincial birth-registration scheme that allowed women to register the surnames of their newborns. The Supreme Court determined this to be sex discrimination against men; that is, the Court unanimously ruled that giving women sole discretion to name their children was against the equality rights of biological fathers. Some cases translated into losses for women on grounds other than sex; one of these was *Law*, which was viewed as the most significant development in equality jurisprudence since *Andrews* and which comes as a response to the 1995 trilogy of *Egan*, *Miron*, and *Thibaudeau* (see Baines 2006, 75).

But again, losses, like wins, can be less than straightforward. What and who gets factored into such assessments? For instance, which women are affected by the 'loss'? In the *Symes* case, a founding member of LEAF sought equality in the application of tax laws to men and women, that is, by being able to deduct childcare expenses as a business expense. In the end, the majority ruled against Beth Symes, but interestingly enough, two women Supreme Court justices on the case dissented. In view of who actually brought the case forward and who dissented from the majority, this 'defeat' was most likely felt by a more privileged class of women (see Macklin 1992). Consequently, *Symes* has been depicted by some as an illustration of 'privileged women trying to take advantage of a privileging tax system in a way that potentially undermines the interests of other, more disadvantaged women' (Majury 2002a, 332).

Furthermore, in cases considered to be 'failures', as with many 'successes', we typically see more of a 'ping pong' effect in the Courts. For example, consider the back and forth, the losses, gains, and losses that occurred with cases such as *Seaboyer* and *O'Connor* and then later *Mills* and *Shearing*.[5] A 'loss' can also, sometimes, become more of a 'win' or at least a more ambivalent outcome. In *Seaboyer,* although LEAF 'unsuccessfully' defended the *Criminal Code*'s so-called 'rape-shield' law against a due-process challenge, the Supreme Court's majority ruling caused a furor and acted as a catalyst for widespread activism by women. A diverse range of women's groups (see McIntyre 1994) worked with the justice minister (Kim Campbell, who, of course, later became Canada's first female prime minister) and provided input into the drafting of a more sensitive and sensible law. 'The new bill seemed to be influenced at least as strongly by Justice L'Heureux-Dubé's dissent which, in turn, resembled LEAF's arguments—as by Justice McLachlin's majority ruling. The net result was a win for LEAF' (MacIvor 2006, 211). But then again, in the final analysis, 'it is unclear whether these rule changes had much impact on the level of violence against women or the actual processing of sexual assault cases' (Manfredi 2004, 195).

In short, this running tally of losses and wins is less important than the concrete repercussions that unfold when the legal, as well as the socio-economic and political, context changes. In the *Law* case, for example, the Supreme Court developed a complicated taxonomy for equality, 'convert[ing] a 46-word guarantee into an elaborate analytic framework whose multipartite content now extends to two detailed pages'. And yet, in spite of the intricate test developed by the unanimous *Law* Court, section 15 decisions are now 'almost completely unpredictable. They are however depressingly consistent in their narrowing of the promise of substantive rights' (McIntyre and Rodgers 2006, 10–11).

## Relapses and Mixed Messages

Ultimately what is most problematic, in my view, is the recent trend of equality backsliding at a time of marketization and the rise of the right, which assumes that equality exists. Despite the less than rosy realities outlined throughout this volume, the general public assumes that women have achieved not only formal, but substantive, equality. And so, when feminist equality seekers and anti-oppression activists point to the contrary, they are dismissed as being outmoded defenders of political correctness.

Yet, numerous legal scholars have tracked the deterioration of broader, purposive understandings of equality as initially articulated in *Andrews* (Faraday et al. 2006; McIntyre and Rodgers 2006). Melanie Randall comments on the 'increasingly impatient reaction to discussions of gender discrimination and "women's issues"' and suggests that it 'appears to be a society-wide phenomenon. But it is also traceable in Canadian case law, in the Supreme Court's tepid reception to discrimination, and in the diminishing rates of success of Charter equality claims' (2006, 280).

Fiona Sampson writes, 'To date, section 15 of the Charter has not fulfilled all of its potential; and more recently, post-*Law*, the Supreme Court's section 15 analyses have become more regressive and confusing in relation to goals of substantive equality and the legal elimination of disadvantage' (2006, 267). One can choose from a range of cases that reflect these tendencies and trends. However, three cases—*Auton*, *NAPE*, and *Gosselin*—are particularly illustrative, not only for their retreat from substantive equality, but also for how this regression becomes intertwined with neo-liberal-inspired market calculations.

In the 2004 *Auton* decision, the Supreme Court ruled on whether expensive therapy for autism should be covered by the British Columbia healthcare system. Here, the parents of autistic children argued that section 15 'imposes an obligation to fund the treatment for their children . . . that children with autism have unique needs and that a refusal by governments to meet those needs has a discriminatory consequence' (Porter 2006, 39). Although the Court relied on the rhetoric of substantive equality, it reverted to formalistic equality calculations by way of a 'highly specified comparator analysis' (Pothier 2006, 149). The chief justice asserted that in order to demonstrate that section 15 had been violated, 'the petitioners in *Auton* must show differential treatment in comparison to a non-disabled person or person suffering a disability other than a mental disability (here autism) seeking or receiving funding for a non-core therapy' (Porter 2006, 40).

As Dianne Pothier perceives, this brings to mind the infamous *Bliss* case of the 1970s; in that pre-Charter, high-watermark of formal equality and Bill of Rights absurdity, a pregnant woman, Stella Bliss, was denied unemployment benefits when the Supreme Court ruled that 'discrimination on the basis of pregnancy was not sex discrimination' (2006, 148). Porter concurs that in *Auton* '[o]ne is reminded . . . of the futile quest for the 'pregnant man' comparator in the Bliss case' (Porter 2006, 40). In *Auton*, then, the Supreme Court's '[e]xcessive pigeonholing leaves room only for formal equality because it does not allow for consideration of different needs and circumstances' (Pothier 2006, 148).

The bottom line here is the bottom line: this therapy was deemed to be too expensive. Financial calculations ultimately trumped both substantive equality and broader views of discrimination. Randall writes: '*Auton* represents a paradigmatic example of a simultaneous failure to grasp the nature of the discrimination at issue and over-sensitivity to the burden on governments which equality claims might pose' (Randall 2006, 289). Such justifications are plain to see in the next two cases that specifically involve women's socio-economic status.

The 2004 *NAPE* case—*Treasury Board v. Newfoundland and Labrador Association of Public and Private Employees (NAPE)*—provides the first explicit example of 'a cost-based justification alone of a claim of sex discrimination' (Young 2006, 66). Here the Supreme Court refused to prompt the Newfoundland and Labrador government to fulfill its $24 million pay-equity obligation to women public-healthcare workers. In *NAPE*, the Court wholeheartedly agreed that yes, discrimination and the violation of women's equality had taken place; nonetheless, it decided not to compel the Newfoundland government to make reparations because of the financial burden that this would impose.

Some might suggest that such calculations were also at the root of the *Bliss* decision, but here Young counters that the budgetary concern 'was understated in *Bliss,* and not the primary mechanism for denying Stella Bliss's claim', whereas in 2004:

> the financial angle is key. Women's equality rights—recognized by the government in its pay equity agreement promises—are cast as threats to the attainment of other public goods such as hospital beds and schoolrooms. And the effect to the judgment is to uphold discriminatory budget balancing: the levying of a targeted tax on an already vulnerable and economically disadvantaged group of female workers in the name of the greater economic good. (Young 2006, 67)

The inequality between men and women is a reality that is being ignored by political leaders, and now the courts seem to have resigned themselves to the fact that, because of the expense, they cannot compel governments to remedy this situation.

In *Gosselin,* the Supreme Court was willing to disregard socio-economic conditions and fall back on stereotypes in order to limit expenditures. This 2002 case challenged social-assistance programs that penalized youth in Quebec. The Court ignored a recession that contributed to high unemployment rates (23 per cent) among adults under 30[6] and some of the specifics involving a young, impoverished woman on social assistance (Kim and Piper 2003).

And, contrary to efforts by feminist activists, academics, and even many judges to transcend problematic portrayals of women (such as the stereotypes involved in *Ewanchuk*), in *Gosselin,* the Supreme Court perpetuated the stereotype of the young, female welfare claimant despite NAWL's efforts to the contrary:

> Chief Justice McLachlin's account of Gosselin's misfortune placed emphasis, explicitly or not, on features about the individual herself: her mental health, her work ethic, her stamina, her range of poor personal choices. NAWL's account was more situational, still individual, but reflective of a broader context of destitution and misfortune. (Young 2006, 60)

This decision cannot be divorced from market rationales. In *Gosselin* the Court became 'clearly overwhelmed by the prospect of "tens of thousands of unidentified people" being owed "hundreds of millions of taxpayer dollars" and dismisses the claim based on the absence of evidence that these tens of thousands have been adversely affected by their social assistance being reduced by two thirds' (Majury 2006, 229).

Nevertheless, rather than chalk up wins or list what would seem to be a growing number of losses, it still is more helpful to consider how circumstances have changed, in order to understand the attenuation of substantive equality.

# Erasing Equality: Political Dynamics

## Changing Institutions and Changing Ideas, Interests, and Identities

It is important to acknowledge the growth in stature of the Supreme Court since the adoption of the Charter and the decline in support for formal political arenas in this same period. The Canadian public has expressed faith in the Courts and in the Charter, and this helps to explain why many believe substantive equality rights to be both apparent and real. Polls released in 2007 show that as many as 53 per cent of Canadians believe the Charter to be a positive development and most Canadians rate the Courts higher than the legislatures (Supreme Court 47 per cent versus Parliament 37 per cent) (Makin 2007, A1). Clearly, a more dynamic, liberal Court in the early days of Charter euphoria sealed these impressions. However, given both marketization and the rise of the right, the blush is off the Court's rose, and the colder climate for equality is setting in.[7]

Courts are not static. Appointments come and go, and they reflect different political mandates. The composition of the court matters when it comes to equality and how it is understood and articulated. Supreme Court justices who were keen to herald a new Charter era by transcending formal equality and legitimizing substantive equality and a 'contextual mode of interpretation', notably Bertha Wilson and Claire L'Heureux-Dubé (Grabham 2002, 661), are now gone. Diana Majury expresses her fear 'that the Court will no longer feel the need to engage in a rigorous sex equality analysis' with the retirement of Justice L'Heureux-Dubé, 'who has been a champion of women's equality rights.

Her sexual assault judgments, often in dissent, are wonderfully affirming for feminist advocates who work on this issue' (2002a, 322).

Even since *Gosselin*, the makeup of the Supreme Court has changed. As Brodsky and Day observe: 'Four of the judges who sat on *Gosselin*, including L'Heureux-Dubé and Arbour JJ. who wrote most imaginatively are no longer on the Court', and they go on to question whether the 'newly-composed Court positioned at a crucial crossroads' will 'revert to a narrow, negative, formalistic conception of equality that is indifferent to material conditions of inequality and deprivation, or move forward with a substantive conception of equality?' (Brodsky and Day 2006, 337). As we have seen, formalism is certainly more in evidence when market forces weigh in, both implicitly and explicitly.

Consider also the influence of right-wing critiques. Recall how the right drummed up opposition to the appointment to the Supreme Court of the renowned equality advocate Rosalie Abella. Indeed, that opposition may help to explain her cautious approach on the bench and her failure to reach the creative heights of Wilson or L'Heureux Dubé.

The political ground shifted further in 2006: right-wing Charter skeptics are not only advising political leaders but are now in power. The Harper government's first chief of staff, Ian Brodie, had made his views clear in 2002 in his book, which, for example, criticized both the Supreme Court and the Court Challenges Program for favouring feminist and gay-rights groups. Echoing his mentors, Morton and Knopff, Brodie castigates the high court for making political decisions under the pretext of interpreting constitutional law (Brodie 2002a). He also specifically targets the Court Challenges Program in an article published in the same year (2002b). It is now obvious that these ideas had been put into practice by the fall of 2006.

Because the Harper government is opposed to how the Supreme Court has operated, especially in its broad and liberal interpretations of equality, it is keen to rein in the Court, as well as to shift the balance of the Court to reflect the current government's more conservative, Charterphobic views. As Peter Russell muses, the Conservatives are thinking ' "We are going to get people on the Bench of our persuasion ... [and in so doing dispense with] judicial and legal establishments [that] all love the *Charter* . . . . [especially the] left-of-centre, civil libertarian judiciary [that] has been totally unbalanced by ideological appointments of Charterphiles" ' (Russell quoted in Schmitz 2006). The Conservatives' first Supreme Court appointment, Marshall Rothstein, was supported by Prime Minister Harper for having 'the appropriate "judicial temperament" . . . manifested by jurists who "apply the law rather than make it, and . . . apply it in a way that uses common sense and discretion, without being inventive" ' (Schmitz 2006). Then, in the fall of 2008, bypassing an all-party selection panel established to open up the Supreme Court appointment process, and ignoring the fact that it was Newfoundland's 'turn' for a Supreme

Court appointment, the prime minister nominated Thomas Cromwell, a bilingual, Nova Scotian appeal judge.

Beyond the Supreme Court, the Conservatives' 'reforms' of the way federal judges are appointed also provide a means to this end of more conservative and Charterphobic judicial appointments. The Canadian Bar Association (CBA) sharply criticized the Harper government's changes to the judicial appointment committees (JACs). Beyond the CBA and leading judges, even columnists in the *Globe and Mail* see this 'reform' for what it is: 'There isn't any other way to put it: The Harper government, by perverting the rules and by appointing party loyalists to key positions, intends to stack Canada's courts with conservatives ... this ideological contamination of the justice system must be seen as by far the worst misdeed committed by this administration' (Ibbitson 2007, A4).

In the end, then, it may not be an 'activist' court but rather an agenda-driven government that proves most decisive (Kelly 2005) when it comes to how the Charter will be interpreted. In other words, anti-court, anti-Charter tendencies are also likely to be exacerbated because the current Harper government is so tightly controlled from the centre. Even as a minority government, the Conservatives were able to change fundamentally the tenor of the courts and eliminate access to justice programs. And 'equality rights have no meaning in Canada if women, and other Canadians who face discrimination, cannot use them' (Day quoted in FAFIA 2006).

Changes to the courts, changes to the government, and even changes to institutions like federalism matter, as do the changing ideas that go with them. Shifts in federalism and the financing of federalism help contextualize why the Court deemed that it was too expensive to have British Columbia health services support therapy for autistic children, even though it had required BC hospitals to provide services for the deaf. Similarly, federal government offloading and cost-cutting has negatively affected healthcare which, in turn has an impact on the sorry state of abortion access in Canada, thereby attenuating the *Morgentaler* outcome.

Beyond changing institutions and ideas, shifts in political interests and identity politics also matter. Clearly, the foregoing political context helps us to understand why certain forms of interest mediation are not having the effect they once had. Some collective identities and interests are 'in', and others are 'out'. As Gregory Hein's work shows, business interest groups have made more inroads with the Charter, and this is not surprising in a climate of marketization (2001). This chapter details how equality seekers, especially feminists, have become more 'out' than 'in', in that there has been a virulent anti-feminist backlash, misconceptions about equality, and growing opposition to an activist court that promotes substantive equality, as well as to activist governments.

Feminist mobilization is obviously compromised from without, but it is also challenged from within. Strategies affect collective identities, and vice versa.

Feminist 'successes' are tempered by equality pursuits that can necessitate either 'over-protection' or problematic categorization. Lesbians, Aboriginal women, racialized women, immigrant women, and women with disabilities, among other women who have multiple, intersecting identities, have challenged equality-seeking feminist groups like LEAF and NAWL for their essentialist tendencies. This, in turn, has prompted analyses that reflected more 'particularity'. Yet, more 'particularity' means more specificity, which may undercut broader equality claims for women in general.

Finally, as the women's movement became more complex, diverse, and dispersed, the right simplified and caricatured the equality seekers' aims and outcomes. This helped to create more rifts. By playing up inconsistencies and using divide-and-conquer tactics, the right effectively delegitimized feminists' multiple identities and their strategies, and thus consolidated its own interests.

## Conclusion

This chapter illustrates that neo-liberalism is not a consistent, immutable force, and that dimensions of neo-liberalism can manifest themselves in different ways, in different realms. Moreover, political mobilization, of various kinds, at multiple levels, can affect the course of neo-liberalism.

The impact of feminist interest mediation, specifically intervenors like LEAF and NAWL, on equality cases was undoubtedly significant, and initially it helped to forestall neo-liberal advances. However, that influence can be exaggerated, as was done deliberately by Charterphobes to promote a right-wing agenda. Moreover, even notable feminist equality 'wins' are not without their limitations given such issues as 'over-protection' and 'oversimplification'. In the end, the outcomes of women's 'wins' and 'losses' are much harder to read in changing political circumstances and a turbulent socio-economic environment. In light of many women's precarious socio-economic, political, and legal status, it is not at all surprising that feminists and left liberals are not cheering, and some might even suggest that the early Charter critics may have been proved right. But what is the alternative? Here it is important not to lose sight of the larger political picture and consider the longer view.

Overall, back-pedalling on substantive equality is a serious problem for women in the current political climate where equality is considered a given, equality seekers' concerns are downgraded, and market concerns are upgraded. To be sure, while 'the courts have been doing poorly on socio-economic rights claims, the legislatures have been doing worse, forcing groups to go to the courts to seek redress against drastic government cutbacks and draconian revisions to social programs.' Still the 'courts have largely failed in providing redress' (Majury 2002a, 330).

Yet, to suggest that women have been either 'winners' or 'losers' is too simplistic an assessment. While it is true that many feminist 'gains' have become 'losses', outcomes are invariably more complicated in changing political circumstances. Any measurement of 'success' is not only fraught with difficulties but also highly contingent. Therefore, it may be more fruitful to focus on the actors and processes involved in the particular socio-economic, political, and cultural context—the institutions, interests, ideas, and identities at play at a particular juncture—their legitimacy, or lack thereof, and changes over time.

In her thoughtful NAWL address, after commenting on women's growing dissatisfaction with the Charter, Bertha Wilson went on to ask: 'Are they right to give up so easily and so early in the Charter's history? I don't think so. Ten years is not very long in the history of a constitution' (Wilson 1993, 1). Now, more than 25 years later, this is still not a very long history. Moreover, as we have seen, politics, broadly defined, both in terms of political contexts and in the multiple strategies of a wide array of political actors, will invariably change. In this there is hope.

## Notes

1   The prime minister's chief of staff in the first few years of the first Harper government was Ian Brodie, formerly a political science professor and a keen student of the Calgary school. When the feminist legal academic and activist Marilou McPhedran questioned Brodie about the Harper government's position on gender equality, he replied, 'We support gender equality . . . in Afghanistan.' (This question and answer exchange took place before a full audience, in which the author of this chapter was present, at the 'Charter at 20 Conference', March 2007, at McGill University.) More on this erasure of equality in the third section of this chapter.

2   As will be discussed in the third section, recent changes made by the Harper government to the judicial appointment committees (JACs) are not likely to add diversity to the ranks of the judiciary. Ironically, for a government worried about judges who are too political and lacking in impartiality, the latest reforms appear to prepare the ground for more conservative and less representative appointments, thereby *increasing* politicization and *decreasing* impartiality.

3   For some recent examples see Jhappan (2002), Green (2003), Faraday et al. (2006), and McIntyre and Rodgers (2006). For an excellent review article that focuses on the women, the Charter, and equality rights see Majury (2002a).

4   Empirical studies show, however, that this 'spectre of an almighty "Court Party" using the Charter to trample majority opinion is overstated' (MacIvor 2006, 200).

5   Majury sums up what was at stake in the *Mills* and *Shearing* cases: 'the Supreme Court of Canada increasingly has been willing to explore the gendered assumptions and values underlying the evidentiary issues. This process culminated in the almost unanimous decision in Mills in which the statutory protocols for the admission of confidential records pertaining to the complainant in a sexual assault trial were upheld. However, the more recent decision in *Shearing* represents a step backwards. The majority ruled that the accused could not cross-examine the complainant on the absence of entries in her diary relating to the abuse in order to raise the presumption that if it was not recorded it must not have happened. Then, in a sleight of hand, the majority ruled that the accused can cross-examine the complainant on the absence of entries in order to test the accuracy and completeness of her recollection of the events around the time she was abused' (Majury 2002a, 321). For a more critical analysis of *Mills*, see Gotell (2001).

6   See statistics cited in note 48 in McIntyre and Rodgers (2006, 15).

7   For instance, in surveys taken in 1987 and 1999, support for the Supreme Court appears stronger than in the most recent surveys. In 1987 and 1999, when Canadians were asked whether the courts or legislatures should have the last word on Charter of Rights conflicts, over 60 per cent replied that the Courts should have the final say (see MacIvor 2006, 129).

## References

Abu-Laban, Yasmeen, and Tim Nieguth. 2000. 'Reconsidering the Constitution, Minorities and Politics in Canada', *Canadian Journal of Political Science* 33 (3): 465–98.

Baines, Beverley. 2006. 'Equality, Comparison, Discrimination, Status'. In Fay Faraday, Margaret Denike, and M. Kate Stephenson, eds, *Making Equality Rights Real: Securing Substantive Equality under the Charter*, 73–98. Toronto: Irwin.

Bakan, Joel, and Michael Smith. 1997. 'Rights, Nationalism, and Social Movements in Canadian Constitutional Politics'. In David Schneiderman and Kate Sutherland, eds, *Charting the Consequences: The Impact of Charter Rights on Canadian Law and Politics*, 218–44. Toronto: University of Toronto Press.

Brodie, Ian. 2002a. *Friends of the Court: The Privileging of Interest-Group Litigants in Canada*. Albany: State University of New York Press.

———. 2002b. 'Interest Group Litigation and the Embedded State: Canada's Court Challenges Program', *Canadian Journal of Political Science* 34 (2): 357–76.

Brodie, Janine, Shelley A.M. Gavigan, and Jane Jenson. 1992. *The Politics of Abortion*. Toronto: Oxford University Press.

Brodsky, Gwen, and Shelagh Day, eds. 1989. *Canadian Charter Equality Rights for Women: One Step Forward or Two Steps Back?* Ottawa: Canadian Advisory Council on the Status of Women.

———, and ———. 2006. 'Women's Poverty Is an Equality Violation'. In Fay Faraday, Margaret Denike, and M. Kate Stephenson, eds, *Making Equality Rights Real: Securing Substantive Equality under the Charter*, 319–44. Toronto: Irwin.

Burstyn, Varda. 1985. *Women against Censorship*. Vancouver: Douglas and McIntyre.

Cairns, Alan C. 1991. *Disruptions: Constitutional Struggles from the Charter to Meech Lake*. Ed. Douglas E. Williams. Toronto: McClelland and Steward.

———. 1992. *Charter versus Federalism: The Dilemmas of Constitutional Reform*. Montreal: McGill-Queen's University Press.

Canadian Abortion Rights Action League (CARAL). 2003. *Protecting Abortion Rights in Canada: A Special Report to Celebrate the 15th Anniversary of the Decriminalization of Abortion*. Ottawa: CARAL.

CARAL. *See* Canadian Abortion Rights Action League.

Cossman, Brenda, Shannon Bell, Lise Gotell, and Becki L. Ross. 1997. *Bad Attitudes on Trial: Pornography, Feminism and the Butler Decision*. Toronto: University of Toronto Press.

Day, Shelagh, and Gwen Brodsky. 1998. *Women and the Equality Deficit: The Impact of Restructuring on Canada's Social Programs*. Ottawa: Status of Women Canada.

Devlin, Richard, Wayne MacKay, and Natasha Kim. 2000. 'Reducing the Democratic Deficit: Representation, Diversity and the Canadian Judiciary, or Towards a "Triple P" Judiciary', *Alberta Law Review* 38 (3): 734–866.

Dobrowolsky, Alexandra. 1997. 'The Charter and Mainstream Political Science: Waves of Contestation and Changing Theoretical Currents'. In David Schneiderman and Kate Sutherland, eds, *Charting the Consequences: The Impact of Charter Rights on Canadian Law and Politics*, 303–42. Toronto: University of Toronto Press.

———. 1998. 'Of "Special Interest": Interest, Identity and Feminist Constitutional Activism', *Canadian Journal of Political Science* 31(4): 707–42.

———. 2000. *The Politics of Pragmatism: Women, Representation, and Constitutionalism in Canada*. Toronto: Oxford University Press.

———. 2008. 'The Women's Movement in Flux: Feminism and Framing, Passion, and Politics'. In Miriam Smith, ed., *Social Movements in Canada*, 159–80. Peterborough, Ont.: Broadview Press.

———, and Jane Jenson. 2004. 'Shifting Representations of Citizenship: Canadian Politics of "Women" and "Children" ', *Social Politics* 11 (2): 154–80.

FAFIA (Feminist Alliance for International Action ). 2006. *Cuts to Status of Women and Court Challenges Programme Undermine Government's Commitment to Women's Equality*. Press release. Ottawa, 25 Sept.

Faraday, Fay, Margaret Denike, and M. Kate Stephenson. 2006. 'In Pursuit of Substantive Equality'. In Fay Faraday, Margaret Denike, and M. Kate Stephenson, eds, *Making Equality Rights Real: Securing Substantive Equality under the Charter*, 9–28. Toronto: Irwin Law.

Gotell, Lise. 1997. 'Shaping Butler: The New Politics of Anti-pornography'. In Brenda Cossman, Shannon Bell, Lise Gotell, and Becki L. Ross, eds, *Bad Attitudes on Trial: Pornography, Feminism, and the Butler Decision*, 48–106. Toronto: University of Toronto Press.

———. 2001. 'Colonization through Disclosure: Confidential Records, Sexual Assault Complainants, and Canadian Law', *Social and Legal Studies* 10 (3): 315–46.

———. 2002. 'Towards a Democratic Practice of Feminist Litigation? LEAF's Changing Approach to Charter Equality'. In Radha Jhappan, ed., *Women's Legal Strategies in Canada*, 135–74. Toronto: University of Toronto Press.

———, and Janine Brodie. 1996. 'Women and Parties in the 1990s: Less Than Ever an Issue of Numbers'. In Hugh Thorburn, ed., *Party Politics in Canada*. 7th edn, 54–71. Scarborough, Ont.: Prentice Hall.

Grabham, Emily. 2002. '*Law v. Canada*: New Directions for Equality under the Charter?' *Oxford Journal of Legal Studies* 22 (4): 641–61.

Green, Joyce. 2001. 'Canaries in the Mines of Citizenship: Indian Women in Canada'. *Canadian Journal of Political Science* 34 (4): 715–38.

———. 2003. 'Balancing Strategies: Aboriginal Women and Constitutional Rights in Canada'. In Alexandra Dobrowolsky and Vivien Hart, eds, *Women Making Constitutions: New Politics and Comparative Perspectives*, 36–51. Houndmills: Palgrave MacMillan.

Hein, Gregory. 2001. 'Interest Group Litigation and Canadian Democracy'. In Paul Howe and Peter H. Russell, eds, *Judicial Power and Canadian Democracy*. Montreal: McGill-Queen's University Press and Institute for Research on Public Policy.

Ibbitson, John. 2007. 'By Stacking Deck with Tories, Ottawa Puts the Court System at Risk', *Globe and Mail*, 12 Feb., A4.

James, Matt. 2004. 'The Politics of Honourable Constitutional Inclusion and the Citizens' Constitution Theory'. In Gerald Kernerman and Philip Resnick, eds, *Insiders and Outsiders: Alan Cairns and the Reshaping of Canadian Citizenship*, 132–47. Vancouver: UBC Press.

Jhappan, Radha, ed. 2002. *Women's Legal Strategies in Canada*. Toronto: University of Toronto Press.

Karaian, Lara. 2005. 'Troubling the Definition of Pornography: *Little Sisters*, a New Defining Moment in Feminists' Engagement with the Law', *Canadian Journal of Women and the Law* 17 (1): 117–33.

Kelly, James B. 2005. *Governing with the Charter: Legislative and Judicial Activism and Framers' Intent*. Vancouver: UBC Press.

Kim, Natasha, and Tina Piper. 2003. '*Gosselin v. Quebec*: Back to the Poorhouse', *McGill Law Journal* 48 (4): 749–81.

Kome, Penney. 1983. *The Taking of Twenty-Eight: Women Challenge the Constitution*. Toronto: Women's Press.

LEAF (Women's Legal Education and Action Fund). 1996. *Equality and the Charter: Ten Years of Feminist Advocacy before the Supreme Court of Canada*. Toronto: Emond Montgomery.

MacIvor, Heather. 2006. *Canadian Politics and Government in the Charter Era*. Toronto: Thomson Nelson.

McIntyre, Sheila. 1994. 'Redefining Reformism: The Consultations That Shaped Bill C-49'. In J.V. Roberts and Renate Mohr, eds, *Confronting Sexual Assault: A Decade of Social and Legal Change*. Toronto: University of Toronto Press.

———. 2006. 'Answering the Siren Call of Abstract Formalism with the Subjects and Verbs of Domination'. In Fay Faraday, Margaret Denike, and M. Kate Stephenson, eds, *Making Equality Rights Real: Securing Substantive Equality under the Charter*, 99–121. Toronto: Irwin Law.

———, and Sanda Rodgers. 2006. 'Introduction: High Expectations, Diminishing Returns—Section 15 at 20'. In Sheila McIntyre and Sanda Rodgers, eds, *Diminishing Returns: Inequality and the Canadian Charter of Rights and Freedoms*, 1–19. Toronto: Butterworths.

Macklin, Audrey. 1992. '*Symes v. M.N.R.*: Where Sex Meets Class', *Canadian Journal of Women and the Law* 5 (2): 498–517.

Majury, Diana. 2002a. 'The Charter, Equality Rights and Women: Equivocation and Celebration', *Osgoode Hall Law Journal* 40 (3–5), 298–336.

———. 2002b. 'Women's (In)Equality before and after the Charter'. In Radha Jhappan, ed., *Women's Legal Strategies in Canada*, 101–34. Toronto: University of Toronto Press.

———. 2006. 'Women Are Themselves to Blame: Choice as a Justification for Unequal Treatment'. In Fay Faraday, Margaret Denike, and M. Kate Stephenson, eds, *Making Equality Rights Real: Securing Substantive Equality under the Charter*, 209–44. Toronto: Irwin.

Makin, Kirk. 2007. 'Judges garner greater trust than politicians, survey finds,' *Globe and Mail*, 9 Apr., A5.

Manfredi, Christopher. 2004. *Feminist Activism in the Supreme Court: Legal Mobilization and the Women's Legal Education and Action Fund*. Vancouver: UBC Press.

Martin, Sheilah L. 2002. 'Abortion Litigation'. In Radha Jhappan, ed., *Women's Legal Strategies in Canada*, 335–78. Toronto: University of Toronto Press.

Morton, F.L., and Avril Allen. 2001. 'Feminists and the Courts: Measuring Success in Interest Group Litigation in Canada', *Canadian Journal of Political Science* 34 (1): 55–84.

———, and Rainer Knopff. 2000. *The Charter Revolution and the Court Party*. Peterborough, Ont.: Broadview Press.

Pal, Leslie A. 1993. 'Advocacy Organizations and Legislative Politics: The Effects of the Charter of Rights and Freedoms on Interest Lobbying of Federal Legislation, 1989–91'. In Leslie Seidle, ed., *Equity and Community: The Charter, Interest Advocacy and Representation*, 119–57. Montreal: Institute for Research on Public Policy.

Palley, Howard A. 2006. 'Canadian Abortion Policy: National Policy and the Impact of Federalism and Implementation on Access to Services', *Publius* 36 (4): 565–86.

Pothier, Dianne. 2006. 'Equality as a Comparative Concept: Mirror, Mirror on the Wall, What's the Fairest of Them All?' In Sheila McIntyre and Sanda Rodgers, eds, *Diminishing Returns: Inequality and the Canadian Charter of Rights and Freedoms*, 135–50. Toronto: Butterworths.

Porter, Bruce. 2006. 'Expectations of Equality'. In Sheila McIntyre and Sanda Rodgers, eds, *Diminishing Returns: Inequality and the Canadian Charter of Rights and Freedom*, 23–44. Toronto: Butterworths.

Randall, Melanie. 2006. 'Equality Rights and the Charter: Reconceptualizing State Accountability to Ending Domestic Violence'. In Fay Faraday, Margaret Denike, and M. Kate Stephenson, eds, *Making Equality Rights Real: Securing Substantive Equality under the Charter*, 275–18. Toronto: Irwin.

Rodgers, Sanda. 2006. 'Misconceptions: Equality and Reproductive Autonomy in the Supreme Court of Canada'. In Sheila McIntyre and Sanda Rodgers, eds, *Diminishing Returns: Inequality and the Canadian Charter of Rights and Freedoms*, 281–89. Toronto: Butterworths.

Russell, Peter H. 2006. Cited in Cristin Schmitz, 'Conservatives aim to replace judicial "Charterphiles" with "Charterphobes" ', *Lawyer's Weekly* 28 (27). http://lawyersweekly.ca/index.php?section=article&aricleid=402 (accessed 6 Nov. 2008).

Ryder, Bruce. 2001. 'The *Little Sisters* Case, Administrative Censorship, and Obscenity Law', *Osgoode Hall Law Journal* 39 (1): 207–27.

Sampson, Fiona. 2006. 'The Law Test for Discrimination and Gendered Disability Inequality'. In Fay Faraday, Margaret Denike, and M. Kate Stephenson, eds, *Making Equality Rights Real: Securing Substantive Equality under the Charter*, 245–74. Toronto: Irwin.

Schmitz, Cristin. 2006. 'Conservatives aim to replace judicial "Charterphiles" with "Charterphobes" ', *Lawyer's Weekly* 28 (27). http://lawyersweekly.ca/index.php?section=article&aricleid=402 (accessed 6 Nov. 2008).

Smith, Miriam. 1999. *Lesbian and Gay Rights in Canada: Social Movements and Equality Seeking, 1971–1995*. Toronto: University of Toronto Press.

———. 2002. 'Ghosts of the JCPC: Group Politics and Charter Litigation in Canadian Political Science', *Canadian Journal of Political Science* 35 (1): 3–29.

Trimble, Linda. 1997. 'Feminist Politics in the Alberta Legislature, 1972–1994'. In Jane Arscott
and Linda Trimble, eds, *In the Presence of Women: Representation in Canadian Governments*,
128–53. Toronto: Harcourt.
———, and Jane Arscott. 2003. *Still Counting: Women in Politics across Canada*. Peterborough,
Ont.: Broadview Press.
Turpel, Mary Ellen. 1991. 'Aboriginal Peoples and the Canadian Charter: Interpretive
Monopolies, Cultural Differences'. In Richard F. Devlin, ed., *Canadian Perspectives on Legal
Theory*. Toronto: Emond Montgomery.
Wilson, Bertha. 1993. 'Women and the Canadian Charter of Rights and Freedoms'. Keynote
address at 'Healing the Past, Forming the Future', the biennial conference of the National
Association of Women and the Law, 19–21 Feb., Vancouver.
Women's Legal Education and Action Fund. *See* LEAF.
Young, Margot. 2006. 'Blissed Out: Section 15 at Twenty'. In Sheila McIntyre and Sanda Rodgers,
eds, *Diminishing Returns: Inequality and the Canadian Charter of Rights and Freedoms*, 45–69.
Toronto: Butterworths.

## Further Reading

Baines, Beverley, and Ruth Rubio Marin. 2004. *The Gender of Constitutional Jurisprudence*.
Cambridge: Cambridge University Press.
Dobrowolsky, Alexandra. 2008. 'The Women's Movement in Flux: Feminism and Framing,
Passion and Politics'. In Miriam Smith, ed., *Group Politics and Social Movements in Canada*,
159–80. Peterborough, Ont.: Broadview Press.
Dobrowolsky, Alexandra. 2000. *The Politics of Pragmatism: Women, Representation, and Constitu-
tionalism in Canada*. Toronto: Oxford University Press.
Dobrowolsky, Alexandra, and Vivien Hart. 2003. *Women Making Constitutions: New Politics and
Comparative Perspectives*. Houndmills: Palgrave Macmillan.
Irving, Helen. 2008. *Gender and the Constitution: Equity and Agency in Comparative Constitu-
tional Design*. Cambridge: Cambridge University Press.
Jhappan, Radha. 2002. *Women's Legal Strategies in Canada*. Toronto: University of Toronto Press.
Canadian Feminist Alliance for International Action. www.fafia-afai.org.
Native Women's Association of Canada. www.nwac-hq.org.
Equal Voice. www.equalvoice.ca.

## Questions for Critical Thought

1. Beyond the symbolic significance, were there any real advantages to enshrining women's
   equality rights in the Canadian constitution?
2. Can equality between men and women be measured? If not, why not? If so, how?
   What benchmarks would you use and why?
3. What are the pros and cons of using the courts to bring about political gains for women?
4. Is there any scope for equality concerns in neo-liberal and/or post–neo-liberal times?

# CHAPTER 11

# 'Show Us the Money':

## Tracking Gender-Equality Commitments and the 'Constraints' of Canadian Budgeting

Isabella Bakker

## Introduction

Over the last few decades, Canada has been a signatory to a number of United Nations (UN) commitments to gender equality and more inclusive economic development, such as the Convention on the Elimination of All Forms of Discrimination against Women (CEDAW), the Beijing Platform for Action, and more recently, the Millennium Development Goals (MDGs). Despite these stated commitments, as the chapters in this volume attest, there remain significant gender inequalities in the life experiences and distribution of opportunities among women and men, and between women, in Canada (Statistics Canada 2006b; Townson 2005).

Government budgets, which are policy statements that reflect the social and economic priorities of governments, are one area of public action that has been identified as an important tool for redressing underlying inequalities and tackling them through the allocation of public resources. In particular, gender budget analysis or gender-responsive budgeting is increasingly recognized by international agencies and some 70 governments as an important way to hold governments accountable for their commitments to human rights and gender equality, as gender budgets help to connect these commitments to the distribution, use, and generation of public resources.[1]

Ironically, in the Canadian case, governments have promised to undertake gender-responsive budgeting analysis yet no systematic effort is underway despite stated commitments as well as the adoption of results-based or performance-based budgeting frameworks (Bakker 2005; Philipps 2006).[2] Furthermore, the capacity within government to undertake gender-sensitive analysis is actually on the decline with cutbacks in funding for women's agencies and gender-analysis units and the discrediting of women's claims-making in the overall policy process (Brodie 2007; Brodie and Bakker 2008). This is a concrete result of both neo-liberal and social investment discourses and practices (see Jenson in this volume). Moreover, the so-called 'sound' macro-economic policies (which promote low inflation and high mobility of capital) that are common to both neo-liberal and social investment perspectives often create policy *incoherence* (Elson 2006). For example, the commitment of the social investment model to poverty alleviation (see the Introduction in this volume) and international covenants that include the promise of gender equality require public spending, not fiscal contraction, to counterbalance deflationary policies (Elson and Cagatay 2000).

Nonetheless, in Canada, federal spending as a share of the economy shrank from 16 per cent of GDP in 1993–4 to 11 per cent in 2000/1, as part of a massive neo-liberal–inspired plan to eliminate budget deficits through cuts in federal spending. According to a 2005 Social Watch report, these cuts were most harsh for the most vulnerable, and, given their place in the distribution of income, women were 'doubly jeopardized' (Yalnizyan 2005c). For instance, the dramatic decline in employment insurance coverage has been reflected in a widening gap between the coverage for women and men. Townson and Hayes note that the main reason is that 'while women's patterns of paid employment and participation in the paid workforce are different from those of men, these differences were not recognized when the EI changes were made' (2007, 8; see also MacDonald in this volume). In a detailed report for Status of Women Canada on Canada's social policy regime and its changes over the last decade, Brodie and Bakker conclude that the continued fragmentation and erosion of the social-assistance regime, along with tax-delivered social policies (seen particularly with the rise of the social investment model) that do not benefit low-income women (since they generally do not have enough taxable income—see Philipps 2006), have left Canada's poorest—who are disproportionately women, children, Aboriginal peoples, and visible minorities—poorer and more insecure than they were before the reforms were enacted (Brodie and Bakker 2007).

With that background, the first section of this chapter will begin by briefly highlighting the main international agreements on gender equality to which Canada has been a signatory, such as the Beijing Platform for Action (and its follow-up) and the Convention for the Elimination of Discrimination against Women. These are important rights instruments that require national governments to achieve substantive equality between women and men through public-resource allocation and mobilization. The second section looks at the budget process and the extent to which a variety of societal interests are represented in budget formulation, thereby raising broader questions of accountability and how it is understood by policy makers. For instance, the current emphasis on market-based performance indicators overshadows social accountability involving desired social outcomes: from the social investment priorities discussed in this volume (for example, social inclusion and social cohesion), to the much broader and deeper goals of gender equality and distributive justice.

The politics of the budget process and its surrounding power relations require further scrutiny, especially given the raft of reforms in budgetary processes over the last decade that have increasingly oriented government expenditure towards being more 'results-based'. This emphasis on 'results' and the use of indicators, targeting, and benchmarking fits well with social investment discourses where present-day expenditures are meant to 'pay off' in future. I consider the implication of the new results-based budgeting (RBB) for tracking the money allocated to gender-equality goals. However, as the third section highlights, the capacity to actually undertake gender-based analysis (GBA) in government has been dramatically reduced as women's machineries have been systematically cut back and sidelined. Many of the chapters in this volume comment on these processes that intensified in the mid-1990s, but here I highlight how they, ironically, coincide with the launch of the Federal Plan for Gender Equality (Box 1) in 1995 and take place alongside promises made in relation to wider, international, gender-equality covenants.

The fourth section scrutinizes the policy incoherence that results from pursuing prevailing 'sound' macro-economic policies while making social commitments to poverty reduction, human rights, and gender equality. As yet, the emphasis has fallen dramatically on the macro-economic policies and not the on the social commitments. In contrast, recent work in heterodox macro-economics, such as contributions by Joe Stiglitz and Dani Rodrik, argues that there needs to be better balancing of the economic and social dimensions of poverty and enhanced policy space and manoeuvrability for governments—a move away from the one-size-fits-all approach of mainstream economic policy that usually has a neo-liberal rationale. Indeed, the fact that distributive justice, particularly, gender equality, can have a significant multiplier effect for the economy is something that is increasingly being recognized by the Bretton Woods institutions. This is being acknowledged in relation to the developing world, but I argue that a similar costing exercise needs to be undertaken in Canada in order to begin to identify the gaps in funding for gender-equality commitments and the economic gains that can come with filling these gaps.

Finally, the fifth section notes that not only must macro-economic policy be informed by the real politics of the use of time, especially the time women spend on unpaid care work; but there also needs to be a link between macro-economic scenarios and different policy models for incorporating the reality of unpaid work into fiscal policy. These are precisely the considerations and calculations that are noticeably absent from both neo-liberal and social investment mandates. Again, as the literature from developing countries over the last two decades has shown, unequal gender relations can often be harmful to overall growth and development goals. For instance, restrictions on women's partici-

~pation in the economic and political life of their countries is costing Asian and Pacific countries between \$42 billion and \$46 billion a year, according to research by the World Bank (2006).

# Delivering on Commitments to Gender Equality

Paradoxically, given the consolidation of neo-liberalism in this decade, the 1990s saw the emergence of an international consensus on poverty eradication and the promotion of gender equality through such policy commitments as the 1995 World Social Summit on Development (WSSD), the Fourth World Conference on Women in Beijing (FWCW) and the International Conference on Population and Development (ICPD). The signatory countries made commitments to integrate the goals of these conferences into their policy plans (see Box 1 for excerpts of the federal government's Plan for Gender Equality 1995). This included mobilizing resources and ensuring transparency and accountability in budget processes, as well as the monitoring of progress toward these goals on the basis of the documented links between gender equality and broader economic and social progress (Box 2). The ten-year reviews in 2005 of the UN Fourth World Conference on Women, however, identified a number of shortfalls in the meeting of these commitments, especially the inadequate allocation of public resources and their ineffective and inequitable use. In January 2003, the UN Committee on the Elimination of Discrimination against Women (CEDAW) also identified under-funding of key social supports, such as the public sector and transfers by governments on which women heavily rely, as an impediment to

---

**Box 1:   The Federal Mandate in Canada: The Federal Plan for Gender Equality 1995**

Objective 1: Implement Gender-based Analysis throughout Federal Departments and Agencies, puts forward a systematic process to inform and guide future legislation and policies at the federal level by assessing any potential differential impact on women and men. Hence, this objective underpins all subsequent objectives.

Objective 2: Improve Women's Economic Autonomy and Well-being, promotes the valuation of paid and unpaid work performed by women, women's equitable participation in the paid and unpaid labour force and the equitable sharing of work and family responsibilities between women and men; encourage women's entrepreneurship; and promote the economic security and well-being of women.

Source: Status of Women Canada 1995.

**Box 2:   The United Nations Mandates That Relate to Gender-Equitable Fiscal Policy Beijing +5**

*To be done by national governments:*

109a.  Incorporate a gender perspective into the design, development, adoption and execution of all budgetary processes, as appropriate, in order to promote equitable, effective and appropriate resource allocation and establish adequate budgetary allocations to support gender equality and development programmes which enhance women's empowerment and develop the necessary analytical and methodological tools and mechanisms for monitoring and evaluation.

*Action by national governments:*

58(d).  Restructure and target the allocation of public expenditures to promote women's economic opportunities and equal access to productive resources and to address the basic social, educational and health needs of women, particularly those living in poverty.

346.  Governments should make efforts to systematically review how women benefit from public sector expenditures; adjust budgets to ensure equality of access to public sector expenditures, both for enhancing productive capacity and for meeting social needs.

165(f).  Conduct reviews of national income and inheritance tax and social security systems to eliminate any existing bias against women.

165(i).  Facilitate, at appropriate levels, more open and transparent budget processes.

Source: United Nations 1996.

Canada's fulfillment of its human-rights commitments to women. This finding was reinforced by Armine Yalnizian's extensive study of federal government budgets from 1995 to 2005. She notes that since the elimination of the federal budget deficit in 1998, more than half of the accumulated fiscal surplus has been dedicated to tax cuts rather than the restoration and augmentation of public spending (Yalnizyan 2005a; see also Philipps 2006). Aside from the distributive implications of tax cuts for women and men broadly speaking, Philipps notes there is also an allocative issue related to how different tax reductions affect women's economic choices. She notes that women and men have different patterns of labour, investment, and consumption and that those patterns will condition their responses to particular incentives such as tax cuts (2006, 159).

All of these preliminary insights suggest the importance of scrutinizing both fiscal policy and the budget process from a gender-responsive viewpoint.

# The Determination of Fiscal Policies and Gender-Equality Goals

## The Budget Process

Currently, access to budget-policy formulation by gender-equality experts and advocates is limited.[3] The decisions about fiscal and monetary policy are still concentrated in the hands of the Department of Finance, the Bank of Canada, the Privy Council Office (PCO), and the Treasury Board. In practice, the final version of the federal budget is written by civil servants in the Department of Finance who are given political direction by the minister of finance and the prime minister. The minister of finance establishes the overall fiscal framework within which policy decisions are made. In addition, the PCO co-ordinates the budget proposals of individual ministers and line departments and the Treasury Board, which is a committee of the Cabinet consisting of six ministers responsible for expenditure management. The governor of the Bank of Canada also holds regular meetings on monetary policy with the minister of finance (Makarenko 2005).

As Philipps has suggested, two developments in the mid-1990s promised openings in this process for gender-responsive budget analysis. The first was the federal government's commitment to the Beijing Platform for Action (discussed above), which called for a gender-based analysis of macro-economic policies; the second was Finance Minister Martin's opening up of the budget process through public pre-budget hearings of the Finance Committee (the House of Commons Standing Committee on Finance), part of the New Public Management (NPM) approach that emphasizes accountability and transparency (Philipps 2006, 151). A number of issues are raised by this potential opening up of the consultative process. These relate both to substantive participation and resources and to the limits of the possible when it comes to the framing of fiscal and monetary policies.

With regards to the first set of issues around process, it has been observed that '[w]hile all are invited to participate in the hearings, there are gross disparities in the level of resources brought to the table' (Philipps 2006, 151). For instance, the wealthier groups, like trade associations and members of the financial sector, have paid staff and consultants such as professional tax experts that allow them to present sophisticated submissions to the hearings. In contrast, women's groups and social-justice advocates are frequently short of money and time, and consequently they often make one combined representation to the Committee. In addition, selective closed-door meetings with Department of Finance officials continue to be held and to exclude those whose ideas of fiscal policy are outside the mainstream, such as gender-equality advocates and experts (Philipps 2006).

Hence, to achieve substantive equal representation from a broad spectrum of civil society, including women's organizations and gender-equality experts, would require funding so that such groups could participate effectively in the annual pre-budget hearings. One solution that has been suggested would be on-line budget-literacy initiatives by the government that would explain the budget process (Philipps 2006). However, the funding trends for women's groups in Canada imply the opposite, as was noted at the beginning of this chapter. Furthermore, the capacity within the federal government to undertake a gender-responsive budget analysis has been shrinking with cuts to the independent policy-research arm of Status of Women Canada (see below under 'Capacity and Funding for Gender-based Analysis'). The Department of Finance has one staff member (a 'GBA Champion') for gender-based analysis of fiscal and monetary policy (House of Commons Standing Committee on the Status of Women 2008); however, that GBA Champion operates within a mainstream macro-economic framework that excludes considerations of gender-based differences (see below under 'Macro-economics and Policy Coherence'). The politics of the budget process reveal the subtle and not so subtle distribution of power that influence the subsequent distribution of public resources and that may enhance or hinder the achieving of gender-equality goals. One thing that has shaped these questions over the last decade has been the raft of reforms in budgetary processes, reforms whose main goal is to make government expenditure more results-based (Sharp 2003). The move to results-based budgeting has led gender-equality experts and advocates to turn their focus on this new approach within government because it suggests that gender-based analysis would improve the outcomes of government in a more streamlined way. The next section will briefly consider the challenges of RBB as they pertain to the financing of gender equality.

### New Public Management and Results-based Budgeting: Better Links between Resources and Gender-Equality Commitments?

In both developed and developing countries, approaches to public policy and public management have been reshaped by 'new public management' (NPM). NPM entails the restructuring of many public services in an attempt to make them run more like businesses. The goal is to enhance the efficiency of firms and government and introduce more competition and private-market discipline, in an attempt to promote a more accountable, results-based, and citizen-oriented government (De Renzio 2004). One limitation of this shift is that it tends to eclipse other concepts of efficiency, such as social and allocative efficiency. In Canada, the move to NPM dovetailed well with neo-liberal mandates that privatized and streamlined, and in which efficiency and cost-effectiveness replaced messier, and more expensive, social realities.

At the same time, NPM also influenced the area of budgeting. Here the emphasis lay increasingly on performance and results, rather than on inputs. With this technique, which is referred to as performance-oriented budgeting or results-based budgeting (RBB), the objectives are twofold: (1) to allocate resources according to government priorities and objectives and (2) to relate the budget's resource allocation, or how the funds are planned to be used, to the results expected. RBB is one component of the NPM approach to economic governance but one that also fits in well with the pervasive benchmarking and performance indicators that are part of the social investment perspective.

Although there are certainly disadvantages to RBB, in some respects its goals may offer an entry point for harmonizing with gender-responsive budgeting. That is to say, the shift to performance-based budgeting or RBB has led gender-equality advocates to ask: does the adoption of budget reform along these lines offer opportunities for new monitoring and accountability mechanisms for linking budgets (resources) and gender-equality commitments? One general study based on country experiences and the availability of data and indicators offers a technical consideration of the strengths and limitations of RBB for gender-responsive budgets. The author of the study, Rhonda Sharp, outlines a number of strategies for achieving more gender-aware outcomes within the RBB framework. She notes that RBB involves a particular approach to budgetary and policy performance that she summarizes in the following manner:

a. What does the government want to achieve? *Outcomes*
b. How does the government achieve this? *Outputs*
c. How does it know if it is succeeding? *Performance Reporting* (2003, 56)

Sharp advocates three means by which gender-responsive budgeting can engage with output and outcomes budgeting:

1. *By developing gender-sensitive indicators of inputs, outputs, and outcomes.* Gender and other disaggregated data enhance the clarification, evaluation, and targeting of all budget outputs and outcomes, which are central aspects of results-based budgeting. At present, most examples pertain to specifically targeted programs for women and girls (for example, health services and social policies).
2. *By extending the existing output and outcomes framework with equity as an explicit indicator of performance.* Equity is defined in terms of access for, or the representation of, different groups. This goes beyond the narrow focus of most RBB models with their economy, efficiency, and effectiveness criteria of performance.
3. *By challenging the existing meanings of economy, efficiency, and effectiveness to include unpaid care activities within budgeting frameworks.* For instance, economy-based measures of performance-oriented budgeting calculate only the monetary costs, but if the non-money costs of inputs are considered, the result is a different measure of total economic activity. Efficiency measures do not take into account the care economy

and the transfer of costs to the unpaid sector that often accompany efficiency measures of performance. Similarly, effectiveness measures do not take into account all contributions to outcomes since none of the unpaid contribution of care activities to outcomes is counted. (Sharp 2003, 53–76)

## Capacity and Funding for Gender-based Analysis

Despite the potentially fruitful links between RBB and GBA, in Canada the capacity to undertake gender-based analysis has been undermined. It is widely recognized that in order to link financing to gender-equality commitments, it is important to fund national machineries for the advancement of women and incorporate those machineries into all stages of the budget process. These connections are made in the Global Framework of the Beijing Platform for Action, and the General Assembly reaffirmed its call for sufficient resources to be allocated to national machineries in its five-year review of the Beijing Platform for Action in 2000.[4] Yet, as Brodie and Bakker (2007, 2008) note, despite a long history of gender-based policy units in the Canadian federal government, since the mid-1990s, broader social and political forces have been eroding the resources assigned to these units. This became starkly apparent in 2006 when, after many years of successive cutbacks to the women's machinery under the Liberals, the new Conservative government under Stephen Harper cut a further 2 billion dollars from the funding of Canada's equality-seeking groups (see other chapters in this volume). Brodie (2007, 2008) argues that this dismantling of GBA in government is part of a broader process of delegitimizing the women's movement and women's claim-making vis-à-vis public policy and that it underscores the disappearance of women as an analytical category in favour of, for example, the child.

These developments suggest that at the very time when we need more effective analysis of expenditures and revenues, and when indeed, governments have made commitments to results-based management of public funds, we have fewer financial and human resources for such analyses. Moreover, this comes on top of the significant cuts to social expenditures over the last decade which have had a disproportionately negative impact on poor women and children (Yalnizyan 2005a).

This neglect of gender-based analysis in budgets raises broader questions about the accountability of policy makers who make fiscal and monetary decisions. Of course the generic taxpayer is the touchstone of accountability. Yet, as feminist economists, lawyers, and activists have pointed out, taxpayers are not generic subjects, and, depending on their gender, race, class, and other social circumstances, they are faced with different life experiences. Hence, the issue of equity among various groups in society becomes an important factor in budget analysis that goes beyond mainstream norms of horizontal and vertical equity, which are formulated exclusively with reference to income and which tend to be silent about social conditions and how these may determine similarity or differences in circumstances (Philipps 2006, 155).

The neo-liberal shift in economic governance has also resulted in a general and indirect form of *market accountability* that attempts to sustain an 'appropriate business climate' for investors, businesses, currency traders, and so on; and a second form of more direct and specific *accountability of borrowers to lenders (creditors)*—in short to all the institutions that might fund budget deficits through loans (Bakker 2002). More broad-based participation in the economic policy process requires a *social accountability* that will support three other types of accountability that underpin a more inclusive and equitable budget process: *political accountability* of institutions such as parliaments; *administrative accountability* for policy delivery based on clear standards and protocols of practice; and *judicial accountability* by which rights incorporated into constitutions and other national legislation provide both protection of citizens' rights and the ability to challenge government legislation and policy deemed to undermine or run counter to such rights (Oxford Policy Management et al. 2008, 10). Elson has illustrated the links between budgets and the Convention for the Elimination of Discrimination against Women (CEDAW) that Canada ratified in 1981 and that oblige the federal government to align its legislation (and resources) with the articles of the Convention (Elson 2004).

## Macro-economics and Policy Coherence

From the recent Report of the Parliamentary Standing Committee on the Status of Women (Canada 2008), it is clear that one key aspect of attaining more gender-responsive budgeting is to scrutinize the approach to economic policy in the prevailing economic and budgetary consensus. For instance, recent studies conclude that too narrow a focus on macro-economic stability can have adverse effects on economic and human development. 'Sound' policy to defeat inflation, for instance, has led to very high interest rates in a number of countries. Higher interest rates in turn have led to increased unemployment, and this has contributed to continuing poverty (Rodrick 2007; Stiglitz 2005). Economic growth does require measures such as employment creation, yet when viewed from a gender-equality perspective, notions of 'full' employment also need to be scrutinized for not taking account of the unpaid work in which most women are engaged. For instance, lower-income women in developing countries often suffer from 'overfull employment' because of the time and energy they spend in fetching fuel and water, producing meals, and so on. Lower-income women in the more developed countries still have many care responsibilities that compromise their ability to seek full employment in the formal labour market, a fact that is reflected in the higher concentration of women in part-time jobs in most countries (Elson 2006, 119–20).

Those points underscore what appears to be a conceptual separation in Finance Canada's thinking between 'structural' policies and 'macro-economics' polices. In her testimony to the Standing Committee on the Status of Women, the newly appointed Gender Based Analysis Champion at Finance notes that:

> Macro-economic policies deal with aggregate economic variables such as fiscal surpluses and fiscal deficit targets and the level of public debt. These policies provide the economic and fiscal framework within which structural policies are developed. Since macro-economic policies are by definition not targeted to any sector or any group of individuals in particular, gender-based analysis is not applicable.
>
> Structural policies, on the other hand, can impact specific sectors and segments of the population. Since these policies could potentially have different measurable impacts on women and men, it is on those policies that gender-based analysis is carried out. Examples of structural policy for which the Department of Finance is responsible include tax, tariff policy, managing federal borrowing, administering transfers to the provinces, and developing an effective system of regulation for the financial sector.[5]

Feminist economists and activists have documented how broader macro-economic strategies and discourses about the role of government, in particular public investment, shape the direction of economic growth, the nature and level of job creation, poverty-reduction efforts, and time spent in social-reproduction activities. These issues are related to the appropriate level of budget deficit and surplus, which neo-liberal economists argue should be in balance. Feminist macro-economists generally tend to support a more Keynesian approach that allows for greater government discretion in managing public finances and deciding how the deficit or surplus is managed (Elson 2004, 626). Yet this approach too may suffer from what Elson coins an implicit or explicit 'breadwinner bias', where priority is given to men's employment and women are treated as dependents with a contingent relationship to public services and social protection (Elson 2004; Bakker 1997).

Another related limitation identified by heterodox and feminist economists is the lack of policy coherence between 'sound' economic policies that emphasize low inflation and mobility of capital on the one hand, and the social commitments to poverty reduction, human rights, and gender equality on the other. The latter often require public spending to support social provisioning and to stabilize the social imbalances that result from deflationary policies. Thus, Elson and Cagatay argue that an 'alternative approach to considering social policies as an afterthought to macro-economic policies would start with the premise that all macro-economic policies are enacted within a certain set of distributive relations and institutional structures; and that all macro-economic policies entail a variety of social outcomes which need to be made explicit' (2000, 1347–8).

That approach would mean that sound economic policies were judged, not only by market criteria (and those that signal the appropriate business climate), but by the social outcomes desired, such as distributive justice, equity, and meeting of needs for all (2000, 1348).

Indeed, better management of the interface between national regulatory and social regimes may be part of the newly emerging approach to growth. Furthermore, not only is a genuine balancing of the economic and social dimensions of policy necessary for meeting gender-equality commitments, but meeting gender-equality commitments may be of economic benefit. The multiplier effect of gender equality has been recognized by the Bretton Woods institutions as a key to meeting the Millennium Development Goal (MDG) targets in 2015. A recent paper prepared for the World Bank specifies the costs of present and future interventions aimed at promoting gender equality and the empowerment of women. The goals are twofold: to identify the minimum resources necessary for meeting these objectives in low-income countries and to estimate the share of all MDG investments that have the potential to improve outcomes for all people in those countries. The authors find that on average the cost of interventions directly aimed at promoting gender equality is $7 to $13 per capita from 2006 to 2015. On the basis of various scenarios for costing, gender-equality investment needs come to about 12 per cent of total MDG needs in 2006 and 15 per cent in 2015. According to such projections, the gender-equality financing gap is $12–$30 billion in 2006 and rises to $24-$83 billion in 2015 (depending on the extent to which resources are raised domestically or externally). What these figures indicate is that achieving gender-equality objectives and the MDGs requires money and a reallocation of existing resources (Grown et al. 2006). A similar costing exercise is required in Canada as a starting point for identifying the gap in meeting gender-equality commitments.

## Macro-economics and Unpaid Work

A final set of issues relates to the critique of the conventional macro-economic framework that guides fiscal, monetary, and exchange-rate policy. Feminist researchers and activists have argued that gender-neutral macro-economic policy will address women's needs and experiences only to the extent to which they conform to male norms. Yet, a substantial part of women's time and resources is dedicated to unpaid work—the work of producing and caring for human beings—which underpins the paid economy. This omission of the activities and values left out of macro-economic inquiry and therefore policy is not simply an omission based on complexities of measurement. Rather, it reflects assumptions built into this model that exclude women's time in unpaid work as a used economic resource. In the last two decades, feminist researchers have documented how neo-liberal economic policies cut social supports and how both neo-liberalism and social investment perspectives rely on women's unpaid labour to fill the gaps. In this sense, current fiscal policies treat women's unpaid work as an externality. As Lahey (2005) reported, women's responsibilities for unpaid work push them in the direction of part-time and other marginal forms of work, which generate smaller incomes and benefits and thus make them more dependent on the very redistributive social policies that have been dramatically scaled back. Policy makers are rarely explicit about how such assumptions guide their decisions. Yet social policy development in Canada is informed by these implicit (and often paradoxical) models of the macro economy (Bakker 1997), the family, and models of social policy. The addition of a social investment approach, which seeks to promote human capital, also serves to encourage women to engage increasingly in paid work without sufficient public-policy attention to the necessity for unpaid work, including childcare.

When we survey existing measures and what we can learn from them about the usefulness of integrating both paid and unpaid labour into national policies, at least three related approaches emerge with regard to the politics of care. One gives *indirect policy recognition* to the relationship between paid and unpaid labour through, for example, pension schemes and employment equity policies that encourage a more equitable choice and distribution of unpaid work. The second *recognizes the importance of unpaid work* through policies such as tax breaks for those staying at home to raise young children. A third approach is *public sector provision of services*, which recognizes women as both mothers and workers and removes some of the individual burden of unpaid labour, such as childcare, by shifting it to the public sphere (see Daly 2001 for a detailed discussion).

Conventional macro-economics sees the household sector only as a source of personal consumption and savings. Heterodox macro-economists have made the argument that the household sector and unpaid labourers are producers of goods and services as well as of future stocks of labour and social citizens. If we take the broader, heterodox view of links between unpaid labour and macro-economics, what have we learned in terms of more equitable and efficient macro-economic policy making?

We do have some empirical findings from developing countries that suggest an important link between macro-economic adjustment packages and gender relations. What is required is further empirical work that assesses the links between gender inequality and loss of aggregate output, and that tracks the gender division of labour and its impact on the reallocation of labour between various sectors. As noted in the previous section, macro-economics is not gender-neutral, precisely because there is inequality of both access to and participation in markets, which is based on the gender division of labour.

- It is largely women who provide a human-resource subsidy to the economy by caring for children and, increasingly, the elderly and the ill.
- Labour markets continue to be segmented along gender lines, partly because of differences in labour mobility between women and men and partly because of restructuring.
- Disparities in wages and poverty along gender lines are firmly entrenched.
- The distribution of wealth and assets (traditional assets such as land and newer assets such as knowledge) is even more unequal than the distribution of income.

These conditions determine women's ability to respond to macro policy and constrain overall human-resource development. They also suggest important limitations to market-led solutions to closing the gender-equality gap. In the end, although there have been a number of innovative new sources of funding proposed for meeting gender-equality commitments, such as more effective and equal tax systems or global private women's funds (see Bakker 2007 for a discussion of these alternatives), it is ultimately states that must ensure they have the funds to meet their human-rights and gender-equality obligations and stated commitments.

In sum, gender-responsive budgeting should be an important focus of government since budgets are instruments for administering various aspects of social policy, particularly through the tax system (the so-called fiscalization of social policy,[6] which predominates in a social investment agenda). Such an emphasis also reflects a broader emerging consensus in heterodox and feminist economics that social policy needs to be mainstreamed into macroeconomic analysis precisely because all macro-economic policies entail a variety of social outcomes and that trade-offs between gains and losses need to be made explicit (Elson and Cagatay 2000, 1348). A heterodox economic approach to public-policy making, it has been suggested, presents the possibility of greater policy space as well as a recognition of the inter-relatedness of women's paid and unpaid work in realizing both growth potential and greater gender-equality goals. The adoption of results-based budgeting, can, it has been furthermore suggested, also create the political space for developing gender-sensitive indicators of inputs, outputs, and outcomes, thus creating a means of tracking progress in meeting gender-equality goals and commitments.

Finally, as this chapter underscores, to go beyond rhetoric requires a sustained and planned commitment of funds to meet stated gender-equality objectives. This includes costing gender-equality commitments and setting out a budgetary plan that recognizes these commitments. The recent recommendations in the Report of the Parliamentary Standing Committee on the Status of Women offer an important road map to begin such a process within government. In tandem with a growing civil-society-based gender-responsive budgeting movement, the so-called 'constraints' of fulfilling gender-equality commitments through the politics of the budget could be significantly challenged.

## Notes

1  See http://www.gender-budgets.org.
2  A recent effort by an outside government group has integrated a gender-based analysis into its annual budget forecast. See CCPA (2008).
3  For a more detailed discussion see Brodie and Bakker (2008).
4  See http://www.un.org/womenwatch/daw/followup/beijing%2B5.htm.
5  See http://cmte.parl.gc.ca/Content/HOC/committee/392/fewo/reports/rp3551119/feworp11/08-chap5-e.htm, note 158.
6  Fiscalization means that social policy goals are pursued only indirectly through the tax system and the spending priorities of families, while taxable income determines both who is eligible for support and the level of support attained. What are the implications of the growing fiscalization of social policy for different women? For one, the use of the tax system and in particular, tax expenditures, to realize social policy objectives is not a gender-neutral public-policy strategy. Lisa Philipps (2006b) has argued that these tax-delivered social policies have two systemic disadvantages for many women. First, tax-based measures generally do not benefit low-income women because they do not have enough taxable income or tax liability to claim deductions, exemptions, or credits. And second, it is assumed that the primary breadwinner will share these gains with the household. This ignores a good deal of evidence about intra-household financial inequalities, assumes that caregivers are in a spousal or partner relationship, and leaves out those where neither partner earns sufficient taxable income to benefit from the credit (Philipps 2006b. See also Yalnizyan 2005a, b, and c).

## References

Bakker, Isabella. 1994. *The Strategic Silence: Gender and Economic Policy*. London: Zed Press/North-South Institute.

———. 1997. *Unpaid Work and Macroeconomics: New Discussions, New Research Directions*. Ottawa: Status of Women Canada.

———. 2002. *Fiscal Policy, Accountability and Voice: The Example of Gender Responsive Budgeting*. Background Study, Human Development Report. New York: United Nations Development Programme.

———. 2005. *Gender Budget Initiatives: Why They Matter in Canada*. Alternative Federal Budget Working Paper No. 1. Ottawa: Canadian Centre for Policy Alternatives.

———. 2007. *Financing for Gender Equality and the Empowerment of Women: Paradoxes and Possibilities*. United Nations Division for the Advancement of Women. Expert Group Meeting on financing for gender equality and the empowerment of women, Oslo, Norway, 4–7 Sept. Available at http://www.womenwatch.org.

———, and Janine Brodie. 1995. *The New Canada Health and Social Transfer (CHST): Implications for Women*. Ottawa: Status of Women Canada.

Brodie, Janine. 1995. *Politics on the Margins: Restructuring and the Canadian Women's Movement*. Halifax: Fernwood.

———. 2002. 'The Great Undoing: State Formation, Gender Politics, and Social Policy in Canada'. In Catherine Kingfisher, ed., *Western Welfare in Decline: Globalization and Women's Poverty*. Philadelphia: University of Pennsylvania Press.

———. 2007. 'Canada's 3 "D"s: Gender and Social Policy in Canada'. In Marjorie Cohen and Janine Brodie, eds, *Remapping Gender in the New Global Order*. London: Routledge.

————. 2008. 'Putting Gender Back In: Women and Social Policy in Canada'. In Yasmeen Abu-Laban, ed., *Gendering the Nation State: Canadian and Comparative Perspectives*. Vancouver: UBC Press.

————, and Isabella Bakker. 2007. *Canada's Social Policy Regime and Women: An Assessment of the Last Decade*. Ottawa: Status of Women Canada. http://www.swc-cfc.gc.ca/pubs/pubspr/0662450870/index_e.html.

————, and ————. 2008. *Where Are the Women? Gender Equity, Budgets and Canadian Public Policy*. Ottawa: Canadian Centre for Policy Alternatives.

Cagatay, Nilufer. 1998. *Engendering Macroeconomics and Macroeconomic Policies*. Social Development and Poverty Elimination Division Working Paper. New York: United Nations Development Programme.

Canada, SWC (Status of Women Canada). 2002. *Canadian Experience in Gender Mainstreaming 2001*. Ottawa: Status of Women Canada. http://www.swc.gc-cfc.gc.ca/resources (accessed Oct. 2006).

————. 2004. *Budget 2004: Status of Women Canada: Gender Equality Review*. Ottawa: Status of Women Canada. http://www.swc.gc-cfc.gc.ca/resources (accessed Oct. 2006).

————. 2005. *Gender Equity Consultation*. http://www.swc-cfc.gc.ca/resources/consultations/ges09-2005/introe.html (accessed Oct. 2006).

Canada. 2005a. Parliament. House of Commons Standing Committee on the Status of Women. *Gender-Based Analysis: Building Blocks for Success*. Ottawa: Minister of Supply and Services.

————. 2005b. *Government Response to Gender-Based Analysis: Building Blocks for Success*. September. http://www.parl.gc.ca/committee/CommitteePublication.aspx?COM=8997&Lang=1&SourceId=129221 (accessed Oct. 2006).

————. 2008. Parliament. House of Commons. Standing Committee on the Status of Women. *Gender Responsive Budgeting: Rising to the Challenge of Achieving Gender Equality*. 39th Parliament, 2nd Session. http://cmte.parl.gc.ca/Content/HOC/committee/392/fewo/reports/rp3551119/feworp11-e.html.

CCPA (Canadian Centre for Policy Alternatives). n.d. www.policyalternatives.ca (accessed Oct. 2006).

————. 2008. *The Alternative Federal Budget 2008*. Ottawa: Canadian Centre for Policy Alternatives.

Commonwealth Secretariat. 2002. *Gender Budgets Make Cents (Understanding Gender Responsive Budgets)*. London: Commonwealth Secretariat.

Condon, Mary, and Lisa Philipps. 2005. 'Transnational Market Governance and Economic Citizenship: New Frontiers for Feminist Legal Theory', *Thomas Jefferson Law Review* 28 (2): 105–50.

Daly, Mary. 2001. 'Care Policies in Western Europe'. In Mary Daly, ed., *Care Work: The Quest for Security*. Geneva: ILO (International Labour Organisation).

De Renzio, Paolo. 2004. *Why Budgets Matter: The New Agenda of Public Expenditure Management*. London: Overseas Development Instituted. Briefing Paper May.

Elson, Diane. 2004. 'Engendering Government Budgets in the Context of Globalization(s)', *International Feminist Journal of Politics* 6 (4): 623–42.

————. 2006. *Budgeting for Women's Rights: Monitoring Government Budgets for Compliance with CEDAW*. New York: UNIFEM.

————, and Nilufer Cagatay. 2000. 'The Social Content of Macroeconomic Policies'. *World Development* 28 (7): 1347–64.

FAFIA (Feminist Alliance for International Action). n.d. http://www.fafia-afai.org.

Grown, Caren, Chandrika Bahadur, Jessie Handbur, and Diane Elson. 2006. *The Financial Requirements of Achieving Gender Equality and Women's Empowerment*. Washington, DC: World Bank.

Lahey, Kathleen. 2005. *Women and Employment: Removing Fiscal Barriers to Women's Labour Force Participation*. Ottawa: Status of Women Canada.

Macdonald, Martha. 1995. 'Feminist Economics: From Theory to Research', *Canadian Journal of Economics* 28 (1): 159–76 .

Makarenko, Jay. 2005. *The Canadian Federal Budget*. http://www.mapleleafweb.com/features/economy/budget/Federal-Budget/ (accessed Oct. 2006).

NCW (National Council of Welfare). 2002. *Welfare Incomes 2000–2001*. Ottawa: Minister of Public Works and Government Services.

———. 1995–2004. *Welfare Incomes*. Ottawa: Minister of Public Works and Government Services. http://www.ncwcnbes.net/htmdocument/principales/online/pub-e.htm (accessed Nov. 2006).

Norton, Andrew, and Diane Elson. 2002. *What's Behind the Budget? Politics, Rights and Accountability in the Budget Process*. London: Overseas Development Institute.

Oxford Policy Management/Social Development Direct/Working Together. 2008. *Making Aid More Effective through Gender, Rights and Inclusion: Evidence from Implementing the Paris Declaration*. Oxford.

Parkinson, Rhonda. 2002. *The Bank of Canada*. http://www.mapleleafweb.com/features/economy/bank-canada/index.html.

Philipps, Lisa. 1996. 'The Rise of Balanced Budget Laws in Canada: Fiscal (Ir)Responsibility', *Osgoode Hall Law Journal* 34 (4): 681–740.

———. 1999. 'Taxing the Market Citizen: Fiscal Policy and Inequality in an Age of Privatization', *Law and Contemporary Problems*. http://www.law.duke.edu/journals/lcp/articles/lcp63dautumn2006 (accessed Nov. 2006).

———. 2006. 'Gender Budgets and Tax Policy Making'. In Miranda Stewart, ed., *Tax Law and Political Institutions*. Annandale, Australia: Federation Press.

Rodrik, Dani. 2007. 'Rethinking Growth Strategies'. In. A.B. Atkinson et al., *WIDER Perspectives on Global Devselopment*. London: Palgrave-Macmillan in association with UNU-WIDER.

Sharp, Rhonda. 2003. Budgeting for Equity: Gender Budgeting Initiatives within a Framework of Performance Oriented Budgeting. New York: UNIFEM.

Statistics Canada. 2006. *Women in Canada: A Gender-based Statistical Report*. Ottawa: Statistics Canada.

Status of Women Canada. 1995. *Setting the Stage for the Next Century: The Federal Plan for Gender Equity*. Ottawa: Status of Women Canada.

Stiglitz, Joseph. 2005. 'Finance for Development'. In Melvin Ayogu and Don Ross, eds, *Development Dilemmas: The Methods and Political Ethics of Growth Policy*. London, New York: Routledge.

Townson, Monica. 2005. *Poverty Issues for Canadian Women*. Prepared for Gender Equality Consultations. Ottawa: Status of Women Canada.

———, and Kevin Hayes. 2007. *Women and the Unemployment Insurance Program*. Ottawa: Canadian Centre for Policy Alternatives. See www.GrowingGap.ca.

United Nations. 1996. *Report of the Fourth World Conference on Women, Beijing, 4–15 September 1995*. United Nations Sales No. E.96.IV. 13. New York: United Nations.

World Bank. 2006. *Gender Equality as Smart Economics: A World Bank Group Gender Action Plan*. http://www.worldbank.org/gender.

Yalnizyan, Armine, 2005a. *Canada's Commitment to Equality: A Gender Analysis of the Last Ten Federal Budgets (1995–2005)*. Ottawa: Canadian Feminist Alliance for International Action.

———. 2005b. 'Assessing the Federal Budget 2005: What's in It for Women'. Paper prepared for the Feminist Alliance for International Action. Ottawa.

———. 2005c. 'Divided and Distracted: Regionalism as Obstacle to Reducing Poverty and Inequality'. Ottawa: Canadian Centre for Policy Alternatives.

## Further Readings

Bakker, Isabella, and Diane Elson. 1998. 'Towards Engendering Budgets in Canada'. In Canadian Centre for Policy Alternatives, ed., *Alternative Federal Budget Papers 1998*. Ottawa: Canadian Centre for Policy Alternatives.

Budlender, Debbie, and Rhonda Sharp with Kerri Allen. 1998. *How to Do a Gender-Sensitive Budget Analysis: Contemporary Research and Practice*. London: Commonwealth Secretariat.

Elson, Diane. 1998. 'Integrating Gender Issues into National Budgetary Policies and Procedures: Some Policy Options', *Journal of International Development* 10.

Hofbauer Balmori, H. 2003. *Gender and Budgets: Overview Report*. Brighton: IDS.

UNIFEM. 2000. *Progress of the World's Women 2000*. New York. http://www.unifem.undp.org/
    progressww/2000/index.html.
Gender Responsive Budgeting. www.gender-budgets.org.
Canadian Centre for Policy Alternatives. www.policyalternatives.ca.
International Budget Partnerships. www.internationalbudget.org.

## Questions for Critical Thought

1. What are the gender impacts of recent tax reforms?
2. What would a gender-sensitive fiscal policy look like?
3. How can the budget process be more responsive to gender-equality commitments?

# Notes on Contributors

YASMEEN ABU-LABAN

Yasmeen Abu-Laban is Professor and Associate Chair (Research) in the Department of Political Science at the University of Alberta. Her research interests centre on the Canadian and comparative dimensions of gender and ethnic politics, nationalism, globalization and processes of racialization, immigration policies and politics, and citizenship theory. She has published over 50 articles, book chapters, and reviews, and is the co-author (with Christina Gabriel) of *Selling Diversity: Immigration, Multiculturalism, Employment Equity and Globalization* (2002), co-editor of *Politics in North America: Redefining Continental Relations* (2008), and editor of *Gendering the Nation-State: Canadian and Comparative Perspectives* (2008).

ISABEL ALTAMIRANO-JIMÉNEZ

Isabel Altamirano-Jiménez is an Indigenous Zapotect from Oaxaca, Mexico, and Assistant Professor in the Department of Political Science and the Faculty of Native Studies at the University of Alberta. She researches the politics of Indigeneity and the construction of women, places, and spaces. Her research interests include Indigenous comparative politics, gender, nationalism, globalization, Indigenous mapping, and Indigenous North American politics.

PAT ARMSTRONG

Pat Armstrong is a Professor of Sociology and Women's Studies at York University and the co-author or editor of various books on healthcare, including *Critical to Care: The Invisible Women in Health Services*; *About Canada: Health Care, Caring For/Caring About*; *Exposing Privatization: Women and Health Reform in Canada*; *Unhealthy Times, Heal Thyself: Managing Health Care Reform*; *Wasting Away: The Undermining of Canadian Health Care*; *Universal Health Care: What the United States Can Learn from Canada*; *Medical Alert: New Work Organizations in Health Care*; *Vital Signs: Nursing in Transition*; and *Take Care: Warning Signals for Canada's Health System*. She has also published on a wide variety of issues related to women's work and to social policy. On the basis of this work, she has been called as an expert witness in more than a dozen cases linked to women's work, pay equity, and women's rights. She has served as Chair of the Department of Sociology at York University and Director of the School of Canadian Studies at Carleton University. She was a partner and acting director in the National Network on Environments and Women's Health and chairs a working group on health reform that crosses the Centres of Excellence for Women's Health. She holds a CHSRF/CHIR Chair in Health Services and Nursing Research and serves on the board of both the Canadian Health Coalition and the Canadian Centre for Policy Alternatives.

## ISABELLA BAKKER

Isabella Bakker is a Professor of Political Science and Political Economy at York University. Appointed a Fulbright New Century Scholar in 2004–05, she worked with a team of international scholars and activists on *Beyond States and Markets: The Challenges of Social Reproduction* (co-edited by Isabella Bakker with Rachel Silvey and published by Routledge). She has worked extensively on gender and macro-economic issues with Status of Women Canada, with the United Nations on two UNDP Human Development Reports, with UNIFEM on the first Progress of the World's Women, and with the Division on the Advancement of Women on gender mainstreaming in the budget and planning process of the United Nations.

## CHERYL N. COLLIER

Cheryl N. Collier is an Assistant Professor in the Department of Political Science at the University of Windsor. She holds a degree in Journalism from Carleton University and a doctorate in Political Science from the University of Toronto. She has published articles in the *Canadian Journal of Political Science* and in a variety of edited texts on violence against women and childcare policy. Her current research interests are in gender and Canadian social policy, federalism and provincial public policy, and contemporary comparative women's movement politics.

## ALEXANDRA DOBROWOLSKY

Alexandra Dobrowolsky is a Professor in and Chair of the Department of Political Science at Saint Mary's University, and an Adjunct Professor in the Faculty of Law, Dalhousie University. She teaches in the areas of Canadian politics, comparative politics, and women, gender, and politics. She has published extensively in national and international volumes and journals on themes of representation and citizenship, and in policy areas that range from constitutional and social policy to security and immigration policy. She is the author of *The Politics of Pragmatism: Women, Representation, and Constitutionalism in Canada* (Oxford 2000), co-editor of *Women Making Constitutions: New Politics and Comparative Perspectives* (Palgrave MacMillan 2003), and *Women, Migration and Citizenship: Making Local, National and Transnational Connections* (Ashgate 2006).

## LOIS HARDER

Lois Harder is an Associate Professor of Political Science at the University of Alberta. Her current research concerns the regulation of intimate life in Canada and the United States. She is the author of several articles on this subject, including 'The Rights of Love: The State and Intimate Relationships in Canada and the United States', *Social Politics* 14 (2) (2007), and 'The State and the Friendships of the Nation: The Case of Non-Conjugal Relationships in Canada and the United States' forthcoming in *Signs* in 2009. In the fall of 2008 she was a Fulbright Scholar at the University of Hawaii.

SARA HAWRYLUK

Sara Hawryluk is a student in the Johnson-Shoyama Graduate School of Public Policy located at the University of Regina. She is currently working on producing a gender budget for Saskatchewan that analyzes the differential outcomes of budget allocations for men and women. She has also worked for non-governmental organizations and is currently employed as a policy analyst in the Saskatchewan Ministry of Health.

JANE JENSON

Since 2001 Jane Jenson has held the Canada Research Chair in Citizenship and Governance at the Université de Montréal, where she is a Professor of Political Science. In August 2008 she became Associate Dean of Graduate Studies and External Relations of the Faculté des arts et des sciences of the Université de Montréal. She is also Editor of *Lien social et Politiques—RIAC*, a social policy journal. Between June 1999 and 2004, she was the Director of the Family Network of Canadian Policy Research Networks, Inc., a policy think tank located in Ottawa. In that position she wrote numerous research reports on the best policy mix for children and families and Canada's social architecture, often from a comparative perspective. In 2005 she was named a Fellow of the Trudeau Foundation and in 2004 a member of the Successful Societies programme of the Canadian Institute for Advanced Research (CIFAR). She has been a visiting professor at a number of European universities, as well as Harvard University, where she held the William Lyon Mackenzie King Chair in Canadian Studies. She was elected a Fellow of the Royal Society of Canada in 1989.

MARTHA MacDONALD

Martha MacDonald is a Professor of Economics and Chair of the Economics Department at Saint Mary's University, where she teaches courses in labour economics and women and the economy. Her current research areas include income-security policy, economic restructuring in rural communities, work-life balance, and precarious employment. She is Past President of the International Association for Feminist Economics.

KATHLEEN McNUTT

Kathleen McNutt is an Associate Professor in the Johnson-Shoyama Graduate School of Public Policy at the University of Regina and is a faculty associate in the Department of Political Science. She completed a PhD in Political Science at Simon Fraser University. Specializing in public-policy analysis and program evaluation, her research interests include e-government, climate change, gender and policy, policy networks, and federal policy-making. Her work has been published in the *Canadian Journal of Political Science*, *Canadian Political Science Review*, *Russian Journal of Political Science*, *Global Social Policy*, *HealthcarePapers*, *Federal Governance*, and *The Encyclopedia of Digital Government*. She also has chapters in *Neo-Liberalism, State Power and Global Governance* and in *The OECD and Global Governance*. Her current research projects include contemporary policy-analysis methods, feasibility study of nuclear power in Saskatchewan, and an evaluation of the closing or downsizing of Status of Women's offices across Canada.

RIANNE MAHON

Rianne Mahon is Director of the Institute of Political Economy and a member of the School of Public Policy and Administration and the Department of Sociology and Anthropology at Carleton University in Ottawa. While her earlier work focused on unions and labour-market restructuring in Canada and Sweden, over the past decade she has produced numerous articles and book chapters on the politics of childcare. Together with Sonya Michel, she edited *Child Care Policy at the Crossroads: Gender and Welfare State Restructuring*. Recent publications include 'Varieties of Liberalism: Canadian Social Policy from the "Golden Age" to the Present' in *Social Policy and Administration* (2008), 'Challenging National Regimes from Below: Toronto Child Care Politics' in *Gender and Politics* (2007), and *The OECD and Transnational Governance*, co-edited with Stephen McBride (UBC Press). Mahon is also co-editor, with Roger Keil, of the forthcoming title *Leviathan Undone? Toward a Political Economy of Scale* (UBC Press). Her current research project focuses on the OECD and 'policy learning' in Canada, Sweden, and Korea as this pertains to 'reconciliation of work and life' policies.

# Index